Fodor's
BAHAMAS

WELCOME TO THE BAHAMAS

Made up of 700 islands—some busy and bustling, some isolated and inhabited by no one but hermit crabs and seagulls—the Bahamas offers an alluring mix of land and sea activities. From Nassau to Eleuthera, you can play golf on a seaside fairway, dive dramatic wrecks and reefs, and sail in crystal clear water. Accommodations run the gamut from simple inns to sophisticated retreats, from practical fishing lodges to romantic honeymoon hideaways. And for those who look a little closer, there's a fascinating and diverse culture to be explored.

TOP REASONS TO GO

★ **Beaches.** The powdery, soft sand creates some of the world's best strands.

★ **Boating.** Ideal conditions draw small dinghies, serious sailboats, and luxury yachts.

★ **Family Fun.** From sprawling water parks to horseback rides along the beach.

★ **Out Islands.** Quiet and uncrowded, these islands are hard to reach but worth the trip.

★ **Fishing.** From fly-casting for tarpon and bonefish to fighting with a giant marlin.

19 ULTIMATE EXPERIENCES

Bahamas offers terrific experiences that should be on every traveler's list. Here are Fodor's top picks for a memorable trip.

1 Scuba Diving

Discover aquatic wonders when you explore the region's ultra-clear waters, from the shallows of the world's third-largest barrier reef to the ocean depths. Coral, blue holes, drop-offs, and sea gardens abound here. *(Ch. 1)*

2 Lucayan National Park

Kayak through wild tamarind and gumbo-limbo trees, a mangrove swamp, and one of the world's largest underwater cave systems at this land preserve on Grand Bahama Island. *(Ch. 3)*

3 The Out Islands

Seek refuge at these sparsely populated islands. Ascend the cut stone staircase to Mount Alvernia, the country's highest natural point, 206 feet above sea level. *(Ch. 8)*

4 Rum Drinks

Revisit the bootlegging days of the Prohibition Era. Treat yourself to a Goombay Smash invented at Miss Emily's Blue Bee Bar in Abaco. *(Ch. 1)*

5 Horseback Riding

Even without prior experience, visitors can take guided tours of several of the islands on horseback; gallop across the sand and even into the sea. *(Ch. 6)*

6 Sailing

The Abacos is the sailing capital of the Bahamas. The region hosts an open regatta where all types of boats can join in for island hopping and racing. *(Ch. 1)*

7 Nurse Sharks

Interact with harmless nurse sharks in their natural habitat at Compass Cay in the Exumas, where a handful of them swim and sunbathe at the private island marina. *(Ch. 1)*

8 Swimming With Pigs

World-famous pigs live on Big Major Cay in the Exumas. The animals swim out to greet tourists, but be respectful on their home turf, and don't pick any up for selfies. *(Ch. 7)*

9 Aquaventure at the Atlantis Resort

This 141-acre aquatic wonderland on Paradise Island has river rides, a 200-foot body slide, and pools. It's the ultimate playground for kids and adventurous adults. *(Ch. 2)*

10 Bonefishing

Shallow waters and mangroves filled with "gray ghosts," or silvery white fish, make bonefishing the fly-fishing sport of choice in the Bahamas. *(Ch. 1)*

11 Private Resorts

Complete your island getaway with a stay at a secluded, all-inclusive luxury resort like Fowl Cay, just a 7-minute boat transfer from Staniel Cay Airstrip. *(Ch. 7)*

12 Dolphin Spotting

Take a boat into Freeport, and a pod of dolphins may splash and dive along beside you. Jump into the water to swim with them in their natural environment. *(Ch. 3)*

13 Fish Fry

At Arawak Cay, brightly colored restaurants serve local fish specialties like fried fish and cracked conch. Wash it down with "sky juice" (gin, coconut water, and milk). *(Ch. 2)*

14 Junkanoo festival

This spirited celebration with dancing, brass bands, and vibrant costumes is the Bahamas' answer to Mardi Gras. Junkanoo happens on Boxing Day and New Year's Day. *(Ch. 2)*

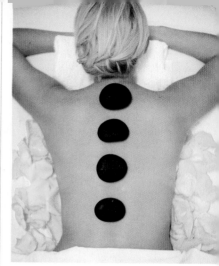

15 Snorkeling

Explore Thunderball Grotto in the Exumas and its limestone cave, or Paradise Point in Bimini where dolphins and black coral await you just offshore. *(Ch. 1)*

16 Spas

Retreat to top-rated spas in idyllic settings throughout the region, where you can indulge in massages, body treatments, aromatherapy, and much more. *(Ch. 2)*

17 The Exumas

Across the Tropic of Cancer lies this chain of hundreds of islands with white sand and calm blue water. Look for exquisite wildlife: giant starfish, iguanas, and pigs. *(Ch. 7)*

18 Beaches

With powdery white and pink sand and kaleidoscopic blue water, beaches extend for a total of 800 miles in the Bahamas and offer parties on the sand or complete solitude. *(Ch. 1)*

19 Harbour Island

Modern but with an old-world feel, Harbour Island is home to pastel-colored clapboard houses, a three and a half mile pink sand beach, and the mysterious lone tree. *(Ch. 6)*

Fodor's BAHAMAS

Editorial: Douglas Stallings, *Editorial Director*; Margaret Kelly, Jacinta O'Halloran, *Senior Editors*; Kayla Becker, Alexis Kelly, and Amanda Sadlowski, *Editors*; Teddy Minford, *Content Editor*; Rachael Roth, *Content Manager*

Design: Tina Malaney, *Design and Production Director*; Jessica Gonzalez, *Production Designer*

Photography: Jennifer Arnow, *Senior Photo Editor*

Maps: Rebecca Baer, *Senior Map Editor*; David Lindroth and Mark Stroud, *Cartographers*

Production: Jennifer DePrima, *Editorial Production Manager*; Carrie Parker, *Senior Production Editor*; Elyse Rozelle, *Production Editor*; David Satz, *Director of Content Production*

Business & Operations: Chuck Hoover, *Chief Marketing Officer*; Joy Lai, *Vice President and General Manager*; Stephen Horowitz, *Director of Business Development and Revenue Operations*; Tara McCrillis, *Director of Publishing Operations*; Eliza D. Aceves, *Content Operations Manager and Strategist*

Public Relations and Marketing: Joe Ewaskiw, *Manager*; Esther Su, *Marketing Manager*

Writers: Bob Bower, Dana McKimmie, Sheri-kae McLeod, Jessica Robertson, Ashleigh Rolle

Editor: Rachael Roth

Production Editor: Jennifer DePrima

31st Edition

ISBN 978-1-64097-018-2

ISSN 1524–7945

SPECIAL SALES

This book is available at special discounts for bulk purchases for sales promotions or premiums. For more information, e-mail SpecialMarkets@fodors.com.

PRINTED IN THE UNITED STATES OF AMERICA

10 9 8 7 6 5 4 3 2 1

CONTENTS

Fodor's Features

CONTENTS

MAPS

ABOUT
THIS GUIDE

Fodor's Recommendations

Everything in this guide is worth doing—we don't cover what isn't—but exceptional sights, hotels, and restaurants are recognized with additional accolades. **Fodor's Choice ★** indicates our top recommendations. Care to nominate a new place? Visit Fodors.com/contact-us.

Trip Costs

We list prices wherever possible to help you budget well. Hotel and restaurant price categories from $ to $$$$ are noted alongside each recommendation. For hotels, we include the lowest cost of a standard double room in high season. For restaurants, we cite the average price of a main course at dinner or, if dinner isn't served, at lunch. For attractions, we always list adult admission fees; discounts are usually available for children, students, and senior citizens.

Hotels

Our local writers vet every hotel to recommend the best overnights in each price category, from budget to expensive. Unless otherwise specified, you can expect private bath, phone, and TV in your room. *For expanded hotel reviews, visit Fodors.com.*

Top Picks	Hotels &
★ **Fodor's** Choice	**Restaurants**
	⬛ Hotel
Listings	⬏ Number of
✉ Address	rooms
✉ Branch address	❏ Meal plans
☎ Telephone	✕ Restaurant
🖷 Fax	🖉 Reservations
⊕ Website	🏛 Dress code
✍ E-mail	▭ No credit cards
🏷 Admission fee	$ Price
⏱ Open/closed	
times	**Other**
Ⓜ Subway	⇨ See also
⊹ Directions or	☞ Take note
Map coordinates	🏌 Golf facilities

Restaurants

Unless we state otherwise, restaurants are open for lunch and dinner daily. We mention dress code only when there's a specific requirement and reservations only when they're essential or not accepted. *For expanded restaurant reviews, visit Fodors.com.*

Credit Cards

The hotels and restaurants in this guide typically accept credit cards. If not, we'll say so.

EUGENE FODOR

Hungarian-born Eugene Fodor (1905–91) began his travel career as an interpreter on a French cruise ship. The experience inspired him to write *On the Continent* (1936), the first guidebook to receive annual updates and discuss a country's way of life as well as its sights. Fodor later joined the U.S. Army and worked for the OSS in World War II. After the war, he kept up his intelligence work while expanding his guidebook series. During the Cold War, many guides were written by fellow agents who understood the value of insider information. Today's guides continue Fodor's legacy by providing travelers with timely coverage, insider tips, and cultural context.

EXPERIENCE
THE BAHAMAS

WHAT'S WHERE

1 **New Providence and Paradise Islands.** Nassau and nearby Paradise Island are the most action-packed places in the Bahamas. From flashy megaresorts Atlantis and Baha Mar to fine dining and high-end shopping, development here is unrivaled on any of the other islands.

2 **Grand Bahama Island.** Urban and deserted vibes mix to create a quieter alternative to fast-paced Nassau. Lucaya has shopping, golfing, scuba diving, and beach parties, but old-island fishing settlements and vast expanses of untouched nature appeal to adventurous travelers.

3 **The Abacos.** Shallow, translucent waters, top-notch marinas, and idyllic, historic settlements spread over 120 miles of cays (some uninhabited) give the Abacos the apt title of "Sailing Capital of the Bahamas."

4 **Andros, Bimini, and the Berry Islands.** In the northwest corner of the Bahamas, these islands share many characteristics, most notably their reputation for excellent fishing and diving. Each exudes a casual, old-island atmosphere and abundant natural beauty.

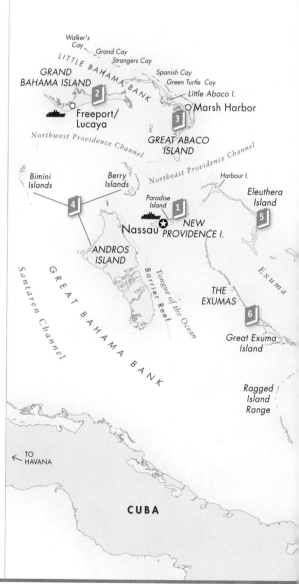

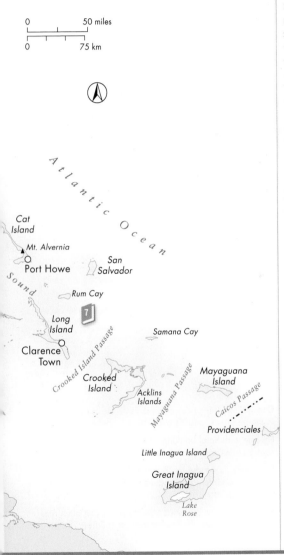

0   50 miles

0   75 km

Atlantic Ocean

Cat Island

Mt. Alvernia

Port Howe

San Salvador

Sound

Rum Cay

Long Island

7

Clarence Town

Samana Cay

Crooked Island Passage

Crooked Island

Acklins Islands

Mayaguana Island

Mayaguana Passage

Caicos Passage

Providenciales

Little Inagua Island

Great Inagua Island

Lake Rose

5 Eleuthera and Harbour Island. The Nantucket of the Bahamas, Harbour Island—rimmed by its legendary pink-sand beach—is the chicest Out Island. Eleuthera is the opposite, with historic churches and pretty fishing villages, unpretentious inns, and a few upscale, intimate beach resorts.

6 The Exumas. Hundreds of islands skip like stones across the Tropic of Cancer, all with gorgeous white beaches and the most beautiful water in the Bahamas. Mainland Great Exuma has friendly locals and great beach parties.

7 The Southern Out Islands. The Bahamas' southernmost islands have so few visitors and so many natural wonders. Cat Island boasts the highest natural point in the country, San Salvador marks Christopher Columbus's discovery of the Western world, and Inagua is home to one of the largest flamingo colonies in the world.

NEED TO KNOW

BAHAMAS
Nassau

Atlantic
Ocean

Caribbean
Sea

AT A GLANCE

Capital: Nassau

Population: 388,019

Currency: Bahamian dollar; pegged to U.S. dollar

Money: ATMs on main islands. USD accepted.

Language: English

Country Code: 1 242

Emergencies: 919

Driving: On the left

Electricity: 120v/60 cycles; plugs U.S. 2- and 3-prong

Time Zone: EST

Documents: Up to 90 days with valid passport; immigration preclearance returning to U.S.

Mobile Phones: GSM

Mobile Company: BTC

WEBSITES

Ministry of Tourism: ⊕ www.bahamas.com

Out Islands Promo Board: ⊕ www.myoutislands.com

Visitors Guide: ⊕ www.bahamasvisitorsguide.com

GETTING AROUND

✈ **Air Travel:** Nassau's Lynden Pindling International Airport and Freeport's Grand Bahama International Airport are principal gateways.

🚌 **Bus Travel:** Larger islands have jitneys (buses). Exuma and some other islands do not have public buses.

🚗 **Car Travel:** Rental cars are available but not recommended.

⛴ **Ferry Travel:** Ferries connect Nassau to several of the Bahamas' Out Islands. Scheduled ferries run to Andros, Eleuthera, Harbour Island, and the Abacos.

PLAN YOUR BUDGET

	HOTEL ROOM	MEAL	ATTRACTIONS
Low Budget	$225	$15	The Pompey Museum of Slavery and Emancipation, $3
Mid-Budget	$350	$25	Half-day snorkel cruise, $60
High Budget	$475	$45	Atlantis Aquaventure Pass (cruise passengers only), $150

WAYS TO SAVE

Conch it up. This pricey delicacy is an inexpensive staple in the Bahamas, and it's available everywhere.

Fly free with hotel booking. The Bahamas Ministry of Tourism often sponsors promotions.

Sail away ... slowly. The Bahamas' old-fashioned mail boats are an interesting and inexpensive way to get to the Out Islands.

Kid freebies. The Bahamas Ministry of Tourism often runs online promotions offering freebies for children.

PLAN YOUR TIME

Hassle Factor	Medium. The majority of the Bahamas' smaller islands require a puddle-jumper from Nassau or Freeport; preplan visits here.
3 days	Relax poolside or beachside at your Bahamas resort. Take a day to explore the island and do some sightseeing.
1 week	Enjoy and explore one of the Bahamas' principal islands: Grand Bahama Island or New Providence Island (Nassau). Take a small plane to one of the Out Islands to experience the real Bahamas.
2 weeks	Choose Nassau as your base and island hop through the Bahamas. First visit Andros (by plane or ferry); then fly to The Abacos, Eleuthera, The Exumas, and more.

WHEN TO GO

High Season: Mid-December through mid-April is the most fashionable and most expensive time to visit, when the weather is typically sunny and warm. Good hotels are often booked far in advance and everything is open—and busy. On more touristy islands, spring breakers are most numerous in February and March.

Low Season: From July to late October, temperatures can grow oppressively hot and the weather muggy, with high risk of tropical storms. However, diving and fishing conditions are at their best. Most resorts remain open, offering deep discounts, but on some of the smaller islands there may not be much else open.

Value Season: From late April to June and again November to mid-December, hotel prices drop 20% to 50% from high-season prices. There are chances of scattered showers, but expect sun-kissed days and comfortable nighttime temperatures, plus fewer crowds.

BIG EVENTS

December–January: Junkanoo celebrations take place on Boxing Day and New Year's Day with festivities that include parades, music, dancing, and food.

February–October: Wooden sloop regattas complete with big parties on land take place on a different island each month.

June–August: The annual Junkanoo Summer festival is held on Saturday throughout July in Nassau.

December: The Bahamas International Film Festival in Nassau offers screenings, receptions, and movie-industry panels. ⊕ www.bintlfilmfest.com

READ THIS

■ *Islands in the Stream,* Ernest Hemingway. Parts take place in Bimini.

■ *Thunderball: James Bond Series,* Ian Fleming. The ninth book in Fleming's Bond series.

■ *The Noble Pirates,* Rima Jean. A fictional historical romance.

WATCH THIS

■ *Casino Royale.* The 21st James Bond film.

■ *Splash.* Daryl Hannah plays a mermaid opposite Tom Hanks.

■ *Cocoon.* Alien encounter filmed in the Bahamas.

EAT THIS

■ *Cracked conch*: pounded, battered, and then fried.

■ *Conch salad*: onion, bell pepper, lime, sour orange, peppers.

■ *Guava duff*: compote in sweet dough, with rum or brandy sauce.

■ *Johnnycake*: thick, slightly sweet dense bread.

■ *Peas 'n' rice*: white rice with salt pork, thyme, tomato paste, pigeon peas.

■ *Bahamian mac 'n' cheese*: baked with cream, Daisy cheese, butter.

BAHAMAS TODAY

Development is no longer on the back burner in the Bahamas. The largest project, the Baha Mar overhaul of the Cable Beach strip on New Providence, was years behind schedule, but the first of several phases was completed in 2017 and is already impacting tourism in the country. Many other new projects are underway across the islands, and Bahamians used the slow period as an opportunity to spruce up existing properties and improve an infrastructure that was starting to show signs of age and neglect.

The British Feel Remains

From driving on the left side of the road, to tea parties, to the wig-wearing lawyers who stroll into court, British influence is still apparent in the Bahamas. Though the country gained independence from England in 1973, Bahamians learn British spelling in school, and the country still uses the Westminster style of government. At the same time, a constant diet of American media has had an impact on the country. Bahamians measure temperature in Fahrenheit instead of Celsius, and although the English gentleman's cricket is the national sport, you'll be hard-pressed to find a local who plays the game.

A Playground for the Rich and Famous

With its near-perfect year-round weather, modern infrastructure and amenities, and proximity to the United States, it's no wonder that the Bahamas is a home away from Hollywood for many celebrities. Sean Connery lives behind the gates of the exclusive Lyford Cay community on New Providence Island. Johnny Depp owns his own private island in the Exumas, as do Tim McGraw and Faith Hill, David Copperfield, and Nicolas Cage. Mariah Carey owns a private Eleuthera estate, and the island is also home to Lenny Kravitz, whose mother, actress Roxie Roker, grew up there.

Many Different Destinations

The majority of the 6 million tourists who visit the Bahamas each year experience only Nassau, Paradise Island, or perhaps Grand Bahama. But with more than 700 islands, there's so much more to see and do. Each island has a different way of life; none of them have the hustle and bustle of big-city life experienced in the capital. The farther south you venture, the slower the pace.

WHAT WE'RE TALKING ABOUT

Bahamians are passionate about their politics. Though elections are only held every five years, everyone is continually vocal about which party will win and which scandals will and will not sway voters.

The Bahamas has a parliamentary system, much like England's. As elsewhere in the British Commonwealth, there is a governor general who serves as the Queen's representative. A prime minister leads the government and bicameral legislature. The upper chamber is called the Senate, whose members are appointed by the prime minister in consultation with the opposition. Members of the lower chamber, the House of Assembly, are elected directly. Perry Christie and the Progressive Liberal Party unseated Hubert Ingraham and the Free National Movement Party for a second time in

Still Developing

Bay Street, once Nassau's Madison Avenue, is on the road to recovery after years of neglect. The esplanade just west of downtown is undergoing a major transformation with new and renovated hotels, and western New Providence continues to be developed. The Lynden Pindling International Airport is now a modern gateway that truly welcomes visitors. And following a number of false starts, the multibillion-dollar Baha Mar transformation of the Cable Beach strip is now a reality. As Nassau continues to develop, the Out Islands remain untouched, preserving the quaint nature that attracts adventure travelers each year.

Sustainable Development

The government works closely with the Bahamas National Trust to identify and develop protected green spaces, adding more and more land each year to the National Park System, and any developer interested in putting up a sizable or potentially environmentally sensitive project anywhere in the country is required to pay for and submit an Environmental Impact Assessment before consideration is granted.

2012. The Democratic National Alliance, led by a former FNM cabinet minister, was the first fringe party to run a full slate of candidates in 2012, and all three parties are likely to be the forerunners in 2017.

Even the most patriotic Bahamian will admit that the country's jewel—downtown Nassau—had lost its luster. As the economy slumped, particularly east of East Street, once-spectacular stores had given way to tacky T-shirt shops or have been left vacant, and sidewalks and building facades had suffered. Now, a resurgence is underway. New restaurants and bars have been popping up, live music and handmade crafts are available at Pompey Square, and extensive renovations and new construction are creating a complete resurgence west of the British Colonial Hilton.

FLAVORS OF THE BAHAMAS

There's nothing fancy about Bahamian food, just fresh ingredients and unique peppery spices.

Breakfasts include standard American fare like eggs, bacon, and pancakes, or Bahamian favorites such as chicken souse, boil' fish, or stew' fish, served with grits and johnnycake. Lunch standards include: fresh fish, conch, or chicken sandwiches, or hamburgers sided with french fries, coleslaw, or local favorites like peas 'n' rice or baked macaroni and cheese with locally grown goat or bird peppers. At dinner you'll find fish, fried chicken, and pasta.

"Steamed" fish means cooked with tomatoes, peppers, and onions. Order any fish "Bahamian style" and it will be baked and smothered in tomatoes and spices.

Conch

(A) You'll find conch, the unofficial dish of the Bahamas, prepared in a variety of ways, on nearly every menu. The sea snail has a mild flavor and taste and texture similar to calamari. Start with conch fritters, tasty fried dough balls packed with chunks of conch. Conch chowder is traditionally tomato-based; cracked conch is battered and fried; grilled conch is wrapped in a foil packet with lime juice, pepper, onion, tomato, and a bit of butter and cooked on top of the barbecue; and, perhaps the most popular entrée, conch salad is akin to ceviche. Fresh-caught conch is diced and mixed with chopped onions and red or green bell peppers. The mix is drizzled with fresh lime and sour orange juice, and spiced with finely minced local hot peppers.

Guava Duff

This local favorite is similar to English pudding. A guava fruit compote is folded into a sweet dough and wrapped up in aluminum foil, and then steamed or boiled for as long as three hours. It's topped with a sweet rum or brandy sauce.

Johnnycake

(B) Johnnycake is not actually a dessert but a thick, heavy, slightly sweet bread that's typically served alongside souses, soups, and stews.

Mac 'n' Cheese

Bahamians bake their macaroni noodles in a mixture of cream, cottage cheese, and butter.

Peas 'n' Rice

This popular side dish is made of white rice cooked with salt pork, thyme, a dab of tomato paste, and fresh or canned pigeon peas.

Rum Cake

(C) Rum cake is an all-time favorite on the islands. Rum is mixed into the batter and then poured in a syrupy glaze over the fresh-out-of-the-oven cake. The alcohol cooks off when it bakes.

Souse, Boil', or Stew'

(D) A peppery bowl of chicken souse or boil' fish—the clear broth has a lime-and-goat-pepper base with pieces of chicken or meaty fish, onions, and potatoes—is an authentic breakfast dish. Variations include pig-feet and sheep-tongue souse. You'll also find stew' fish or conch on most menus. The soup in bowls of stew is a Bahamian variation on the traditional French roux made with flour, water, and browning sauce, and seasoned with pepper and fresh thyme.

IT'S 5 O'CLOCK SOMEWHERE

Rum has played a particularly interesting role in Bahamian history since the days of the U.S. Prohibition, when entrepreneurial Bahamians got rich smuggling liquor across the Atlantic from Britain; a ready supply less than 50 miles away made the island nation a key trans-shipment point for contraband.

The Bahamas still has two breweries and two rum distilleries. **Kalik,** brewed on the southwestern end of New Providence at Commonwealth Brewery, is a nice, light ale and comes in regular, Kalik Lite, Kalik Radler (including a nonalcoholic version), and the stronger Kalik Gold. The beer was awarded four Monde Selection Gold Medals. Commonwealth also has a distillery, turning out **Ole Nassau** and **Ron Ricardo** rums. Brewery and distillery tours are not available there,

but you're encouraged to tour the artisanal John Watling's Distillery located on the site of the former Buena Vista hotel in Nassau. After your tour, take a seat, enjoy the breeze off the harbor, and enjoy their signature Rum Dum cocktail. The newer **Sands Beer,** brewed on Grand Bahama, comes in regular and light. The line recently expanded to include stouts and lagers. Tours are available at this 20-acre brewery (242/352–4070).

Bahamian Cocktails

Bahama Mama. Light rum, coconut rum, vanilla-infused rum, orange and pineapple juices.

(A) Goombay Smash. Light rum, coconut rum, pineapple juice, a dash of Galliano, grenadine. Created at Miss Emily's Blue Bee Bar on Green Turtle Cay, where her daughter and granddaughter still serve them daily.

Rum Punch. Campari, light rum, coconut rum, orange and pineapple juices.

Sky Juice. Gin, fresh coconut water, condensed milk, a sprinkle of nutmeg. Served over crushed ice. In Grand Bahama, this concoction is called Gully Wash.

Best Beach Bars

(B) Chat 'N' Chill, the Exumas. The restaurant and 9-acre playground—an amazing white-sand beach—is the Exumas' party central, particularly for the famous all-day Sunday pig roasts and the Friday-night bonfire beach bash. Play volleyball in the powdery sand, slam the notorious Goombay Smash, order what's cooking on the outdoor grill—fresh fish, ribs—or just chat and chill.

(C) Nippers, the Abacos. Guana Cay's infamous party spot is a lively bar with spectacular views of the Abaco Great Barrier Reef. The Frozen Nipper—a slushy rum-and-fruit-juice beverage—goes down well on a hot day. Don't miss the Sunday pig roasts, which draw everyone on the island.

Pete's Pub, Abaco. This beachside tiki hut in Little Harbour is jumping from 11 am to sunset. Take a dip in the shallow harbor or luxuriate on the beach with a cup of their special rum punch—the Blaster.

GREAT ITINERARIES

ISLAND-HOPPING FOR 1 WEEK

The Bahamas is comprised of more than 700 islands, yet many visitors experience just one in a single visit. With limited scheduled transportation between the islands, it's difficult to island-hop without going back to Nassau for each leg, but this itinerary shows how you can use mail boats, speedboats, and scheduled flights to experience Nassau, Paradise Island, Rose Island, Sandals Island, mainland Exuma, and a handful of the Exuma cays and do it all in just a week, provided you arrive in Nassau on a Monday since the mail boat to George Town leaves on Tuesday.

1 Day: Nassau

Explore the sprawling marine habitat, face your fears on the exhilarating waterslides (including a clear acrylic slide that plunges through a shark tank), and get up close with sea lions and dolphins at the iconic Atlantis Resort. A new policy limits Aquaventure access to resort guests or cruise-ship passengers (with a day pass) so you'll need to plan on at least one night in the sprawling resort or at Comfort Suites next door. Dine at one of the 21 restaurants on-property, and then dance the night away at Aura nightclub.

1 Day: Mail Boat Passage

On Day 2, head downtown and take in the history, architecture, culture, and (most importantly) the food of historic Nassau on the Bites of Nassau Food Tour. With your belly full, head to the eastern side of Potter's Cay Dock to the *Grand Master* mail boat (☎ 242/393–1041). Once you get your tickets (no need to book in advance), head over

to the colorful stalls to enjoy a game of dominoes and an ice cold Sands or Kalik beer. The mail boat, which leaves port between 4 and 5:30 every Tuesday afternoon, will be your transportation, overnight accommodations, and dinner restaurant on your way to George Town, Exuma, all for less than $60 per person one-way. Don't expect anything fancy; you'll get only a basic bunk in one of two small and stark (yet air-conditioned) cabins. For dinner it's a plate full of the same hearty meal enjoyed by the crew.

1 Day: George Town, Exuma

Following your 14-hour overnight passage—complete with unbelievable sunsets, a strong possibility of dolphin spotting, and space shared with everything from cars to mail to sheep and goats—you'll arrive in George Town bright and early. Make Club Peace and Plenty your first stop for a Bahamian breakfast staple: boiled fish and johnny-cake. Drop your bags at the hotel and take the water taxi from the Government Dock for a day of sun and fun at Chat 'N' Chill on Stocking Island, just a mile offshore. Swim with some wild stingrays that pop in daily for lunch, and treat yourself to tropical libations and conch salad prepared right before your eyes. After, head back over to the mainland for a restful night; evening activities are more or less limited to Fish Fry Friday or the annual Regatta.

1 Day: Exuma Cays

The next day, island-hop the stunning Exuma cays on a half-day excursion with Four C's Adventures *(see Sports and the Outdoors in The Exumas)*. Skim through the azure, crystal-clear waters from island to island, feeding iguanas on Allan's Cay petting the swimming pigs on Big Major

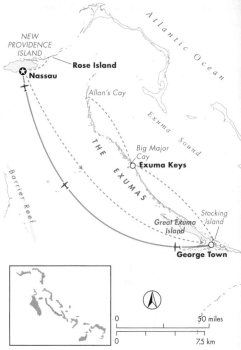

Cay, taking the perfect selfie at one of the beautiful beaches, and snorkeling in ocean blue holes. Catch the last scheduled flight back to Nassau, where you'll spend another night.

1 Day: Rose Island

Just 8 miles off the eastern coast of New Providence lies Rose Island. A popular weekend boating drop for locals, the long island is uninhabited. Book a night at the new Sandy Toes Retreat (☎ 242/363–8637 ⊕ *www.sandytoesroseisland.com*; starting at $795 a night), a beautifully appointed two-bedroom cottage with unbelievable ocean views. Your boat transportation is included, and once the excursion day-trippers leave at 3:45, you'll have the island to yourself.

1 Day: Nassau

Catch the 20-minute boat ride back to Nassau, and head west to end your island-hopping week with a luxurious massage on the Sandals resort private island. A day pass gives you access to an array of restaurants, unlimited beverages, and all the amenities, including a private offshore island where you can be pampered in a tiki hut as the waves break on the northern shore, explore the three beaches, or lounge in the pool, and either head home late in the afternoon or early evening or spend one final night on New Providence.

TIPS

Because of the mail boat schedule, this itinerary should begin on a Monday.

The *Grand Master* departs Tuesday between 4 and 5:30. Arrive a few hours early to buy your passenger ticket.

Mail boat has two rooms with six bunks each and no shower facilities on board.

Arrange provisioning for your meals on Rose Island, or stop at a food store in Nassau and stock up.

GREAT ITINERARIES

ISLAND-HOPPING FOR 2 WEEKS

While you could easily spend two weeks soaking up the sun, snorkeling, scuba diving, beach combing, and enjoying local cuisine on any single island, this itinerary lets you see more of the Bahamas, taking you to Nassau, the Exuma Cays, Grand Bahama, and the Abacos over two weeks.

1 Day: Nassau

Plan on arriving early and dropping your bags at your hotel. Explore downtown Nassau this morning on foot, stopping in at the National Art Gallery, the Straw Market, and the Graycliff Cigar Factory, then rent a scooter and head west. Baha Mar is a good spot to take a break and grab a drink, then continue west. Have lunch at Dino's Gourmet Conch Salad stand and carry on to Clifton Heritage National Park, where you can immerse yourself in the slave and plantation history and snorkel out to the Atlas underwater statue just offshore.

2 Days: Ship Channel Cay, Exuma

Powerboat Adventures offers an exciting day trip to a private island called Ship Channel Cay, near the top of the Exuma Cays. Enjoy a day feeding iguanas and stingrays, watching the shark feeding, and snorkeling in the beautiful waters. Retreat to your private cottage for a night on a deserted island. After breakfast on the second day, head to the side of the island few day-trippers even know exists for a day of complete sunbathing privacy. Lunch and an open bar are provided, and you'll head back to Nassau in the afternoon with the day-trippers. Try your luck tonight at one of the world-class casinos at Atlantis or Baha Mar and spend one more night in Nassau.

2 Days: Grand Bahama

Fly to Grand Bahama, where you'll spend two nights, and head to UNEXSO to swim with dolphins in their natural open-ocean habitat. Once back on land, head next door to Port Lucaya Marketplace for some shopping, drinks, live music, and dinner in Count Basie Square. The next morning, rent a car and venture east to the Lucayan National Park, timing your visit for low tide. After exploring the fascinating caves, walk across the street along the boardwalk over the mangroves to Gold Rock Beach. You can walk for miles along the rippled sand and lounge in the tide pools.

1 Day: Treasure Cay, Abaco

Catch the 8:30 am Pinder's Ferry from McClean's Town, Grand Bahama, to Crown Haven at the northern tip of Abaco. The Great Abaco Express charter bus will take you the 45-minute drive into Treasure Cay, where you'll spend the night. Grab a towel and relax on the world-famous pink-sand beach.

2 Days: Green Turtle Cay, Abaco

Indulge in one of the delicious cinnamon buns from Café La Florence near the marina before you catch the ferry to nearby Green Turtle Cay, where you'll spend the night. Head out for a memorable scuba or snorkel day trip with Brendals; you'll likely experience another wild-dolphin encounter. The next morning, brush up on Bahamian history as you wander around New Plymouth by golf cart. Be sure to stop in at Miss Emily's Blue Bee Bar for an authentic Goombay Smash. Get the last ferry (4:30 pm) back to Treasure Cay and take a taxi south to Marsh Harbour for the night.

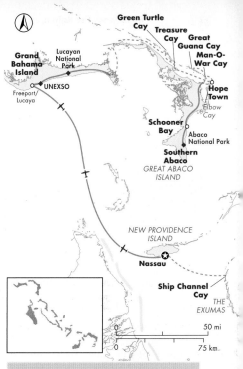

2 Days: Hope Town

Rent a small speedboat and head over to Elbow Cay, making the lighthouse your first stop. The views from the top are breathtaking. Cruise on over to Hope Town to explore the quaint town by foot. Enjoy a spectacular sunset and incredible dinner at FireFly. The next morning, pack a cooler and head back out in your boat to Tahiti Beach for a day of sunning and shelling. Spend a final night in historic Hope Town.

1 Day: Man O' War and Guana Cays

At your leisure, head out to Man O' War Cay to watch the men build traditional wooden boats. Lunch is at Nippers on nearby Great Guana Cay. Expect huge crowds if you happen to catch it on a Sunday, but otherwise you'll likely have the sprawling bar, pool, and beach to yourself. Before sundown, head back to Marsh Harbour to check into a hotel.

1 Day: Schooner Bay

Rent a car and drive south to Schooner Bay. Book a room and dinner well in advance at one of the upscale bonefishing lodges in the area so you can try your hand at bonefishing on the world-famous marls. After dinner walk out to the observation deck for a night of stargazing.

1 Day: Southern Abaco

Early the next morning, head deep into the Abaco National Park at the southernmost tip of the island with DSB excursions, where you'll explore caves and abandoned plantation buildings, climb to the top of the lighthouse, and picnic on a beach that probably hasn't been seen by anyone else in a very long time. Drive back to Marsh Harbour and fly home direct or via Nassau.

TIPS

If you're not comfortable handling a speedboat, you can do this island-hopping itinerary using Albury's Ferry service, but you will have to go back and forth to Marsh Harbour to make connections.

Prebook a taxi to meet you, or if you're with a small group, call Great Abaco Express charter ($10 per person) to Treasure Cay (☎ 242/646-7072) or risk being stuck in Crown Haven.

KIDS AND FAMILIES

It might not be an exaggeration to say that the Bahamas is a playground for children—or anyone else who likes building castles in the sand, searching for the perfect seashell, and playing tag with ocean waves.

Although water-related activities are the most obvious enticements, these relaxed and friendly islands also offer a variety of land-based options, particularly in Nassau and on adjacent Paradise Island. For tales of the high seas, **Pirates of Nassau** has artifacts and interactive exhibits of the original pirates of the Caribbean.

The **Ardastra Gardens, Zoo and Conservation Center** is home to a variety of animals, like pink flamingos, a pair of guenons, and Madagascar lemurs.

Let the kids pick out their favorite pony at the **Surrey Horse Pavilion** on Prince George Wharf and take a leisurely clip-clopping ride through the old city of Nassau. For a few extra dollars, most guides will extend your tour beyond the typical route to include other sites.

Megaresort **Atlantis** has lots of appeal, with everything from pottery painting to remote-control car-making and racing, to an 8,000-square-foot, state-of-the-art kids' camp, and the Bahamas' and Caribbean's largest casino and water park.

In Freeport, older children and adults can spend a day learning how dolphins are trained from **UNEXSO** (one of whose founders was Jacques Cousteau) at Sanctuary Bay, a refuge for dolphins.

For water-sports enthusiasts, snorkeling, parasailing, and boating opportunities abound. In the Exumas, rent a power-boat and take the kids to Big Major's Cay to see the famous **swimming pigs**. If you are staying in Nassau, book a day trip to see the pigs with **Harbour Safaris.** Don't forget some scraps! Kids will also get a kick out of the hundreds of **iguanas** on nearby Allan's Cay and the **giant starfish** near mainland Great Exuma.

Much of the Bahamas' most incredible scenery is underwater, but kids of all ages can enjoy the scenes beneath the sea without even getting wet. At **Stuart Cove's Dive Bahamas** in Nassau, kids 12 and up can go 15 feet under with a SUB (Scenic Underwater Bubble) and zoom around the reefs. **Seaworld Tours'** semisubmarine explores Nassau Harbour and Paradise Island for 1½ hours with sightseeing above and below water.

GREAT WATER ADVENTURES

In an archipelago nation named for shallow seas that amaze even astronauts in space, don't miss having a close marine encounter. Water adventures range from a splash at the beach to shark diving. Or, stay between the extremes with fishing and snorkeling.

WHERE TO DIVE AND SNORKEL IN THE BAHAMAS

Although most water in the Bahamas is clear enough to see to the bottom from your boat, snorkeling or diving gets you that much closer to the country's true natives. Coral reefs, blue holes, drop-offs, and sea gardens abound.

BEST DIVE SITES

Andros Barrier Reef/Tongue of the Ocean. Go from the shallows of the world's third-largest barrier reef to the depths of the ocean.

Fowl Cay Reef, the Abacos. The government-protected reef is near the north coast of Man-O-War Cay. A dive operator can take you through the reef holes.

Sandy Cay Reef, the Abacos. Experience shallow-water diving in Pelican Cays National Park. The reef is full of life (turtles, spotted eagle rays, tarpon), thanks to its protected status.

Shark Wall, New Providence. Off southwest New Providence, this drop is a must for experienced divers. James Bond movies *Thunderball* and *Never Say Never Again* were filmed here.

The Wall, Crooked Island. The famed dive site about 50 yards off Crooked Island's coast drops from 45 feet to thousands.

Diving near New Providence Island

BEST SNORKEL SITES

The Current Cut, Eleuthera. Near the Current settlement in North Eleuthera there is great drift snorkel with the right tide.

Exuma Cays Land and Sea Park. This 176-square-mile park was the first of its kind. Since the park is protected and its waters have essentially never been fished, you can see what the ocean looked like before humanity.

Paradise Point, Bimini. Off northern Bimini, this area is rich in sea life and is famous for the underwater stone path some believe marks the road to the lost city of Atlantis. Dolphins and black coral gardens are just offshore.

Sandy Cay Reef, the Abacos. The water surrounding this reef is just 25-feet deep, making it great for snorkeling or diving.

Thunderball Grotto, the Exumas. This three-story limestone-ceiling cave at the northern end of the Exumas chain was featured in the James Bond movie of the same name.

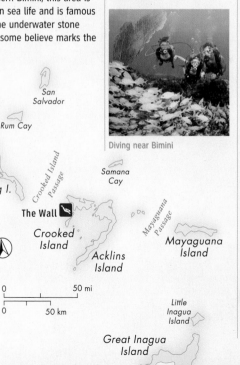

Diving near Bimini

San Salvador

Rum Cay

Long I.

Crooked Island Passage

The Wall

Crooked Island

Acklins Island

Samana Cay

Mayaguana Passage

Mayaguana Island

0   50 mi
0   50 km

Little Inagua Island

Great Inagua Island

EXTREME DIVING ADVENTURES

Various outfitters on Grand Bahama and New Providence offer shark dives. With **Caribbean Divers** (☎ 242/373–9111 ⊕ www.bellchannelinn.com) and **UNEXSO** in Grand Bahama and **Stuart Cove's** in New Providence, you'll watch dive masters feed reef sharks which brush by you—no cage included. Dive masters control the ferocity and location of the frenzy, so the sharks' attention is on the food.

Incredible Adventures (☎ 800/644–7382 ⊕ www.incredible-adventures.com) in Grand Bahama offers cage diving with tiger sharks. You'll sit in the water as giant sharks come breathtakingly close, the only thing between you a few strips of metal.

Feeding sharks when humans are present make these dives controversial, especially when multiple sharks are involved and there's the possibility of a frenzy. Dive operators doing these extreme adventures are experienced and knowledgeable about shark-feeding patterns and signs of aggression, but partake in these dives at your own risk.

French Angelfish

Four-Eyed Butterflyfish

Grunt

Nassau Grouper

Parrotfish

Queen Triggerfish

Sergeant Major

Snapper

Tang

Barracuda*

Lionfish*

Shark*

*dangerous fish

WHAT YOU'LL SEE UNDER THE SEA

Reefs in the Bahamas are alive with colorful life. Vibrant hard corals—such as star, brain, staghorn, and elk—and waving purple sea fans are home to schools of myraid fish, some pictured above. Be on the lookout for lionfish; a prick from the fins of this poisonous fish is painful and could send you to the hospital. The most common sharks in the Bahamas

are nurse sharks (typically non-threatening to humans) and Caribbean reef sharks. The deeper you dive, the bigger and more varied shark species get.

Generally, the further the reef is from a developed area the more abundant the marine life, but even sites around developed islands might surprise you.

ISLAND-HOPPING

The Bahamas is a boater's paradise, with shallow protected waters and secluded, safe harbors. In small island groups, travel takes just a few hours, even minutes. The Abacos archipelago and the Exuma Cays are the best and most convenient islands to hop.

THE ABACOS

If you're cruising from Florida, clear customs in West End, Grand Bahama; the Abaco Cays start just north.

Grand Cay, at the northern end of the chain, has a small community of 200 people. Most yachters find the anchorage off the community dock adequate, and the docks at Rosie's Place can take boats up to 80 feet. Double anchors are advised to handle the harbor's tidal current.

Fox Town, on the "mainland" of Little Abaco, is a good fuel stop, the first if you're traveling east from West End. Farther south, stock up on provisions in **Coopers Town,** Little Abaco's largest community. Just northeast is an 80-slip marina at **Spanish Cay.**

Cruising south, **Green Turtle Cay** has excellent yachting facilities. The Green Turtle Club dominates White Sound's northern end, whereas Bluff

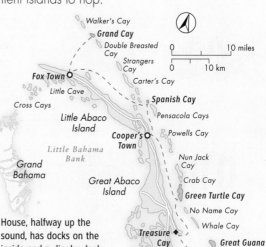

House, halfway up the sound, has docks on the inside and a dinghy dock below the club on the Sea of Abaco side.

South of Green Turtle, back on mainland Great Abaco, **Treasure Cay** Hotel Resort and Marina is one of the largest marinas on the island. Here you can play golf, dine, or relax on a beautiful beach.

Straight back out in the Sea of Abaco is **Great Guana Cay** and its gorgeous 7-mi strip of pristine sand. On Sunday don't miss the famous pig roast at Nipper's Bar. Just south is New England–style charmer **Man-O-War Cay,** a boatbuilding settlement with deserted beaches and 28-slip Man-O-War Marina. Fowl Cay

Park offers great snorkeling and diving just to the north.

Back on Great Abaco, **Marsh Harbour** is the capital and most populated settlement in the Abacos. Boaters consider it one of the easiest harbors to enter. It has several full-service marinas, including the 190-slip Boat Harbour Marina and the 80-slip Conch Inn Marina. This is the stop to catch up on banking and business needs. There are great restaurants and shops, too.

Fishing near Green Turtle Cay

Exuma Cays Land and Sea Park

THE EXUMA CAYS

To really get off the beaten path, the Exuma Cays are where it's at. This 120-mi archipelago is made up of small cays, many of which are still uninhabited or privately owned, and interspersed with sand banks and spits. Throughout is excellent diving and snorkeling. Boaters usually stock up and clear customs in Nassau, cross the yellow banks to the north of the chain, and slowly make their way south.

BOAT TOURS

If you don't have your own boat, these outfitters will take you on island-hopping adventures.

Captain Plug.
☎ 242/577–0273. $200 for a full day of island hopping in the Abacos.

Four C's Adventures.
☎ 242/355-5077
⊕ www.exumawatertours. com. $2,000 for a full day private charter from Great Exuma through the cays.

High Seas Private Excursions. ☎ 242/376-4234 ⊕ www.highseasex-cursions.com. $3,500 for a full day excursion to the Exuma Cays from Nassau.

Highbourne Cay at the chain's northern end has a marina and food store. You can explore many of the surrounding cays by tender if you prefer to dock here. Nearby, **Allan's Cay** is home to hundreds of iguanas that readily accept food.

Norman's Cay has an airstrip and Norman's Cay Beach Club has a fantastic restaurant and bar. Just south is the 176-sq-mi **Exuma Cays Land and Sea Park**. It has some of the country's best snorkeling and diving. Warderick Wells Cay houses the park headquarters, which has nature trail maps and a gift shop. Just below, **Compass Cay** has a marina known for its friendly nurse sharks and a small convenience store. **Pipe Creek,** which winds between Compass and Staniel Cays, has great shelling, snorkeling, diving, and bonefishing. **Staniel Cay** is the hub of activity in these parts and a favorite destination of yachters. That's thanks to the Staniel Cay Yacht Club, the only full-service marina in the cays. It makes a good base for visiting **Big Major Cay**, where wild pigs swim out to

The Abacos

The Exumas

Ship Channel Cay
Allan's Cay
Highbourne Cay
Lang Cay
Norman's Cay
Shroud Cay
Hawksbill Cay   Exuma Cays Land
Cistern Cay   and Sea Park
Waderick Wells Cay
Halls Pond Cay   O'Brian's Cay
Bells Cay   Compass Cay
Pipe Creek   Joe Cay
                     Thomas Cay
Big Major Cay   Staniel
Thunderball   Cay
Grotto

0   10 miles
0   10 km

meet you, and **Thunderball Grotto,** a beautiful marine cave that snorkelers (at low tide) and experienced scuba divers can explore.

BONEFISHING

WHAT IS BONEFISHING?

Bonefishing is the fly-fishing sport of choice in the Bahamas. The country is full of pristine shallow flats and mangroves where stealthy "gray ghosts"—silvery white, sleek fish—school in large groups. Hooking one is a challenge, as the fish are fast, strong, and perfectly camouflaged to the sand and water.

To catch bonefish you need the right mix of knowledge, instinct, and patience. Guides are the best way to go, as their knowledge of the area and schooling patterns gives them an uncanny ability to find bonefish quickly.

EQUIPMENT

Basics include a fly-fishing rod and reel and the right lure. Experienced anglers, guides, and fishing-supply dealers can help you gear up with the best and latest technology. Bonefishing is catch and release, so always use barbless hooks and work quickly when removing them to avoid stressing the fish. Wear comfortable, light clothing that protects much of your body from the sun, as you'll be out for hours without shade.

In many places you can just walk offshore onto the flats. Some anglers use shallow draft boats with a raised platform in the back, where they pole into extremely shallow areas.

BEST PLACES TO BONEFISH

Bonefish hang out in shallow flats and mangrove areas. Andros, Bimini, and the Exumas have the best bonefishing; Abaco, Eleuthera, and Long Island also provide excellent adventures. If you have the time, visit the southernmost islands, like Crooked, Acklins, or Inagua, where these gray ghosts are "uneducated" to anglers.

WHERE TO STAY

Bonefishing lodges are common in the Bahamas and often include top-notch guides. Accommodations are usually basic. Here are our top bonefishing lodges:

- Andros Island Bonefishing Club

- Bishop's Bonefish Resort, Grand Bahama

- Crooked Island Lodge

- Peace and Plenty Bonefish Lodge, the Exumas

- Rickmon Bonefish Lodge, the Abacos

- Small Hope Bay Lodge, Andros

(left pg) Bonefishing in Andros.
(right) A prize catch.

OTHER TYPES OF FISHING

Make sure you are familiar with fishing regulations before you begin your adventure. Visit ⊕ *www.bahamas.com/things-do/fishing.*

DEEP-SEA FISHING

Deep water is just a few miles off most islands, where anglers try for large ocean fish—tuna, wahoo, mahi mahi, shark, and marlin. Like bonefishing, the fight is what most anglers are after; however, a day on the ocean can provide a great meal. The Abacos has great deep-sea fishing, and many tournaments are held there each year.

REEF/SHOAL FISHING

Fishing with a rod, or Bahamian "handlining" can be a great family fishing adventure. Anchoring near a shoal or reef, or even trolling with a lure, can be relaxing. The Out Islands are home to shoals, reefs, and wrecks that are less visited by fishing enthusiasts.

SPEARFISHING

Most reefs are okay for free-dive spear fishing, but spear guns (guns that fire spears) are illegal in the Bahamas. Spear is the traditional Bahamian fishing method, so reefs close to more developed islands tend to have fewer fish. The Out Islands still have lesser-known spots good for spearfishing.

SAILING

Sailing is popular in the Bahamas, and there are many regattas held here throughout the year. The Abacos, the sailing capital of the Bahamas, also host an open regatta, inviting all classes of boats and sailors to join in for a week of island hopping and racing. Large sailboats are available for charter in Marsh Harbour and Hope Town.

NEW PROVIDENCE AND PARADISE ISLANDS

WELCOME TO NEW PROVIDENCE AND PARADISE ISLANDS

TOP REASONS TO GO

★ **Beach-hop:** New Providence beaches, though less secluded than those on the Out Islands, still tempt travelers with their balmy breezes and aquamarine water. Choose between the more remote beaches on the island's western end, action-packed strips on Cable Beach, or public beaches in downtown Nassau.

★ **Dine with the best of 'em:** New Providence is the country's culinary capital. Eat at a grungy local dive for one meal, then feast in a celebrity-chef restaurant for the next.

★ **Experience Atlantis:** Explore the world's largest outdoor aquarium, splash around in the something-for-everyone water park, or dine at one of the 40-plus restaurants, all while never leaving the resort property.

★ **Celebrate Junkanoo:** This uniquely Bahamian carnival takes place the day after Christmas and again on New Year's Day. If you miss it, there are smaller parades in Marina Village on Paradise Island each Wednesday and Saturday at 9:30 pm.

New Providence Island is often referred to by the name of its historic capital city, Nassau. More than two dozen hotels and at least twice as many restaurants lure more than 2 million tourists to the city, and nearby Paradise Island and Cable Beach, annually. The heart of commerce and government and the bulk of the country's 378,000 people are crammed onto the 21 mile by 7 mile island, less than 200 miles from Miami. Venturing outside the three main tourist areas will give you a better idea of true Bahamian life and a glimpse at some under-visited attractions that are worth the trek.

1 Nassau. Pink buildings dating back to the colonial era are interspersed with modern-day office complexes; horses pull their wooden carriages alongside stretch limousines; and tourists browse the local craft-centric straw market or shop for luxurious handbags at Gucci, all in this historic capital city.

2 Paradise Island. P. I. (as locals call the island) is connected to downtown Nassau's east end by a pair

of bridges. Atlantis is a beachfront resort complete with a gamut of dining options, a huge casino, and some of the region's fanciest shops. Most memorable, however, are the water-based activities, slides, and aquariums, which make it a perfect family destination. Love it or hate it, it's today's face of paradise.

Northeast Providence Channel

Northwest Point

West Bay St.

Old Fort Bay

Windsor

West Bay St.

Lyford Cay

Pleasant Bay

4

Clifton Point

Clifton Heritage Park

Adelaide

South West Bay

| 0 | | 2 miles |
| 0 | | 3 km |

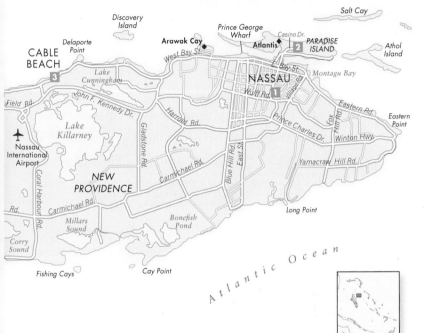

Discovery Island
Delaporte Point
Salt Cay
CABLE BEACH
Prince George Wharf
Arawak Cay
Casino Dr.
Atlantis **2** *PARADISE ISLAND*
Athol Island
West Bay St.
Lake Cunningham
E. Bay St.
Montagu Bay
NASSAU **1**
John F. Kennedy Dr.
Field Rd.
Wulff Rd.
Villiage Rd.
Lake Killarney
Harrold Rd.
Gladstone Rd.
Prince Charles Dr.
Eastern Rd.
Eastern Point
Nassau International Airport
Fox Hill Rd.
Winton Hwy.
NEW PROVIDENCE
Carmichael Rd.
Blue Hill Rd.
East St.
Yamacraw Hill Rd.
Coral Harbour Rd.
Carmichael Rd.
Bonefish Pond
Long Point
Rd.
Millars Sound
Corry Sound
Atlantic Ocean
Fishing Cays
Cay Point

3 **Cable Beach.** The crescent-shape stretch of sand west of Nassau is being transformed into Baha Mar, a 1,000-acre destination to rival Paradise Island. Three brand-new resorts; a top-class golf course; the largest casino in the Caribbean; a sprawling upscale spa; a snorkeling sanctuary; and a vast array of restaurants, bars, and nightlife guarantee there is something to suit everyone. A short walk west of the resort complex is a smattering of restaurants and cafés.

4 **Western New Providence.** West of Cable Beach's high-rise hotels, New Providence becomes primarily residential, with small restaurants and bars along the way. West Bay Street hugs the coastline, providing spectacular ocean views. This part of the island is the least developed, so it's the perfect spot to find a secluded beach or go bird-watching.

Updated
by Jessica
Robertson

An incongruous mix of glitzy casinos and quiet shady lanes, splashy megaresorts and tiny settlements that recall a distant simpler age, land development unrivaled elsewhere in the Bahamas, and vast stretches of untrammeled territory. This is New Providence Island, a grab-bag destination. The island, home to two-thirds of all Bahamians, provides fast-paced living, nightlife that lasts until dawn, and high-end shopping strips. And when all the hustle and bustle becomes too much, it's easy to find quiet stretches of sandy white beach where the only noise is the waves rolling in.

In the course of its history, the island has weathered the comings and goings of lawless pirates, Spanish invaders, slave-holding British Loyalists who fled the United States after the Revolutionary War, Civil War–era Confederate blockade runners, and Prohibition rum-runners. Nevertheless, New Providence remains most influenced by England, which sent its first royal governor to the island in 1718. Although Bahamians won government control in 1967 and independence six years later, British influence is felt to this day.

Nassau is the nation's capital and transportation hub, as well as its banking and commercial center. The fortuitous combination of tourist-friendly enterprise, tropical weather, and island flavor with a European overlay has not gone unnoticed: each year more than 2.5 million cruise-ship passengers arrive at Nassau's Prince George Wharf.

PLANNING

WHEN TO GO

With the warm Gulf Stream currents swirling and balmy trade winds blowing, New Providence is an appealing year-round destination. Temperatures usually hover in the 70s and 80s and rarely get above 90°F on a midsummer's day or below 60°F on a winter's night. June to October tend to be the hottest and wettest months, although rain is often limited to periodic afternoon showers.

The best time to visit the island is December to May, especially if you're escaping the cold. Don't mind the locals, who'll likely tell you it's too chilly to hit the beach in winter, but you may want to pack a light sweater if you plan on dining outdoors. Visitors from colder climates may find the humid summer days and nights a bit stifling. Be aware that tropical depressions, tropical storms, and hurricanes are a possibility in New Providence during the Atlantic hurricane season from early June to late November. Expect to pay between 15% and 30% less off-season at most resorts.

TOP FESTIVALS

WINTER **Bahamas International Film Festival.** In early December, the Bahamas International Film Festival in Nassau celebrates cinema in paradise, with screenings, receptions, and movie-industry panels. ⊠ *Nassau* ⊕ *www. bintlfilmfest.com.*

Christmas Jollification. This ongoing arts-and-crafts fair with Bahamian Christmas crafts, food, and music is held at the Retreat in Nassau the third weekend in November. ⊠ *Nassau* ⊕ *www.bnt.bs.*

Junior Junkanoo Parade. The island's schoolchildren compete for bragging rights in the Junior Junkanoo Parade in mid-December. The parade starts at 6 pm and kids in preschool through high school dress up in crepe paper costumes and put on an exciting show.

Junkanoo. Once Christmas dinner is over, the focus shifts to Junkanoo. The first major parade of the season starts just after midnight in downtown Nassau. There's a second parade on New Year's Day. ⊠ *Nassau.*

SPRING **Festival Rum Bahamas.** Spend three days in late February learning about
Fodor's Choice and drinking rum, dancing to live bands, eating Bahamian food, and
★ experiencing the history and culture of the islands at this festival located in the moat, inside and atop historic Fort Charlotte. ⊠ *Nassau* ⊕ *www. festivalrumbahamas.com.*

SUMMER **Junkanoo Summer Festival.** Bay Street is transformed during the annual Junkanoo Summer festival held every Saturday night 7 pm to midnight during the month of July. Watch some of the island's top Junkanoo groups and sample local foods. ⊠ *Nassau* ⊕ *www.bahamas.com/ summerfestivals.*

Fox Hill Festival. The Nassau Fox Hill Festival in early August pays tribute to Emancipation with church services, Junkanoo parades, music, cookouts, games, and other festivities.

FALL   **International Cultural Weekend.** Eat and drink your way around the world at the International Cultural Weekend, hosted at the Botanic Gardens the third weekend of October.

HOTELS

If you want to mix with locals and experience a little more of Bahamian culture, choose a hotel in downtown Nassau. Its beaches are not dazzling; if you want to be beachfront on a gorgeous white strand, stay on Cable Beach or Paradise Island's Cabbage Beach. Reasons to stay in Nassau include proximity to shopping and affordability (although the cost of taxis to and from the better beaches can add up).

The plush Cable Beach and Paradise Island resorts are big and beautiful, glittering and splashy, and have the best beaches, but they can be overwhelming. In any case, these big, top-dollar properties generally have more amenities than you could possibly make use of, a selection of dining choices, and a full roster of sports and entertainment options. Stay in Cable Beach if you don't plan to visit Nassau or Paradise Island often; you need to take a cab, and the costs add up.

RESTAURANTS

Find everything from shabby shacks to elegant eateries. You'll recognize celebrity chef names like Todd English, Jean-Georges Vongerichten, and Nobu Matsuhisa, all of whom have restaurants here. On a budget? Eat brunch at one of the myriad all-you-can-eat buffets at the larger hotels on Paradise Island and Cable Beach

Note: A gratuity (15%) is often added to the bill automatically.

HOTEL AND RESTAURANT PRICES

Restaurant prices are based on the median main course price at dinner, excluding gratuity (typically 15%) and VAT (7.5%), which are automatically added to the bill. Hotel prices are for two people in a standard double room in high season, excluding service and 6%–12% hotel tax plus 7.5% VAT.

WHAT IT COSTS IN DOLLARS			
$	**$$**	**$$$**	**$$$$**
Restaurants	under $20	$20–$30	$31–$40	over $40
Hotels	under $200	$200–$300	$301–$400	over $400

VISITOR INFORMATION

The Ministry of Tourism operates tourist information booths at the airport, open daily from 8:30 am to 11:30 pm, and at Festival Place, which is adjacent to Prince George Wharf and open daily from 9 am to 5 pm. The Ministry of Tourism's People-to-People Program sets you up with a Bahamian family with similar interests to show you local culture firsthand.

Contacts Ministry of Tourism. ☎ 242/302–2000 ⊕ www.bahamas.com. **People-to-People Program.** ☎ 242/324–9772 ⊕ www.bahamas.com/people-to-people.

2

GETTING HERE AND AROUND

AIR TRAVEL

Lynden Pindling International Airport (NAS) is 8 miles west of Nassau. Many major U.S. airlines fly to Nassau from several different gateways; in addition, the nation's flag carrier, Bahamasair, flies to Nassau from four airports in Florida: Fort Lauderdale (FLL), Miami (MIA), Orlando (MCO), and West Palm Beach (PBI). There is no public bus service from the airport to hotels. Many smaller airlines depart from Nassau to the other islands of the Bahamas. Major car-rental companies are represented at the airport. A taxi ride for two people from the airport to downtown Nassau costs $32; to Paradise Island, $38 (this includes the $2 bridge toll); and to Cable Beach, $25. Each additional passenger is $3, and excess baggage costs $2 a bag.

BOAT AND FERRY TRAVEL

Water taxis travel between Prince George Wharf and Paradise Island during daylight hours at half-hour intervals. The one-way cost is $3 per person, and the trip takes 12 minutes. Nassau is also the primary hub for Bahamas mail boats and ferries to the Out Islands.

BUS TRAVEL

The frequent jitneys are the cheapest choice on routes such as Cable Beach to downtown Nassau. Fare is $1.25 each way, and exact change is required. Hail one at a bus stop, hotel, or public beach. In downtown Nassau jitneys wait on Frederick Street and along the eastern end of Bay Street. Bus service runs throughout the day until 7 pm.

CAR TRAVEL

Rent a car if you plan to explore the whole island. Rentals are available at the airport, downtown, on Paradise Island, and at some resorts for $55–$120 per day. Gasoline costs between $5 and $6 a gallon. Remember to drive on the left. Virgo Car Rental, a local company, doesn't have a website or an airport rental desk, but it does offer a courtesy shuttle to its nearby office.

Contacts Avis Rent A Car. ✉ *Lynden Pindling International Airport, Nassau* ☎ *242/377–7121* ⊕ *www.avis.com.* **Budget Rent-A-Car.** ✉ *Lynden Pindling International Airport, Nassau* ☎ *242/377–9000* ⊕ *www.budget.com.* **Dollar/ Thrifty Rent A Car.** ✉ *Lynden Pindling International Airport, Nassau* ☎ *242/377–8300* ⊕ *www.dollar.com.* **Hertz Rent-A-Car.** ✉ *Lynden Pindling International Airport, Nassau* ☎ *242/377–8684* ⊕ *www.hertz.com.* **Virgo Car Rental.** ☎ *242/377–1275.*

SCOOTER TRAVEL

Two people can rent a motor scooter for about $65 for a half day, $85 for a full day.

TAXI TRAVEL

Unless you plan to jump all over the island, taxis are the most convenient way to get around. The fare is $9 plus a $2 bridge toll between downtown Nassau and Paradise Island, $22 from Cable Beach to Paradise Island (plus $2 toll), and $22 from Cable Beach to Nassau. Fares are for two passengers; each additional passenger is $3. It's customary to tip taxi drivers 15%.

Contacts Bahamas Transport. ☎ *242/323–5111.*

The Royal Bahamas Police Force Band performs in front of Government House.

EXPLORING

NASSAU

Nassau's sheltered harbor bustles with cruise-ship activity, while a block away Bay Street's sidewalks are crowded with shoppers who duck into air-conditioned boutiques and relax on benches in the shade of mahogany and lignum vitae trees. Shops angle for tourist dollars with fine imported goods at duty-free prices, yet you'll find a handful of stores overflowing with authentic Bahamian crafts, food supplies, and other delights.

With a revitalization of downtown ongoing, Nassau is trying to recapture some of its past glamour. Nevertheless, modern influences are completely apparent: fancy restaurants and trendy coffeehouses have popped up everywhere. These changes have come partly in response to the growing number of upper-crust crowds that now supplement the spring breakers and cruise passengers who have traditionally flocked to Nassau. Of course, you can still find a wild club or a rowdy bar, but you can also sip cappuccino while viewing contemporary Bahamian art or dine by candlelight beneath prints of old Nassau, serenaded by soft, island-inspired calypso music.

A trip to Nassau wouldn't be complete without a stop at some of the island's well-preserved historic buildings. The large, pink colonial-style edifices house Parliament and some of the courts, while others, like Fort Charlotte, date back to the days when pirates ruled the town. Take a tour via horse-drawn carriage for the full effect.

2

TOP ATTRACTIONS

Arawak Cay. Known to Nassau residents as "The Fish Fry," Arawak Cay is one of the best places to knock back a Kalik beer, chat with locals, watch or join in a fast-paced game of dominoes, or sample traditional Bahamian fare. The two-story Twin Brothers and Goldie's Enterprises are two of the most popular places. Local fairs and craft shows are often held in the adjacent field. ⊠ *W. Bay St. and Chippingham Rd., Nassau* ⊠ *Free.*

John Watling's Distillery. The former Buena Vista Estate, which featured in the James Bond film *Casino Royale* has been painstakingly transformed and taken back to its glory days, emerging as the new home of the John Watling's Distillery. Parts of the home date back to 1789 and the actual production of the line of John Watling's artisanal rums, gins, vodkas, and liquors are handmade, hand bottled, and hand labeled just as they would have been in that era. Take a self-guided tour through the grounds and working estate to learn the fascinating history of the home and then walk out back to watch the rum production line from an overhead mezzanine. Sit in the Red Turtle Tavern with an internationally acclaimed Rum Dum or just a great mojito and pick up a unique Bahamian souvenir in the on-site retail store. ⊠ *17 Delancy St., Nassau* ☎ *242/322–2811* ⊕ *www.johnwatlings.com* ⊠ *Free.*

Fodor's Choice ★ **National Art Gallery of the Bahamas.** Opened in 2003, the museum houses the works of esteemed Bahamian artists such as Max Taylor, Amos Ferguson, Brent Malone, John Cox, and Antonius Roberts. The glorious Italianate-colonial mansion, built in 1860 and restored in the 1990s, has double-tiered verandahs with elegant columns. It was the residence of Sir William Doyle, the first chief justice of the Bahamas. Don't miss the museum's gift shop, where you'll find books about the Bahamas as well as Bahamian quilts, prints, ceramics, jewelry, and crafts. ⊠ *West and W. Hill Sts., across from St. Francis Xavier Cathedral, Nassau* ☎ *242/328–5800* ⊕ *www.nagb.org.bs* ⊠ *$10* ☉ *Closed Mon.*

FAMILY **Pirates of Nassau.** Take a self-guided journey through Nassau's pirate days in this interactive museum devoted to such notorious members of the city's past as Blackbeard, Mary Read, and Anne Bonney. Board a pirate ship, see dioramas of intrigue on the high seas, hear historical narration, and experience sound effects re-creating some of the gruesome highlights. It's a fun and educational (if slightly scary) family outing. Be sure to check out the offbeat souvenirs in the Pirate Shop. ⊠ *George and King Sts., Nassau* ☎ *242/356–3759* ⊕ *www.pirates-of-nassau.com* ⊠ *$13.*

The Retreat. Nearly 200 species of exotic palm trees grace the 11 verdant acres appropriately known as The Retreat, which serves as the headquarters of the Bahamas National Trust. Stroll in blessed silence through the lush grounds, and be on the lookout for native birds. It's a perfect break on a steamy Nassau day. The Retreat hosts the Jollification—the unofficial start to the Christmas season—the third weekend in November. Carols, festive food and drinks, a kids' holiday craft center, and local artisans selling native and Christmas crafts make this a must-do event. ⊠ *Village Rd., Paradise Island* ☎ *242/393–1317* ⊠ *$2* ☉ *Closed weekends.*

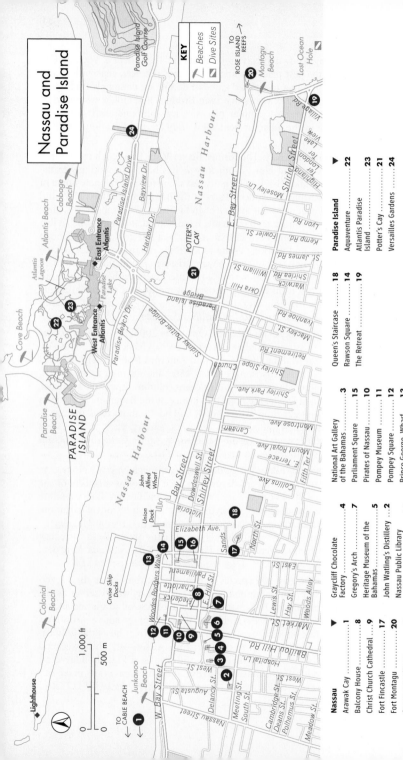

Nassau and Paradise Island

KEY

⚓ Beaches

▧ Dive Sites

TO ROSE ISLAND REEFS →

Nassau ▶

Paradise Island ▶

0 — 1,000 ft
0 — 500 m

WORTH NOTING

Balcony House. A delightful 18th-century landmark—a pink two-story house named aptly for its overhanging balcony—this is the oldest wooden residential structure in Nassau and its furnishings and design recapture the elegance of a bygone era. A mahogany staircase, believed to have been salvaged from a ship during the 19th century, is an interior highlight. A guided tour through this fascinating building is an hour well spent. ⊠ *Market St. and Trinity Pl., Nassau* ☎ *242/302–2621* ✉ *Donations accepted.*

Christ Church Cathedral. It's worth the short walk off the main thoroughfare to see the stained-glass windows of this cathedral, which was built in 1837 when Nassau officially became a city. Don't miss the flower-filled Garden of Remembrance. Sunday Mass is held at 7:30 am, 9 am, 11:15 am, and 6 pm. Drop by the cathedral Christmas Eve and New Year's Eve to see the glorious church at night, and hear the music and choir. Call ahead to find out the time of the service. ⊠ *George and King Sts., Nassau* ☎ *242/322–4186* ⊕ *www.christchurchcathedralbahamas. com* ✉ *Free.*

Fort Fincastle. Shaped like the bow of a ship and perched near the top of the Queen's Staircase, Fort Fincastle—named for Royal Governor Lord Dunmore (Viscount Fincastle)—was completed in 1793 to be a lookout post for marauders trying to sneak into the harbor. It served as a lighthouse in the early 19th century. A 15- to 20-minute tour costs just $1 per person and includes the nearby Queen's Staircase. The fort's 126-foot-tall water tower is more than 200 feet above sea level (and the island's highest point). ⊠ *Top of Elizabeth Ave. hill, south of Shirley St., Nassau* ☎ *242/356–9085* ✉ *Nonresident adults $3; seniors, residents, and children $2.*

Fort Montagu. The oldest of the island's three forts, Montagu was built of local limestone in 1741 to repel Spanish invaders. The only action it saw was when it was occupied for two weeks by rebel American troops—among them a lieutenant named John Paul Jones—seeking arms and ammunition during the Revolutionary War. The small fortification is quite simple, but displays a lovely elevated view of Nassau Harbour. The second level has a number of weathered cannons. A public beach looks out upon Montagu Bay, where many international yacht regattas and Bahamian sloop races are held annually. ⊠ *East of Bay St. on Eastern Rd., Nassau* ✉ *$2.*

Government House. The official residence of the Bahamas governor-general, the personal representative of the Queen since 1801, this imposing pink-and-white building on Duke Street is an excellent example of the mingling of Bahamian-British and American colonial architecture. Catch the changing of the guard ceremony, which takes place every second Saturday of the month at 11 am. The stars of the pomp and pageantry are members of the Royal Bahamas Police Force Band. There is a tea party open to the public from 3 to 4 pm on the last Friday of the month from January to June as part of the People-to-People program. ☒ *Duke and George Sts., Nassau* 🕾 *242/356–5415 ceremony schedule, 242/397–8816 tea party, 242/322–2020 Government House.*

FAMILY **Graycliff Chocolate Factory.** Go behind the scenes at this boutique chocolate factory where can make your own sweet souvenirs. The tour lasts about an hour, and after watching master chocolatiers in action and learning the history of chocolate production around the world, guests enter the chocolate classroom where they get to design their own creations, including a signature Graycliff chocolate bar. There is also a kids' classroom for younger chocolate lovers as well as a chocolates and spirits pairing for adults. ☒ *Graycliff Hotel, W. Hill St., Nassau* 🕾 *242/302–9150* ⊕ *www.graycliff.com* 💶 *$49.95* ☉ *Closed Sun.*

Gregory's Arch. Named for John Gregory (royal governor 1849–54), this arch, at the intersection of Market and Duke streets, separates downtown from the "over-the-hill" neighborhood of Grant's Town, where much of Nassau's population lives. Grant's Town was laid out in the 1820s by Governor Lewis Grant as a settlement for freed slaves. Visitors once enjoyed late-night mingling with the locals in the small, dimly lighted bars; nowadays you should exhibit the same caution you would if you were visiting the commercial areas of a large city. ☒ *Nassau* 💶 *Free.*

FAMILY **Heritage Museum of The Bahamas.** So many artifacts are on display in this small but interesting museum that you can easily spend an hour wandering. Opt for a guided tour, or use the audio tour to take in everything at your own pace. You'll learn about Bahamian history from the days of pirates through the days of slavery to the present. One of the best exhibits is the life-size replica of the old Bay Street General Store. Quite by a series of coincidences, the collection box from the oldest church ended up in this museum—right across the street from the remains of the very same church. ☒ *8–14 W. Hill St., Nassau* 🕾 *242/302–9150* ⊕ *www.graycliff.com/heritage-village-at-graycliff* 💶 *$18.50 guided tour* ☉ *Closed Sun.*

Nassau Public Library and Museum. The octagonal building near Parliament Square was the Nassau Gaol (the old British spelling for jail), circa 1797. You're welcome to pop in and browse. The small prison cells are now lined with books. The museum has an interesting collection of historic prints and old colonial documents. Computers with Internet access are available for rent ($1 for 15 minutes, $4 for an hour). ☒ *Shirley St. between Parliament St. and Bank La., Nassau* 🕾 *242/322–4907* 💶 *Free* ☉ *Closed Sun.*

Parliament Square. Nassau is the seat of the national government. The Bahamian Parliament comprises two houses—a 16-member Senate (Upper House) and a 39-member House of Assembly (Lower House). If the House is in session, sit in to watch lawmakers debate. Parliament Square's pink, colonnaded government buildings were constructed in the late 1700s and early 1800s by Loyalists who came to the Bahamas from North Carolina. The square is dominated by a statue of a slim young Queen Victoria that was erected on her birthday, May 24, in 1905. ⊠ *Bay St., Nassau* ☎ *242/322–2041* ▣ *Free* ⊙ *Closed weekends.*

Pompey Museum. The building, where slave auctions were held in the 1700s, is named for a rebel slave who lived on the Out Island of Exuma in 1830. The structure and historic artifacts inside were destroyed by fire in December 2011, but have been painstakingly re-created and new exhibits have been acquired and produced. Exhibits focus on the issues of slavery and emancipation and highlight the works of local artists. A knowledgeable, enthusiastic young staff is on hand to answer questions. ⊠ *Bay and George Sts., Nassau* ☎ *242/356–0495* ⊕ *www. ammcbahamas.com* ▣ *$3* ⊙ *Closed Sun.*

FAMILY **Pompey Square.** This open space at the western end of Bay Street overlooks the busy Nassau Harbour and is the spot to catch local festivals and events, live music, and Bahamian craft shows. With 24-hour security, public restrooms, an interactive water feature that delights kids of all ages, and a host of small restaurants and bars nearby, this square, which pays tribute to a slave who fought for his freedom, is the start of a strategic redevelopment of downtown Nassau. ⊠ *Bay St., Nassau* ▣ *Free.*

Prince George Wharf. The wharf that leads into Rawson Square is the first view that cruise passengers encounter after they tumble off their ships. Up to a dozen gigantic cruise ships call on Nassau at any one time, and passengers spill out onto downtown, giving Nassau an instant, and constantly replenished, surge of life. Even if you're not visiting via cruise ship, it's worth heading to Festival Place, an outdoor Bahamian village–style shopping emporium. Here you'll find booths for Bahamian artisans; live music; vendors selling diving, fishing, and day trips; scooter rentals; and an information desk offering maps, directions, and suggestions for sightseeing. You can also arrange walking tours of historic Nassau here. ⊠ *Waterfront at Rawson Sq., Nassau* ▣ *Free.*

Queen's Staircase. A popular early-morning exercise regime for locals, the "66 Steps" (as Bahamians call them) are thought to have been carved out of a solid limestone cliff by slaves in the 1790s. The staircase was later named to honor Queen Victoria's reign. Pick up some souvenirs at the ad hoc straw market along the narrow road that leads to the site. ⊠ *Top of Elizabeth Ave. hill, south of Shirley St., Nassau* ▣ *Free.*

Rawson Square. This shady square connects Bay Street to Prince George Wharf. As you enter off Bay Street, note the statue of Sir Milo Butler, the first postindependence (and first native Bahamian) governor general. Horse-drawn surreys wait for passengers along Prince George Wharf (expect to pay about $30 for a half-hour ride through Nassau's streets). Between Rawson Square and Festival Place, check out (or perhaps stop inside) the open-air **hair-braiding pavilion,** where women work their magic at prices ranging from $2 for a single strand to $100 for an elaborate do. Often-overlooked is the nearby Randolph W. Johnston's bronze statue, *Tribute to Bahamian Women*. The prime minister meets with his cabinet every Tuesday in the building that lines the eastern side of the square. ⊠ *Bay St., Nassau* ▣ *Free.*

The Cloisters in Versailles Gardens is possibly the most peaceful spot on the island.

PARADISE ISLAND

The graceful, arched bridges of Paradise Island ($2 round-trip toll for cars and motorbikes; free for bicyclists and pedestrians) lead to and from the extravagant world of Paradise Island. Until 1962 the island was largely undeveloped and known as Hog Island. A&P heir Huntington Hartford changed the name when he built the island's first resort complex. In 1994 South African developer Sol Kerzner transformed the existing high-rise hotel into the first phase of Atlantis. Many years, a number of new hotels, a water park, and more than $1 billion later, Atlantis has taken over the island. Home to multimillion-dollar homes and condominiums and a handful of independent resort properties, you can still find a quiet spot on Cabbage Beach, or Paradise Beach which west of Atlantis.

FAMILY
Fodor's Choice
★
Aquaventure. From near-vertical slides that plunge through shark tanks to a quarter-mile-long lazy river ride, this 141-acre water park allows you to both unwind and get your adrenaline pumping. Spend the day going from ride to ride, or relax under an umbrella on the white sand of three unique beaches, or one of 11 swimming pools. Three pools are designed especially for the youngest of guests, including Splashers, a Mayan-themed water playground. Day passes for nonresort guests are limited so be sure to plan well ahead. ⊠ *Atlantis Paradise Island, Paradise Island* ☎ *242/363–3000* ⊕ *www.atlantisbahamas.com* ☑ *Day pass $161 high season, $150 low season; beach pass $70.*

FAMILY
Fodor's Choice
★
Atlantis Paradise Island. This pink fantasia with its sunstruck Royal Towers comes into view before you cross one of the Paradise Island bridges. With luxury shops, a glitzy casino, and many choices for dining and drinks (40 restaurants, bars, and lounges), Atlantis is as much

a tourist attraction as a resort hotel. At Dolphin Cay you can interact with dolphins, sea lions, and stingrays. The 63-acre Aquaventure water park provides thrilling waterslides and high-intensity rapids as well as a lazy-river tube ride through the sprawling grounds. Celebrity sightings are frequent at both Nobu restaurant and Aura nightclub. The on-site comedy club, Joker's Wild, brings top comedians to the stage. Many of the resort's facilities, including the restaurants and casino, are open to nonguests, but the leisure and sports facilities are open only to resort guests and those who purchase a day pass. Atlantis has the world's largest man-made marine habitat, consisting of 11 lagoons. To see it, take the guided Discover Atlantis tour. ⊠ *Casino Dr., Paradise Island* ☎ *242/363–3000* ✆ *Discover Atlantis tour $42; Aquaventure day pass $150–$161; beach day pass $70; lockers $15–$25 per day; casino free.*

Potter's Cay. Walk the road beneath the Paradise Island bridges to Potter's Cay to watch sloops bringing in and selling loads of fish and conch—pronounced *konk*. Along the road to the cay are dozens of stands where you can watch the conch being extracted from its glistening pink shell, straight from the sea. If you don't have the know-how to handle the tasty conch's preparation—getting the diffident creature out of its shell requires boring a hole at the right spot to sever the muscle that keeps it entrenched—you can enjoy a conch salad on the spot, as fresh as it comes, and take notes for future attempts. Empty shells are sold as souvenirs. Many locals and hotel chefs come here to purchase the fresh catches; you can also find vegetables, herbs, and such condiments as fiery Bahamian peppers preserved in lime juice, and locally grown pineapples, papayas, and bananas. Join in on a raucous game of dominoes outside many of the stalls. Some stalls are closed on Sunday. There's also a police station and dockmaster's office, where you can book an inexpensive trip on a mail boat headed to the Out Islands. Be aware that these boats are built for cargo, not passenger comfort, and it's a rough ride even on calm seas. ⊠ *Nassau* ✆ *Free.*

Versailles Gardens. Fountains and statues of luminaries and legends adorn Versailles Gardens, the terraced lawn at the One & Only Ocean Club, once the private hideaway of Huntington Hartford. At the top of the gardens stand the **Cloisters,** the remains of a stone monastery built by Augustinian monks in France in the 13th century, imported to the United States in the 1920s by newspaper baron William Randolph Hearst. ⊠ *One & Only Ocean Club, Paradise Island Dr., Paradise Island* ☎ *242/363–2501* ✆ *Free.*

CABLE BEACH

From downtown Nassau, West Bay Street follows the coast west past Arawak Cay to the Cable Beach strip. If you're not driving, catch the No. 10 jitney for a direct ride from downtown. This main drag runs the length of the new Baha Mar resort development, separating the golf course and green space from the resorts and beach. Walk or drive west of the megaresort for a smattering of smaller restaurants and local neighborhoods.

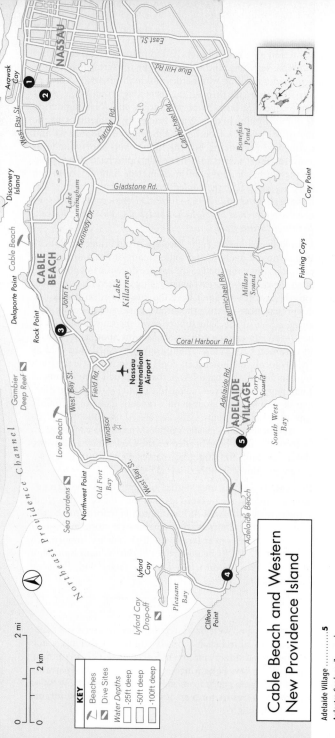

Cable Beach and Western
New Providence Island

KEY

◢ Beaches
◢ Dive Sites

Water Depths
-25ft deep
-50ft deep
-100ft deep

Northeast Providence Channel

NASSAU

Arawak Cay
West Bay St.
Harold Rd.
Blue Hill Rd.
Carmichael Rd.
East St.

Discovery Island

Gladstone Rd.

Lake Cunningham

CABLE BEACH

Cable Beach
Delaporte Point
Rock Point

Kennedy Dr.
John F.

Lake Killarney

Bonefish Pond

Cay Point

Gambier Deep Reef
Love Beach

Sea Gardens

Northwest Point

Old Fort Bay

West Bay St.

Field Rd.
West Bay St.

Windsor

Nassau International Airport

Coral Harbour Rd.

Carmichael Rd.

Millars Sound

Fishing Cays

Adelaide Rd.

Corry Sound

ADELAIDE VILLAGE

South West Bay

Lyford Cay
Lyford Cay Drop-off

Pleasant Bay

Clifton Point

Adelaide Beach

0   2 mi
0   2 km

WORTH NOTING

The Caves. These large limestone caverns that the waves sculpted over the eons are said to have sheltered the early Arawak Indians. An oddity perched right beside the road, they're worth a glance—although in truth, there's not much to see, as the dark interior doesn't lend itself to exploration. Across the street is a concrete viewing platform overlooking the ocean. Just a short drive west beyond the caves, on an island between traffic lanes, is **Conference Corner,** where U.S. president John F. Kennedy, Canadian prime minister John Diefenbaker, and British prime minister Harold Macmillan planted trees on the occasion of their 1962 summit in Nassau. ⊠ *W. Bay St. and Blake Rd., Cable Beach* ☎ *Free*.

WESTERN NEW PROVIDENCE

Immediately west of Cable Beach, the hotel strip gives way to residential neighborhoods interspersed with shops, restaurants, and cafés. Homes become more and more posh the farther west you go; Lyford Cay—the island's original gated community—is home to the original 007, Sean Connery. Hang a left at the Lyford Cay roundabout, and you'll eventually come across the historic Clifton Heritage Park, the local brewery where Kalik and Heineken are brewed and bottled, a new upscale second home development whose financiers include golfers Ernie Els and Tiger Woods, and finally the sleepy settlement of Adelaide.

The loop around the island's west and south coasts can be done in a couple of hours by car or scooter, but take some time for lunch and a swim along the way. Unless you're being taken around by a taxi or local, it's best to return along the same route, as internal roads can get confusing.

WORTH NOTING

Adelaide Village. The small community on New Providence's southwestern coast sits placidly, like a remnant of another era, between busy Adelaide Road and the ocean. It was first settled during the early 1830s by Africans who had been captured and loaded aboard slave ships bound for the New World. They were rescued on the high seas by the British Royal Navy, and the first group of liberated slaves reached Nassau in 1832. Today, there are two sides to Adelaide—the few dozen families who grow vegetables, raise chickens, and inhabit well-worn, pastel-painted wooden houses, shaded by casuarina, mahogany, and palm trees; and the more upscale beach cottages that are mostly used as weekend getaways. The village has a primary school, a few small grocery stores, and a few restaurants serving native foods. ⊠ *Adelaide* ☎ *Free*.

FAMILY **Ardastra Gardens, Zoo, and Conservation Centre.** Marching flamingos give a parading performance at Ardastra daily at 10:30 am, 2:15 pm, and 4 pm. Children can walk among the brilliant pink birds after the show. The zoo, with more than 5 acres of tropical greenery and ponds, also has an aviary of rare tropical birds including the bright-green Bahama parrot, native Bahamian creatures such as rock iguanas, the little (harmless) Bahamian boa constrictors, and a global collection of small animals. ⊠ *Chippingham Rd., south of W. Bay St., Nassau* ☎ *242/323–5806* ⊕ *www.ardastra.com* ☎ *$18*.

Cable Beach is the busiest island beach west of Nassau and Paradise Island. It's home to the upcoming Baha Mar resort, as well as several other resorts.

Clifton Heritage Park. It's quite a distance from just about any hotel you could stay at, but for history and nature buffs, this national park, rescued from the hands of developers, is worth the drive. Situated on a prehistoric Lucayan Village dating back to AD 1000–1500, Clifton Heritage Park allows you to walk through the ruins of slave quarters from an 18th-century plantation. The site can claim ties to pop culture as well because a number of hit movies have been filmed on land and sea here. Book one of the many tours ahead of time—they offer snorkeling out to the Coral Reef Sculpture Garden, nature walks, bush medicine and bird-watching tours, and ATV and buggy tours. Be sure to walk the path from the main parking lot toward the west, where you can enjoy the peace and quiet of the Sacred Space and admire the African women carved out of casuarina wood by local artist Antonius Roberts. Naturalists will enjoy walking along the paths lined with native flora and fauna that lead to wooden decks overlooking mangrove swamps. ⊠ *Clifton Pier, W. Bay St.* ☎ *242/362–4368* ⊕ *www.cliftonheritage.org.*

FAMILY **Fort Charlotte.** Built in 1788, this imposing fort features a waterless moat, drawbridge, ramparts, and a dungeon with a torture device. Local guides bring the fort to life (tips are expected), and tours are suitable for children. Fort Charlotte was built by Lord Dunmore, who named the massive structure after George III's wife. The fort and its surrounding 100 acres offer a wonderful view of the cricket grounds, the beach, and the ocean beyond. On Wednesday and Friday enjoy fully regaled actors reenacting life as it was in the Bahamas in the 18th and 19th centuries. An historic military parade and canon firing takes place daily at noon. ⊠ *W. Bay St. at Chippingham Rd., Nassau* ⊕ *Opposite Arawak Cay* ⊠*Nonresident adults $5; seniors and residents $3; children $2* ⊙ *Closed Christmas Day.*

BEACHES

New Providence is the Bahamas' most urban island, but that doesn't mean you won't find beautiful beaches. Powdery white sand, aquamarine waves, and shade-bearing palm trees are easy to come by. Cable Beach and the beaches near Atlantis are where you'll typically find loud music, bars serving tropical drinks, and vendors peddling everything from parasailing and Jet Ski rides to T-shirts and hair braiding. Downtown Nassau only has man-made beaches, the best being Junkanoo Beach just west of the British Colonial Hilton. Yet the capital city's beaches can't compare to the real thing. For a more relaxed environment, drive out of the main tourist areas. You'll likely find stretches of sand populated by locals only, or, more likely, no one at all.

> **SNAKES ALIVE!**
>
> The Bahamas has five types of snakes (none poisonous), but the most interesting is the Bahamian boa constrictor, threatened with extinction because Bahamians kill them on sight. The Bahamian boa is extremely unusual in that it has remnants of legs, called spurs. The male uses his spurs to tickle the female. Ask one of the trainers at Ardastra Gardens and Zoo to show you the boa up close.

NASSAU

Junkanoo Beach. Right in downtown Nassau, this beach is spring-break central from late February through April. The man-made beach isn't the prettiest on the island, but it's conveniently located if you only have a few quick hours to catch a tan. Music is provided by bands, DJs, and boom boxes; a growing number of bars keep the drinks flowing. **Amenities:** food and drink; parking (no fee); toilets; water sports. **Best for:** partiers; swimming. ⊠ *Immediately west of British Colonial Hilton, Nassau* ⊠ *Free.*

PARADISE ISLAND

FAMILY
Fodor's Choice
★

Cabbage Beach. At this beach you'll find 3 miles of white sand lined with shady casuarina trees, sand dunes, and sun worshippers. This is the place to go to rent Jet Skis or get a bird's-eye view of Paradise Island while parasailing. Hair braiders and T-shirt vendors stroll the beach, and hotel guests crowd the areas surrounding the resorts, including Atlantis. For peace and quiet, stroll east. **Amenities:** food and drink; lifeguards; parking (fee); water sports. **Best for:** solitude; partiers; swimming; walking. ⊠ *Paradise Island* ⊠ *Free.*

CABLE BEACH AND WESTERN NEW PROVIDENCE

FAMILY **Adelaide Beach.** Time your visit to this far-flung beach on the island's southwestern shore to catch low tide, when the ocean recedes, leaving behind sandbanks and seashells. It's a perfect place to take the kids for a shallow-water dip in the sea, or for a truly private rendezvous. Popular with locals, you'll likely have the miles-long stretch all to yourself unless it's a public holiday. **Amenities:** none. **Best for:** solitude; swimming; walking. ✉ *Adelaide* 🎟 *Free.*

Cable Beach. Hotels, including the massive Baha Mar resort development, dot the length of this 3-mile beach, so don't expect isolation. Music from hotel pool decks wafts out onto the sand, Jet Skis race up and down the waves, and vendors sell everything from shell jewelry to coconut drinks right from the shell. Access via new hotels may be limited, but join the locals and park at Goodman's Bay park on the eastern end of the beach. **Amenities:** parking (no fee); water sports. **Best for:** partiers; sunset; swimming; walking. ✉ *Cable Beach.*

Love Beach. If you're looking for great snorkeling and some privacy, drive about 20 minutes west of Cable Beach. White sand shimmers in the sun and the azure waves gently roll ashore. About a mile offshore are 40 acres of coral reef known as the Sea Gardens. Access is not marked, just look for a vacant lot. **Amenities:** none. **Best for:** solitude; snorkeling; sunset ✉ *Gambier Village.*

OFFSHORE ADVENTURES

For a true beach getaway, head to one of the tiny islands just off the coast of Paradise Island. A 20-minute boat ride from Nassau, Blue Lagoon Island has a number of beaches, including one in a tranquil cove lined with hammocks suspended by palm trees. Enjoy a grilled lunch and then rent a kayak or water bike if you're feeling ambitious.

WHERE TO EAT

NASSAU

$$ GREEK 🍴 **Athena Café and Bar.** You're greeted with a welcoming "Opa!" at this family-owned authentic Greek spot where they serve up tasty lunches at moderate prices seven days a week. This Greek restaurant provides a break from the Nassau culinary routine. **Known for:** the best Greek salad around; flaming cheese; the cries of "Opa!" as guests walk in. [$] *Average main: $20* ✉ *Bay St. at Charlotte St., Nassau* ☎ *242/326–1296* ⏲ *No dinner.*

$ BAHAMIAN Fodor's Choice ★ 🍴 **Bahamian Cookin' Restaurant.** Three generations of Bahamian women treat patrons as if they were guests in their own home. And the Bahamian food whipped up in the kitchen is as close to homemade as you can get in a restaurant. **Known for:** home-style cooking; tasty conch fritters; friendly service. [$] *Average main: $13* ✉ *Trinity Pl., Nassau* ✥ *Turn left off Bay St. onto Market St. toward Central Bank, then left onto Trinity Pl.* ☎ *242/328–0334* ⏲ *Closed Sun. No dinner.*

2

$ | **✕ The Bearded Clam Sports Bar.**
AMERICAN | Nestled in the middle of the Inter-
Fodor's Choice | national Arcade linking Bay Street
★ | and the wharf is this lively bar and restaurant serving up tasty appetizers and meals. There's the traditional Bahamian cracked conch or conch balls. **Known for:** daily happy hour 5–8; tasty bar fare; lively atmosphere. $ *Average main: $15* ✉ *Nassau* ☎ *242/323–4455* ⊕ *www.beardedclamnassau.com.*

POP THE BUBBLY

A meandering maze underneath historic Graycliff's sprawling kitchen and dining area houses more than 200,000 bottles of wine and Champagne, making this wine cellar one of the most extensive and impressive in the world. It costs $1,000 to book the elegant private cellar dining room, but tours are free.

$ | **✕ Biggity.** The Bahamian term "big-
CAFÉ | gity" means bold or brash. The food served up at this small upstairs Bay Street café certainly lives up to the name, but the atmosphere is anything but—it's a welcome reprieve from the constant traffic and pedestrian noise of downtown's main drag. **Known for:** off the beaten path; Bahamian bush teas; in-house line of scented candles. $ *Average main: $14* ✉ *Southern Bay St., just east of Parliament St., Nassau* ⊕ *www.biggity242.com* ☾ *Closed Sun.*

$$$ | **✕ Café Matisse.** Low-slung settees, stucco arches, and reproductions
ITALIAN | of the eponymous artist's works set a casual and refined tone at this
Fodor's Choice | restaurant owned by a husband-and-wife team. He's Bahamian, she's
★ | northern Italian, and the fare perfectly blends the two cultures. **Known for:** Italian cuisine with a Bahamian spin; biannually changing menu; delicious handmade cookies. $ *Average main: $36* ✉ *Bank La. and Bay St., behind Parliament Sq., Nassau* ☎ *242/356–7012* ⊕ *cafe-matisse. com* ☾ *Closed Sun., Mon., and Sept.*

$$$ | **✕ East Villa Restaurant and Lounge.** In a converted Bahamian home, this
CHINESE | is one of the most popular Chinese restaurants in town. The Chinese-Continental menu includes entrées such as conch with black-bean sauce, *hung shew* (walnut chicken), and steak *kew* (cubed prime fillet served with baby corn, snow peas, water chestnuts, and vegetables). **Known for:** traditional Chinese cuisine; broiled NY strip steaks. $ *Average main: $33* ✉ *E. Bay St. near Nassau Yacht Club, Nassau* ☎ *242/393–3377* ⊕ *www.eastvillabahamas.com* ☾ *No lunch Sat.*

$$$$ | **✕ Graycliff Restaurant.** A meal at this hillside mansion's formal restaurant
EUROPEAN | begins in the elegant parlor, where drinks are served over the sounds of a
Fodor's Choice | live piano. It's a rarefied world, where waiters wear tuxedos and Cuban
★ | cigars and cognac are served after dinner. **Known for:** only five-star rating in town; signature Kobe beef; one of the largest wine cellars in the world. $ *Average main: $55* ✉ *Graycliff, W. Hill St. at Cumberland Rd., across from Government House, Nassau* ☎ *242/302–9150* ⊕ *www. graycliff.com* 🎩 *Jacket required.*

$$ | **✕ The Green Parrot.** Two locations—Green Parrot Harbourfront and
AMERICAN | Green Parrot Hurricane Hole—mean you get incomparable views of Nassau Harbour and a fresh breeze, whichever way the wind is blowing. The large burgers are a favorite at these casual, all-outdoor restaurants and bars. **Known for:** harbor views; simple but tasty American fare; large, lively bars. $ *Average main: $28* ✉ *E. Bay St., west of bridges to Paradise Island, Nassau* ☎ *242/322–9248, 242/328–8382* ⊕ *greenparrotbar.com.*

$$$$ BRAZILIAN 🍴 **Humidor Churrascaria Restaurant.** Each table here comes with a coaster (green on one side, red on the other, to signify stop and go, respectively), and waiters will serve you a never-ending selection of delicious skewered meats and fresh fish until you flip your coaster to red and declare uncle The salad bar offers everything from simple salad fixings to scrumptious seafood salads and soups. The terrace out back serves wood-fired pizzas; Friday happy hour means $20 pizza and a bucket of three beers. **Known for:** wood-fired pizzas; smoking lounge; great for meat-lovers. [$] *Average main: $50* ✉ *W. Hill St. off Cumberland Rd., next to Graycliff Hotel, Nassau* ☎ *242/302–9150* 🌐 *www.graycliff.com* 🕒 *No lunch.*

$$$ ITALIAN 🍴 **Luciano's of Chicago.** Green Roofs, the sprawling former residence of the late Sir Roland Symonette (the country's first premier), houses this harborside restaurant. The mansion's mahogany woodwork, gardens, and terraces create a romantic setting for enjoying Tuscan fare that features local seafood, including the fisherman's soup, grouper, and homemade pastas—try the delicious frutti di mare over linguine. **Known for:** Tuscan fare; views of Paradise Island at sunset; rum-soaked Bahamian-style bread pudding. [$] *Average main: $40* ✉ *E. Bay St., 2 blocks west of Paradise Island bridges, Nassau* ☎ *242/323–7770* 🌐 *www.luciano snassau.com* 🕒 *No lunch Sat.*

$$ BAHAMIAN Fodor's Choice ★ 🍴 **Lukka Kairi.** Lukka Kairi means "people of the Islands," and at this hot spot you can experience the food, live music, and hospitality Bahamian people are known for. The tapas-style menu lets you sample a variety of traditional Bahamian dishes with a twist. **Known for:** some of the best conch fritters around; live Bahamian music on stage; great harbor views. [$] *Average main: $22* ✉ *Woodes Rodgers Walk, Nassau* ☎ *242/326–5254* 🌐 *www.lukkakairi.com.*

$$ SEAFOOD 🍴 **Montagu Gardens.** Angus beef and fresh native seafood—flame-grilled and seasoned with home-mixed spices—are the specialties at this simple but romantic restaurant in an old Bahamian home on Lake Waterloo. The dining room opens to a walled courtyard niched with Roman-style statues and gardens that lead to a waterside balustrade. **Known for:** complimentary transportation; bring your own catch and they'll cook it; sumptuous Fort Montagu mud pie. [$] *Average main: $25* ✉ *E. Bay St., Nassau* ☎ *242/394–6347* 🌐 *stenigh8.wix.com/montagugardens* 🕒 *Closed Sun.*

$ JAMAICAN 🍴 **Pepper Pot Grill and Juice Bar.** Jamaican transplant Keron Williams takes his role of cooking and serving up the most authentic Jamaican food in Nassau very seriously. His small, simple restaurant draws an international crowd of cruise ship workers and immigrants from the Caribbean diaspora. **Known for:** authentic Jamaican cooking; fresh fruit and vegetable juices; cheap but filling eats. [$] *Average main: $12* ✉ *King St., Nassau* ✥ *From Bay St., turn south onto Market St., then right onto King St.* ☎ *242/323–8177* 🕒 *Closed Sun. No dinner.*

$$ BAHAMIAN 🍴 **The Poop Deck.** Just east of the bridges from Paradise Island and a quick cab ride from the center of town is this favorite local haunt that is always busy. Start with the conch fritters, then move on to the fish (it's usually served head to tail, so if you're squeamish, ask your waiter to have the head cut off before it comes out on your plate). **Known for:** pick your own fish; calypso coffee spiked with secret ingredients;

marina and harbor views. $\boxed{\$}$ *Average main: $30 ⊠ E. Bay St. at Nassau Yacht Haven Marina, Nassau ⌖ East of bridges from Paradise Island* ☎ *242/393–8175* ⊕ *www.thepoopdeck.com.*

$$
SUSHI
Fodor'sChoice
★

✕ **Seafront Sushi.** One of Nassau's hot spots, this simple restaurant has an extensive menu including traditional rolls, sushi, and sashimi, as well as more innovative options that incorporate conch and other local delicacies. The volcano roll topped with their special conch sauce is a favorite. **Known for:** volcano roll; reservations not accepted; traditional tatami rooms. $\boxed{\$}$ *Average main: $20* ⊠ *E. Bay St., Nassau* ☎ *242/394–1706* ⊕ *www.seafrontsushibahamas.com* ⊗ *Closed Sun. No lunch Sat.*

$$
BAHAMIAN

✕ **Sharkeez Bar & Grill.** If you arrive in Nassau aboard a cruise ship, you won't miss the sign for this second-floor bar and grill emblazoned atop its thatched roof. You may have a hard time picking your drink from the extensive menu of frozen concoctions. **Known for:** creative frozen concoctions; lively setting; theme nights. $\boxed{\$}$ *Average main: $20* ⊠ *Woodes Rodgers Walk, Nassau* ☎ *242/322–8519* ⊕ *sharkeezcaribbean.com.*

PARADISE ISLAND

Restaurants at Atlantis Paradise Island tend to close one or two nights a week (but not always the same nights each week), and their schedules vary with the resort's occupancy levels. Check with the reservations desk at Atlantis if you want to dine there. Reservations are essential at most of the upscale spots and a good idea at all restaurants that accept them.

$$
AMERICAN

✕ **Anthony's.** This lively, casual spot is one of the most affordable spots for breakfast, lunch, or dinner this side of Nassau Harbour, but that doesn't mean it's cheap. The baby back ribs with a homemade barbecue sauce are among the most popular on this Bahamian and American fare menu. **Known for:** one of few nonresort restaurants on PI; extensive menu; affordable (by PI standards) dining. $\boxed{\$}$ *Average main: $30* ⊠ *Paradise Village Shopping Plaza, Paradise Island* ☎ *242/363–3152* ⊕ *www.anthonysparadiseisland.com.*

$$$$
EUROPEAN

✕ **Bahamian Club.** Reminiscent of a British country club, this handsome restaurant has walls lined with dark oak, overstuffed chairs, and leather banquettes. Meat is the house specialty—rib-eye steak, veal chop, lamb loin, and chateaubriand for two—but grilled swordfish steak, Bahamian lobster, salmon fillet, and other fresh seafood dishes are all prepared with finesse. **Known for:** upscale ambience; outstanding service; enough-to-share chateaubriand. $\boxed{\$}$ *Average main: $55* ⊠ *Atlantis Paradise Island, Coral Towers, Paradise Island* ☎ *242/363–3000* ⊕ *www.atlantisbahamas.com* ⊗ *No lunch.*

$$$$
SEAFOOD

✕ **Blue Lagoon Seafood Restaurant.** This harbor-front seafood restaurant is a good choice for a quiet meal away from the bustle of Atlantis. Hurricane lamps and brass rails fill this narrow third-floor dining room, which looks out at Nassau on one side and Atlantis on the other. **Known for:** seafood prepared to perfection; great spot to escape the crowds; live one-man brass band and jazz quartet. $\boxed{\$}$ *Average main: $45* ⊠ *Club Land'Or, Paradise Island* ☎ *242/363–2400* ⊕ *www.bluelagoonseafood.com* ⊗ *Closed Sun. No lunch.*

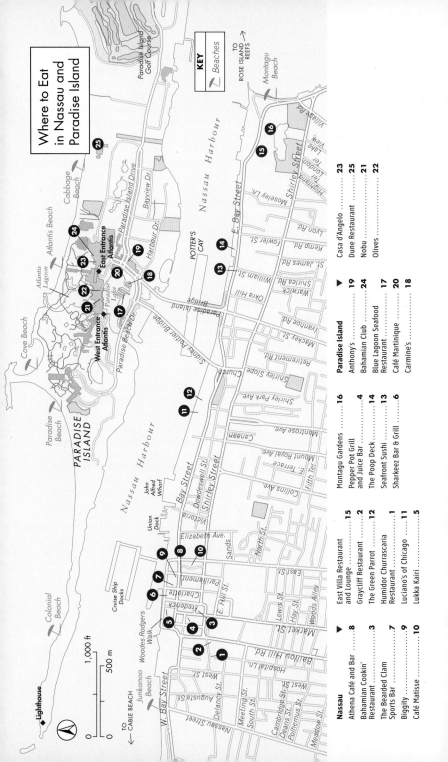

Where to Eat in Nassau and Paradise Island

KEY

▼ Beaches

TO ROSE ISLAND REEFS

$$$$
FRENCH
Fodor's Choice
★

×**Café Martinique.** The original restaurant, which was made famous in the 1965 James Bond film *Thunderball*, has long been bulldozed, but with the help of renowned international chef Jean-Georges Vongerichten and New York designer Adam D. Tihany, this resurrected a classic remains one of the hottest tables in Atlantis. **Known for:** white-glove service; table-side filleted Dover sole; rich chocolate soufflé. $ *Average main: $60 ⊠ Atlantis Paradise Island, Marina Village, Paradise Island* ☎ *242/363–3000* ⊕ *www.atlantisbahamas.com.*

$$$$
ITALIAN
FAMILY
Fodor's Choice
★

×**Carmine's.** This Italian restaurant is a great place to go with a small group. Appetizers, entrées, and desserts come in extralarge portions meant to feed a crowd and are served family-style, so the prices can be more affordable (by Paradise Island standards, at least) than they seem at first, especially if you share among several people. **Known for:** huge portions meant for sharing; Titanic (ice cream-laden chocolate torte); options for every member of the family. $ *Average main: $55 ⊠ Atlantis Paradise Island, Marina Village, Paradise Island* ☎ *242/363–3000* ⊕ *www.atlantisbahamas.com* ⊗ *No lunch.*

$$$$
ITALIAN

×**Casa D'Angelo.** At this restaurant, an outpost of the wildly popular Casa d'Angelo chain in south Florida, chef Angelo Elia brings his famous Tuscan-style cuisine to Paradise. The antipasti display whets the appetite for succulent seafood, hearty pasta dishes, and prime cuts of beef. **Known for:** wine pairings with every course; standard Italian fare; delectable pastries. $ *Average main: $50 ⊠ Atlantis Paradise Island, Coral Towers, Paradise Island* ☎ *242/363–3000* ⊕ *www.atlantisbahamas.com* ⊗ *No lunch.*

$$$$
MODERN FRENCH

×**Dune Restaurant.** Feast on Jean-Georges Vongerichten's intricately prepared dishes while overlooking Cabbage Beach at the renowned One&Only Ocean Club. Go for breakfast or lunch for the most (relatively) reasonable prices. **Known for:** Chef Jean-Georges's signature touch; fine dining overlooking the ocean; divine salted caramel banana cake. $ *Average main: $55 ⊠ One & Only Ocean Club, Ocean Club Dr., Paradise Island* ☎ *242/363–2501* ⊕ *oceanclub.oneandonlyresorts.com.*

$$$$
SUSHI

×**Nobu.** Sushi connoisseurs, celebrities, and tourists pack this Atlantis restaurant night after night. The rock shrimp tempura, yellowtail sashimi with jalapeño, and miso-glazed black cod are Nobu favorites, but this restaurant also takes advantage of fresh Bahamian seafood—try the lobster shiitake salad or the cold conch shabu-shabu with Nobu sauces. **Known for:** traditional Japanese sushi; sake cellar; delicious miso-glazed black cod. $ *Average main: $60 ⊠ Atlantis Paradise Island, Royal Towers, Paradise Island* ☎ *242/363–3000* ⊕ *www.atlantisbahamas.com* ⊗ *No lunch.*

Humidor Churrascaria Restaurant is in the Graycliff Hotel.

$$$$ MEDITERRANEAN 🍴 **Olives.** Todd English has paired up with Atlantis to give his signature Mediterranean style a taste of the Caribbean. Enjoy the shellfish, clams, and oysters from the Raw Bar; pick the fish you want to see on your plate; or satisfy your meat craving with the huge Tomahawk rib eye—all steaks are 100% Akaushi Wagyu beef. **Known for:** late-night kitchen; extensive raw bar; homemade pasta dishes. [$] *Average main: $50* ✉ *Atlantis Paradise Island, Royal Towers, Paradise Island* ✣ *In casino* ☎ *242/363–3000* 🌐 *www.atlantisbahamas.com.*

CABLE BEACH

$$$$ STEAKHOUSE 🍴 **Black Angus Steakhouse & Grill.** This steak house offers some of the best certified Angus beef on the island. Bring your appetite if you're going to try the gigantic cowboy steak (28 or 32 ounces), which is carved right in front of you. **Known for:** plate-sized steaks; melt-in-your-mouth mashed potatoes; live jazz. [$] *Average main: $50* ✉ *Meliá Nassau Beach Resort, W. Bay St., Cable Beach* ☎ *242/327–6200* 🌐 *www.melia.com* 🕓 *No lunch.*

$$ BAHAMIAN 🍴 **Nesbitt's Delaporte Restaurant & Lounge.** The vibe in this hole-in-the-wall restaurant is set by whomever controls the jukebox, which has everything from current hits to old-school R&B, to local Rake 'n' Scrape. The food is simple but hits the spot, and the lounge is a great place to meet some locals. **Known for:** late-night libations; greasy savory bites; hangout for tourists and locals. [$] *Average main: $20* ✉ *Cable Beach* ✣ *West of BTC Delaporte phone tower* ☎ *242/327–6036.*

$$$ ASIAN FUSION 🍴 **Nikkei.** The menu at this Japanese-Peruvian restaurant is small but eclectic. There's a sushi bar in the main dining room, but book ahead and reserve a space in the real draw, the Teppanyaki Experience room,

where your main course will be prepared right in front of you. **Known for:** hibachi experience; delicious conch ceviche; only local spot for Peruvian cuisine. $ *Average main: $35* ⊠ *Meliá Nassau Beach Resort, W. Bay St., Cable Beach* ☎ *242/327–6000* ⊗ *No lunch*.

$$
MEDITERRANEAN ✕ **Olive's Meze Grill.** Hip and trendy, this restaurant puts a fresh twist on Mediterranean classics. The fare is simple, but locally grown greens and fish caught in nearby waters make the meals special. **Known for:** flaming cheese lit table-side; all-you-can-drink mimosa or sangria weekend brunch; late-night weekend hot spot. $ *Average main: $30* ⊠ *W. Bay St., Cable Beach* ☎ *242/327–6393*.

$$$
SEAFOOD ✕ **The Poop Deck at Sandyport.** A more upscale version of the other Poop Deck in Nassau, this waterside restaurant has soaring ceilings, a pastel pink and aqua color scheme, and a dazzling view of the ocean. Seafood is the star on the menu here: shrimp, lobster, calamari, grouper, and, of course, conch. **Known for:** pick-your-own catch of the day; great ocean views; option to dine on the beach. $ *Average main: $36* ⊠ *W. Bay St., Cable Beach* ☎ *242/327–3325* ⊕ *www.thepoopdeckrestaurants.com* ⊗ *Closed Mon.*

$$
NORTHERN
ITALIAN
FAMILY ✕ **Spritz Restaurant and Bar.** This casual, open-air restaurant and bar overlooks the Sandyport Canal and the pedestrian-only streets of the Old Towne at Sandyport. Seating is limited, so reservations are recommended, especially for busy weekend nights. **Known for:** hand-tossed thin-crust pizzas; great spot for kids to run around; will cater to special dining needs. $ *Average main: $28* ⊠ *Sandyport Olde Towne Marina Plaza, Cable Beach* ☎ *242/327–0762* ⊕ *www.spritzrestaurant.com* ⊗ *No lunch Mon.*

$$
AMERICAN ✕ **The Swimming Pig Gastropub.** This bustling gastropub pays homage to the world famous swimming pigs with its name and a few small paintings. The menu is mostly American-inspired—hearty burgers and flat breads—with a few touches of English pub fare like the oxtail, Guinness pie, and fish-and-chips. **Known for:** 24 beers on tap; 24-hour kitchen service; hearty American and English bar and pub fare. $ *Average main: $28* ⊠ *Baha Mar, Cable Beach* ☎ *242/677–9000*.

$$
AMERICAN ✕ **Twisted Lime.** This busy sports bar has something for everyone: indoors, the dining room and bar feature games on flat-screen TVs; outdoors, casual canal-front dining (think pub food like burgers and nachos) and drinks are available at high-tops or on plush sofas. The menu is quite extensive: fish tacos or nachos fiesta are good options for starters with local flair. **Known for:** dock and dine; sports fans' hangout; late-night food spot. $ *Average main: $28* ⊠ *Sandyport Marina Village, Cable Beach* ☎ *242/327–0061* ⊕ *www.twistedlimebar.com*.

WESTERN NEW PROVIDENCE

$$$
AMERICAN ✕ **Compass Point.** This restaurant and bar with friendly service is one of the best sunset-watching spots on the island. Sit indoors or out on the terrace overlooking the ocean and enjoy the simple but tasty Bahamian and island-style American fare for breakfast, lunch, and dinner. **Known for:** incredible sunsets; live music; late-night kitchen. $ *Average main: $35* ⊠ *W. Bay St., Gambier Village* ☎ *242/327–4500* ⊕ *www.compasspointbeachresort.com*.

$ BAHAMIAN Fodor's Choice ★ 🍴 **Dino's Gourmet Conch Salad.** Conch salad is the draw at the popular roadside joint; it might take half an hour to get your food, but you can grab a stool and order a refreshing (and intoxicating) gin and coconut water while you wait. If you're in a hurry, call ahead to try and cut down on the wait. **Known for:** cash only; great photo-op spot; "tropical" conch salad. [$] *Average main: $12* ✉ *Gambier Village* ☎ *242/377–7798* 💳 *No credit cards.*

$$$$ ECLECTIC Fodor's Choice ★ 🍴 **Mahogany House.** A favorite with the upscale Lyford Cay crowd, Mahogany House is sophisticated simplicity at its best. Whether you're dressed to the nines or sporting flip-flops, you're bound to feel both comfortable and welcome at this dining spot and lively bar. **Known for:** private wine cellar dining room; specialty ingredients like buffalo pork belly; vast selection of cured meats and cheeses. [$] *Average main: $45* ✉ *Western Rd.* ☎ *242/362–6669* 🌐 *www.the-island-house.com/dining* 🕒 *No lunch weekends.*

$$$ ASIAN FUSION Fodor's Choice ★ 🍴 **Shima.** Enjoy authentic Southeast Asian–inspired cuisine at this popular restaurant and bar with views overlooking the ritzy Lyford Cay Marina. The little fire symbols peppered throughout the menu indicate their propensity for spice, but they're happy to tone things down if you ask. **Known for:** authentic Asian cuisine; happening weekend brunch; extremely spicy food. [$] *Average main: $34* ✉ *Lyford Cay* ☎ *242/698–6300* 🌐 *www.the-island-house.com.*

WHERE TO STAY

NASSAU

$$$$ HOTEL 🏨 **British Colonial Hilton Nassau.** This 1899 landmark hotel is the social heart of Nassau; it's the setting for political meetings and events, and offers sophisticated guestrooms with unmatched views of the harbor and old Nassau. **Pros:** right on Bay Street; quiet but trendy beach and pool area; centrally located. **Cons:** busy with local meetings and events; man-made beach; hard to access at peak traffic times. [$] *Rooms from: $477* ✉ *1 Bay St., Nassau* ☎ *242/322–3301* 🌐 *www.bchiltonnassauhotel.com* 🛏 *288 rooms* 🍽 *No meals.*

$ HOTEL 🏨 **Grand Central Hotel.** Not as grand as the name suggests, this four-story hotel is clean, safe, cheap, and central. **Pros:** in the heart of downtown Nassau; guesthouse quality; friendly, personalized service. **Cons:** on busy street that can feel dodgy after dark; no pool or beach; extremely basic. [$] *Rooms from: $90* ✉ *Charlotte St., Nassau* ☎ *242/322–8356* 🛏 *35 rooms* 🍽 *No meals.*

$$$$ HOTEL Fodor's Choice ★ 🏨 **Graycliff Hotel.** The old-world flavor of this Georgian colonial landmark—built in the 1720s by ship captain Howard Graysmith—has made it a perennial favorite among both the rich and the famous (past guests have included the Duke and Duchess of Windsor, Winston Churchill, Aristotle Onassis, and the Beatles). **Pros:** exceptionally luxurious accommodations; lush tropical gardens; cigar and chocolate factories on-site. **Cons:** near busy restaurant and bar area; not easily accessible for handicapped; no beach. [$] *Rooms from: $435* ✉ *W. Hill St., Nassau* ☎ *242/322–2796, 800/476–0446* 🌐 *www.graycliff.com* 🛏 *20 rooms* 🍽 *Breakfast.*

PARADISE ISLAND

You'll find several hotels and apartment buildings on Paradise Island, but the sprawling Atlantis resort is the main attraction. It's a bustling fantasy world—at once a water park, entertainment complex, megaresort, and beach oasis. Other than the new Baha Mar resort complex in Cable Beach, it's the largest resort in the country. The public areas are lavish, with fountains, glass sculptures, and gleaming shopping arcades. There is plenty of nightlife on the premises; the casino, ringed by restaurants, is one of the largest in the Bahamas and the Caribbean. Some of these facilities can be visited by nonguests (restaurants, shops, the casino, and nightspots), but the famed Aquaventure Water Park is limited to guests of Atlantis, a handful of affiliated hotels, and cruise passengers.

$$
RESORT
FAMILY
Beach Tower (Atlantis). Located at the easternmost edge of Atlantis, the Beach Tower offers a bit of a reprieve from the hustle and bustle of the rest of the megaresort, with a large inviting pool and lazy river that are less congested than the more elaborate Aquaventure. **Pros:** less congestion at beach and pools; close to kids' activities; best value for Atlantis Resort. **Cons:** far from the main attractions of Atlantis; oldest part of the property; only one restaurant in this section. $ *Rooms from: $239* ⊠ *Atlantis Paradise Island, Paradise Island* ☎ *242/363–3000, 888/877–7525 reservations* ⊕ *www.atlantisbahamas.com* ⟿ *423 rooms* ⦿ *Some meals.*

$$
HOTEL
FAMILY
Best Western Bay View Suites. This 4-acre condominium resort has a lush, intimate character, and guests can socialize around three pools (two for general use, one reserved for the villas) that are surrounded by tropical plants, including several hibiscus and bougainvillea varieties. **Pros:** children 12 and under stay free; private "at-home" vibe; free Wi-Fi in pool area. **Cons:** long walk from beach; no restaurant serving dinner on property; no organized activities on-site. $ *Rooms from: $280* ⊠ *Bay View Dr., Paradise Island* ☎ *242/363–2555, 800/757–1357* ⊕ *www.bayviewsuitesparadiseisland.com* ⟿ *25 rooms* ⦿ *No meals.*

$$
RESORT
FAMILY
The Coral (Atlantis). The newly renovated family-friendly Coral is at the heart of the Atlantis Resort, giving you the good access to all the top amenities—including the casino and Aquaventure—at a moderate price point. **Pros:** on-site movie theater (included in resort fee); family-exclusive swimming pool; Marina Village steps away. **Cons:** always busy lobby area; guest rooms lack some of the pizazz you might expect at Atlantis; many kids running around. $ *Rooms from: $279* ⊠ *Atlantis Paradise Island, Paradise Island* ☎ *242/363–3000, 888/877–7525 reservations* ⊕ *www.atlantisbahamas.com* ⟿ *693 rooms* ⦿ *Some meals.*

$$$
HOTEL
FAMILY
Comfort Suites Paradise Island. This all-suites, three-story pink-and-white hotel in the middle of the Paradise Island action allows guests of its neighbor, Atlantis, to use its facilities for free. **Pros:** kids can enroll in Atlantis's Kids Camp; near shops, restaurants, and Cabbage Beach; full cooked breakfast included. **Cons:** not on a beach; busy traffic surrounds; activities are only at the Atlantis Resort. $ *Rooms from: $350* ⊠ *Paradise Island Dr., Paradise Island* ☎ *242/363–3680, 800/424–6423* ⊕ *www.comfortsuitespi.com* ⟿ *223 rooms* ⦿ *Breakfast.*

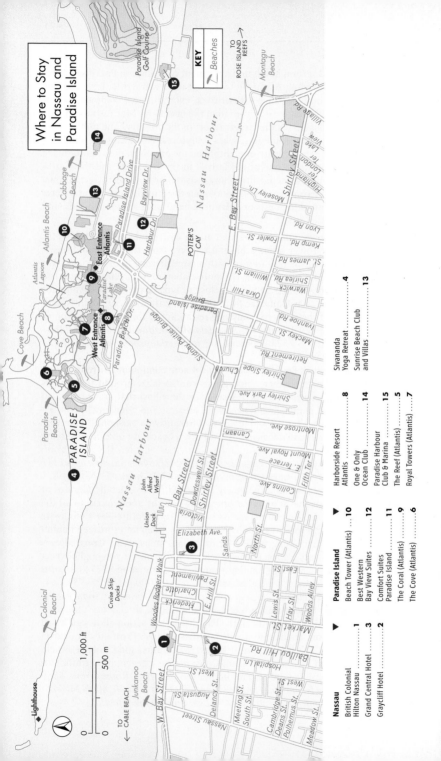

Where to Stay in Nassau and Paradise Island

KEY

↙ Beaches

Nassau

British Colonial
Hilton Nassau **1**
Grand Central Hotel **3**
Graycliff Hotel **2**

Paradise Island

Beach Tower (Atlantis) ... **10**
Best Western
Bay View Suites **12**
Comfort Suites
Paradise Island **11**
The Coral (Atlantis) **9**
The Cove (Atlantis) **6**

Harborside Resort
Atlantis **8**
One & Only
Ocean Club **14**
Paradise Harbour
Club & Marina **15**
The Reef (Atlantis) **5**
Royal Towers (Atlantis) ... **7**

Sivananda
Yoga Retreat **4**
Sunrise Beach Club
and Villas **13**

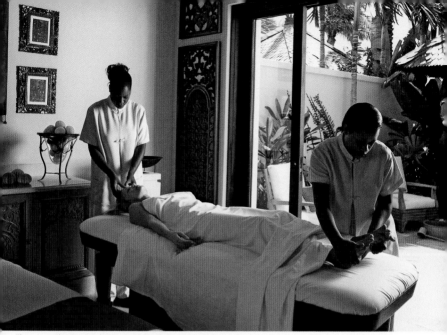

The spa at the One&Only Ocean Club offers indulgent massages.

$$$$ 🏨 **The Cove (Atlantis).** Worlds away from the other properties within the
RESORT Atlantis Resort in terms of overall look, experience, and sophistication,
Fodor'sChoice this high-rise overlooking two stunning white-sand beaches is a true
★ grown-ups' getaway. **Pros:** highly exclusive adult-only pool; incredible
private beaches; amenities of Atlantis, but separated from the hustle
and bustle. **Cons:** a long walk to Atlantis amenities; limited dining and
bar options on-site; pricey. $ *Rooms from: $545* ⊠ *Atlantis Paradise
Island, Paradise Island* ☎ *242/363–3000, 888/877–7525 reservations*
⊕ *www.atlantisbahamas.com* ➪ *600 suites* ❑ *Some meals.*

$$$$ 🏨 **Harborside Resort Atlantis.** It you want more space to stretch out during
RENTAL your Paradise Island vacation, consider these one-, two-, and three-bed-
FAMILY room town-house-style villas that can accommodate up to nine guests
and are fully equipped with separate living/dining areas, kitchens, and
private laundry facilities. **Pros:** lots of space to stretch out; pool area
is less crowded than Aquaventure; right next door to Nassau water
taxi dock. **Cons:** Wi-Fi is extra; long walk to Atlantis restaurants and
amenities; no room service. $ *Rooms from: $470* ⊠ *Paradise Beach Dr.,
Paradise Island* ☎ *242/363–3000* ⊕ *www.atlantisbahamas.com* ➪ *392
villas* ❑ *Some meals.*

$$$$ 🏨 **One & Only Ocean Club.** Once the private hideaway of A&P heir Hun-
RESORT tington Hartford, this exclusive resort on magnificent Cabbage Beach's
Fodor'sChoice quietest stretch provides the ultimate in understated—and decidedly
★ posh—elegance. **Pros:** ultraexclusive; lovely beach; top-rated amenities.
Cons: not within walking distance of Atlantis; limited (and very expensive) on-site dining; free Wi-Fi only in certain public areas. $ *Rooms
from: $689* ⊠ *Ocean Club Dr., Paradise Island* ☎ *242/363–2501,
866/552–0001* ⊕ *oceanclub.oneandonlyresorts.com* ➪ *110 rooms.*

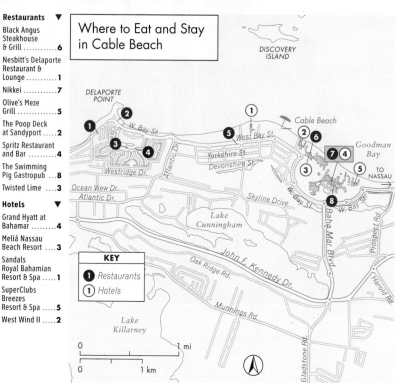

Restaurants ▼

Black Angus Steakhouse & Grill 6
Nesbitt's Delaporte Restaurant & Lounge 1
Nikkei 7
Olive's Meze Grill 5
The Poop Deck at Sandyport 2
Spritz Restaurant and Bar 4
The Swimming Pig Gastropub ... 8
Twisted Lime 3

Hotels ▼

Grand Hyatt at Bahamar 4
Meliá Nassau Beach Resort 3
Sandals Royal Bahamian Resort & Spa 1
SuperClubs Breezes Resort & Spa 5
West Wind II 2

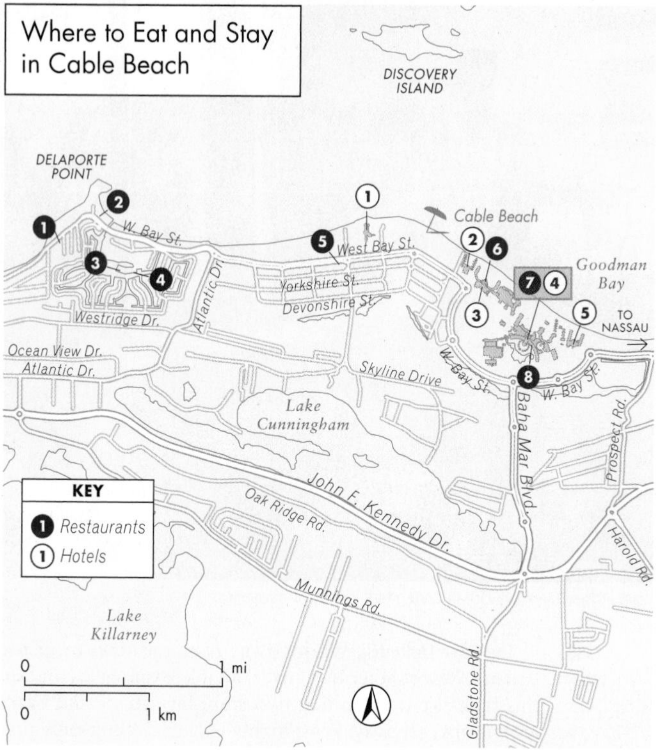
Where to Eat and Stay in Cable Beach
DISCOVERY ISLAND
DELAPORTE POINT
Cable Beach
Goodman Bay
TO NASSAU
W. Bay St.
West Bay St.
Yorkshire St.
Devonshire St.
Westridge Dr.
Atlantic Dr.
Ocean View Dr.
Atlantic Dr.
Skyline Drive
W. Bay St.
W. Bay St.
Baha Mar Blvd.
Prospect Rd.
Lake Cunningham
John F. Kennedy Dr.
Oak Ridge Rd.
Harold Rd.
Munnings Rd.
Lake Killarney
Gladstone Rd.
KEY
Restaurants
Hotels
0
1 mi
0
1 km

$ HOTEL FAMILY

🏨 **Paradise Harbour Club & Marina.** With a marina and an enviable location, this collection of oversize, comfortable apartments is a great choice for those who want the freedom of a private residence with the facilities of a large resort. **Pros:** quiet location; cooking facilities; scheduled beach and grocery store shuttle. **Cons:** need to walk or be shuttled to and from the beach; condo built nearby towers over property; no restaurant on-site. [$] *Rooms from: $169* ✉ *Paradise Island Dr., Paradise Island* ☎ *242/363–2992* 🌐 *www.paradiseharborclub.com* 🛏 *23 units* 🍴 *No meals.*

$$$$ RESORT FAMILY

🏨 **The Reef (Atlantis).** This 497-suite tower has exquisitely outfitted studios or one- and two-bedroom condominium-style accommodations. **Pros:** units fully equipped with kitchens or kitchenettes; quiet; cost-effective option with Atlantis benefits. **Cons:** no restaurants or bars on property; long walk to Atlantis amenities; no grocery stores nearby. [$] *Rooms from: $850* ✉ *Atlantis Paradise Island, Paradise Island* ☎ *242/363–3000, 888/877–7525 reservations* 🌐 *www.atlantisbahamas.com* 🛏 *497 apartments* 🍴 *No meals.*

$$$ RESORT FAMILY Fodor's Choice ★

🏨 **Royal Towers (Atlantis).** At the centrally located Royal Towers, spend your days riding the slides at Aquaventure, and your nights in the casino and the nightclub. **Pros:** access to top amenities including spa and Aquaventure water park; larger rooms than other Atlantis towers; plenty of on-site activities. **Cons:** full balconies only in suites; noisy; pricey on-site dining, subpar fast-food options. [$] *Rooms from: $349* ✉ *Atlantis*

CLOSE UP

Baha Mar

The Cable Beach strip has been completely transformed by the sprawling, multibillion dollar Baha Mar resort. New hotels, which include a Grand Hyatt, Rosewood, and SLS Lux, have altered the skyline and can be seen from across the island of New Providence. Following multiple delays, the property finally opened its first phase in April 2017. The Grand Hyatt was first to welcome guests—opening just 600 of its 1,800 rooms. SLS Lux was scheduled for a late 2017 launch with Rosewood set to open its doors in early 2018. The casino, spa, golf course, and a number of the projected 40 restaurants and bars are all open to guests and additional amenities come on stream constantly as they work to create the exciting multihotel resort complex the world has been waiting on.

Paradise Island, Paradise Island ☎ *242/363–3000, 888/877–7525 reservations* 🌐 *www.atlantisbahamas.com* 🛏 *1201 rooms* 🍴 *Some meals.*

$ B&B/INN ★ **Sivananda Yoga Retreat.** Accessible only by boat, this resort features guest rooms in the main house and one-room bungalows overlook a gorgeous white-sand beach in a 5-acre compound that stretches from Nassau Harbour to the ocean; air-conditioning is an additional $10 per day. **Pros:** ideal for peace and quiet; inexpensive accommodations; free shuttle to and from Nassau. **Cons:** several night minimum stay during certain times of year; basic accommodations; no road access. [$] *Rooms from: $140* ✉ *Paradise Island* ☎ *242/363–2902, 866/559–5167* 🌐 *www.sivanandabahamas.org* 🛏 *190 rooms* 🍴 *All meals.*

$$$ HOTEL FAMILY ★ **Sunrise Beach Club and Villas.** Lushly landscaped with crotons, coconut palms, bougainvillea, and hibiscus, this low-rise, family-run resort on Cabbage Beach has a tropical wonderland feel. **Pros:** on one of the best beaches on the island; lively bar on property; great for families. **Cons:** no activities; lots of walking to get to rooms; a distance from the activities at Atlantis. [$] *Rooms from: $365* ✉ *Casino Dr., Paradise Island* ☎ *242/363–2234, 800/451–6078* 🌐 *www.sunrisebeachclub.com* 🛏 *40 rooms* 🍴 *No meals.*

CABLE BEACH

$$$ RESORT ★ **Grand Hyatt at Baha Mar.** The largest property within the Baha Mar Resort is steps away from the ESPA spa and the Baha Mar Casino—the largest in the Caribbean—and offers guests access to an array of other amenities even if it does lack some of the exclusivity of other hotels within the resort complex. **Pros:** plenty to do right on property; steps away from the casino, spa, and convention center; resort-view rooms face the nightly fountain show. **Cons:** long walk to the beach; hard to get away from it all; many features are not yet open due to phased launch. [$] *Rooms from: $375* ✉ *Baha Mar Blvd., Cable Beach* ☎ *242/788–7800, 844/800–2242 reservations* 🌐 *www.bahamar.grand.hyatt.com* 🛏 *1800 rooms* 🍴 *No meals.*

$$$
RESORT
FAMILY
Meliá Nassau Beach Resort. Although the Meliá is not part of the Baha Mar resort next door, the property has embarked on a series of upgrades to keep pace with the changes to the neighborhood. **Pros:** guests get preferred rates at Baha Mar; lots of activities included; situated on a beautiful beach. **Cons:** rooms have yet to be upgraded; hotel immediately to east will remain closed for foreseeable future; restaurants are hit or miss. *$ Rooms from: $360 ✉ Cable Beach ☎ 242/327–6000 ⊕ www. melia.com ⬳ 694 rooms ⫮◯⫯ All-inclusive.*

$$$$
RESORT
Sandals Royal Bahamian Resort & Spa. Cable Beach's most expensive all-inclusive has elegantly furnished rooms with views of the ocean, pool, or grounds replete with pillars and faux-Roman statuary, as well as personal butler service and a room that opens up to a private pool for the ultimate indulgence. **Pros:** no children; lovely setting; private offshore cay. **Cons:** couples only; need car or taxi to go into town; convention center popular for local functions. *$ Rooms from: $750 ✉ W. Bay St., Cable Beach ☎ 242/327–6400, 800/726–3257 ⊕ www. sandals.com ⬳ 404 rooms ⫮◯⫯ All-inclusive.*

$$
RESORT
SuperClubs Breezes Resort & Spa. This affordable all-inclusive is ideally situated right on beautiful Cable Beach and next door to the sprawling Baha Mar resort complex. **Pros:** Situated on the popular Cable Beach; walking distance to Baha Mar casino; lots of activities. **Cons:** not family friendly; need car or taxi to access town; packed with spring breakers during March and April. *$ Rooms from: $216 ✉ W. Bay St., Cable Beach ☎ 242/327–5356, 800/467–8737 ⊕ www.breezes.com ⬳ 392 rooms ⫮◯⫯ All-inclusive.*

$$
RESORT
FAMILY
West Wind II. Privacy is the lure of these cozy time-share villas, with balconies and patios overlooking oceans and pools on Cable Beach's west end, 6 miles from downtown. **Pros:** fully stocked kitchens; condos sleep six; right on Cable Beach. **Cons:** no major activities; need car or taxi to go downtown; housekeeping, beach towels, and toiletries additional. *$ Rooms from: $300 ✉ W. Bay St., Cable Beach ☎ 242/327–7211, 242/327–7019 ⊕ www.westwindii.com ⬳ 54 villas ⫮◯⫯ No meals.*

WESTERN NEW PROVIDENCE

$$
B&B/INN
A Stone's Throw Away. Featuring seaside comfort in fashionable surroundings, this hotel advertised as a bed-and-breakfast is actually a luxurious hideaway. **Pros:** serene; secluded public-beach access; friendly staff. **Cons:** in flight path; long distance from anything else; hotel access up a steep staircase cut out of the limestone hill. *$ Rooms from: $235 ✉ Tropical Garden Rd. and W. Bay St., Gambier Village ☎ 242/327–7030 ⊕ www.astonesthrowaway.com ⬳ 10 rooms ⫮◯⫯ No meals.*

$$$
RESORT
Compass Point. This whimsical-looking hotel made up of brightly colored one- and two-story cottages offers a relaxing alternative to many of the area's major resorts. **Pros:** fun and funky accommodations; access to incredible private beach; romantic sunset views. **Cons:** in flight path; not ideal for children; expensive taxi ride to town. *$ Rooms from: $375 ✉ W. Bay St., Gambier Village ☎ 242/327–4500 ⊕ www. compasspointbeachresort.com ⬳ 18 cottages ⫮◯⫯ Breakfast.*

The cottages at Compass Point are known for their whimsical colors.

$$$$ B&B/INN Fodor's Choice ★ **The Island House.** The antithesis of the big resorts typically found in New Providence, The Island House delivers casual sophistication with high-end yet understated amenities and features at every turn. **Pros:** tranquil and private; near the airport; variety of amenities for sports and wellness enthusiasts. **Cons:** far from main attractions; no beach nearby; caters primarily to fitness-lovers. [$] *Rooms from: $550* ✉ *Mahogany Hill, Western Rd.* ☎ *242/698–6300* 🌐 *www.the-island-house.com* 🛏 *30 suites* 🍴 *No meals.*

$ B&B/INN **Orange Hill Beach Inn.** If you prefer down-home coziness over slick glamour, then this basic hotel—on the site of a former orange plantation perched on a hilltop overlooking the ocean—is the place to stay. **Pros:** across from a pleasant beach; humble; family-style service. **Cons:** long distance from town; not many activities; basic accommodations. [$] *Rooms from: $140* ✉ *W. Bay St., Gambier Village* ☎ *242/327–7157* 🌐 *orangehill.com* 🛏 *32 rooms* 🍴 *No meals.*

NIGHTLIFE

NASSAU

BARS AND CLUBS

Bambu. Pop into this open-air club overlooking Nassau Harbour where the DJ often plays the latest hits. Wait a few moments and Europe's sexiest house beats will change the atmosphere. It's popular with hip young locals and cruise passengers and staff. The club is open on Friday and Saturday nights (or any night a cruise ship is in port) from 9 pm to 5 am. ✉ *Upstairs Prince George Plaza, Bay St., Nassau.*

Sharkeez Bar & Grill. Every night brings a different theme and vibe at this popular restaurant and gathering spot. A DJ spins a varied range of music from Top 40 to reggae, soca, calypso, and Latin. Most nights they're open til midnight, but on Saturdays the party keeps going until 2 am. The drinks menu is extensive, including Nassau's largest offering of frozen cocktails. ⊠ *Woodes Rodgers Walk, Nassau* ☎ *242/601–5325* ⊕ *www.sharkeezcaribbean.com.*

Via Caffe. This lively restaurant and café is transformed most nights (every night but Sunday, really) into a lively locale for late-night entertainment with no cover charge. Depending on the night, you might find yourself learning salsa techniques while sipping a margarita, dancing to the hottest tunes spun by the house DJ, listening to a live band, or wowing the crowd at karaoke. For a late bite, the kitchen is open until the early morning hours. ⊠ *Scotiabank Bldg., Corner of Parliament St. and Woodes Rogers Walk, Nassau* ☎ *242/322–7203.*

PARADISE ISLAND

BARS AND CLUBS

Aura. This is the country's hottest nightclub, located upstairs from the Atlantis Casino. It's the place to see and be seen on Paradise Island, though many of the celebrities who frequent the club opt for the ultra-exclusive private lounge. Dancing goes on all night, and bartenders dazzle the crowd with their mixing techniques. The music varies, depending on the night. ⊠ *Atlantis Paradise Island Royal Towers, Paradise Island* ☎ *242/363–3000* ⊕ *www.atlantisbahamas.com* ⌁ *Closed Sun.–Wed.*

Oasis Lounge. There's live piano or vocal music here every night except Sunday from 7:30 to midnight. Go early to get a good seat and take advantage of one of the buy one, get one free drink specials and the complimentary hors d'oeuvres, offered from 5 to 7 pm. The lounge is open until midnight every night. ⊠ *Club Land'Or, Paradise Island* ☎ *242/363–2400* ⊕ *www.clublandor.com.*

CASINOS

PARADISE ISLAND

Atlantis Casino. Featuring a spectacularly open and airy design, the 50,000-square-foot (100,000 if you include the dining and drinking areas) casino is ringed with restaurants and offers more than 1,100 slot machines, baccarat, blackjack, roulette, craps tables, and such local specialties as Caribbean stud poker. There's also a high-limit table area, and most of the eateries have additional games. The sports book with the massive video wall looks out over the luxury yachts in the marina. The casino is always open, with gaming tables open from 10 am to 4 am daily. ⊠ *Atlantis Paradise Island Royal Towers, Paradise Island* ☎ *242/363–3000* ⊕ *www.atlantis.com.*

SHOPPING AND SPAS

Most of Nassau's shops are on Bay Street between Rawson Square and the British Colonial Hotel, and on the side streets leading off Bay Street. Some stores are popping up on the main shopping thoroughfare's eastern end and just west of the Cable Beach strip. Bargains abound between Bay Street and the waterfront. Upscale stores can also be found in Marina Village, in the Crystal Court at Atlantis, and at Baha Mar on Cable Beach.

You'll find duty-free prices—sometimes as much as 25% to 50% less than U.S. prices—on imported items such as crystal, linens, watches, cameras, jewelry, leather goods, and perfumes, but you really need to know the prices before you buy. Not everything is a bargain.

NASSAU

SHOPS
CIGARS

Be aware that some merchants on Bay Street and elsewhere in the islands are selling counterfeit Cuban cigars—sometimes unwittingly. If the price seems too good to be true, chances are it is. Check the wrappers and feel to ensure that there's a consistent fill before you make your purchase.

Graycliff Hotel. Graycliff carries one of Nassau's finest selections of hand-rolled cigars, featuring leaves from throughout Central and South America. Graycliff's operation is so popular that it has been expanded by the hotel to include an entire cigar factory, which is open to the public for tours, purchases, and even a cigar-rolling lesson. A dozen Cuban men and women roll the cigars; they live on the premises and work here through a special arrangement with the Cuban government. True cigar buffs will seek out Graycliff's owner, Enrico Garzaroli. In addition to the shop in the hotel, there's another Graycliff boutique at Lynden Pindling International Airport. ⊠ *W. Hill St., Nassau* ☎ *242/302–9150* ⊕ *www.graycliff.com.*

CLOTHING AND ACCESSORIES

Brass and Leather. Here you can find leather goods for men and women, including bags, shoes, and belts. Pick up one of the unique soft leather passport covers that come in an array of colors emblazoned with your country's coat of arms. ⊠ *Charlotte St., off Bay St., Nassau* ☎ *242/322–3806.*

Cole's of Nassau. This is a top choice for everything from ball gowns and cocktail dresses to resort wear and bathing suits with all the shoes and accessories for every look. ⊠ *Parliament St., Nassau* ☎ *242/322–8393* ⊕ *www.colesofnassau.com.*

La Casita. This quaint and humble boutique offers high-end straw bags and purses, as well as costume jewelry. ⊠ *Bay St., near Straw Market, Nassau* ☎ *242/328–5988.*

FOOD

Bahamas Rum Cake Factory. At the Bahamas Rum Cake Factory, delicious Bahamian rum-soaked cakes are made and packaged in tins right on the premises (peek into the bakery) and make a great souvenir. Just make sure you take one home for yourself. ☒ *602 E. Bay St., Nassau* ☏ *242/328–3750* ⊕ *thebahamasrumcakefactory.com.*

Mortimer Candies. Mortimer Candies whips up batches of uniquely Bahamian sweet treats daily. Pop in for a sno-cone on a hot day, or buy some bags of bennie cake, coconut-cream candy, or their signature Paradise Sweets in a swirl of the Bahamian flag colors. ☒ *E. St. Hill, Nassau* ☏ *242/322–5230* ⊕ *www.mortimercandies.com.*

GIFTS

Fodor's Choice ★ **Bahama Handprints.** Bahama Handprints fabrics emphasize local artists' sophisticated tropical prints in an array of colors. Also look for leather handbags, a wide range of women's clothing, housewares, and bolts of fabric. Ask for a free tour of the factory in back. ☒ *Island Traders Bldg. Annex, off Mackey St., Nassau* ☏ *242/394–4111* ⊕ *www.bahamahandprints.com.*

The Craft Cottage. This small shop situated in a traditional wooden structure is a great place to buy locally made souvenirs and gifts including soaps and oils, hand-painted glassware, jewelry, straw bags, and textiles. The artists and artisans are often on-site. ☒ *20 Village Rd., Nassau* ☏ *242/446–7373* ⊕ *www.craftcottagebahamas.com.*

Doongalik Studios Art Gallery. This gallery, housed in a traditional Bahamian-style building, features a large exhibition gallery showcasing local artists. There's also a small shop where you an buy authentic Bahamian art and crafts and on Saturday morning a bustling farmers' market takes place on the grounds. ☒ *18 Village Rd., Nassau* ☏ *242/394–1886* ⊕ *www.doongalik.com.*

Linen Shop. This shop sells fine embroidered Irish linens and lace and has a delightful Christmas corner. ☒ *Bay St., Nassau* ☏ *242/322–4266.*

My Ocean. Here you can find candles, soaps, salt scrubs, and lotions in island- and ocean-inspired scents and colors, all locally made. A second location is found at Festival Place. ☒ *Prince George Plaza, Nassau* ☏ *242/328–6167* ⊕ *www.myocean-bahamas.com.*

JEWELRY, WATCHES, AND CLOCKS

Coin of the Realm. Coin of the Realm has Bahamian coins, stamps, native conch pearls, tanzanite, and semiprecious stone jewelry. ☒ *Charlotte St. off Bay St., Nassau* ☏ *242/322–4862, 242/322–4497* ⊕ *www.coin-realm.net.*

Colombian Emeralds International. Colombian Emeralds International is the local branch of this well-known jeweler; its stores carry a variety of fine jewelry in addition to its signature gem. In addition to a location in downtown Nassau, there are also branches in Marina Village and at the Atlantis Paradise Island Royal Towers and Beach Towers. ☒ *Bay St. near Rawson Sq., Nassau* ☏ *242/322–2230* ⊕ *www.colombianemeralds.com.*

Continued on page 86

JUNKANOO IN THE BAHAMAS
by Jessica Robertson

It's after midnight, and the only noise in downtown Nassau is a steady buzz of anticipation. Suddenly the streets erupt in a kaleidoscope of sights and sounds—Junkanoo groups are parading down Bay Street. Vibrant costumes sparkle in the light of the street lamps, and the revelers bang on goatskin drums and clang cowbells, hammering out a steady celebratory beat. It's Junkanoo time!

Junkanoo is an important part of the Bahamas' Christmas season. Parades begin after midnight and last until midday on Boxing Day (December 26), and there are more on New Year's Day. What appears to be a random, wild expression of joy is actually a well-choreographed event. Large groups (often as many as 500 to 1,000 people) compete for prize money and bragging rights. Teams choose a different theme each year and keep it a closely guarded secret until they hit Bay Street. They spend most of the year preparing for the big day at their "shacks," which are tucked away in neighborhoods across the island. They practice dance steps and music, and they design intricate costumes. During the parade, judges award prizes for best music, best costumes, and best overall presentation.

Junkanoo costume, Grand Bahama

JUNKANOO HISTORY

Junkanoo holds an important place in the history and culture of the Bahamas, but the origin of the word *junkanoo* remains a mystery. Many believe it comes from John Canoe, an African tribal chief who was brought to the West Indies as a slave and then fought for the right to celebrate with his people. Others believe the word stems from the French *gens inconnus*, which means "the unknown people"—significant because Junkanoo revelers wear costumes that mask their identities.

The origin of the festival itself is more certain. Though its roots can be traced back to West Africa, it began in the Bahamas during the 16TH or 17TH century when Bahamian slaves were given a few days off around Christmas to celebrate with their families. They left the plantations and had elaborate costume parties at which they danced and played homemade musical instruments. They wore large, often scary-looking masks, which gave them the freedom of anonymity, so they could let loose without inhibition.

Over the years, Junkanoo has evolved. Costumes once decorated with shredded newspaper are now elaborate, vibrant creations incorporating imported crepe paper, glitter, gemstones, and feathers.

MUSIC'S ROLE

There's something mesmerizing about the simple yet powerful beat of the goatskin drum. Couple that steady pounding with the "kalik-kalik" clanging of thousands of cowbells and a hundreds-strong brass band, and Junkanoo music becomes downright infectious.

Music is the foundation of Junkanoo. It provides a rhythm for both the costumed revelers and crowds of spectators who jump up and down on rickety bleacher seats. The heavy percussion sound is created by metal cowbells, whistles, and oil barrel drums with fiery sternos inside to keep the animal skin coverings pliant. In the late 1970s, Junkanoo music evolved with the addition of brass instruments, adding melodies from Christmas carols, sacred religious hymns, and contemporary hits.

If you're in Nassau anytime from September through the actual festival, stand out on your hotel balcony and listen carefully. Somewhere, someone is bound to be beating out a rhythm as groups practice for the big parade.

DRESS TO IMPRESS

Each year, talented artists and builders transform chicken wire, cardboard, Styrofoam, and crepe paper into magnificent costumes that are worn, pushed, or carried along the Junkanoo parade route. Dancers and musicians tend to wear elaborate head dresses or off-the-shoulder pieces and cardboard skirts completely covered in finely fringed, brightly colored crepe paper—applied a single strip at a time until every inch is covered. Gemstones, referred to as "tricks" in the Junkanoo world, are painstakingly glued onto costumes to add sparkle. In recent years, feathers have been incorporated, giving the cardboard covered creations an added level of movement and flair.

In order to wow the crowd, and more importantly, win the competition, every member of the group must be in full costume when they hit Bay Street. Even their shoes are completely decorated. Massive banner pieces so big they graze the power lines and take up the entire width of the street are carried along the route by men who take turns. Every element, from the smallest costume to the lead banner, as well as the entire color scheme, is meticulously planned out months in advance.

EXPERIENCE JUNKANOO

SECURE YOUR SEATS

■ Junkanoo bleacher seat tickets ($10–$50) can be hard to come by as the parade date approaches. Contact your hotel concierge ahead of time to arrange for tickets.

■ Rawson Square bleachers are the best seats. This is where groups perform the longest and put on their best show.

■ If you don't mind standing, make your way to Shirley Street or the eastern end of Bay Street, where the route is lined with barricades. Judges are positioned all along the way so you'll see a good performance no matter where you end up.

■ Junkanoo groups make two laps around the parade route. Each lap can take a few hours to complete, and there are many groups in the lineup, so most spectators stay only for the first round. Head to Bay Street just before dawn, and you'll be sure to score a vacant seat.

BEHIND THE SCENES

■ During the parade, head east along Bay Street and turn onto Elizabeth Avenue to the rest area. Groups take a break in the parking lot here before they start round two. Costume builders frantically repair any pieces damaged during the first rush (Bahamian slang for parading), revelers refuel at barbeque stands, goatskin drums are placed next to a giant bonfire to keep them supple, and in the midst of all the noise and hubbub, you'll find any number of people taking a nap to ensure they make it through a long and physically demanding night.

■ If star-stalking is your thing, scour the crowds in the VIP section in Parliament Square or look across the street on the balcony of the Scotiabank building. This is where celebrities usually watch the parades. Some who've been spotted include Michael Jordan and Rick Fox.

■ When the parade ends, wander along the route and surrounding streets to score a one-of-a-kind souvenir. Despite the many hours Junkanoo participants spend slaving over their costumes, by the time they're done rushing the last thing they want to do is carry it home. Finders keepers.

■ If you're in Nassau in early December, watch the Junior Junkanoo parade. School groups compete for prizes in various age categories. The littlest ones are usually offbeat and egged on by teachers and parents, but are oh-so-cute in their costumes. The high school groups put on a show just as impressive as the groups in the senior parade.

JUNKANOO TRIVIA

■ Kalik beer, brewed in the Bahamas, gets its name from the sound of clanking cowbells.

■ An average costume requires 3,000 to 5,000 strips of fringed crepe paper to completely cover its cardboard frame.

■ During the height of sponge farming in the Bahamas, a major industry in the early 1900s, many Junkanoo participants used natural sponge to create their costumes.

Junkanoo parade in Nassau

JUNKANOO ON OTHER ISLANDS

Nassau's Junkanoo parade is by far the biggest and most elaborate, but most other islands hold their own celebrations on New Year's Day. Nassau's parades are strictly a spectator sport unless you are officially in a group, but Out Island parades are more relaxed and allow visitors to join the rush.

JUNKANOO YEAR-ROUND

Not satisfied with limiting Junkanoo to Christmastime, the Bahamas Ministry of Tourism hosts an annual **Junkanoo Summer Festival**. Smaller scale parades are held on alternating weekends in June and July on most major islands, including Nassau. In addition to the traditional Junkanoo rush, these festivals offer arts and crafts demonstrations, conch cracking, crab catching, coconut-husking competitions, concerts featuring top Bahamian artists, and of course, lots of good Bahamian food. ☎ 242/302–2000.

Marina Village on Paradise Island hosts **Junkanoo rushouts** on Wednesday and Saturday (9:30 pm). There are no big stand-alone pieces, but dancers and musicians wear color-coordinated costumes and headpieces. The parade is much less formal, so feel free to jump in and dance along.

The **Educulture Museum and Workshop** in Nassau gives a behind-the-scenes look at Junkanoo. Some of each year's best costumes are on display, as well as costumes from years gone by when newspaper and sponges were used as decoration. The diehard Junkanoo staff will help you make your own Junkanoo creations. Be sure to arrange your visit ahead of time. ☎ 242/328–3786.

John Bull. Established in 1929 and magnificently decorated in its Bay Street incarnation behind a Georgian-style facade, John Bull fills its complex with wares from Tiffany & Co., Cartier, Mikimoto, Nina Ricci, and Yves Saint Laurent. The company has eight locations throughout Nassau and Paradise Island and also owns a number of the better-known high-end boutique brand stores. ⊠ *284 Bay St., Nassau* ☎ *242/302–2800* ⊕ *www.johnbull.com.*

LIQUOR

Fodor's Choice ★ **Pirate Republic Brewing Company.** When you spot a pirate hanging out on Woodes Rogers Walk, you know you've found the home of the Bahamas' only craft brewery. Inside the shop is Pirate Republic beer to sample—Long John Pilsner, Gold and Haze of Piracy, and the Island Pirate Ale—as well as live music most nights and a limited but tasty grub menu. For a look at how the brew is made, take one of the tours offered twice a day. ⊠ *Woodes Rodgers Walk, Nassau* ☎ *242/328–0612* ⊕ *www.piraterepublicbahamas.com.*

MARKETS AND ARCADES

International Bazaar. This collection of shops under a huge, spreading bougainvillea, sells linens, jewelry, souvenirs, and offbeat items. There's often a small band playing all sort of music along this funky shopping row. ⊠ *Bay St. at Charlotte St., Nassau.*

Prince George Plaza. Prince George Plaza, which leads from Bay Street to Woodes Rogers Walk near the cruise-ship docks, just east of the International Bazaar, has about two dozen shops with varied wares. ⊠ *Bay St., Nassau.*

Straw Market. This towering colonial-style marketplace houses hundreds of straw vendors selling straw bags, T-shirts, and other souvenirs. The Straw Market is one place in the Bahamas where bartering is accepted, so it's best to wander around and price similar items at different stalls before sealing a deal. Besides the wood-carvers on the western side of the market you're not likely to find any local made items here. ⊠ *Bay St., Nassau.*

PERFUMES AND COSMETICS

The Cosmetic Boutique. This shop has beauty experts on hand to demonstrate the latest cosmetics offerings, including M.A.C., Clinique, Bobbi Brown, and La Mer. ⊠ *Bay St. near Charlotte St., Nassau* ☎ *242/323–2731.*

Perfume Bar. This shop carries the best-selling French fragrance Boucheron and the Clarins line of skin-care products, as well as scents by Chanel, Fendi, and other well-known designers. ⊠ *Bay St., Nassau* ☎ *242/325–1258.*

SPAS

Baha-Retreat. This spa, situated in an old wooden two-story Bahamian home, is popular with locals and offers a full range of spa and salon services seven days a week. Reservations are suggested, but walk-ins are welcome. Specialties include body sugaring and threading for hair removal, but massages are also good here. Book a Couples Spa Day for a complete pampering treat: aromatherapy body polish, aromatherapy massage, spa manicure and pedicure, and gourmet lunch with a glass of wine each. ⊠ *E. Bay St., Nassau* ☎ *242/323–6711* ⊕ *www.baharetreat.com.*

Windermere Day Spa at Harbour Bay. This day spa offers a variety of spa treatments—such as hydrotherapy and salt glows—as well as facials, massages, manicures, and pedicures. They also have a location in Caves Village in Western New Providence. Get to the Lynden Pindling International Airport early for a final massage or manicure at their nail and massage bar in the departure lounge. ⊠ *E. Bay St.* ☎ *242/393–8788* ⊕ *www.windermeredayspa.com.*

PARADISE ISLAND

SHOPS

ARTS AND CRAFTS
Bahamacraft Centre. Bahamacraft Centre offers some top-level Bahamian crafts, including a selection of authentic straw work. Dozens of vendors sell everything from baskets to shell collages inside this vibrantly colored building. You can catch a shuttle bus from Atlantis to the center. ⊠ *Paradise Island Dr., Paradise Island.*

CIGARS
Havana Humidor. Havana Humidor has the largest selection of authentic Cuban cigars in the Bahamas. Watch cigars being made, or browse through the cigar and pipe accessories. ⊠ *Atlantis Paradise Island Crystal Court, Paradise Island* ☎ *242/363–5809.*

SPAS
Fodor's Choice ★ **Mandara Spa at Atlantis.** Located at Atlantis but open to the public, the expansive, multistory Indonesian-inspired Mandara Spa has treatments utilizing traditions from around the world. Plan to spend more time than your treatment or service requires to enjoy the unisex relaxation lounge, hot and cold plunge pools, and the sauna and steam room. Use of the 15,000-square-foot fitness center is complimentary for a day when you spend more than $99 on spa or salon services. The full-service salon offers hair and nail treatments as well as tooth whitening, hair extensions, and waxing. Men can get the works at the barbershop. Both the spa and fitness center are open until 9 pm daily. ⊠ *Atlantis Paradise Island Royal Towers, Casino Dr.* ☎ *242/363–3000* ⊕ *www. mandaraspa.com.*

Fodor's Choice ★ **One&Only Spa.** Paradise Island's One&Only Ocean Club has one of the island's most luxurious and indulgent spa retreats. The space is so lovely, be sure to allow additional time just to lounge and relax. For the ultimate indulgence, treat yourself to the signature One&Only Massage—two therapists perform a perfectly choreographed blend of five styles of massage; finish it up with the Ultimate Bathing ritual including fresh local and exotic flower petals. Take your break from reality a step further and book a treatment for two in a private Bali-inspired villa with private courtyard, canopied daybed, and open-air hydrotherapy bath; this romantic spot is designed for shared treatments, but you can book individually. With just eight villas, it's a good idea to book well in advance, particularly during high season. ⊠ *Paradise Island* ☎ *242/363–2501* ⊕ *www.oneandonlyoceanclub.com.*

DID YOU KNOW?

Marina Village, an open-air marketplace at Atlantis, is a popular tourist destina tion. The bazaar features five restaurants, a craft market, and upscale stores.

CABLE BEACH

SPAS

ESPA at Baha Mar. Encompassing 30,000 square feet, the only ESPA flagship spa in the Caribbean is also one of the largest spas in the region. Indulge in massages, facials, and body treatments using a variety of local products designed to soothe and relax. Treatments are done in one of 24 rooms, two of which are designed to accommodate couples. Plan some extra time before and after to relax in the sauna and steam rooms—there are male- and female-specific as well as unisex areas—or in the serene Relax Lounge, the social Chill Zone, or on the outdoor Ocean View Terraces. ⊠ *Baha Mar Casino & Hotel, Baha Mar Blvd., Cable Beach* ☎ *242/788–7800* ⊕ *www.espaatbahamar.com.*

Red Lane Day Spa. If you're not a guest at Sandals Royal Bahamian, you can still enjoy pampering services at the Red Lane Day Spa on the outskirts of the all-inclusive property. Facials, massages, wraps, and scrubs utilize an array of tropical scents and ingredients from coffee to frangipani, sugarcane, and even seaweed to guarantee relaxation. To indulge at the full spa or have a massage in a private hut overlooking the ocean on a private island, consider booking a Sandals day pass for access. ⊠ *Sandals Royal Bahamian, W. Bay St., Cable Beach* ☎ *242/327–6400* ⊕ *www.sandals.com.*

WESTERN NEW PROVIDENCE

SHOPS

Pasión Tea & Coffee Company. Pop into this hilltop shop to purchase locally made souvenirs or to grab a spot of tea ($3) or coffee ($3.50) on the breezy deck. The Pasión tea line is made locally in a nearby warehouse. The shop has a great array of teas, coffees, and spices as well as trinkets and soaps, lotions, and scrubs. On a hot day, enjoy a scoop of homemade soursop ice cream. Local bush medicine plants adorn the garden where roosters roam around. ⊠ *Plantation Hill, Caves Rd., off W. Bay St., Gambier Village* ☎ *242/327–7011* ⊕ *www. pasionteas.com.*

SPORTS AND THE OUTDOORS

BOATING

From Chub Cay—one of the Berry Islands 35 miles north of New Providence—to Nassau, the sailing route goes across the mile-deep Tongue of the Ocean. The Paradise Island Lighthouse welcomes yachters to Nassau Harbour, which is open at both ends. The harbor can handle the world's largest cruise liners; sometimes as many as eight tie up at one time. Two looming bridges bisect the harbor connecting Paradise Island to Nassau. Sailboats with masts taller than the high-water clearance of 72 feet must enter the harbor from the east end to reach marinas east of the bridges.

Atlantis Marina. The marina at Atlantis has 63 megayacht slips and room for yachts up to 240 feet. Stay here and you can enjoy all the amenities at Atlantis, including Aquaventure. ⊠ *Atlantis Paradise Island, Paradise Island* ☎ *242/363–6068.*

Bay Street Marina. With 89 slips accommodating yachts up to 150 feet, this modern, centrally located marina on the Nassau side of the harbor has all the amenities you might need. The marina is within walking distance to Paradise Island as well as downtown Nassau and has a lively restaurant and bar on-site. ⊠ *E. Bay St., Nassau* ☎ *242/676–7000* ⊕ *www.baystreetmarina.com.*

Brown's Boat Basin. On the Nassau side, Brown's Boat Basin offers a place to tie up your boat, as well as on-site engine repairs. ⊠ *E. Bay St., Nassau* ☎ *242/393–3331.*

Hurricane Hole Marina. Ninety-slip Hurricane Hole Marina is on the Paradise Island side of the harbor and accommodates yachts over 200 feet. ⊠ *Paradise Island* ☎ *242/363–3600* ⊕ *www.hurricaneholemarina.com.*

Lyford Cay. At the western end of New Providence, Lyford Cay, a posh development for the rich and famous, has an excellent 74-slip marina, but there is limited availability for the humble masses. ☎ *242/362–4131.*

Nassau Yacht Haven. On the Nassau side of the harbor, the island's oldest marina, Nassau Yacht Haven, has 150 berths and also arranges fishing charters. ⊠ *E. Bay St., Nassau* ☎ *242/393–8173* ⊕ *www.nassauyachthaven.com.*

Palm Cay Marina. The easternmost marina on New Providence offers 194 slips and all the amenities, including a full restaurant, pool, and beach. ⊠ *Palm Cay, Yamacraw Hill Rd., Nassau* ☎ *242/676–8554* ⊕ *www.palmcay.com.*

FISHING

The waters here are generally smooth and alive with many species of game fish, which is one of the reasons why the Bahamas has more than 20 fishing tournaments open to visitors every year. A favorite spot just west of Nassau is the Tongue of the Ocean, so called because it looks like that part of the body when viewed from the air. The channel stretches for 100 miles. For boat rental, parties of two to six will pay $600 or so for a half day, $1,600 for a full day.

Born Free Charters. This charter company has five boats and guarantees a catch on full-day charters—if you don't get a fish, you don't pay. Pickup is included from various locations, and the company will make the arrangements for you. ⊠ *Nassau* ☎ *242/698–1770, 954/526–1956 U.S. phone number* ⊕ *www.bornfreefishing.com.*

Charter Boat Association. The Charter Boat Association has 15 boats available for fishing charters. Pickup is from Paradise Island Ferry Terminal or Nassau Harbour in front of the Straw Market. ☎ *242/393–3739.*

Chubasco Charters. This charter company has four boats for deep-sea and light tackle sportfishing. Half- and full-day charters are available. Pickup is from Paradise Island Ferry Terminal or Nassau Harbour in front of the Straw Market. ☎ *242/324–3474* ⊕ *www.chubascocharters.com.*

Paradise Island's One&Only Ocean Club has a scenic golf course.

Nassau Yacht Haven. Nassau Yacht Haven can put you in touch with one of the private fishing charter captains operating out of its 150-slip marina. ⊠ *Nassau Yacht Haven, E. Bay St., Nassau* ☎ *242/393–8173* ⊕ *www.nassauyachthaven.com.*

GOLF

Ocean Club Golf Course. Designed by Tom Weiskopf, the Ocean Club Golf Course is a championship course surrounded by the ocean on three sides, which means that the views are incredible, but the winds can get stiff. Call to check on current availability and up-to-date prices (those not staying at Atlantis or the One&Only Ocean Club can play at management's discretion, and at a higher rate). The course is open daily from 6 am to sunset. ⊠ *One&Only Ocean Club, Paradise Island Dr., Paradise Island* ☎ *242/363–6682* ⊕ *www.oceanclub.oneandonlyresorts.com* ✉ *$225–$295 for 18 holes (discounted after 1 pm); $70 club rentals* ⌟ *18 holes, 6805 yards, par 72.*

Royal Blue Golf Course. You will get two different golf experiences in one golf course at Baha Mar, which was created from the island's oldest course. It has stunning ocean views on the front nine and a back nine taking players through a native forest all the way to the natural Lake Cunningham. A bat cave on the course features a protected indigenous bat species, and more than 70 species of birds have been spotted on the course and surrounding lake. This new course is challenging for players at all levels. Nonresort guests are welcome to book a tee time. Rates vary for guests and nonguests and on weekdays versus weekends. ⊠ *Baha Mar Resort, Baha Mar Blvd., Cable Beach*

☎ *242/327–6000* ⊕ *www.bahamar.com* ✎ *$250–$275 resort guests;*
$295–$325 nonresort guests ⚐ *18 holes, 7189 yards, par 72.*

HORSEBACK RIDING

Happy Trails Stables. Happy Trails Stables gives guided 90-minute trail
rides, including basic riding instruction, through remote wooded areas
and beaches on New Providence's southwestern coast. Two morning
group rides are offered, but private rides can be arranged at any time.
Courtesy round-trip bus transportation from hotels is provided (about
an hour each way). Tours are limited to eight people. There's a 200-
pound weight limit, and children must be at least 12 years old. Reservations are required. ☎ *242/362–1820* ⊕ *www.ridingbahamas.com*
✎ *$150 per person.*

PADDLEBOARDING

FAMILY   **Pappasurf.** There's no better way to explore the crystal-clear blue Baha-
Fodor'sChoice mian ocean than gliding along the surface. Experienced paddlers can
★   rent boards from this outfitter, or you can sign up for lessons. For a truly
unique experience, book a sunset ($85) or nightglow ($65) tour. Both
last for about 90 minutes and include all equipment and experienced
guides. ⊠ *Henrea Carlette Bldg., W. Bay St., Cable Beach* ⊕ *For tours,*
lessons, and rental drop-offs head to Goodman's Bay beach opposite
Goodman's Bay Corporate Center; the office is across the road and just
east of Sandals ☎ *242/327–3853* ⊕ *www.pappasurf.com.*

SCUBA DIVING AND SNORKELING

DIVE SITES

Coral Reef Sculpture Garden. Created by the Bahamas Reef Environment
Education Foundation (BREEF), this underwater art gallery is suitable for SCUBA divers and snorkelers. The highlight is the 17-foot-tall
"Ocean Atlas" crouching on the ocean floor. The site is situated just off
Clifton Heritage Park on southwestern New Providence and is accessible from land or boat. Be sure to take an underwater camera for a
spectacular photographic souvenir.

Gambier Deep Reef. Off Gambier Village about 15 minutes west of Cable
Beach, Gambier Deep Reef goes to a depth of 80 feet.

Lost Ocean Hole. The elusive (and thus exclusive) Lost Ocean Hole (east
of Nassau, 40–195 feet) is aptly named because it's difficult to find. The
rim of the 80-foot opening in 40 feet of water is studded with coral
heads and teeming with small fish—grunts, margate, and jacks—as well
as larger pompano, amberjack, and sometimes nurse sharks. Divers will
find a thermocline at 80 feet, a large cave at 100 feet, and a sand ledge
at 185 feet that slopes down to 195 feet.

Lyford Cay Drop-Off. Lyford Cay Drop-Off (west of Nassau, 40–200-plus
feet) is a cliff that plummets from a 40-foot plateau almost straight into
the inky blue mile-deep Tongue of the Ocean. The wall has endless
varieties of sponges, black coral, and wire coral. Along the wall, grunts,

grouper, hogfish, snapper, and rockfish abound. Off the wall are pelagic game fish such as tuna, bonito, wahoo, and kingfish.

Rose Island Reefs. The series of shallow reefs along the 14 miles of Rose Island is known as Rose Island Reefs (Nassau, 5–35 feet). The coral is varied, although the reefs are showing the effects of the heavy traffic. Still, plenty of tropical fish live here, and the wreck of the steel-hulled ship *Mahoney* is just outside the harbor.

Sea Gardens. This site is off Love Beach on the northwestern shore beyond Gambier.

DIVE OPERATORS

All recommended New Providence dive shops are PADI-affiliated (Professional Association of Diving Instructors) facilities. Expect to pay about $65 to $99 for a two-tank dive or beginner's course. Shark dives run $100 to $125, and certification costs $450 and up.

Bahama Divers Ltd. The largest and most experienced dive operation in the Bahamas offers two-tank morning dives, single-tank afternoon dives, and twice-daily snorkeling excursions. Introduction to SCUBA and PADI certification courses are available, and there's a full line of scuba equipment for rent. Destinations are drop-off sites, wrecks, coral reefs and gardens, and an ocean blue hole. Bus pickup is scheduled twice daily from hotels throughout New Providence. ⊠ *Nassau* ☎ *242/393–5644, 866/234–8322, 954/602–7731* ⊕ *www.bahamadivers.com.*

Stuart Cove's. Located on the island's south shore, this operator is considered by aficionados to be the island's leading dive shop. Although they're pros at teaching beginners (scuba instruction and guided snorkel tours are available), experienced thrill-seekers flock to Stuart Cove's for the famous shark dives. The company runs dive trips to the south-shore reefs twice a day, weather permitting. The minisub adventure, which requires no experience, is $129; snorkeling expeditions cost $75 for adults and $35 for kids 11 and under. The shark dives are $170 for a three-hour dive. Complimentary shuttle service from all major hotels is included. ☎ *242/362–4171, 800/879–9832* ⊕ *www.stuartcove.com.*

TOURS

DAY SAILS

Barefoot Sailing Cruises. The company offers regularly scheduled half-day snorkeling trips, full-day sailing tours of New Providence, and sunset Champagne trips, not to mention private charters. ⊠ *Bayshore Marina, E. Bay St.* ☎ *242/393–5817* ⊕ *www.barefootsailingcruises.com* 🖃 *Half-day sail and snorkel $90; half-day sail, snorkel, and beach $115; full day $140.*

Flying Cloud. This 57-foot catamaran based at the Paradise Island Ferry Terminal offers half-day sailing and snorkeling tours, full-day cruises on some Sundays, as well as sunset sails. Private charters can also be arranged. Price includes round-trip ground transportation from your hotel. ⊠ *Paradise Island Ferry Terminal, Paradise Island* ☎ *242/394–5067* ⊕ *www.flyingcloud.com* 🖃 *Half day (Mon.–Sat.) $80; Sun. full day $95; evening cruise $70.*

OUT ISLANDS TRIPS

You can visit a number of islands and cays on a day trip by boat from Nassau. Bahamas Ferries does a day trip to Harbour Island: 2½ hours in an air-conditioned ferry (or with the ocean breeze blowing through your hair on the upper deck) and enough time onshore to explore the quaint island via golf cart, have lunch, and stroll the beautiful pink-sand beach. A number of operators offer daily powerboat trips to the upper cays in the Exuma chain where you can see wild iguanas, stingrays, and sharks up close and enjoy their private islands for the day, and there are also excursions to Blue Lagoon Island and Rose Island—both a short boat ride away from Nassau. If you want to get up close to the world-famous swimming pigs, you'll need to plan a day or two in George Town or Staniel Cay farther south in the Exumas (*see Island Hopping Itineraries in the Experience chapter*).

Bahamas Fast Ferries. This isn't just a transportation company: Bahamas Fast Ferries also offers day trips from Nassau to Harbour Island, including lunch and pickups at major hotels. ⊠ *Potter's Cay, Nassau* ☎ *242/323–2166* ⊕ *www.bahamasferries.com* ✉ *$225.*

Fodor'sChoice ★ **Harbour Safaris.** Head to Big Major Cay to visit the world-famous swimming pigs on one of this outfit's two saddle-style Parker RIB vessels. On the way you'll stop off to feed some native iguanas. The full-day tour also includes lunch and a stop at a deserted beach or sandbank. Children under 12 are not permitted. ⊠ *Nassau* ☎ *242/394–8687* ⊕ *www. harboursafaris.com* ✉ *$389.*

Island World Adventures. The company, which operates two 45-foot speedboats, offers regularly scheduled full-day or private-charter tours to the northern Exumas from the Paradise Island Ferry Terminal. ⊠ *Paradise Island Ferry Terminal, Paradise Island* ☎ *242/363–3333* ⊕ *www. islandworldadventures.com* ✉ *$200.*

Fodor'sChoice ★ **Powerboat Adventures.** The company offers speed-filled day trips to the Exuma Cays on two custom-made powerboats. You can feed wild iguanas and stingrays, go on a snorkeling safari where you are pushed along by the ocean currents, and watch the daily shark-feeding. For a true adventure, overnights on the company's island, Ship Channel Cay, are also available. ⊠ *Paradise Island* ☎ *242/363–2265* ⊕ *www. powerboatadventures.com* ✉ *$192.53.*

SPECIAL-INTEREST TOURS

Bahamas Outdoors Ecoventures. This outfitter offers half- and full-day birding and nature tours through some of the national parks on New Providence Island. Charters can be arranged to Andros or even Eleuthera. There's a two-person minimum for tours. ☎ *242/362–1574* ⊕ *www.bahamasoutdoors.com* ✉ *$79–$129.*

Bowcar Bahamas. Rent a scooter, ATV, or buggy and head off on your own adventure or sign up for one of their guided tours—you'll drive your own buggy while following a tour guide to Nassau's hot spots. ⊠ *Nassau* ☎ *242/477–6778* ⊕ *www.bowcarbahamas.com.*

FAMILY **Dolphin Encounters.** On Blue Lagoon Island, the company offers dolphin and sea lion interactions with bona fide movie stars—three of their dolphins starred in the movie *Flipper* and their sea lions played the lead in a number of Hollywood films. Ferry transportation is included with departure from the Paradise Island Ferry Terminal. Make a day of it by adding a beach day on the island before or after your animal encounter. ⊠ *Paradise Island* ☎ *242/363–1003* ⊕ *www.dolphinencounters.com* 🖾 *Dolphin Swim $185; Dolphin Encounter $115; Sea Lion Encounter $109; Blue Lagoon Day $69.*

WALKING TOURS

Fodor'sChoice **Tru Bahamian Food Tours.** If you have three hours in Nassau, this is a
★ great way to spend it. The ecofriendly walking tour combines the food, history, and culture of the Bahamas in a way that's sure to leave you satisfied. The six tasting stops include some popular hot spots as well as some off-the-beaten-path gems. They have also partnered with five-star restaurant Graycliff to offer a 3½-hour cooking class. ⊠ *George St. and King St., Nassau* ⊹ *Meet outside Christ Church Cathedral* ☎ *800/656–0713, 242/601–1725* ⊕ *www.trubahamianfoodtours.com* 🖾 *$69* ☞ *Not suitable for visitors in wheelchairs.*

GRAND BAHAMA ISLAND

WELCOME TO GRAND BAHAMA ISLAND

TOP REASONS TO GO

★ **Take endless strolls on your own private beach.** Sprawling, reef-protected shoreline and cays offer more than 50 miles of secluded white-sand beaches along the southern shore.

★ **Go down under.** Between the shipwrecks, caves, coral reefs, and abundant marine life are some of the country's most varied and vivid snorkeling and diving.

★ **Get your green on.** Learn about the island's ecology underwater and among the mangroves where you can feed stingrays or catch sight of spotted dolphins and their calves.

★ **Party at the weekly fish fry or a beach bonfire.** Head to Smith Point to feast and party with locals, or dance around the bonfire at Taino by the Sea with all-you-can-eat authentic Bahamian cuisine and Bahama Mama cocktails.

★ **Swim with the dolphins or feed the sharks.** Several professional dive shops stand ready to introduce you to some of the ocean's most interesting characters.

Only 52 miles off Palm Beach, Florida, 96-mile-long Grand Bahama is one of the chain's northernmost islands. Freeport and Lucaya are its main cities, comprising the second-largest metropolitan area in the Bahamas. Lucaya sees the most action, as Freeport struggles to regain ground lost in the hurricanes and financial setbacks of the last decade. The town of West End, once a quiet, colorful fishing village, was nearly decimated during Hurricane Matthew in October 2016. The residents have pulled together to reconstruct their homes, and the conch shacks that lined the road along the coastline are slowly being rebuilt. Its upscale Old Bahama Bay Resort and marina are the extent of tourism on this end of the island. East of Freeport-Lucaya, small fishing settlements, secluded beaches, and undeveloped forest stretch for 60 miles to the outlying cays, and luxury bonefishing lodge, Deep Water Cay.

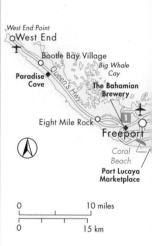

1 **Freeport.** The working end of Grand Bahama, Freeport is convenient to the airport and harbor for visitors in transit. Rand Nature Centre and The Bahamian Brewery make the area worth a visit, although downtown looks depressed and forlorn as developers await economic recovery.

Great Sale
Cay

Little Abaco
Island

Sponge Cay

Mangrove
Rocks

andy Cay

LITTLE   BAHAMA   BANK

Water
Cay

Water Cay

Halls
Point

Riding
Point

Rocky
Creek

Pelican
Point

McLean's August Cay
Town

over
ound

Rand Nature
Centre

Lucayan
National
Park

Bevans
Town   Grand Bahama Hwy.

Deep Water Cay

Sweeting's Cay

Big
Cross
Cay

High Rock

Sweetings Cay

4 Freetown

Lighthouse Cay

Michael's Cay

Long
Cay

Lucaya

2 **3** Fortune
Beach

Villiam's
Town

Smith Point

Taino
Beach

Northwest Providence
Channel

2 **Port Lucaya.** Freeport's beachfront counterpart is dominated by two of the island's largest hotels and resorts and Port Lucaya Marketplace (the island's best shopping).

3 **Greater Lucaya.** Lucayan Beach along Port Lucaya can get crowded, but Taino Beach, Coral Beach, and Fortune Beach are nearby for those who prefer more space and solitude; you'll find additional hotels and restaurants here as well.

4 **Greater Grand Bahama.** The bulk of the island lies on either side of the neighboring metropolitan duo of Freeport and Lucaya. Escaping town means discovering treasures such as Paradise Cove and Lucayan National Park, in addition to remote beaches, time-stilled fishing villages, and wooded land the locals refer to as the "bush."

LUCAYAN NATIONAL PARK

In this extraordinary 40-acre land preserve, trails and elevated walkways wind through a natural forest of wild tamarind and gumbo-limbo trees, past an observation platform, over a mangrove swamp, along a postcard-worthy beach, and in and around one of the world's largest explored underwater cave systems (more than 6 miles long).

Twenty-five miles east of Lucaya, the park contains examples of the island's five ecosystems: beach, hardwood forest, mangroves, rocky coppice, and pine forest. From the designated parking lot, you can enter the caves at two access points; one is closed in June and July for the bat-nursing season. Across the highway from the caves, two trails form a loop. Creek Trail's boardwalk showcases impressive interpretive signage, and crosses a mangrove-clotted tidal creek to Gold Rock Beach, claimed by Grand Bahama's Ministry of Tourism to be the island's "welcome mat." A narrow strand of white sand at high tide, and an expansive white-sand playground at low tide, this lightly visited beach is edged by some of the island's highest dunes and a picturesque jewel-tone sea.

Visitors will find subtle treasures no matter what time of year they explore. Summer can be overbearingly hot for walking. However, that's also when certain orchids and other plants flower. Migrating birds and cooler temperatures make October–April optimal, especially mornings and low tide, when birds are most plentiful.

BEST WAYS TO EXPLORE

By Kayak. A kayak launch, near a beach where parts of the *Pirates of the Caribbean* movies were filmed, lies just east of the park's parking lot on the south side. From here paddlers can work their way through mangrove forest to the beach and Gold Rock Creek.

Underwater. Snorkeling is popular around Gold Rock Beach and its eponymous offshore Gold Rock. Certified cave divers can explore the intricate underwater network with Underwater Explorers Society (UNEXSO).

On Foot. Trails come in two parts. On the north side of the highway at the parking lot, one trail takes you into Ben's Cave and the Burial Mound Cave, where ancient Lucayan remains and artifacts have been discovered. A tricky spiral staircase descends into the dark depths of the former, and an easier wooden staircase to the latter. At both, observation platforms accommodate visitors who want to peer into the caves' clear depths. Across the highway, two flat, easy trails form a loop to the beach. Creek Trail (0.2 mile) is the easiest because its boardwalk is newer and more elevated. Birds are more abundant here in the tidal creek with its low forest of mangroves at your feet. Mangrove Swamp Trail (0.3 mile) tends to be wet at high tide, and its boardwalk more difficult to negotiate (especially for small feet). Take one

to the beach and the other to return to see the full range of environment here.

PETERSON CAY NATIONAL PARK

Only accessible by boat or a long swim, Peterson Cay National Park, one of the Bahamas' smallest national parks, takes up 1½ acres 1 mile offshore from Barbary Beach. The gorgeous, usually deserted beach and lively marine life make it worth the effort of snorkeling the reef or enjoying a quiet picnic. However, vegetation on the cay is salt-stunted and scrubby, so shade is scarce, but lively hermit crabs are abundant. All wildlife is protected in the park by the Bahamas National Trust, including ¼ mile of surrounding marine environment. Local ecotour operators lead kayak and snorkel excursions.

FUN FACT

A species of crustacean labeled *Speleonectes lucayensis* was discovered here and exists exclusively in the caverns of Lucayan National Park, where its population is protected. The rare, cave-dwelling Remipedia has no eyes or pigmentation.

Updated by Dana MacKimmie

Natural beauty conspires with resort vitality to make Grand Bahama Island one of the Bahamas' most well-rounded, diverse destinations. In its two main towns, Freeport and Lucaya, visitors can find what the more bustling Nassau has to offer: resort hotels, a variety of restaurants, golfing, and duty-free shopping. But unlike New Providence, the touristy spots take up only a small portion of an island that, on the whole, consists of uninhabited stretches of sand and forest.

Prior to the development of Freeport, West End (the capital of Grand Bahama Island) was the epicenter of the Bahamas' logging industry and a playground for the wealthy in the 1920s. The fate of Grand Bahama changed in the 1950s when American financier Wallace Groves envisioned Grand Bahama's grandiose future as a tax-free shipping port. The Bahamian government signed an agreement that set in motion the development of a planned city, an airport, roads, waterways, and utilities as well as the port. From that agreement, the city of Freeport—and later, Lucaya—evolved. The past decade's hurricanes and economic downfall have demolished Freeport's resort glamour, and the tourism center has shifted to Lucaya, now home to the island's largest resorts.

Not much else on the island has changed since the early days, however. Outside of the Freeport-Lucaya commercial and resort area, fishing settlements remain, albeit now with electricity and paved roads. The East End is Grand Bahama's "back-to-nature" side, where Caribbean yellow pine–and-palmetto forest stretches for 60 miles, interrupted by the occasional small settlement. Little seaside villages with white churches and concrete-block houses painted in bright pastels once filled in the landscape between Freeport and West End, however a category 4 hurricane in 2016 nearly wiped them all out, and with the poor economy, rebuilding has been slow. Many of these settlements are more than 100 years old.

PLANNING

WHEN TO GO

As one of the northernmost Bahama Islands, Grand Bahama experiences temperatures dipping into the 60s with highs in the mid-70s in January and February, so you may need a jacket and wet suit. On the upside, the migrant bird population swells and diversifies during that time of year. High tourist season (which means seasonal crowds and increased room rates) runs from Christmas to Easter, peaking during spring break (late February to mid-April), when the weather is the most agreeable. October through mid-December can also exhibit good weather, so long as there hasn't been a particularly active hurricane season. Almost daily isolated thunderstorms never last more than a half hour, and the average temperatures steadily decrease from the high 80s at the beginning of October, to high 70s by mid-December.

Summers can get oppressively hot (into the mid and high 90s) and muggy; unless you're planning on doing a lot of snorkeling, diving, and other water sports, you may want to schedule your trip for cooler months. Afternoon thunderstorms and occasional tropical storms and hurricanes are also common in summer. The island averages around 20 days of rain per month from June to September, but it usually falls briefly in the afternoon. The good news is that hotel rates plummet and diving and fishing conditions are great.

TOP FESTIVALS

WINTER **Festival Noel.** Since 1993, Festival Noel has marked the official start to the Christmas season. Traditionally held the first Friday evening in December at the Rand Nature Centre, this wine- and food-tasting event and art show displays local talent. Proceeds aid the Bahamas National Trust for the development and restoration of national parks on Grand Bahama Island. ⊠ *Rand Nature Centre, East Settler's Way, Freeport, Freeport* ✛ *Across street from Sir Jack Hayward Junior High School* ☎ *242/352–5438.*

New Year's Day Junkanoo Parade. Junkanoo is the national festival of the Bahamas, named after an African tribal chief named "John Canoe," who demanded the right to celebrate with his people after being brought to the West Indies in slavery. Starting in the evening on January 1, and into the early morning hours, the downtown streets of Freeport come alive with larger-than-life costumed dancers jumping to the sounds of drums, whistles, and cowbells. At the end of January, watch local primary and secondary students take to the streets in the same colorful, cultural garb for Junior Junkanoo.

SPRING **Pelican Point Coconut Festival.** This homecoming celebration on the East End of the island held annually on Easter Monday features live music, coconut food sampling, coconut crafts, coconut bowling, and more.

FAMILY **Dog Days Half Marathon.** Held every March, this fund-raiser for the Grand Bahama Humane Society has grown in popularity since its inception in 2015. There's something for everyone: if you can't handle a half marathon, try out the 10k, 5k, or just the 1-mile fun run, where locals run, walk, and clown around with their dogs in tow. Stay after the race to swim at the beach beside the finish line, and to join the after-party. ⊠ *Bahamas Adventures, Jolly Roger Dr., Lucaya* ⊹ *On Jolly Roger Dr., next to Taino Beach Resort* ⊕ *www.grandbahama-dogdayshalfmarathon.com.*

Extreme Kayak Fishing Tournament. Usually held in April, sportfishing enthusiasts gather on the beach at Taino Beach Resort to watch competing anglers haul in fish nearly the size of the their kayaks. For those interested in participating, three-day packages start at approximately $595. ⊕ *www.extremekayakfishingtournament.org.*

SUMMER **BASRA's Bernie Butler Swim Race and Beach Party.** Every summer a party crowd gathers for the Bahamas Air Sea Rescue Association's annual swim race and daylong beach bash. Grand Bahama residents of all ages swim the sea in honor and support of BASRA's volunteer force, who in conjunction with the Bahamas Defense Force and the U.S. Coast Guard help people in distress. Live music, food and drink tents, and a bikini-friendly, end-of-summer party atmosphere make this a memorable event. ⊠ *Coral Beach, behind Coral Beach Bar, Just off Royal Palm Way and Coral Rd.* ⊕ *basragrandbahama.com.*

Grand Bahama Regatta and Heritage Festival. Sailing sloops from throughout the country meet in July for various sailing races, and crowd-pleasing favorite, the sculling competition. Onshore festivities take place at Taino Beach and include Junkanoo parades, dancing, live music, and food and drink. ⊠ *Taino Beach.*

FALL **Conchman Triathlon.** The annual Conchman Triathlon at Taino Beach in November is a swimming-running-bicycling competition for amateurs of all ages that raises funds for local charities. International applicants welcome. ⊠ *Taino Beach* ⊕ *www.conchmantriathlon.com.*

McLean's Town Conch Cracking Festival. McLean's Town's annual homecoming event on the East End began in 1972 and includes conch-cracking competitions, games, live music, crafts, and various conch dishes for sample. The best conch-cracker goes home with an authentically Bahamian-designed conch trophy. ⊠ *East End* ☎ *242/350–8600.*

HOTELS

Grand Bahama accommodations remain some of the Bahamas' most affordable, especially those away from the beach. The majority of these provide free shuttle service to the nearest stretch of sand. The island's more expensive hotels are beachfront, with the exception of Pelican Bay. These include the all-inclusive Lighthouse Pointe at The Grand Lucayan; Viva Wyndham Fortuna Beach, an all-inclusive east of Port Lucaya; West End's elegant Old Bahama Bay Resort & Yacht Harbour; and the east-end luxury bonefishing resort, Deep Water Cay. Small apartment complexes and time-share rentals are economical alternatives, especially if you're planning to stay for more than a few days.

Rates post-Easter through December 14 tend to be 25%–30% lower than those charged during the rest of the year.

RESTAURANTS

The Grand Bahama dining scene stretches well beyond traditional Bahamian cuisine. The resorts and shopping centers have eateries that serve up everything from West Indian rotis to fine Continental and creative Pacific Rim specialties. For a true Bahamian dining experience, look for restaurants named after the owner or cook—such as TB's Conch Shack, Ian's on the Bay, or Bishop's.

A native fish fry takes place every Wednesday evening at Smith's Point, east of Port Lucaya (taxi drivers know the way). Here you can sample fresh fish, sweet-potato bread, conch salad, and all the fixings cooked outdoors at the beach. It's a great opportunity to meet local residents and taste real Bahamian cuisine—and there's no better place than seaside under the pines and palms.

Note: A gratuity or "service charge" (15%) is often added to the bill automatically; be sure to check your total before adding an additional tip. Restaurant prices are based on the median main course price at dinner, excluding gratuity, typically 15% and VAT, which is often automatically added to the bill. Hotel prices are for two people in a standard double room in high season, excluding service and 6%–12% of various taxes.

WHAT IT COSTS IN DOLLARS			
	$	$$	$$$	$$$$
Restaurants	under $20	$20–$30	$31–$40	over $40
Hotels	under $200	$200–$300	$301–$400	over $400

VISITOR INFORMATION

Tourist information centers are open weekdays at the Grand Bahama International Airport (9–5), Freeport Harbour (according to cruise ship arrivals), and Port Lucaya Marketplace (10–6). The People-to-People Program matches your family with hospitable locals who share like interests.

Contacts Ministry of Tourism Grand Bahama Office. ⊠ *Fidelity Financial Center, Poinciana Dr., 1st fl., Freeport* ☎ *242/350-8600* ⊕ *www.bahamas. com.* **People-to-People Program.** ☎ *242/302-2000* ⊕ *www.bahamas.com/ people-to-people.*

GETTING HERE AND AROUND

AIR TRAVEL

Grand Bahama International Airport (FPO) is about 6 minutes from downtown Freeport and about 10 minutes from Port Lucaya. Several international carriers offer direct service to Grand Bahama from various U.S. gateways, but you can also connect in Nassau on regional carriers, including Bahamasair. No bus service is available between the airport and hotels. Metered taxis meet all incoming flights, although most of the resorts can make arrangements ahead of time for you, for a fee. Rides cost about $15 for two to Freeport, or $22 to Lucaya; see posted signs for fixed rates. The price drops to $4 per person with larger groups. There's also an airport in **West End (WTD)**, but it's strictly for private planes and charters.

Contacts Grand Bahama Airport Company (MYGF). ⊠ *Grand Bahama International Airport* ☎ *242/352–6020, 242/350–4211* ⊕ *www.freeportcontainerport.com.*

BOAT AND FERRY TRAVEL

Balearia Bahamas Express sails from Fort Lauderdale's Port Everglades and provides fast-ferry service, making a day trip possible, while Bahamas Paradise Cruise Line sails overnight from West Palm Beach, offering a more traditional cruise-ship experience, with two-night Grand Bahama hotel packages available. Taxis meet all ships.

BUS TRAVEL

Buses (usually minivans) are an inexpensive way to travel the 4 miles between downtown Freeport and Port Lucaya Marketplace daily until 8 pm. The fare is $1. Buses from Freeport to the West End cost $5 each way; to the East End, $15. Exact change is required. It should be noted that although this is a good way for the budget-conscious traveler to get around, these buses don't run to an exact schedule, and are often not in prime mechanical condition.

CAR TRAVEL

If you plan to drive around the island, it's cheaper and easier to rent a car than to hire a taxi. You can rent vehicles from local and major U.S. agencies at the airport. Calling ahead to reserve a car is recommended. Cars can range from $40/day to $125/day depending on the agency and length of rental.

Contacts AVIS. ⊠ *Grand Bahama International Airport* ☎ *242/351–2847, 242/351–2847* ⊕ *www.avis.com.* **Brad's Car Rental.** ⊠ *Grand Bahama International Airport* ☎ *242/352–7930, 954/703–5246* ⊕ *www.bradscarrental.com.* **Hertz Rent-a-Car.** ⊠ *Grand Bahama International Airport* ☎ *242/352–3297* ⊕ *www.hertz.com.* **KSR Car Rental.** ⊠ *Grand Bahama International Airport* ☎ *242/351–5737, 954/703–5819* ⊕ *www.ksrrentacar.com.*

SCOOTER TRAVEL

Contacts Island Jeep and Car Rentals. ⊠ *Island Seas Resort* ☎ *242/373–4001, 242/727–2207* ⊕ *www.islandjeepcarrental.com.*

TAXI TRAVEL

Taxi fares are fixed (but generally you're charged a flat fee for routine trips; see posted trip fares at the airport) at $3 for the first ¼ mile and 40¢ for each additional ¼ mile. After two people, additional passengers are $3 each. Taxis are available outside of the big resorts or you can call the Grand Bahama Taxi Union for pickup.

Contacts Grand Bahama Taxi Union. ☎ *242/352–7101.*

EXPLORING

FREEPORT

Freeport, once an attractive, planned city of modern shopping centers, resorts, and other convenient tourist facilities, took a bad hit from the 2004 and 2005 hurricanes and subsequent economy downturn; its main resort and casino have not reopened. An Irish firm purchased the former Royal Oasis Resort & Casino but no plans have been made to rebuild or renovate. The International Bazaar next door is currently an abandoned ghost town with only a few crafts vendors and shops. Despite all this, Freeport's native restaurants, Rand Nature Centre, Bahamian Brewery, and beaches make it worth the visit. It's close to Lucaya (a 15-minute drive), and the airport and harbor are just a few minutes from downtown.

The Bahamian Brewery. One hundred percent Bahamian-owned, this 20-acre brewery opened in 2007, bringing to the Bahamian islands five new beers including Sands, High Rock Lager, Bush Crack, and Strong Back Stout. The brewery even makes a signature red ale served exclusively at the Atlantis Resort on Paradise Island. The brewery does everything on-site including bottling and labeling, and offers 45-minute to hour-long tours on weekdays that take you along each step in the brewing process. The tour ends in the tasting room where you can belly up to the bar or cocktail tables to sample each beer. Walk-ins are accepted. Beer, wine, and liquor can be purchased in the retail store; Bahamian Brewery souvenirs are available in the gift shop. ⊠ *Just off Queen's Hwy., east of turn to West End, Freeport* ☎ *242/352–4070* ⊕ *www.bahamianbrewery.com* ⊠ *$10 for tours* ⊘ *No tours on weekends, but liquor store open Sat. Closed Sun.*

Bahamas National Trust Rand Nature Centre. Established in 1939 on 100 acres just minutes from downtown Freeport, a half mile of self-guided botanical trails shows off 130 types of native plants, including many plants known for their use in bush medicine. The remaining tracts of land are left natural and undisturbed to serve as wildlife habitat. The center is also one of the island's birding hot spots, where you might spy a red-tailed hawk or a Cuban emerald hummingbird. Visit Donni, the one-eyed Bahama parrot the center has adopted, and the two Bahamian boas, a species that inhabits most Bahamian islands, but not Grand Bahama. The visitor center also hosts changing local art exhibits. The center survives on admissions, gift shop purchases, and donations alone, but has plans for a future face-lift and new exhibits. ⊠ *E. Settlers Way, Freeport* ☎ *242/352–5438* ⊕ *www.bnt. bs* ⊠ *$5* ⊘ *Closed weekends.*

More than 300 bird species call the Bahamas home, including this Bananaquit.

LUCAYA

On the beach and harbor of Grand Bahama's southern coast is resort center Lucaya, developed after its neighbor Freeport. Colorful Port Lucaya Marketplace grew up along the safe harbor, known for its duty-free shops, bars, restaurants, straw market, and outdoor bandstand. This is also the home of UNEXSO, the island's famous diving and dolphin encounter attraction. Surrounding the port are the island's biggest hotels: Lighthouse Pointe at The Grand Lucayan, and Pelican Bay.

PORT LUCAYA

Port Lucaya Marketplace. Lucaya's capacious and lively shopping complex is on the waterfront across the street from the Grand Lucayan Hotel, and right in front of the Pelican Bay. The outdoor shopping center, whose walkways are lined with hibiscus, bougainvillea, and croton, has more than 100 well-kept, colorfully painted establishments, among them waterfront restaurants and bars, water-sports operators, and shops that sell clothes, silver, jewelry, perfumes, and local arts and crafts. The marketplace's centerpiece is **Count Basie Square,** where live entertainment featuring Bahamian bands appeals to joyful nighttime crowds every weekend. Lively outdoor watering holes line the square, which is also *the* place to celebrate the holidays: a tree-lighting ceremony takes place in the festively decorated spot at the beginning of December and fireworks highlight New Year's Eve, July 4, and Bahamian Independence Day, July 10. ✉ *Across from Grand Lucayan , Sea Horse Rd., Port Lucaya Marketplace* ☎ *242/373–8446* ⊕ *www.portlucaya.com.*

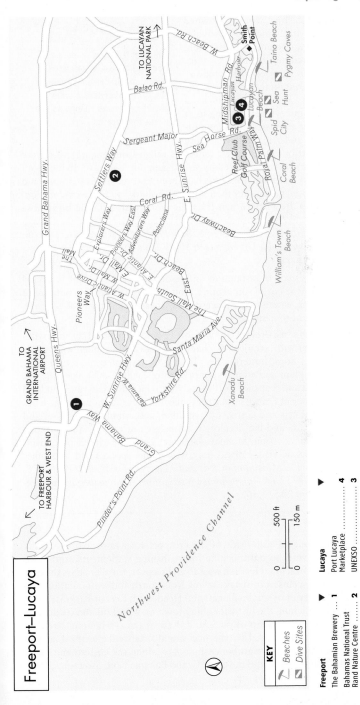

KEY

↗ Beaches
⬛ Dive Sites

Ⓝ

Freeport
The Bahamian Brewery **1**
Bahamas National Trust
Rand Nature Centre **2**

▶

Lucaya
Port Lucaya
Marketplace **4**
UNEXSO **3**

FAMILY
Fodor's Choice
★

UNEXSO. This world-renowned scuba-diving facility provides rental equipment, guides, and boats. Facilities include a 17-foot-deep training pool with windows that look out on the harbor, changing rooms and showers, docks, a full boutique with everything from swimwear to hostess gifts, an outdoor bar and grill, and an air-tank filling station. Daily dive excursions range from one-day discovery courses and dives, to specialty shark, dolphin, and cave diving. Both the facility and its dive masters have been featured in international and American magazines for their work with sharks and cave exploration. UNEXSO are also known for their work with Atlantic bottlenose dolphins. ⊠ *Port Lucaya, next to Pelican Bay Hotel, Port Lucaya Marketplace* ☎ *242/373–1244, 800/992–3483* ⊕ *www.unexso.com* ✉ *Discover Scuba Diving $129; Shark Dive $109.*

> **DID YOU KNOW?**
>
> The term "Lucayan" is derived from the Arawak Indian word Lukka-Cairi, or "Island People." The early indigenous people gave the Bahama Islands its first name, the Lucayas.

GREATER LUCAYA

The lion's share of restaurants and resorts in Lucaya is located around Port Lucaya, but if you venture a bit farther you'll find a handful of attractions, eateries, and places to stay that are slightly removed from the crush of tourists.

The Garden of the Groves. This vibrant, 12-acre garden and certified wildlife habitat with a trademark chapel and waterfalls, is filled with native Bahamian flora, butterflies, birds, and turtles. Interpretative signage identifies plant and animal species. First opened in 1973, the park was renovated and reopened in 2008; additions include a labyrinth modeled after the one at France's Chartres Cathedral, colorful shops and galleries with local arts and crafts, a playground, and a multideck indoor and outdoor café and bar. Explore on your own or take a half-hour-long guided tour at 10 am (Monday–Saturday). Enjoy the garden under twinkling lights on Friday nights only, with dinner specials and sometimes live music. ⊠ *Midshipman Rd. and Magellan Dr.* ☎ *242/374–7778, 242/374–7779 Fri. night dinner reservations* ⊕ *www.thegardenofthegroves.com* ✉ *$16.50.*

GREATER GRAND BAHAMA

Farther out on either side of the Freeport–Lucaya development, the island reverts to natural pine forest, fishing settlements, and quiet secluded beaches. Heading west from Freeport, travelers pass the harbor area, a cluster of shacks selling fresh conch and seafood at Fishing Hole, a series of small villages, and Deadman's Reef at Paradise Cove before reaching the historic fishing town of West End and its upscale resort at the very tip of the island. East of Lucaya lie long stretches of forest interrupted by the occasional small village, the Lucayan National Park, myriad bonefishing flats along the eastern end up to McClean's Town, and the outer Grand Bahama cays: Sweetings, Deep Water, and Lightbourne.

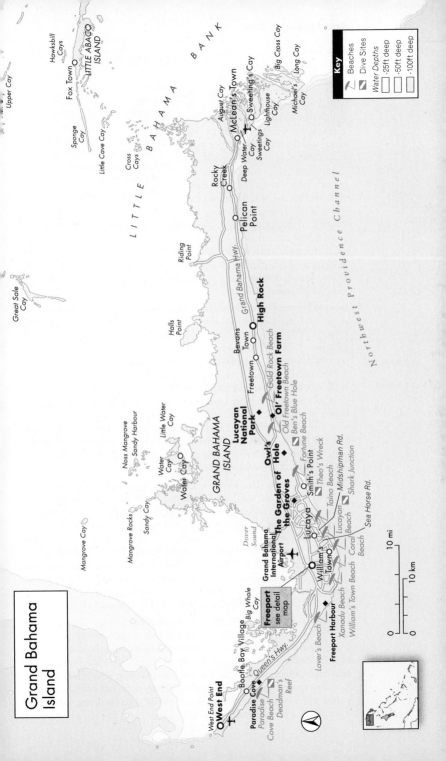

High Rock. About 45 miles east of Lucaya and 8 miles from Lucaya National Park, it's worth the extra drive to visit an authentic, old-time island settlement affected only lightly by tourism. Its beach spreads a lovely white blanket of plump sand, with two beach bars for food and drink, including Bishop's Place. Time spent at the bar with Bishop himself (aka Ruben "Bishop" Roberts) and his dog will make you feel like a local. Take a walk along the beach and its parallel road (rock outcroppings interrupt the sand in places) past the cemetery to the faux lighthouse that makes a nice photographic punctuation. Although the welcome sign identifies the village as "Home of Hospitality," it holds just two small lodges and offers only simple fried Bahamian fare. The service is friendly and the beer is cold. ⊠ *Eastern Grand Bahama.*

> ## ISLAND DOGS
>
> Island dogs, known as "potcakes"—a reference to the bottom of the rice pans they clean up—run wild, so be careful when driving. Efforts in recent years by the active Grand Bahama Humane Society have raised awareness of the need for neutering and spaying.

Lucayan National Park. Considered the crown jewel of the four national parks on Grand Bahama, Lucayan National Park is the only place to find all six Bahamian ecosystems in a single, 40-acre expanse of land: pine forest, blackland coppice (ferns, bromeliads, orchids), rocky coppice (hardwoods), mangrove swamp, whiteland coppice (rich plant life, poisonwood), and beach/shoreline. Because it is 25 miles east of Lucaya, booking a tour or renting a car is necessary in order to experience all the park has to offer. Explore two caves, hike around the nature trails, bird watch across the raised boardwalks through the mangroves, or stroll along the spectacular Gold Rock Beach during low tide as the shoreline sets out its "welcome mat"—sand ripples created by tidal pools as the water recedes. ⊠ *Grand Bahama Hwy., Freetown* ☎ *242/353–4149, 242/352–5438* ⊕ *www.bnt.bs* ☑ *$5.*

FAMILY **Ol' Freetown Farm.** This family-owned and -operated farm offers farm tours to meet, greet, feed, and pet the resident animals, including horses, ponies, peacocks, turkeys, goats, sheep, rabbits, and guinea pigs, among others. The farm also grows its own fruit and vegetables, available for purchase at their farm stand along with fresh-pressed sugarcane juice and eggs straight from the chicken coop. Horseback riding lessons are also available. Opening hours change with the seasons and daily weather, so call ahead before you visit. ⊠ *Grand Bahama Hwy., 6 miles east of College of the Bahamas, before Lucayan National Park, Freetown* ☎ *242/441–8611, 242/441–8611* ⊙ *Closed Sun. and Mon.*

Owl's Hole. Named for the mama owl who nests here every year, this vertical freshwater cave (a limestone sinkhole formed by the collapse of a section of a cavern's roof) is a popular local swimming hole. It's rimmed by a 24-foot cliff if you're up for taking a plunge. The less adventuresome can climb down a ladder into the cool but refreshing water. Take snorkel gear down with you to experience the beauty at its full potential, and if you're a certified cavern diver you can join local scuba diving excursions to explore even deeper. If your timing is right, you will see a nest full of fuzzy owlets (April and May) tucked under the ledge as you descend the ladder. The drive here feels a bit like a ride on a Bahamian bush roller coaster but it's worth it—finding the hole is half the adventure. ⊠ *Off Grand Bahama Hwy.* ✛ *From Grand Bahama Hwy., turn right on last dirt road before "Dangerous Curve" sign (before Lucayan National Park). Drive 1.6 miles to tiny parking area on left. You've gone too far if you reach beach.*

West End. Once a rowdy, good-time resort area, West End was nearly leveled by Hurricane Matthew in

2016, and is slowly rebuilding. It still attracts small crowds on Sunday evenings for friendly, casual street gatherings, and small fish fry shacks on weekend afternoons, offering up some of the island's best traditional Bahamian fare. Today's visitors stop at Paradise Cove for snorkeling, and farther west at the bay-front conch shacks for conch salad straight from the shell (try Shebo's or Ian's on the Bay) or at other tiny eateries along the way like Chicken's Nest, known for having the best conch fritters on island. Overnighters stay at Old Bahama Bay Resort & Yacht Harbour, an upscale gated resort. Nonguests are welcome at the hotel's beachside Tiki Bar for breakfast and lunch, or at the Dockside Grill for dinner. ⊠ *Western Grand Bahama.*

BEACHES

Grand Bahama Island stretches for 96 miles, with beautiful beaches fringing its south coast, and a few remote ones along the west coast. This guide will lead any beach enthusiast to a fitting seaside spot.

FREEPORT

William's Town Beach. When the tide is high, this 1.9-mile slice of relatively hidden beach (from East Sunrise Highway, take Coral Road south, turn right onto Bahama Reef Boulevard, then left on Beachway Drive) can get a little narrow, but there's a wide area at its East End on Silver Point Beach near Island Seas Resort, where a food stand called Bernie's Tiki Hut serves fresh local delicacies such as cracked conch, fried snapper, or grilled lobster tail. Bernie's also hosts a bonfire on Tuesday nights. Just west of here, a sidewalk runs the length of the beach along the road and at low tide the beach expands far and wide for easy walking on the shore. Across the road, a number of forlorn roadside beach bars dot the landscape. Island Seas Resort has its own modern interpretation of the local beach shack, called CoCoNuts Grog & Grub. **Amenities:** food and drink; parking (no fee); water sports. **Best for:** solitude; swimming; walking. ⊠ *Next to Island Seas Resort, Silver Point Dr. at Beachway Dr., Williams Town.*

LUCAYA

PORT LUCAYA

Lucayan Beach and Coral Beach. This stretch of sand divides into separately named beaches at the intersection of Sea Horse Road and Royal Palm Way. The eastern end is Lucayan Beach, monopolized by the broad spread of the Lighthouse Pointe at The Grand Lucayan resort, where nonguests can purchase day passes from the hotel which include use of pools, nonmotorized water equipment, and access to restaurants. Feed jack fish, snorkel at Rainbow Reef, parasail, or take a WaveRunner tour. Near the long-standing Ocean Motion Watersports, there is no admission fee for the beach. Go west from here along Coral Beach, where the shore widens for easier strolling and the crowds thin considerably on the way to Coral Beach Bar. **Amenities:** food and drink; lifeguards; parking (no fee); water sports. **Best for:** partiers; snorkeling; sunrise; swimming, walking. ⊠ *Sea Horse Dr., Royal Palm Way, behind Grand Lucayan, and Coral Beach Bar, Freeport.*

GREATER LUCAYA

FAMILY **Fortune Beach.** Fortune Beach lies between two canal channels, and in the middle sits the Wyndham Viva Fortuna all-inclusive resort, where visitors can purchase day passes to use water-sports equipment and resort facilities. Steps from the resort the secluded beach offers exceptional strolling, off-shore snorkeling, and swimming. The western end backs the Margarita Villa Sand Bar and the private homes along Spanish Main Drive, known as "Millionaire Row." The eastern end is home to Banana Bay Restaurant, where at low tide a shallow lagoon forms alongside a drawn-out sandbar, allowing you to walk yards out to sea with cold drink in hand. **Amenities:** food and drink; parking near east end only (no fee). **Best for:** solitude; snorkeling; sunrise; swimming; walking. ⊠ *Fortune Bay Dr., Greater Lucaya.*

FAMILY **Taino Beach.** A short walk down the long, gently coved beach takes you to Pirates Cove Water Park, where the kids can bounce to their hearts' content on giant trampolines in the water. Rent kayaks, paddleboards, and jet skis, or beach chairs and umbrellas. A bar with a small food menu is also available. A few steps farther is Outriggers Beach Club, home to the popular fish fry held every Wednesday night. Plenty of green space edges the beach, and there's also a playground. **Amenities:** food and drink; parking (no fee); toilets; water sports. **Best for:** partiers; sunset; swimming; walking. ⊠ *W. Beach Rd., near Smith's Point, Greater Lucaya.*

GREATER GRAND BAHAMA

Fodor's Choice ★ **Gold Rock Beach.** Located just off the Grand Bahama Highway 26 miles outside town, this secluded beach is accessible via a lovely 10-minute walk through the Lucayan National Park, spanning for yards into the sea when the tide is low. The turquoise water is exceptionally clear, calm, and shallow. Occasional cruise-ship tours visit for a couple of hours around midday, but there is enough space that you will never feel crowded. The beach is almost nonexistent when the tide is high and shade is sparse, so time your visit appropriately. **Amenities:** none. **Best for:** solitude; swimming, walking. ⊠ *Grand Bahama Hwy., Freetown.*

Lover's Beach. This beach on the island's west side is relatively unknown and rarely visited by tourists, and its sand is far less fine and powdery than what's found along the southern shores. However, it's the only spot on Grand Bahama to find sea glass. Adding to its uniqueness is its view of the large tanker and container ships anchored at sea for the island's industrial businesses, and the pastel-painted heavy-equipment tires planted in the sand for seating. **Amenities:** parking (free). **Best for:** walking. ✉ *Hepburn Town in Eight Mile Rock, across the channel from Freeport Harbour, West End.*

3

Old Freetown Beach. This lightly visited beach will take you far from the tourist crowds and resorts. Considered one of the prettiest beaches on the island, with a wide scattering of sea biscuits, blinding white sand, and shallow turquoise water, you will most likely have the whole stretch of sand to yourself. **Amenities:** none. **Best for:** solitude; swimming; walking. ✉ *Off Grand Bahama Hwy., just west of Ol' Freetown Farm* ✣ *Turn south on dirt road that lies just east of Grand Bahama Hwy.'s "Dangerous Curve" sign. Road to Owl's Hole will also land you at this beach.*

Paradise Cove Beach. A 20-minute drive from Freeport, this beach's spectacular swim-to reef (called Deadman's Reef) is its best asset. Close to shore, you'll also find the longest man-made reef (composed of a long line of concrete reef balls) in the Bahamas, with spectacular marine life that includes various rays, sea turtles, and barracudas. Paradise Cove is a small native-owned resort with many different adventure packages, which all include return transportation. The beach is short but wide with scrubby vegetation and swaying palm trees. Snorkel equipment and kayaks are available to rent, and refreshments flow at the Red Bar. There is a $4/person fee just to hang at the beach. **Amenities:** food and drink; parking (no fee); showers; toilets; water sports. **Best for:** snorkeling. ✉ *Warren J. Levarity Hwy., between Eight Mile Rock and West End, West End* 🌐 *www.deadmansreef.com* 🎟 *$4.*

WHERE TO EAT

FREEPORT

$$ SUSHI Fodor's Choice ★

🍴 **East Sushi at Pier One.** Pier One has one of the most unique settings of any restaurant in Grand Bahama, and two different menus to choose from: sushi or cooked continental fare. Built on stilts above the ocean near Freeport Harbour, it offers one-of-a-kind views of magnificent sunsets, larger-than-life cruise ships departing, and sharks swimming for chum. **Known for:** fresh, quality sushi; great views; shark-watching. [$] *Average main: $25* ✉ *Next to Freeport Harbour, and a 2nd location in Port Lucaya Marketplace, Freeport* ☎ *242/352–6674* 🌐 *pieroneandeast.com* 🕒 *No lunch Sun.*

$ VEGETARIAN

🍴 **Livity Vegetarian Juice Bar & Take-Out.** Offering the healthiest food alternative on the island, this little shop (located in a shabby strip mall) doesn't look like much, but the quality of the food tells a different story. Livity blends up fresh fruit and vegetable juices and smoothies with names like Flu Shot, Pressure Reliever, and Incredible Hulk. **Known for:**

vegetarian fare; delicious smoothies; healthy lunch alternatives. $ *Average main: $8* ⊠ *West Atlantic Dr., in Rolle's Furniture Plaza, Freeport* ☎ *242/352–1855* ⊟ *No credit cards* ⊗ *Closed weekends. No dinner.*

$ ✕ **Mary Ann's Restaurant and Lounge.**

BAHAMIAN This native restaurant tucked in a Freeport strip mall attracts a steady local clientele for its home-cooked Bahamian cuisine. Named after owner Mary Ann Ward, who runs the place with her husband, the little diner is known for its cracked or curried lobster, along with traditional favorites like chicken souse, tuna and grits, peas 'n' rice, johnnycake, and a slightly spicy baked mac 'n cheese. **Known for:** local cuisine; delicious curried lobster; nontouristy atmosphere. $ *Average main: $12* ⊠ *West Settler's Way, Elite Plaza, Freeport* ☎ *242/352–8875, 242/477–8040.*

$ ✕ **Merport Bistro.** Offering French cuisine with a strong Bahamian influ-

FRENCH FUSION ence, Merport Bistro is popular with locals and tourists alike. Located in downtown Freeport, their weekly specials are worth checking out, and although the menu changes constantly, there is something for everyone, from seafood wraps and lobster bisque, to coq au vin, to stuffed snapper with corn and zucchini salsa. **Known for:** fresh ingredients; daily changing specials; friendly staff. $ *Average main: $19* ⊠ *3 Merport Bldg., Pioneer's Way, 1 Town Center, Freeport* ✛ *Across from BTC* ☎ *242/602–7506* ⊗ *Closed weekends.*

$ ✕ **Senor Frog's Restaurant Bar & Souvenir Shop.** This Mexican-themed party

MEXICAN place fills with cruise-ship passengers in port for the day, and sends them back to the boat happy, fed, and full of rum drinks. The location at the Freeport Harbour is open-air and full of life, complete with a dance stage, large flat-screen TVs, a wraparound bar, and seating for more than 100 people. **Known for:** Mexican cuisine; party atmosphere; lots of tequila. $ *Average main: $17* ⊠ *Freeport Harbour, Freeport* ☎ *242/351–3764* ⊕ *www.senorfrogs.com* ⊗ *Closed when there are no docked cruise ships.*

LUCAYA

Most of the dining in Lucaya is in or around the Port Lucaya Marina or Port Lucaya Marketplace, which means that nearly all the restaurants are within walking distance of each other and of the hotels in the immediate vicinity.

$ ✕ **Banana Bay Restaurant.** Directly on Fortune Beach, Banana Bay is

CARIBBEAN a great place for lunch or daytime cocktails, whether you sit on the

FAMILY restaurant's shaded deck or on a lounger in the sand. As the tide rolls

Fodor's Choice out the beach grows, creating a wonderful shallow lagoon and sandbar,

★ perfect for wading and for frolicking kids. **Known for:** fresh fish daily

> **DID YOU KNOW?**
>
> Sands Beer made its first appearance with the opening of The Bahamian Brewery in 2008 and is now a favorite local brew, available throughout the Bahamas. Subsequently, the brewery, and its logo of a man sculling in a boat, have been a catalyst in bringing back one of the country's oldest pastimes: "Man in the Boat" sculling races are now part of sailing regattas all over the Bahamas, after a 20-plus-year absence.

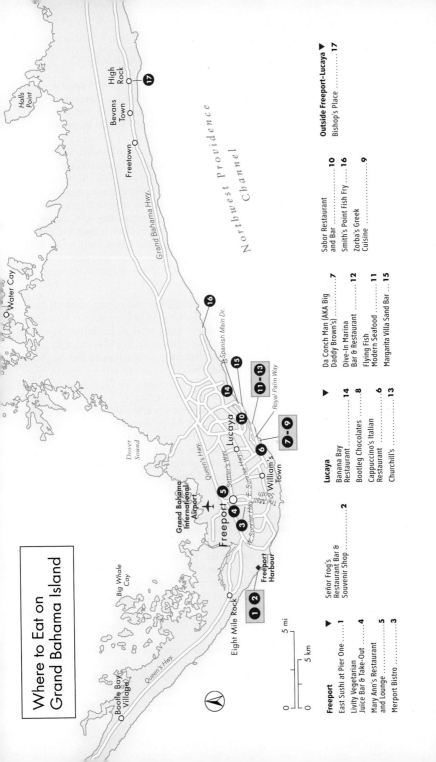

Where to Eat on Grand Bahama Island

Freeport ▼

East Sushi at Pier One	1
Livity Vegetarian Juice Bar & Take-Out	4
Mary Ann's Restaurant and Lounge	5
Merport Bistro	3
Señor Frog's Restaurant Bar & Souvenir Shop	2

Lucaya ▼

Banana Bay Restaurant	14
Bootleg Chocolates	8
Cappuccino's Italian Restaurant	6
Churchill's	13
Da Conch Man (AKA Big Daddy Brown's)	7
Dive-In Marina Bar & Restaurant	12
Flying Fish Modern Seafood	11
Margarita Villa Sand Bar	15
Sabor Restaurant and Bar	10
Smith's Point Fish Fry	16
Zorba's Greek Cuisine	9

Outside Freeport-Lucaya ▼

Bishop's Place	17

specials; beautiful beach views; warm homemade banana bread. $ *Average main: $18* ✉ *Fortune Beach, Fortune Bay Dr., Lucaya* ☎ *242/373–2960* ⊗ *No dinner.*

$

CAFÉ

× **Bootleg Chocolates.** This cozy little café offers strong gourmet coffees, delicious pastries, and creative and delicious chocolates, handcrafted in-store. Try inventive flavors, such as black tea and ginger, goat pepper and balsamic caramel, or Bahamian seas salt and hibiscus caramel—a unique taste of the Bahamas to take home. **Known for:** strong coffee; inspired chocolate flavors; locally made chocolates. $ *Average main: $10* ✉ *Port Lucaya Marketplace, on waterfront, Port Lucaya Marketplace* ☎ *242/373–6303* ⊕ *www.bootlegchocolates.com* ▭ *No credit cards.*

$

ITALIAN

Fodor's Choice

★

× **Cappuccino's Italian Restaurant.** This Italian family-run cozy restaurant offers consistently good food and great service. Traditional comfort pasta dishes adorn the menu, like pesto gnocchi and seafood linguine, in addition to steaks and daily fresh fish specials. **Known for:** delightful Italian cuisine; daily fresh fish specials; romantic atmosphere. $ *Average main: $18* ✉ *Port Lucaya Marketplace, Sea Horse Rd., Lucaya* ☎ *242/373–1584* ⊗ *Closed Wed. No lunch.*

$$

STEAKHOUSE

× **Churchill's.** Unwind in the handsome wood piano bar before enjoying a four-course dinner in the dining room, surrounded by white wainscoting and French windows. The menu is Mediterranean inspired, with house specialties such as lobster and wild mushroom risotto and veal marsala, but also includes create-your-own pasta dishes, steaks, and seafood. **Known for:** formal dining (strict dress code); Mediterranean-inspired cuisine; great steaks. $ *Average main: $30* ✉ *Lighthouse Pointe at Grand Lucayan Resort, Lucaya* ☎ *242/373–1333* ⊕ *www. grandlucayan.com* ⊗ *Closed Mon.–Wed. No lunch.*

$

BAHAMIAN

× **Da Conch Man (AKA Big Daddy Brown's).** Located in Port Lucaya Marketplace along the water, Big Daddy Brown's offers fresh conch salad and authentic Bahamian staples. Watch this family team prepare mouthwatering conch fritters, cracked conch, and fried lobster right in front of you; grab a cold Sands beer at any of the open-air bars surrounding the stand and enjoy it all while people-watching in Market Square. **Known for:** authentic fried Bahamian staples; fresh conch salad; central location. $ *Average main: $10* ✉ *Port Lucaya Marketplace, Lucaya* ▭ *No credit cards.*

$

CARIBBEAN

FAMILY

× **Dive-In Marina Bar & Restaurant.** This relaxing outdoor poolside bar and grill at UNEXSO is great for lunch and weekend brunch, with delicious and creative menu items. Kids can splash in the pool (which has underwater windows to the marina, so bring goggles!) while adults sip spicy Bloody Marys and tropical drinks. **Known for:** casual lunches; weekend

CONCHING OUT

Conch harvesting is illegal in the United States and closely regulated in other tropical locations to guard against overfishing. Currently, conch harvesting is limited to six per vessel in the Bahamas, but populations, while still plentiful, are slowly becoming depleted. The Bahamas National Trust launched a "Conchservation" campaign in 2013 in an effort to educate and preserve Queen Conch fishing in the Bahamas. Read more about it at ⊕ www.bnt.bs/conchservation.

This sailboat is in front of Grand Lucayan.

brunch; patrons can use the pool. $ *Average main: $17* ✉ *UNEXSO, Lucaya* ✛ *Next to Pelican Bay Hotel* ☎ *242/373–1244.*

$$$
SEAFOOD
Fodor's Choice
★

✕ **Flying Fish Modern Seafood.** Flying Fish offers one of the finest culinary experiences in the Caribbean. You'll find quality service with an eclectic collection of seafood and Bahamian favorites, made with local ingredients and done with a gourmet and artistic twist. **Known for:** eclectic and inspired menu; good wine list; casual Sunday evenings. $ *Average main: $38* ✉ *1 Sea Horse Rd., Lucaya* ✛ *Next to Pelican Bay Hotel* ☎ *242/373–4363* ⊕ *www.flyingfishbahamas.com* ☾ *Closed Tues. and all public holidays. No lunch Mon.* ☞ *Docking facilities for boaters.*

$
AMERICAN

✕ **Margarita Villa Sand Bar.** There is no flooring in this cozy little beach bar, just sand, along with a few bar-top tables and some stools along the bar. The bartender will make you feel like an old friend. **Known for:** right on the beach; warm service; party atmosphere. $ *Average main: $12* ✉ *Fortune Beach, off Spanish Main Rd., Mather Town, Lucaya* ☎ *242/373–4525* ⊕ *www.sandbarbahamas.com.*

$$
ECLECTIC

✕ **Sabor Restaurant and Bar.** The setting makes this restaurant the perfect place for an evening cocktail whether you sit overlooking the Port Lucaya Marina or nestled among the twinkling lights and palm trees around the pool deck. The lunch and dinner menu is a fun fusion of Bahamian and American favorites with tropical twists, such as O.M.G. jalapeño shrimps, Grand Cay cracked conch, blackened grouper, spice-rubbed seared tuna, and steaks and burgers to boot. **Known for:** Bahamian-American cuisine; friendly staff; pleasant, intimate atmosphere. $ *Average main: $20* ✉ *Pelican Bay Hotel, Lucaya* ☎ *242/373–5588* ⊕ *www.sabor-bahamas.com.*

DID YOU KNOW?

Grand Bahama is one of the most eco-oriented islands in the Bahamas. Kayaks are readily available across the island.

$ ╳ **Smith's Point Fish Fry.** For Bahamian food fixed by Bahamians, head
BAHAMIAN to Smith Point for the famous weekly fish fry. Every Wednesday night
this little settlement by Taino Beach comes to life with both locals
and tourists, when the open-air beach shacks along the street serve up
fried fish (with the head and tail still on), cracked conch (pounded and
fried), lobster tail, fried grouper, and barbecue chicken down-home
style. **Known for:** traditional Bahamian food; party atmosphere; on
the beach. $ *Average main: $10* ⊠ *Smith's Point, Off W. Beach Rd.,
Lucaya* ⊹ *Next to Taino Beach* ⊕ *www.bahamas.com/vendor/fish-fry-
smiths-point* ▭ *No credit cards.*

$ ╳ **Zorba's Greek Cuisine.** Besides Greek favorites, this longtime Port
GREEK Lucaya tenant serves popular Bahamian dishes, too. Join the port's
yacht-in clientele, shoppers, and locals alike, for breakfast, lunch, or
dinner on the white-and-blue-trimmed sidewalk porch. New in 2017,
Zorba's expanded to include a café next door to the main restaurant,
with daily fresh pastries and breads, coffee, and espresso. **Known for:**
traditional Greek menu items; central location; casual dining. $ *Aver-
age main: $17* ⊠ *Port Lucaya Marketplace, Lucaya* ☎ *242/373–6137*
⊕ *www.zorbasbahamas.com.*

GREATER GRAND BAHAMA

$ ╳ **Bishop's Place.** A longtime favorite of locals and visitors who venture
BAHAMIAN out to Lucayan National Park (about 6 miles away) and into the East
End's settlements, Bishop's serves all the fried Bahamian favorites with
a view of the sea. The beach bar itself doesn't sell food, so you'll have
to make the short walk across the parking lot to order in the restaurant
and they will bring it out to you. **Known for:** traditional Bahamian
menu favorites; relaxing bar on outstanding beach; casual, friendly
atmosphere. $ *Average main: $15* ⊠ *High Rock* ☎ *242/353–5485*
⊕ *www.bishopsresort.net* ▭ *No credit cards* ☉ *Closed weekdays during low season. Best to call ahead, to avoid a trek out for nothing.*

WHERE TO STAY

Grand Bahama has a selection of time-shares in addition to regular
hotels and resorts. For more information about time-share houses,
apartments, and condominiums, contact the Ministry of Tourism Grand
Bahama Office (☎ *800/224–2627* ⊕ *www.bahamas.com*).

FREEPORT

$ ▦ **Island Seas Resort.** This time-share property also accommodates non-
RESORT members looking for fun on the beach away from urban traffic. **Pros:**
FAMILY on-site restaurant; fun pool and bar area; great beach. **Cons:** fitness
center is below par; service can be slow; property is worn and room
decor is outdated. $ *Rooms from: $150* ⊠ *123 Silver Point Dr., Williams Town* ☎ *242/373–1271, 800/801–6884* ⊕ *www.islandseas.com*
⊅ *190 rooms* ⎟○⎟ *No meals.*

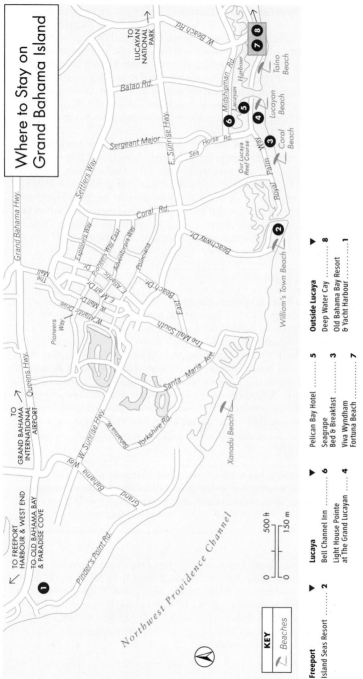

Where to Stay on Grand Bahama Island

KEY

Beaches

| 0 | 500 ft |
| 0 | 150 m |

Freeport ▶

Island Seas Resort 2

Lucaya ▶

Bell Channel Inn 6

Light House Pointe
at The Grand Lucayan 4

Pelican Bay Hotel 5

Seagrape
Bed & Breakfast 3

Viva Wyndham
Fortuna Beach 7

Outside Lucaya ▶

Deep Water Cay 8

Old Bahama Bay Resort
& Yacht Harbour 1

Northwest Providence Channel

LUCAYA

$ **Bell Channel Inn.** Right on the water and a short walk from Port
HOTEL Lucaya Marketplace, this charming family-run (through three generations) inn with newly updated, simple-yet-spacious rooms has quick and
easy access to the island's best down-under sites, making it perfect for
scuba-oriented and budget-minded travelers. **Pros:** friendly, longtime
staff; clean, affordable rooms; bar/restaurant on-site. **Cons:** no beach
but on the canal; 10-minute walk from shopping and restaurant scene;
rooms are not fancy but well maintained. $ *Rooms from: $127 ⊠ Kings
Rd., just off Midshipman, Lucaya* ☎ 242/373–1053, 242/373–1053
dive shop ⊕ *bellchannelinn.com* ↷ *31 rooms* ¹⊙¹ *No meals.*

$$ **Lighthouse Pointe at The Grand Lucayan.** The damage caused by Hur-
RESORT ricane Matthew in 2016 shrunk The Grand Lucayan down from
FAMILY two hotels to one, and currently only Lighthouse Pointe remains
as a two-story structure that replicates Caribbean-style plantation
manors housing all-water-view rooms and suites removed from the
resort's hustle and bustle. **Pros:** across the street from Port Lucaya
Marketplace; great beachfront activities; eight on-site eateries and
bars. **Cons:** service can be spotty; all-inclusive meals can be repete-
tive and lack choice. $ *Rooms from: $210 ⊠ Sea Horse Rd., Lucaya*
☎ 242/373–1333, 855/708–6671 ⊕ *www.grandlucayan.com* ↷ *196
rooms* ¹⊙¹ *All meals.*

$ **Pelican Bay Hotel.** Close to the beach with rooms overlooking Port
HOTEL Lucaya Marina or waterfront along the canal, Pelican Bay has a funky
Fodor'sChoice modern appeal, and suites overflow with character and decorative
★ elements collected from around the world. **Pros:** stylish and comfort-
able; water views; trendy on-site bars and restaurants. **Cons:** no beach;
poolside/marina-front rooms can be noisy. $ *Rooms from: $175 ⊠ Sea
Horse Rd., Lucaya* ☎ 242/373–9550, 800/852–3702 ⊕ *www.pelican-
bayhotel.com* ↷ *90 rooms, 96 waterside suites* ¹⊙¹ *Breakfast.*

$ **Seagrape Bed & Breakfast.** This quiet B&B offers tourists something
B&B/INN more intimate, away from the hustle and bustle of Port Lucaya yet
mere steps from the beach and a short walk from everything else.
Pros: free airport pickup; central location to beach and amenities;
bikes for rent. **Cons:** only two rooms; fee for return trip to airport.
$ *Rooms from: $95 ⊠ Off Royal Palm Way, Lucaya* ☎ 954/234–
2387, 242/373–1769 ⊕ *www.seagrapehouse.com* ▭ *No credit cards*
↷ *2 rooms* ¹⊙¹ *Breakfast.*

$$ **Viva Wyndham Fortuna Beach.** Popular with couples, families, and
RESORT spring breakers, this secluded resort provides a casual, all-inclusive
getaway where one price covers meals, drinks, tips, nonmotorized water
sports, and nightly entertainment. **Pros:** snorkeling and paddleboarding right offshore; trapeze lessons; beautiful, secluded beach. **Cons:**
need a car or taxi to Port Lucaya; rooms are small; resort bustles with
spring breakers. $ *Rooms from: $220 ⊠ Churchill Dr. at Doubloon
Rd., Lucaya* ☎ 242/373–4000, 800/996–3426 in U.S. ⊕ *vivaresorts.
com* ↷ *276 rooms* ¹⊙¹ *All-inclusive.*

These handwoven souvenirs can be purchased at Port Lucaya Marketplace.

GREATER GRAND BAHAMA

$$$$
RESORT
Fodor'sChoice
★

Deep Water Cay. Founded in 1958 by Gil Drake and iconic *Field and Stream* editor A.J. McClane, Deep Water Cay is the longest established bonefishing lodge in the Bahamas. **Pros:** secluded, Out Island feel; great on-site dining; unmatched bonefishing and expert fishing guides. **Cons:** far from other amenities on Grand Bahama; pricey. $ *Rooms from: $700* ⊠ *Off Grand Bahama's East End* ✛ *A 5-min boat ride from McLean's Town, with reservations at resort* ☎ *970/208–9306, 888/420–6202* ⊕ *www.deepwatercay.com* ☻ *Closed mid-July–Oct.* ⤷ *7 oceanfront cottages, 6 villas* ⦿| *Some meals.*

$$
RESORT
FAMILY
Fodor'sChoice
★

Old Bahama Bay Resort & Yacht Harbour. Fishing enthusiasts, yachters, and families can relax in relative seclusion at this West End resort, made up of colorful beachfront and poolside suites decorated with island charm. **Pros:** top-shelf marina; quiet and secluded; on-site activities including tennis and basketball courts. **Cons:** limited dining choices; far from main airport, shopping, and other restaurants; need a car to explore the rest of the island. $ *Rooms from: $250* ⊠ *West End* ☎ *242/350–6500, 888/800–8959* ⊕ *www.oldbahamabay.com* ⤷ *73 rooms* ⦿| *No meals.*

NIGHTLIFE

For evening and late-night entertainment, Port Lucaya is filled with restaurants and bars. Throughout the week there's live entertainment in the middle square; the best nights are Friday and Saturday. Other options include bonfire beach parties at Taino by the Sea, the Wednesday-night fish fry at Smith's Point, or taking a sunset cruise through the canals.

LUCAYA

BARS

Fodor'sChoice ★ **Bones Bar.** This trendy spot on the waterfront at Pelican Bay Hotel is a cool and classy fishermen's clubhouse, with swim-up seating at the adjacent pool. Sip high-end tasting rums or fresh-squeezed cocktails like the Silver Fox (lime juice, homemade simple syrup, and vodka), rent fishing gear, and hear bonefish stories. They don't have a menu, but have recently started serving freshly made individual savory pies. ⊠ *Pelican Bay Hotel, Sea Horse Rd., on the canal next to Flying Fish Modern Seafood, Lucaya* ☏ *242/374–4899* ⊕ *www.bones-bar.com.*

Club Neptune's Lounge and Nightclub. Adorned with Tiffany lamps, couch seating, and a swanky bar all circling the dance floor, this place is *the* place to get your groove on at night. The small lounge upstairs provides a quieter environment if you need a break from dancing. Happy hour is nightly from 7 to 9 pm, and other events including karaoke and Ladies' Night grace a changing weekly schedule. ⊠ *Port Lucaya Marketplace, Lucaya* ☏ *242/374–1221* ⊕ *neptunesportlucaya.com* ☉ *Closed Sun. and Mon.*

Coral Beach Bar and Restaurant. At the popular and long-standing condominium property Coral Beach Hotel, this spacious, open-air bar bustles with visitors and locals, too. Bartenders serve up tropical drinks and cold beer to a lively crowd with music in the background. The menu boasts Bahamian favorites like conch fritters along with burgers and sweet-potato fries. Situated poolside and beachfront to Coral Beach, this spot is fun for lunch and a daytime drink, too. ⊠ *Coral Rd., off Royal Palm Way, Lucaya* ☏ *242/373–2468* ⊕ *www.coralbeachonline.com.*

FAMILY **Market Square.** The stage at Market Square at the center of the Port Lucaya Marketplace becomes lively after dark, with live or piped-in island music and other performances (made all the more festive by surrounding popular watering holes: the Corner Bar, Kalypzo, and Rum Runners). Entertainment includes live Bahamian bands on weekend evenings, fire dancers, fashion shows, classic movie showings, and special holiday events. ⊠ *Port Lucaya Marketplace, Sea Horse Rd., Lucaya* ☏ *242/373–8446* ⊕ *www.portlucaya.com.*

Rum Runners. This busy outdoor bar in Count Basie Square specializes in keeping bar hoppers young and old supplied with free Wi-Fi, tropical frozen drinks and punches, and piña coladas served in coconuts. ⊠ *Port Lucaya Marketplace, Lucaya* ☏ *242/373–7233.*

SHOPPING AND SPAS

In the stores, shops, and boutiques in Port Lucaya Marketplace you can find duty-free goods costing up to 40% less than what you might pay back home. At the numerous perfume shops, fragrances are often sold at a sweet-smelling 25% below U.S. prices. Be sure to limit your haggling to the straw markets.

Shops in Lucaya are open Monday–Saturday from 9 am to 6 pm. Stores may stay open later at the Port Lucaya Marketplace. Straw markets, grocery stores, some boutiques, and drugstores are open on Sunday.

FREEPORT

SPAS

La Belle Spa & Boutique. This small but charming luxury day spa offers top-of-the-line treatments and specialty services such as gel manicures and pedicures, advanced facials and enzyme peels, microdermabrasion, reflexology, and hot stone massages. The technicians are knowledgeable and friendly, and you can relax with provided refreshments to the sounds of trickling water and meditative music. ⊠ *W. Atlantic Blvd., Freeport* ☎ *242/351–3565* ⊘ *Closed Sun. and Mon.*

Renu Day Spa. This simple yet elegant spa situated in the bright blue, statuesque Millenium House offers many general spa services including nail treatments, waxing, facials, body wraps and scrubs, massage, and Reiki. They use Essie and OPI nail products and Guinot skin products, in addition to several other organic lines. ⊠ *Millenium House, E. Mall Dr., Freeport* ☎ *242/352–7368* ⊕ *www.renudayspabahamas.com* ⊘ *Closed Sun. and Mon., except by appointment.*

LUCAYA

SHOPS
ART
Leo's Art Gallery. This little shop showcases the expressive Haitian-style paintings and colorful Bahamian impressionism of famed local artist Leo Brown, each piece with its own story. This storefront is both his studio and his showroom. This place is worth a visit, if only to meet the charming Leo and witness his inspiring work and creativity. ⊠ *Port Lucaya Marketplace, across from Zorba's, Lucaya* ☎ *242/373–1758.*

FASHION
Bandolera. Bandolera sells European-style women's fashions and accessories, such as classic Joseph Ribkoff designs. Find that perfect little chic dress, and everything from casual wear to gowns ⊠ *Port Lucaya Marketplace, Lucaya* ☎ *242/373–7691.*

JEWELRY AND WATCHES
Colombian Emeralds. Colombian Emeralds purveys a line of Colombian's famed gems plus other jewelry and crystal. ⊠ *Port Lucaya Marketplace, Lucaya* ☎ *242/373–8400* ⊕ *www.colombianemeralds.com.*

John Bull. With locations throughout the Bahamas, this 85-year-old family business sells high-end items including gemstones; gold and designer

jewelry like David Yurman and Antica Murrina; fine leather bags and accessories such as Dooney & Bourke and Michael Kors; and designer sunglasses by Maui Jim, Guccis, and Ray-Ban. John Bull has also been the official Rolex retailer in the Bahamas since 1955. ⊠ *Port Lucaya Marketplace, Lucaya* ☎ *242/374–6614* ⊕ *www.johnbull.com.*

MARKETS AND ARCADES

Arawak Crafts Center. This independent collection of 27 small shops and booths on the west side of the Port Lucaya Marketplace is comprised of individual Bahamian artisans, each selling unique arts and home-made handicrafts, many customized on request. Items for sale include seashell ornaments, candles, soaps, straw goods, dolls, and more. ⊠ *Port Lucaya Marketplace, across from Dominos Pizza, Lucaya* ⊕ *www.portlucaya.com.*

FAMILY **Port Lucaya Marketplace.** This quaint harborside shopping, dining, and entertainment village is one of the liveliest locales on the island. New owners have pumped lots of money into ongoing renovations and new shops, and restaurants continue to pop up, including a chocolate factory and a coffee shop. There's also an extensive straw market and 20-plus local crafts vendors. Live music and entertainment bring the center bandstand to life on weekend nights, and additional entertainment is brought along on busy cruise ship days. ⊠ *Sea Horse Rd., Lucaya* ⊹ *Across from Grand Lucayan and Memories Resort* ☎ *242/373–8446* ⊕ *www.portlucaya.com.*

Port Lucaya Straw Markets. Come to this collection of 100 wooden stalls at Port Lucaya Marketplace's East and West ends to bargain for straw goods, T-shirts, and souvenirs. ⊠ *Port Lucaya Marketplace, Sea Horse Rd., Lucaya* ⊕ *www.portlucaya.com.*

MISCELLANEOUS

Photo Specialist. Photo Specialist carries photo and video equipment, memory cards, rechargeable batteries, cell phone chargers, and any other electronic accessory you may have forgotten to bring with you. ⊠ *Port Lucaya Marketplace, Lucaya* ☎ *242/373–7858.*

Sun & Sea Outfitters at UNEXSO. This retail shop at UNEXSO offers the biggest shopping selection in Lucaya, including water-sports equipment, toys, jewelry and accessories, brand-name apparel and swimsuits for both men and women, island-style housewares, and books by local authors. ⊠ *UNEXSO, next to Pelican Bay Hotel, Lucaya* ☎ *242/373–1244, 800/992–3483* ⊕ *www.unexso.com.*

SPAS

Senses Spa at Grand Lucayan. This three-level spa offers a variety of luxury services including body wraps and scrubs, facials, various mas-sage techniques, and manicures and pedicures, in addition to a full-service salon. On the top floor you will find state-of-the-art exercise equipment, including free weights and elliptical machines, a spin class studio, and daily exercise classes for every interest. Senses is open to nonguests as well, and a daily fee includes use of the locker room, lap pool, hot tubs, and sauna facilities. All spa services are by appointment. ⊠ *Grand Lucayan, Lighthouse Point, Lucaya* ☎ *242/350–5281* ⊕ *www. grandlucayan.com.*

SPORTS AND THE OUTDOORS

BIKING

By virtue of its flat terrain, broad avenues, and long straight stretches of highway, Grand Bahama is perfect for bicycling. There's a designated biking lane on Midshipman Road.

Inexpensive bicycle rentals are available from some resorts, and the Viva Wyndham Fortuna Beach allows guests free use of bicycles. In addition to its other ecotouring options, Grand Bahama Nature Tours offers 10-mile biking excursions that include a visit to a native settlement and Garden of the Groves.

CocoNutz Cruisers. CocoNutz is locally owned and operated and offers the only motorized (electric) bicycle experience on the island. Alfredo Bridgewater or one of his knowledgeable guides takes tourists along the southern shores of the island, offering island history and stops along the way for unique Grand Bahamian experiences. The 5½-hour ride can take up to 12 bikers, and includes bottled water and lunch. The guides even take photos along the way to send to you later. Find them behind the Port Lucaya Marketplace parking lot at the water's edge. ⊠ *Port Lucaya Marketplace, Lucaya* ☎ *242/374–6889, 954/354–6889* ⊕ *www.coconutzcruisers.com.*

BOATING AND FISHING

CHARTERS

Private boat charters for up to four people average about $100 per person and up for half a day. Bahamian law limits the catching of game fish to six each of dolphinfish, kingfish, tuna, and wahoo per vessel.

Bonefish Folley & Sons at Blue Marlin Cove. Committed to giving you the best fishing experience possible, Bonefish Folley & Sons will take you deep-sea fishing or through the flats for bonefish and permit. The late "Bonefish Folley" is a legend here, and delighted in taking people on bonefish tours for more than 60 years. He passed away in 2012 at the age of 91, but his two sons, Tommy and Carl, are continuing on in his footsteps. They offer a series of different packages from fishing and snorkeling to romantic sunset cruises. ⊠ *Blue Marlin Cove, West End* ☎ *242/646–9504, 242/349–4101* ⊕ *www.bluemarlincove.com.*

Captain Phil & Mel's Bonefishing Guide Service. This independent bonefishing group provides a colorful and expert foray into the specialized world of bonefishing around the East End of Grand Bahama. A whole day (eight hours) for up to two people will run you $450, transportation included; a half day costs $350. ⊠ *East End* ☎ *242/441–0863* ⊕ *www.bahamasbonefishing.net.*

H2O Bonefishing. Clients of this professional saltwater fly fishing outfitter book well ahead of their arrival on island. H2O's fleet of flats boats and professional guides are available as part of a prearranged multiday package that typically includes three to six days of fishing. They cater exclusively to their anglers both on and off the water for the length of their stay, including waterfront lodging at one of Grand Bahama's finest hotels. Fish year-round for trophy-sized bonefish and permit as well as seasonal tarpon, or fish offshore for yellowfin tuna and mahimahi from spring through summer. Light tackle and conventional fishing is also available. Check out their trendy clubhouse, Bones Bar. ⊠ *Lucaya* ☎ *242/359–4958, 954/364–7590* ⊕ *www.h2obonefishing.com.*

Reef Tours. This family-owned company has been offering various tours on Grand Bahama since 1969. Deep sea and bottom-reef fishing tours are three to four hours in duration. Full-day trips are also available, as are paddleboard and kayak rentals, bottom-fishing excursions, glass-bottom-boat tours, snorkeling trips, wine and cheese evening cruises, parasailing, and even guided tours by Segway, Harley, and 4X4. Reservations are essential. ⊠ *Port Lucaya Marketplace, Lucaya* ☎ *242/373–5880, 242/373–5891* ⊕ *www.reeftoursfreeport.com.*

Fodor's Choice
★

West End Ecology Tours. "Ecology and fishing to benefit humanity" is the mission statement for these ecotours run by husband and wife Keith and Linda Cooper. The duo provides educational fishing experiences focused on Grand Bahama's historical West End and the conservation and preservation of the area and its marine life. Their tours include deep-sea fishing, feeding stingrays, discovering and learning about birds, and more. Their company started as a community organization initiative to educate young people about the island's ecology, but it has evolved into much more; clients agree it's an enjoyable way to give back to the environment. Ask about their complete ecovacation packages. ⊠ *West End* ☎ *242/727–1156, 561/370–7583* ⊕ *www.westendecologytours.com.*

GOLF

Fortune Hills Golf & Country Club. On 17 acres of some of the highest ground in Freeport, Fortune Hills Golf & Country Club is a 3,453-yard, 9-hole, par-36 course—a Dick Wilson and Joe Lee design—with a restaurant, bar, and pro shop. This is the least expensive of the three golf courses open on Grand Bahama and is usually quiet, so you'll most often have the course to yourself. The staff is friendly but neither the course nor the equipment are tremendously well maintained. Although the price listed for playing (cart included) is high, rates seem to be negotiable. ⊠ *E. Sunrise Hwy., Freeport* ☎ *242/373–4500* ⊠ *Listed price is $83, including cart, but more favorable rates are often negotiable* ⅄ *9 holes, 3453 yards, par 36* ☉ *Restaurant closed Mon.*

Reef Club Golf Course. The Reef Course is a par-72, 6,930-yard links-style course. Designed by Robert Trent Jones Jr., it features lots of water (on 13 of the holes), wide fairways flanked by strategically placed bunkers, and a tricky dogleg left on the 18th. While it is the most expensive and most pristine golf course on the island, budget constraints have left it comparable to an average municipal course in the States. Club rentals are available. Golf at The Reef is complimentary for all-inclusive guests of The Grand Lucayan; mandatory cart rental is extra. ⊠ *Sea Horse Rd., Lucaya* ☎ *242/373–2002, 866/870–7148* ⊕ *www.grandlucayan. com* ⅄ *18 holes, 6930 yards, par 72.*

Pinetree Stables can take you horseback riding on the beach.

HORSEBACK RIDING

Pinetree Stables. Horseback rides are offered on ecotrails and the beach twice a day, starting at 9 am. All two-hour rides are accompanied by a guide—no previous riding experience is necessary, but riders must be at least eight years old. Plan to bring a waterproof camera because you will get wet! Reservations are essential and drinks are available for purchase. Pinetree Stables offers free shuttles from hotels and the harbor. ⊠ *N. Beachway Dr., Freeport* ☎ *242/602–2122* ⊕ *www.pinetree-stables.com* ✉ *$165 for 2-hr ride.*

KAYAKING

FAMILY **Calabash Eco Adventures.** This tour company, run by Grand Bahama local and avid diver Shamie Rolle, offers a variety of ecoexcursions to areas all over Grand Bahama for sport, history, and education. Options include kayaking, snorkeling, birding, bicycling, and cavern diving into some of the island's famous inland blue holes. All tours include pickup and drop-off at your lodging. ☎ *242/727–1974* ⊕ *www.calabashecoadventures.com.*

Fodor'sChoice **Grand Bahama Nature Tours.** One of the most well-known ecotour operators on the island for more than 20 years, Grand Bahama Nature Tours is continually updating and adding to their wide variety of excursions, run mostly by Grand Bahama natives who are both entertaining and full of island insight. Popular adventures include snorkeling around Peterson Cay, kayaking through the mangroves at Lucayan National Park, jeep safaris, off-road ATV tours, and birding through the Garden of the Groves. All tour prices include air-conditioned pick-ups at your lodging and any necessary equipment. ☎ *242/373–2485, 866/440–4542 ⊕ www.grandbahamanaturetours.com.*

SCUBA DIVING

An extensive reef system runs along Little Bahama Bank's edge; sea gardens, caves, and colorful reefs rim the bank all the way from the West End to Freeport–Lucaya and beyond. The variety of dive sites suits everyone from the novice to the advanced diver, and ranges from 10 to 100-plus feet deep. Many dive operators offer a "discover" or "resort" course where first-timers can try out open-water scuba diving with a short pool course and an instructor at their side.

SITES

A horseshoe-shaped ledge overlooks **Ben's Blue Hole,** which lies in 40 to 60 feet of water. Certified cavern divers can further explore the depths of the cave with guided groups from UNEXSO or Calabash Adventure Tours. Otherwise, interested visitors can view it aboveground when visiting the Lucayan National Park.

For moderately experienced divers, **Pygmy Caves** provides a formation of overgrown ledges that cut into the reef. The high-profile corals here form small caves.

One of Grand Bahama Island's signature dive sites, made famous by the UNEXSO dive operation, **Shark Junction** is a 45-foot dive where 4- to 6-foot reef sharks hang out, along with moray eels, stingrays, nurse sharks, and grouper. UNEXSO provides orientation and a shark feeding with its dives here.

Spid City has an aircraft wreck, dramatic coral formations, blue parrot fish, and an occasional shark. You'll dive about 40 to 60 feet down.

For divers with some experience, **Theo's Wreck,** a 228-foot cement hauler, was sunk in 1982 in 100 feet of water, and was the site for the 1993 IMAX film *Flight of the Aquanaut.*

OPERATORS

Caribbean Divers. This family-owned and -operated dive shop offers personalized and uncrowded trips to coral reefs, wrecks, tunnels, and caverns, as well as shark dives. They also rent equipment and offer NAUI, PADI, and SSI instruction. A resort course allows you to use equipment in a pool and then in a closely supervised open dive. The professionally trained dive staff has more than 30 years of experience and the boat resides right on the channel leading out to the sea, so rides to most major sites are about 5–10 minutes. Lodging packages with Bell Channel Inn are available, in addition to snorkeling trips and private charters. ⊠ *Bell Channel Inn, King Rd., Lucaya* ☎ *242/373–9111, 242/373–9112 ⊕ www.bellchannelinn.com.*

Sunn Odyssey Divers. This family-run shop has been on island for more than 20 years. You'll dive with Nick Rolle, the owner him-self, who caters to smaller dive groups for a more personalized experience. Full PADI certifications available. ⊠ *Beach Way Dr., Williams Town ✛ Near Island Seas Resort and Williams Town Beach*

☏ *242/373–4014, 866/652–3483*
⊕ *www.sunnodysseydivers.com.*

UNEXSO (*Underwater Explorers Society*). This world-renowned scuba diving facility provides rental equipment, guides, and boats. Facilities include a 17-foot-deep training pool with windows that look out on the harbor, changing rooms and showers, docks, an outdoor bar and grill, and an air tank filling station. Daily dive excursions range from one-day discovery courses and dives, to specialty shark, dolphin, and cave diving. Both the facility and its dive masters have been featured in international and American magazines for their work with sharks and cave exploration. UNEXSO and its sister company, the Dolphin Experience, are known for their work with Atlantic bottlenose dolphins. ⊠ *Port Lucaya, Lucaya* ⚓ *Next to Pelican Bay Hotel* ☏ *242/373–1244, 800/992–3483* ⊕ *www.unexso.com* ⚲ *One-tank reef dives $59, Discover Scuba course $129, night dives $79, dolphin dives $219, shark dives $109.*

> **HERE'S WHERE**
>
> The last time locals spotted pirates on Grand Bahama Island was in 2005, when Johnny Depp and his crew were filming the second and third installments in the *Pirates of the Caribbean* series. They used a special device in Gold Rock Creek at one of the world's largest open-water filming tanks to give the illusion that the pirate ship was pitching and yawing. You can view the set near Gold Rock Beach.

Viva Dive Shop, a Reef Oasis Diving Center. Part of the Reef Oasis Dive Club, this shop offers daily dives and snorkels to various reefs and wrecks on a large boat seating 21 divers straight off Fortune Beach at Viva Wyndham Fortuna Resort. This professional PADI-licensed shop also offers certifications for all levels (all equipment is included). ⊠ *Viva Wyndham Fortuna Resort, Churchill and Doubloon Rd., Lucaya* ☏ *242/441–6254* ⊕ *www.reefoasisdiveclub.com.*

SNORKELING

FAMILY **Pat & Diane Tours.** This company offers two snorkel trip options: one tour goes to the vibrant mile-long Rainbow Reef; another is a longer tour to a private beach and includes lunch. Or if you're a landlubber, check out the brewery tour for three hours of shopping and a visit to Sands Brewery. Free pickup and return to all hotels is included. ⊠ *Port Lucaya Marina, Lucaya* ☏ *242/373–8681, 888/439–3959, 954/323–1975* ⊕ *www.snorkelingbahamas.com.*

WATER SPORTS

Fodor's Choice **Ocean Motion Water Sports.** In business since 1990, Ocean Motion Water ★ Sports is one of the largest water-sports companies on Grand Bahama, and operates all water sports at the Grand Lucayan Resort. Located on Lucayan Beach next to the public beach access across from Port Lucaya Marketplace, they offer everything from a water trampoline and Banana Boat rides, to guided Waverunner tours through the canals and to Peterson Cay. They offer parasailing, kayaks, Hobie Cat sailboats, waterskiing, and windsurfing instruction. Or, rent snorkel equipment for the day, and regular ferries will take you to Rainbow Reef and back so you get more beach time. ✉ *Lucayan Beach, Lucaya* ☎ *242/373–2139, 242/373–9603* ⊕ *www.oceanmotionwatersports-bahamas.com.*

Paradise Watersports. This company offers a variety of tours and sports excursions from two locations, including glass-bottom boats, Waverunner tours, snorkeling cruises, and fishing trips. There's another location at Taino Beach Resort. ✉ *Island Seas Resort, Lucaya* ☎ *242/373–4001, 954/237–6660 in U.S., 905/231–1689 in Canada* ⊕ *www.the-bahamas-watersports.com/paradisewatersports/index.html.*

THE ABACOS

WELCOME TO THE ABACOS

TOP REASONS TO GO

★ **Bonefish the Marls:** One of the most spectacular bonefishing flats anywhere, the Marls is an endless maze of lush mangrove creeks, hidden bays, and sandy cays. Hire a professional guide to show you the best spots.

★ **Cay-hop:** Rent a boat and spend a day (or more) skipping among 150 cays. Settle onto your own private strip of beach and enjoy.

★ **Beach bash:** When the Gully Roosters play on Green Turtle Cay, the island rocks. Stop in at Miss Emily's Blue Bee Bar first for a mind-altering rum, pineapple juice, and apricot brandy Goombay Smash; it's where the popular drink was born. On Great Guana Cay, Nippers's Sunday pig roast is the best beach party of the year—and it happens every week.

★ **Swim with the fishies:** With clear shallow waters and a series of colorful coral reefs extending for miles, the Abacos provide both the novice and the experienced underwater explorer plenty of visual stimulation.

The Abacos, 200 miles east of Palm Beach, Florida, are the northernmost chain of cays in the Bahamas. Covering 120 miles, this mini-archipelago offers both historic settlements and uninhabited islands. Great Abaco is the main island, the chain's largest and its most populated. Up north on Little Abaco, a smaller cay connected by bridge, tourism is less prominent and locals live as they have for the last 100 years. Running parallel 5 miles off the east coast of these islands are the Abaco Cays, including Green Turtle, Great Guana, Man-O-War, and Elbow. The majority of the other 146 cays are uninhabited.

1 Great Abaco Island. The Abacos' commercial center still boasts fishing and farming communities, blue holes, caves, wild parrots, and pine forests. Marsh Harbour, the island's main hub, has great restaurants and bustling nightlife. Treasure Cay has a large marina, the only public golf course, and one of the best beaches in the world. Other communities are quiet and tucked away, each with its own personality that makes them worthy day trips.

2 Elbow Cay. Home of the famous candy cane–striped Hope Town Lighthouse, this cay balances a historic getaway with modern conveniences. Hope Town, the main settlement, is known for neat clapboard cottages painted in pastel hues.

3 Man-O-War Cay. Proud of its stance as a traditionally dry island (liquor sold only at one of the two restaurants on the island), this community holds fast to its history. It's famous for its boat-building, which can still be seen here daily on the waterfront, where men work by hand.

4 Great Guana Cay. A real getaway island, here you'll find modern luxuries and empty beaches. Guana also has Nippers, a restaurant–bar with the best party scene in Abaco.

5 Green Turtle Cay. This idyllic island, with homes still built with Loyalist architecture and painted in pastels, is quiet by day but bumping at night when the local band plays.

4

Atlantic Ocean

Carter's Cay

Great Sale Cay

Fish Cays

Upper Cay

Umbrella Cay

Hawksbill Cays

Pensacola Cays

Sponge Cay

Fox Town

Cedar Harbour

Powells Cay

Cooper's Town

Grand Bahama Island

Little Abaco Island

LITTLE BAHAMA

Nun Jack Cay

Crab Cay

Rocky Creek

McLean's Town

Green Turtle Cay 5

New Plymouth

No Name Cay

Sweetings Cay

Lighthouse Cay

Whale Cay

Michael's Cay

BANK

Big Joe Downer Cay

Treasure Cay

Sea of Abaco

Great Guana Cay 4

Man-O-War Cay 3

Dundas Town

Hope Town Lighthouse

Northwest Providence Channel

Marsh Harbour

◆ **The Marls**

Marsh Harbor Airport

Hope Town

Elbow Cay

Tilloo Cay

Hard Bargain

Moore's Island

1

Great Abaco Island

Wilson City

Lynyard Cay

Top Cay

Southern Cay

Little Harbour

Casuarina Point

Cherokee Sound

Eight Mile Bay

◆ Castaway Cay

Disney Cruise Ship Dock

Crossing Rocks

Sandy Point

Abaco National Park

0   10 mi

0   10 km

ABACO NATIONAL PARK

The Abaco National Park was established in 1994 as a sanctuary for the endangered Abaco parrot, of which there are fewer than 3,000. Many other birds call the park home, including the Bahama yellow-throat and pine warbler.

A 15-mile dirt track passes through the 20,500 protected acres, ending at the Hole-in-the-Wall lighthouse, a starkly beautiful and desolate location overlooking the ocean. The drive from the paved highway all the way to the lighthouse takes about 1½ hours, and can only be done in a 4x4 vehicle. The lighthouse is not technically open to visitors, but people still do climb the rickety stairs to the top where views of the island and the sea are mesmerizing. *South end of Great Abaco Island, before you make the final turn on the main road leading to Sandy Point* ☎ *242/367–3067.*

BEST TIME TO GO
Berries ripen in fall and spring, and the parrots become active. The best time to spot the birds is early morning, when they move out of the forest to feed. Temperatures then are also ideal, in the 70s and 80s. The annual bird counts in North and South Abaco held at the beginning of each year are a good opportunity to work with other bird-watchers to gather information on the parrots, which is sent to the Audubon Society.

BEST WAYS TO EXPLORE

By Car on Your Own. Take the 15-mile, 1½-hour drive along a dirt trail out to the lighthouse. This is the only part of the park you can drive. This lighthouse has spectacular views of the coast. Take a packed lunch and have a picnic on a ledge overlooking the ocean.

By Guided Tour. For the best experience, arrange a guided tour with the tourist office. A knowledgeable guide will walk or drive you through the park, pointing out plant and animal species. If you're an early riser, join a bird-watching tour to find the endangered Abaco parrot, as well as other avian beauties that reside here. Walking the park alone is not recommended, as poisonous wood saplings are a problem if you don't know how to identify them.

Friends of the Environment (☎ 242/367–2721) is a local education organization that offers more information on the park and the parrots.

FUN FACT

The park's pine forest is prone to summer lightning fires, but the Abaco pine is extremely resistant and actually depends on the fires to remove dense underbrush that would otherwise smother it. The Abaco parrots nest in holes in the limestone floor to escape the flames. Unfortunately, this makes them vulnerable to feral cats and raccoons that threaten their population.

FOWL CAY NATIONAL RESERVE

This quarter-mile reef located on the ocean side of Fowl Cay is a great snorkeling and dive spot. It's well known among divers for its tunnels and wide variety of fish. On the opposite side of Fowl Cay is a small sand spit, which makes a great spot to reconvene for a sun-soaked picnic.

PELICAN CAYS LAND AND SEA PARK

This 2,000-acre land and marine park is protected and maintained by the Bahamas National Trust. The park's preserved reef is only 25 feet underwater, making it an easy snorkel excursion. It's also a great dive site, as the variety of life here is astounding. Nearby is an incredibly soft beach, great for a post-swim picnic.

(above) Abaco parrot (lower left) Hole-in-the-Wall Lighthouse

Updated
by Jessica
Robertson

The attitude of the Abacos might best be expressed by the sign posted in the window of Vernon's Grocery in Hope Town: "If you're looking for Wal-Mart—it's 200 miles to the right." In other words, the residents of this chain of more than 100 islands know that there's another world out there, but don't necessarily care to abandon theirs, which is a little more traditional, slow-paced, and out of the way than most.

Ecotourism is popular here, and aficionados have revitalized exploration of Abacos' Caribbean pine forests, which are home to wild boar, wild horses, the rare Abaco parrot, and myriad other bird and plant life. Hiking and biking through these forests and along abandoned beaches at the forest's edges are popular activities. Sea kayaking in pristine protected areas also provides a rewarding sense of adventure, and more conventional activities such as golf, tennis, and beach volleyball are available, too.

One of the region's best assets is the water; snorkeling and diving have long been staple activities for visitors. Abaconians are proud of their marine environment and have worked with the government to protect some of the more vibrant reefs. The islands' calm, naturally protected waters, long admired for their beauty, have also helped the area become the Bahamas' sailing capital. Man-O-War Cay remains the Bahamas' boat-building center; its residents turn out traditionally crafted wood dinghies as well as high-tech fiberglass craft. The Abacos play host annually to internationally famous regattas and to a half dozen game-fish tournaments.

PLANNING

WHEN TO GO

June, July, and early August are the best months for sailing, boating, and swimming, precisely why the most popular regatta and fishing tournaments are held during this time. Afternoon thunderstorms are common but usually clear quickly. Temperatures often reach the 90s.

December through May is a pleasant time to visit, with temperatures in the 70s and 80s, though sometimes dropping into the 50s at night when cold fronts blow through. Fishing, particularly deep-sea fishing, is good during this time of year.

From mid-August to late October, typically the peak of hurricane season, visitors drop to a trickle and many hotels and restaurants shut down for two weeks to two months. If you're willing to take a chance on getting hit by a storm, this can still be a great time to explore, with discounts of as much as 50% at the hotels that remain open.

4

TOP FESTIVALS

WINTER **Junkanoo.** Many Abaco communities have their own Junkanoo celebrations; Hope Town has a New Year's Eve children's rushout for locals and visitors to join in. Parades in the Abacos are much smaller and more intimate than in Nassau, and far less competitive. ⊠ *Hope Town.*

SPRING **Heritage Day.** Hope Town's annual Heritage Day in March celebrates the Loyalist settlement's history with traditional songs, speeches, and exhibits on historical topics, and a boat parade. ⊠ *Hope Town.*

Island Roots Festival. The Island Roots Festival celebrates Bahamian traditions with an outdoor party on tiny Green Turtle Cay the first weekend in May. ⊠ *Green Turtle Cay* ⊕ *www.islandrootsheritagefestival.com.*

SUMMER **Junkanoo Summer Festival.** Junkanoo Summer Festival—traditional summertime parties with dance troupes, musical groups, and lots of local food—take place in Marsh Harbour. ⊠ *Marsh Harbour.*

Regatta Time. Regatta Time in Abaco, the first week of July, stretches over several islands, with races and plenty of onshore parties. ⊠ *Green Turtle Cay* ⊕ *www.regattatimeinabaco.com.*

Treasure Cay Billfish Championship. There are big cash prizes that increase with the number of registered boats at the Treasure Cay Billfish Championship in June. The final day includes a Lionfish Tournament designed to help save the Bahamas indigenous marine life from this relatively new predator. ⊠ *Treasure Cay* ⊕ *treasurecay.com.*

HOTELS

Intimate hotels, cottage-style resorts, and rental homes are the rule in the Abacos. There are a few full-scale resorts in Marsh Harbour, Treasure Cay, Green Turtle Cay, and Hope Town—with multiple restaurants, bars, pools, and activities—but most accommodations are more homey. What you might give up in modern amenities you'll gain in privacy and beauty. Many hotels have water views, and with a cottage or private house you may even get your own stretch of beach. Air-conditioning is a standard feature, and more places are adding luxuries like cable TV and wireless Internet. Small and remote doesn't equate with inexpensive, though; it's almost impossible to find lodging for less than $100 a night, and not uncommon to pay more than $300 a night for beachside accommodations with all the conveniences. Both restaurant meals and hotel rooms as well as just about every other goods or service you purchase also now incur an additional 7.5% government VAT.

RESTAURANTS

Fish, conch, land crabs, and rock lobster—called crawfish by the locals—have long been the bedrock of local cuisine. Although a few menus, mostly in upscale resorts, feature dishes with international influences, most restaurants in the Abacos still serve simple Bahamian fare, with a few nods to American tastes. There are some fancier restaurants in Marsh Harbour, Treasure Cay, and Hope Town, but most restaurants are relaxed about attire and reasonably priced. Some offer live music, and shape the nightlife scene on weekends.

HOTEL AND RESTAURANT PRICES

Restaurant prices are based on the median main course price at dinner, excluding gratuity. Most Abaco restaurants do not add the customary 15% gratuity, leaving it up to the customer. Hotel prices are for two people in a standard double room in high season, excluding service and 6%–12% tax.

WHAT IT COSTS IN DOLLARS			
$	$$	$$$	$$$$
Restaurants	under $20	$20–$30	$31–$40	over $40
Hotels	under $200	$200–$300	$301–$400	over $400

SHIPPING

GPS Bahamas. Renting a beach house for a week or longer? Maybe you can't take everything with you, but GPS Bahamas has air-freight service for everything from perishable foods to electronics and computers. It beats the mail boat. ⊠ *Marsh Harbour* ☎ *242/475–5480, 954/689–6761* ⊕ *gpsbahamas.com.*

VISITOR INFORMATION

Contacts Abaco Tourist Office & Information Center. ⊠ *Harbor Place Bldg., Queen Elizabeth Dr., Marsh Harbour* ☎ *242/699-0152* ⊕ *www.bahamas.com.*

GETTING HERE AND AROUND

AIR TRAVEL

Most flights land at the international airports in **Marsh Harbour (MHH)** or **Treasure Cay (TCB)**. Taxis wait at the main airports, and the fare to most resorts is between $15 and $30 for the first two passengers and $3 for each additional person. Cab fare between Marsh Harbour and Treasure Cay or the ferry dock is $85 each way.

Contacts Marsh Harbour Airport. ☎ *242/367-5500.* **Treasure Cay Airport.** ☎ *242/365-8602.*

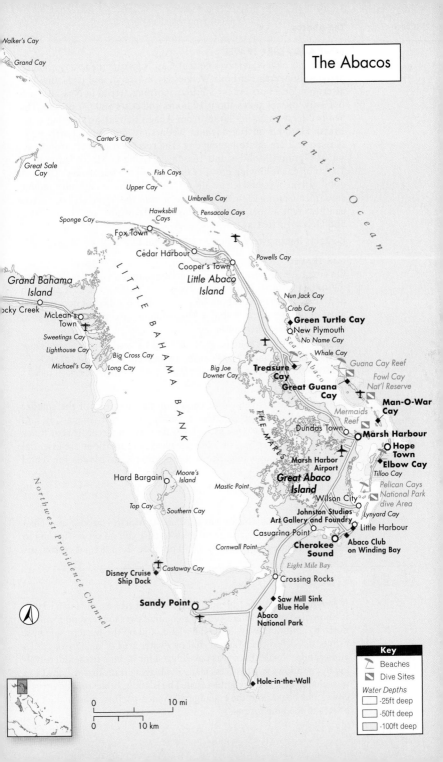

BOAT AND FERRY TRAVEL

The *Legacy* mail boat leaves Potter's Cay, Nassau, on Tuesday evening, arriving in Marsh Harbour Wednesday morning, and departing late afternoon on Thursday for a Friday morning arrival in Nassau. Each one-way journey takes about 10 hours and costs $60 per person. The *Sealink* ferry takes 13 hours from Abaco to Nassau, leaving from Marsh Harbour on Tuesday and Wednesday at 1 pm and arriving in Nassau at 2 am the following day. The reverse trip leaves from Nassau at 9 pm on Monday and Tuesday, arriving in Marsh Harbour at 10 am on the following day. For details, call the **Dockmaster's Office.** A good system of public ferries allows you to reach even the most remote cays. *(See Getting Here and Around within the island sections.)* You can also rent a boat at Marsh Harbour, Treasure Cay, Hope Town, and Green Turtle Cay.

Contacts Dockmaster's Office. ☎ *242/393–1064.*

CAR TRAVEL

On Great Abaco, renting a car is the best option if you plan on exploring outside Marsh Harbour or Treasure Cay. Rentals start at $70 a day, and gasoline costs about $6 per gallon. Cars are not necessary on most of the smaller cays in the Abacos; in fact, rental cars aren't even available in most locations.

Contacts A & P Auto Rentals. ☎ *242/367–2655* ⊕ *www.aandpautorentals.com.* **Bargain Car Rentals.** ☎ *242/367–0500.* **Cornish Car Rentals.** ☎ *242/365–8623.* **Rental Wheels of Abaco.** ☎ *242/367–4643* ⊕ *www.rentalwheels.com.*

GOLF CART TRAVEL

Golf carts are the vehicle of choice on the majority of the smaller cays, including Elbow Cay, Green Turtle Cay, Great Guana Cay, and Man-O-War Cay, as well as in Treasure Cay on Great Abaco. Rates are $40 to $50 per day, or $245 per week. Reservations are essential from April through July. See sections on specific islands for rental recommendations.

Contacts Blue Marlin Rentals. ☎ *242/365–8687.*

TAXI TRAVEL

Taxi service is available on Great Abaco in Marsh Harbour and Treasure Cay. Hotels will arrange for taxis to take you on short trips and to the airport. Fares are generally $1.50 per mile. A 15% tip is customary.

GREAT ABACO ISLAND

If arriving by air, your trip will begin on Great Abaco, the main island. It's bordered on its eastern side by a chain of cays that extend from the north to about midway down the island, and on the western side by a fishing flat called the Marls, a shallow-water area of mangrove creeks and islands. Great Abaco was once logged for its pine trees, and traveling by car allows you to access many old logging trails that will lead you to secluded beaches along the coast. The island is home to wild horses, cows, and boars, and the endangered Abaco parrots, who make their homes in the pine forests.

Marsh Harbour is the main hub of activity on the island, and where most visitors stay. Heading north on the S.C. Bootle Highway will take you to **Treasure Cay** peninsula, a resort development. There's another, smaller, airport here. Farther north are **Cooper's Town** and the small communities of **Little Abaco**, which don't provide much for visitors aside from near-total seclusion. South of Marsh Harbour off the Ernest Dean Highway are artists' retreat **Little Harbour,** and **Cherokee Sound** and **Sandy Point**, both small fishing communities. There is also the quaint yet upscale second home and vacation community **Schooner Bay.**

> **DID YOU KNOW?**
>
> Bahamian currency includes a $3 bill. There's also a half-dollar bill and a 15-cent piece, which is square and decorated with a hibiscus. These three currencies are not frequently seen today, and can make great souvenirs if you come across one.

GETTING HERE AND AROUND

To travel around Great Abaco you'll need a vehicle. Renting a car is the most convenient and economical option, but if you plan on spending most of your vacation in one town, hiring a taxi is also viable. Taxis are available all over the island, but the farther you travel from Marsh Harbour, the more extreme rates get, sometimes in excess of a hundred dollars. The closest settlement worth a visit out of Marsh Harbour is Little Harbour, about 30 minutes away.

From Marsh Harbour you can boat to Little Harbour and Cherokee Sound to the south, and Treasure Cay in the north. Golf carts are used to travel locally within Treasure Cay and Cherokee Sound.

MARSH HARBOUR

Most visitors to the Abacos make their first stop in Marsh Harbour, the Bahamas' third-largest city and the Abacos' commercial center. Besides having the Abacos' largest international airport, it offers what boaters consider to be one of the easiest harbors to enter. It has several full-service marinas, including the 190-slip Boat Harbour Marina and the 80-slip Conch Inn Marina.

Marsh Harbour has a more diverse variety of restaurants, shops, and grocery items than other communities. **Maxwell's Supermarket** and one of the larger liquor stores to stock up on supplies are standard stops on the way to other settlements or islands. The downtown area has several other supermarkets, as well as a few department and hardware stores. If you need cash, this is the place to get it; banks here are open every day and have ATMs, neither of which you will find on the smaller, more remote settlements or cays.

WHERE TO EAT

$$$
BAHAMIAN
Fodor's Choice
★

✕ **Angler's Restaurant.** Dine on roasted rack of lamb with garlic mashed potatoes or a broiled lobster tail while overlooking gleaming rows of yachts moored in the Boat Harbour Marina at the Abaco Beach Resort. Crisp tablecloths with fresh orchid arrangements and napkins folded like seashells create an experience a step up from typical island dining. **Known for:** breakfast and dinner buffets; casual elegance; island-style fine dining. [$] *Average main: $35* ✉ *Abaco Beach Resort, off Bay St.* ☎ *242/367–2158, 800/468–4799* 🌐 *abacobeachresort.com.*

$ BAHAMIAN

🍴 **Jamie's Place.** There's nothing fancy about this clean, bright, diner-style eatery, but the welcome is warm, the Bahamian dishes are well executed, and the prices are right, with most meals clocking in under $15. Choose cracked conch or lobster, or fresh-caught dolphin (also called mahimahi), with your choice of hearty Bahamian sides. Jamie's is also an ice-cream parlor, with a wide selection of flavors. **Known for:** simple but hearty meals; friendly service; bustling takeout business. [$] *Average main: $18* ✉ *Queen Elizabeth Dr.* ☎ *242/367–2880.*

$$ BAHAMIAN

🍴 **Jib Room.** Expect casual lunches of hot wings, conch burgers, fish nuggets, and steak wraps in this harbor-view restaurant and bar, located inside the Marsh Harbour Marina. Dinner is served twice a week, and these "barbecue nights" are especially popular; on Wednesday it's baby back ribs, fish, chicken, potato salad, slaw, and baked beans. **Known for:** rib night; steak night; live local music and entertainment. [$] *Average main: $25* ✉ *Pelican Shores* ☎ *242/367–2700* 🌐 *www.jibroom.com* 🕒 *Closed Sun.–Tues. No dinner Thurs. and Fri.*

$ BAHAMIAN Fodor's Choice ★

🍴 **Junovia's Diner.** A steady stream of locals flow in and out of this unassuming diner to either dine in or grab breakfast or lunch on the run. Chicken souse is usually on the menu board. **Known for:** best spot for early breakfast; peppery chicken souse; authentic Bahamian fare. [$] *Average main: $14* ✉ *Don Mackay Blvd.* ☎ *242/367–1271* 🕒 *No dinner. No lunch weekends.*

$ BAHAMIAN

🍴 **Meke's Snack Shack.** If you're looking for a simple but tasty lunch at a great price, check out this octagonal wooden takeout-only restaurant on the western end of Bay Street. The burgers are hand-formed and served up on homemade buns—the spicy bacon cheeseburger is a local favorite. **Known for:** delicious burgers; cheap eats; ice cream on a hot day. [$] *Average main: $9* ✉ *Bay St.* ☎ *242/367–4005* 🕒 *Closed Sun.* 💳 *No credit cards.*

$$ BAHAMIAN

🍴 **Snappas.** Savvy boat people and in-the-know locals hang out here in the Harbour View Marina. The wood bar is the center of gravity around which the dining room sprawls outward toward the open-air waterside deck. **Known for:** amazing sunsets; live music; tasty mix of Bahamian and American dishes. [$] *Average main: $25* ✉ *Harbour View Marina, Bay St.* ☎ *242/367–2278* 🌐 *www.snappasbar.com.*

$$ BAHAMIAN Fodor's Choice ★

🍴 **Wally's.** This two-story, pink colonial villa sits across Bay Street from the marina, fronted by green lawns, hibiscus, and white-railed verandahs. This is Marsh Harbour's most popular restaurant—*the* place to go for good food, potent rum cocktails, and serious people-watching. **Known for:** pricey but delicious food; front-porch dining; sweet key lime pie. [$] *Average main: $30* ✉ *E. Bay St.* ☎ *242/367–2074* 🕒 *Closed Sun.*

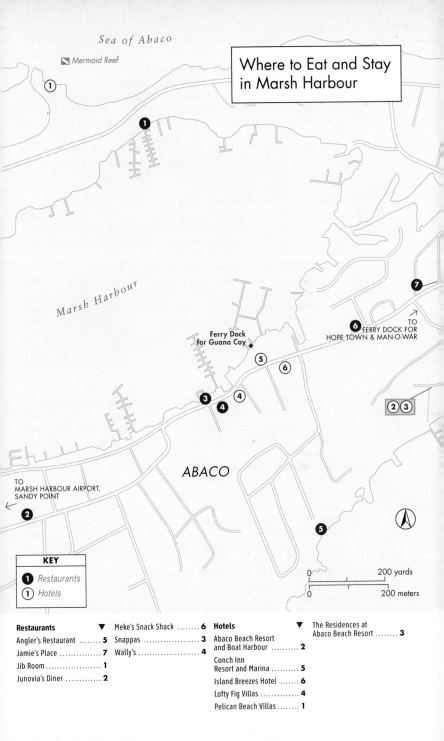

Sea of Abaco

Mermaid Reef

Where to Eat and Stay in Marsh Harbour

Marsh Harbour

Ferry Dock
for Guana Cay

TO
FERRY DOCK FOR
HOPE TOWN & MAN-O-WAR

ABACO

TO
MARSH HARBOUR AIRPORT,
SANDY POINT

KEY	
● 1	*Restaurants*
①	*Hotels*

0   200 yards

0   200 meters

WHERE TO STAY

$$ RESORT FAMILY Fodor's Choice ★ **Abaco Beach Resort and Boat Harbour.** The largest hotel in Marsh Harbour is lively at spring break and during fishing tournaments throughout the year, but can also be very quiet outside the high season. **Pros:** ideal location for all water-related activities; easy access to town shops and restaurants; one of the best marinas in the Abacos. **Cons:** can be crowded and noisy during fishing tournaments; pricey accommodations; long walk from car to rooms (call front desk for golf cart pick up). [$] *Rooms from: $297 ✉ East of Conch Sound Marina ☎ 242/367–2158, 877/533–4799 🌐 www.abacobeachresort.com 🛏 80 rooms 🍴 No meals.*

$ HOTEL **Conch Inn Resort and Marina.** This low-key, one-level marina hotel is a good choice for budget or business travelers, but make reservations well in advance. **Pros:** centrally located; easy to arrange boat rentals and diving; good value for comfortable rooms. **Cons:** far from beaches; small pool area; basic amenities only. [$] *Rooms from: $190 ✉ E. Bay St. ☎ 242/367–4000 🌐 www.conchinn.com 🛏 10 rooms.*

$ HOTEL **Island Breezes Hotel.** This simple, no-frills motel is ideal if you plan to spend your days exploring the mainland by car or the surrounding cays by ferry or boat and just need a place for a cold shower and a good sleep before starting all over the next day. **Pros:** lowest rates in Marsh Harbour; large rooms; right in main tourist area. **Cons:** very simple accommodations; no indoor common area; no pool. [$] *Rooms from: $150 ✉ Bay St. ☎ 242/367–3776 🌐 islandbreezeshotel.com 🛏 8 rooms.*

$ HOTEL **Lofty Fig Villas.** Run by exceptionally friendly and attentive owners and staff, this intimate compound has six spacious villas with pool or harbor views. **Pros:** centrally located; great pool; warm and friendly service. **Cons:** dated furnishings; no place to dock a rental boat; some room porches face busy main road. [$] *Rooms from: $198 ✉ Marsh Harbour ☎ 242/367–2681 🌐 www.loftyfig.com 🛏 6 villas.*

$$ RENTAL **Pelican Beach Villas.** On a quiet private peninsula opposite the main settlement of Marsh Harbour sit seven waterfront clapboard cottages cheerily painted in pale pink, yellow, blue, and green. **Pros:** tranquil beach location; near some of the best snorkeling in the Abacos; many repeat guests. **Cons:** no restaurant; need to rent a car or boat; pricey for less than full-service accommodations. [$] *Rooms from: $250 ✉ Northwest of Marsh Harbour Marina ☎ 877/326–3180 🌐 www.pelicanbeachvillas.com 🛏 7 cottages.*

$$$$ RESORT **The Residences at Abaco Beach Resort.** Lots of room, contemporary upscale island decor, and large balconies where you can sit and enjoy amazing views of the Sea of Abaco make these two- and three-bedroom condos a popular choice. **Pros:** lots of room for a family; upscale accommodations; restaurant and chef service on property. **Cons:** pricey accommodations; noise from marina below; beach is a far walk from rooms. [$] *Rooms from: $725 ✉ Abaco Beach Resort & Marina, Bay St. ☎ 242/367–2158, 800/468–4799 🌐 abacobeachresort.com 🛏 9 condos.*

The Abacos are the sailing capital of the Bahamas.

NIGHTLIFE

The Jib Room. If you're looking for live music and dockside dancing, make reservations at this casual open-air restaurant on Wednesday and Saturday nights. ⊠ *Marsh Harbour* ☎ *242/367–2700* ⊕ *www.jibroom.com.*

Snappas. Friday and Saturday nights feature live music. ⊠ *Harbour View Marina, Bay St.* ☎ *242/367–2278* ⊕ *www.snappasbar.com.*

SHOPPING

Abaco Neem. More than 30 different products are made using locally grown neem trees at this shop and production plant. Salves, soaps, and lotions are organic and in many cases claim to offer medicinal benefits against skin conditions, arthritis, and even hypertension. Abaco Neem also produces an entire range of pet products. Call or email in advance to arrange a tour of the production facility and nearby farm. Tours take about 1½ hours and are free, although a $10 per person donation is welcomed. ⊠ *Don Mackay Blvd.* ☎ *242/367–4117* ⊕ *www.abaconeem.com.*

Abaco Treasures. At Marsh Harbour's traffic light, look for the lime green Abaco Treasures, purveyors of fine china, crystal, perfumes, Bahamian books, and gifts. ⊠ *Don Mackay Blvd.* ☎ *242/367–3460.*

Bliss Coffee House. Sip an iced latte or a strong mug of Hope Town roasted coffee, or indulge in a made-from-scratch Nutella Blissuccino while admiring the smattering of ceramics, paintings, carved wooden boats, and other locally produced creations. ⊠ *E. Bay St.* ☎ *242/367–5523.*

Iggy Biggy. This store, inside a bright peach-and-turquoise building, is your best bet for hats, sandals, tropical jewelry, sportswear, and souvenirs. If you are looking for gifts to take back home, you should be able to find something cool here. ⊠ *E. Bay St.* ☎ *242/367–3596.*

Sand Dollar Shoppe. This shop sells resort wear and jewelry. Look for the locally made Abaco gold necklaces and earrings. ⊠ *E. Bay St.* ☎ *242/367–4405.*

SPORTS AND THE OUTDOORS

BIKING

Rental Wheels of Abaco. You can rent bicycles for $10 a day or $55 a week here. It's located on the main strip between Conch Inn Marina and the turnoff to Boat Harbour Marina. ⊠ *E. Bay St.* ☎ *242/367–4643* ⊕ *www.rentalwheels.com.*

BOATING

Abaco Beach Resort & Boat Harbour Marina. The marina has 198 fully protected slips and a slew of amenities, including on-site customs and immigration clearance and accommodations at the Abaco Beach Resort. ⊠ *Bay St.* ☎ *242/367–2158, 877/533–4799* ⊕ *www.abacoeachresort.com.*

Conch Inn Marina. This is one of the busiest marinas and has 72 slips and full amenities with accommodations available at the Conch Inn. ⊠ *Bay St.* ☎ *242/367–4000* ⊕ *www.conchinn.com.*

Harbour View Marina. The first marina on the west end of Bay Street, across from Wally's Restaurant, has extra-wide slips and 100-foot piers to accommodate boats with unlimited beam size, a private heated swimming pool, wireless Internet, and Snappas Restaurant. ⊠ *Bay St.* ☎ *242/367–3910* ⊕ *www.harbourviewmarina.com.*

Mangoes Marina. This marina has 29 slips and a full range of amenities, including onshore showers, a pool, and a small cabana where you can grill your day's catch. ⊠ *Bay St.* ☎ *242/367–4996* ⊕ *www.mangoesinabaco.com.*

Marsh Harbour Marina. Marsh Harbour Marina has 68 slips and is the only full-service marina on the far side of the harbor, near Pelican Shores. It is a 10-minute drive from most shops and restaurants. ⊠ *Marsh Harbour* ☎ *242/367–2700* ⊕ *www.jibroom.com.*

BOAT RENTALS

The best way to explore the Abacos is by renting a small boat from one of the many rental companies in Marsh Harbour.

Bluewave Boat Rentals. Boats range from 21 to 33 feet, and rental includes access to the pool and other marina facilities as well as free dockage. ⊠ *At Harbour View Marina, Bay St.* ☎ *242/367–3910.*

PLAY THE TIDES

If you're going bonefishing, tide pooling, or snorkeling, you'll want up-to-date tide information for the best results. A low incoming tide is usually best for bonefishing, though the last of the falling is good, too. Low tides are best for beachcombing and tide pools, although higher tides can give better coverage to your favorite reef. Ask at your hotel or a local dive shop for current tide information.

Dream Yacht Charter. Choose from 18 catamarans and two monohull sailboats that range from a 40-foot boat that sleeps 8, up to a 52-foot boat that sleeps 14, to sail from island to island, beach to beach. ⊠ *E. Bay St.* ☎ *866/469–0912* ⊕ *www.dreamyachtcharter.com.*

The Moorings. What better way to truly enjoy the beautiful waters and islands of the Abacos than on board your own private yacht? The Moorings rents single- and double-hull boats with up to four cabins. You can set sail on your own or hire a skipper and even a private chef, or you can simply arrange full provisioning. There is a three-day minimum and you must have good boating skills. ⊠ *Marsh Harbour* ☎ *242/367–4000* ⊕ *www.moorings.com.*

Rainbow Rentals. Single- and twin-engine boats are available for rental from this outfitter. You'll have to get special written approval to head out for deep-sea fishing, but there are plenty of spots in shallow waters to explore. ⊠ *Marsh Harbour* ☎ *242/367–4602* ⊕ *www.rainbowboatrentals.com.*

FISHING

You can find bonefish on the flats, yellowtail and grouper on the reefs, or marlin and tuna in the deeps of the Abacos.

Justin Sands. Premier fly-fishing guide Justin Sands works out of a state-of-the-art Hell's Bay flats skiff that will put you in the shallowest of water. Justin was the Abacos bonefish champ for two years running, and he will guide you in the Marls or around Snake Cay, Little Harbour, and Cherokee Sound. Advance reservations are a must. ⊠ *Marsh Harbour* ☎ *242/367–3526* ⊕ *www.justfishjs.com.*

Pinder's Bonefishing. Buddy Pinder has decades of experience in the local waters, and professional Pinder's Bonefishing provides year-round excursions in the Marls, a maze of mangroves and flats on the western side of Abaco. Advance reservations are essential. ⊠ *Marsh Harbour* ☎ *242/366–2163.*

SCUBA DIVING AND SNORKELING

There's excellent diving throughout the Abacos. Many sites are clustered around Marsh Harbour, including the reef behind **Guana Cay,** which is filled with small cavelike catacombs, and **Fowl Cay National Reserve,** which contains wide tunnels and a variety of fish. **Pelican Cays National Park** is a popular dive area south of Marsh Harbour. This shallow, 25-foot dive is filled with sea life; turtles are often sighted, as are spotted eagle rays and tarpon. The park is a 2,000-acre land-and-marine park protected and maintained by the Bahamas National Trust. Hook up your own boat to one of the moorings, or check with the local dive shops to see when trips to the park are scheduled. All of these sights can be easily snorkeled. Snorkelers will also want to visit **Mermaid Beach,** just off Pelican Shores Road in Marsh Harbour, where live reefs and green moray eels make for some of the Abacos' best snorkeling.

Dive Abaco. Located at the Conch Inn, Dive Abaco offers scuba and snorkeling trips on custom dive boats. Sites explored include reefs, tunnels, caverns, and wreck dives. ⊠ *Marsh Harbour* ☎ *800/247–5338, 242/367–2787, 800/247–5338* ⊕ *www.diveabaco.com.*

TENNIS

Abaco Beach Resort & Boat Harbour Marina. The two lighted courts here are open to visitors who purchase a resort day pass. Rackets and balls are available for use, and there are round-robin tournaments for guests. ⊠ *Marsh Harbour* ☎ *242/367–2158.*

TOURS

Abaco Eco Kayak Tours and Rentals. Get up close and personal with Abaco's amazing ecosystem while on a kayak tour with this environmentally sensitive operator. If you want to go it alone, rent a kayak for half a day or up to a week. ⊠ *Hope Town* ☎ *242/366–0398* ⊕ *www.abacoeco.com.*

Brendal's Dive Center. Whether you're looking for a close encounter with a shark, a dolphin, a turtle, or a swimming pig, this dive operator has a tour designed just for you. They also offer scuba courses, island-hopping adventures, and sunset cruises. ⊠ *Green Turtle Cay* ☎ *242/365–4411* ⊕ *www.brendal.com.*

Froggies Out Island Adventures. Take a day trip to one of the Bahamas' protected national parks. If you're visiting on a Sunday, catch a ride to the infamous Nippers pig roast on neighboring Guana Cay. This operator offers a variety of snorkeling and scuba combination tours and also certifies divers. ⊠ *Hope Town* ☎ *242/366–0431.*

WINDSURFING

Abaco Beach Resort & Boat Harbour Marina. Small sailboats and sea kayaks are available free of charge to hotel and marina guests at the Abaco Beach Resort. If you're not staying there, purchase a $50 beach day pass. ⊠ *Marsh Harbour* ☎ *242/367–2158* ⊕ *www.abacobeachresort.com.*

TREASURE CAY

Twenty miles north of Marsh Harbour is Treasure Cay, technically not an island but a large peninsula connected to Great Abaco by a narrow spit of land. This was once the site of the first Loyalist settlement in Abaco, called Carleton.

While Treasure Cay is a large-scale real estate development project, it's also a wonderful small community where expatriate residents share the laid-back sun-and-sea vibe with longtime locals. The development's centerpiece is the Treasure Cay Hotel Resort and Marina, with its Dick Wilson–designed golf course and a 150-slip marina that has boat rentals, a dive shop, pool, restaurant, and lively bar. Treasure Cay's commercial center consists of two rows of shops near the resort as well as a post office, self-service laundries, restaurants, a couple of well-stocked grocery stores, and BTC, the Bahamian telephone company. You'll also find car-, scooter-, and bicycle-rental offices here.

EXPLORING

Carleton Settlement Ruins. Tucked away toward the northwestern end of the Treasure Cay development are the ruins of the very first settlement in Abaco, founded by the Loyalists that left the Carolinas during the American Revolutionary War. The sight is not well marked, but a local can point you in the right direction. ⊠ *Treasure Cay.*

Treasure Cay Blue Hole. You'll need a car or at least a bicycle to visit this natural wonder, but it's worth the trek. Scientists believe the Treasure Cay Blue Hole is 200 feet deep, but feel free to dip your toes into the crystal-clear blue waters or make a splash swinging from one of the rope swings tied to surrounding pine trees. The water is both salt and fresh and there is no known marine life in the blue hole. ⊠ *Off S.C. Bootle Hwy.* ✛ *Turn left off S.C. Bootle Hwy. just before entrance to Green Turtle Cay Ferry Dock. Take wide dirt road about 2½ miles and follow narrow dirt road at left 500 feet to blue hole.*

BEACHES

FAMILY
Fodor'sChoice
★

Treasure Cay Beach. This beach is world famous for its expanse of truly powder-like sand and breathtaking turquoise water. In front of the handful of hotels lining the beach are bar and grill spots with a couple of shade-bearing huts. The rest of the beach is clear from development, since the land is privately owned, and almost clear of footprints. With a top-notch marina across the road and lunch a short stroll away, you have luxury; a walk farther down the beach gives you a quiet escape. **Amenities:** food and drink; parking (no fee); toilets; water sports. **Best for:** sunrise; sunset; swimming; walking. ⊠ *Treasure Cay.*

WHERE TO EAT

$
BAKERY
Fodor'sChoice
★

✕ **Café La Florence.** Stop off at this bakery-café in the Treasure Cay resort's main shopping strip for just-made muffins and some of the best cinnamon rolls you'll ever try. You'll know you've found it by the smell of those fresh-baked treats and the line of people waiting to indulge. **Known for:** sinfully good cinnamon buns; catered lunches for boat excursions; only ice-cream parlor in town. $ *Average main: $10* ⊠ *Treasure Cay* ☎ *242/365–8185* ▭ *No credit cards* ☉ *No lunch, dinner Sun.*

$
BAHAMIAN
FAMILY

✕ **Coco's Beach Bar & Sea Grille.** Enjoy the stunning scenery of one of the world's top-rated beaches while enjoying lunch or a cocktail at this casual, laid-back spot. Sit at the bar or on the open deck, or, for the best views, enjoy your meal under one of the thatched shades right on the beach. **Known for:** beautiful beach views; Sunday brunch buffet; bonfire cookouts on the beach. $ *Average main: $15* ⊠ *Treasure Cay* ☎ *242/365–8470* ⊕ *www.treasurecay.com* ▭ *No credit cards* ☉ *No dinner Wed.–Mon.*

$$$
BAHAMIAN

✕ **Spinnaker Ocean Grille & Wine Bar.** Ceramic-tiled floors, rattan furniture, and floral-print tablecloths accent this large resort restaurant—250 guests fit in the air-conditioned main dining area and the adjacent screened-in outdoor patio—and bar at the Treasure Cay Marina. Dinner boasts an international flair and each night there's a special theme: Sunday is Italian pasta night; Monday and Saturday choose from prime rib, duck, lamb, steaks, and lobster on the Deluxe menu; Wednesday is Caribbean Delights; and Friday is the popular Bahamian Buffet. **Known for:** theme nights; prime rib on Saturday. $ *Average main: $35* ⊠ *Treasure Cay Marina* ☎ *242/365–8801* ⊕ *www.treasurecay.com* ☉ *No lunch.*

$$
BAHAMIAN

✕ **Touch of Class.** Ten minutes north of Treasure Cay Resort, this locals'-favorite, no-frills restaurant serves traditional Bahamian dishes such as grilled freshly caught grouper and minced local lobster stewed with

Treasure Cay beach is one of the most beautiful beaches on Great Abaco Island.

tomatoes, onions, and spices. Reasonably priced appetizers such as conch chowder and conch fritters, and a full bar make this a perfect option for a night out. **Known for:** authentic Bahamian menu; complimentary transportation from Treasure Cay resort area. [$] *Average main: $28* ✉ *Queen's Hwy. at Treasure Cay Rd.* ☎ *242/365–8195* 🕓 *No lunch.*

$$$ BAHAMIAN Fodor's Choice ★ 🍴 **Treasure Sands Club.** Be sure to make a reservation for a Friday or Saturday night dinner especially during the season, as this restaurant just outside the entrance to the Treasure Cay Resort town draws locals and snowbirds from all over the Abacos. If it's not too cool, the restaurant will be converted to an open-air space, and you're right on the world-famous Treasure Cay beach. **Known for:** cool vibe; amazing views; best food in town. [$] *Average main: $35* ✉ *Treasure Cay* ☎ *242/365–9385* 🌐 *www.treasuresandsclub.com.*

WHERE TO STAY

$$ HOTEL Fodor's Choice ★ 🏨 **Bahama Beach Club.** Ideal for families and small groups, these two- to four-bedroom condos are right on the famous Treasure Cay beach. **Pros:** luxury accommodations on one of the most sublime beaches in the world; large pool area with Jacuzzi; walking distance to the marina, restaurants, and shops. **Cons:** check-in can be slow; housekeeping is separate cost; closed September and October. [$] *Rooms from: $300* ✉ *Treasure Cay* ☎ *800/284–0382, 242/365–8500* 🌐 *www.bahamabeachclub.com* 🛏 *87 condos* 🍽 *No meals.*

$ HOTEL FAMILY 🏨 **Treasure Cay Beach, Marina & Golf Resort.** Treasure Cay is known for its 18-hole golf course, one of the few open to the public in Abaco; its first-class 150-slip marina; and its location across the street from one of the most beautiful beaches in the world. **Pros:** convenient location; multiple on-site restaurants and bar; golf course. **Cons:** restaurant reservations essential in high season; pool area can get crowded; rooms need updating. [$] *Rooms from: $179* ✉ *Treasure Cay Marina* ☎ *242/365–8801, 800/327–1584* 🌐 *www.treasurecay.com* 🛏 *64 rooms* 🍴 *No meals.*

NIGHTLIFE

Tipsy Seagull Pool Bar. This outside bar and grill is a fun happy-hour spot. There's usually live music on the weekend and Thursday night's Pizza Night is a big hit with locals and visitors alike. Throw on your bathing suits and join in Saturday's afternoon pig roast and pool party followed by dancing to '70s and '80s music on the deck. ✉ *Treasure Cay Marina* ☎ *242/365–8801* 🌐 *www.treasurecay.com.*

SHOPPING

Fodor's Choice ★ **Abaco Ceramics.** Near Treasure Cay Resort is Abaco Ceramics, which offers its signature white-clay pottery with a variety of designs. The Royal fish pattern remains a favorite. ✉ *Treasure Cay* ☎ *242/365–8489* 🌐 *www.abacoceramics.com* 🕓 *Closed weekends.*

SPORTS AND THE OUTDOORS

BIKING

Wendell's Bicycle Rentals. Rent mountain bikes by the half day, day, or week. ✉ *Treasure Cay* ☎ *242/365–8687.*

BOATING

Treasure Cay Beach, Marina & Golf Resort has 150 slips and can accommodate large yachts. It's a great base for jaunting to outer uninhabited cays for day fishing or diving trips, or to Green Turtle Cay.

Contacts Treasure Cay Boat Rentals. ☎ *242/365–8582* 🌐 *www.treasurecay-boatrentals.com.*

FISHING

Justin Sands. Reservations are a must to fish with Justin Sands, Abaco's award-winning angler and guide. ✉ *Marsh Harbour* ☎ *242/367–3526* 🌐 *www.justfishjs.com.*

O'Donald Macintosh. Top professional bonefishing guide O'Donald Macintosh meets clients each day at the Treasure Cay Marina for full or half days of guided bonefishing in the northern Marls or outside Coopers Town. This guiding hall-of-famer has built up a large base of repeat clients, so you'll need to book him well in advance—especially in the prime months of April, May, and June. ✉ *Treasure Cay* ☎ *242/365–0126.*

Treasure Cay Beach. Marina & Golf Resort. Arrange for local deep-sea fishing or bonefishing guides through Treasure Cay Beach, Marina & Golf Resort. ✉ *Treasure Cay* ☎ *242/365–8250* 🌐 *www.treasurecay.com/fishing.*

GOLF

Treasure Cay Beach, Marina & Golf Resort. A half mile from the Treasure Cay Beach, Marina & Golf Resort is the property's par-72, Dick Wilson–designed course, with carts available. There's no need to reserve tee times, and the course is usually delightfully uncrowded—ideal for a leisurely round. A driving range, putting green, and small pro shop are also on-site. ✉ *Treasure Cay* ☎ *242/365–8045* 🌐 *www.treasurecay.com/golf* 🎟 *$85–$105* ⛳ *18 holes, 6985 yards, par 72.*

SCUBA DIVING AND SNORKELING

No Name Cay, Whale Cay, and the **Fowl Cay Preserve** are popular marine-life sites. The 1865 wreck of the steamship freighter *San Jacinto* also affords scenic diving and a chance to feed the resident green moray eel.

TENNIS

Treasure Cay Beach, Marina & Golf Resort. The tennis courts here are six of the best courts in the Abacos, four of which are lighted for night play. Make your reservations at the resort reception desk. ✉ *Treasure Cay* ☎ *242/365–8801* ⊕ *www.treasurecay.com/tennis* ⌨ *$25 per hr.*

WINDSURFING

Treasure Cay Hotel Resort & Marina. Hobie Cats and a complete line of nonmotorized watercraft are available for rent here. ✉ *Treasure Cay* ☎ *242/365–8250* ⊕ *www.treasurecay.com.*

SOUTH OF MARSH HARBOUR

Thirty minutes south of Marsh Harbour, the small, eclectic artists' colony of **Little Harbour** was settled by the Johnston family more than 50 years ago. Randolph Johnston moved his family here to escape the consumerist, hectic lifestyle he felt in the United States and to pursue a simple life where he and his wife could focus on their art. The family is well known for their bronze sculptures, some commissioned nationally.

Just to the south of Little Harbour is the seaside settlement of **Cherokee Sound,** home to fewer than 100 families. Most of the residents make their living catching crawfish or working in the growing tourism industry; many lead offshore fishing and bonefishing expeditions. The deserted Atlantic beaches and serene salt marshes in this area are breathtaking, and though development at Winding Bay and Little Harbour are progressing, the slow-paced, tranquil feel of daily life here hasn't changed. **Schooner Bay** is a new, by-design village just a bit farther south. Initially intended as a living, breathing community, it has turned into more of a second home and vacation destination, but it maintains a quaint island village feel. **Sandy Point,** a fishing village with miles of beckoning beaches and a couple of bonefishing lodges, is slightly more than 50 miles southwest of Marsh Harbour, about a 40-minute drive from Cherokee.

EXPLORING

Abaco Club on Winding Bay. Twenty-five minutes south of Marsh Harbour this glamorous private golf and sporting club is set on 534 acres of stunning oceanfront property. The clubhouse, restaurant, and pool, which sit on 65-foot-high white limestone bluffs, offer guests and members a mesmerizing view of the purple-blue Atlantic Ocean, and the bay has more than 2 miles of sugar-sand beaches. Amenities and activities at the club include an 18-hole tropical links golf course, a luxurious European-style spa and fitness center, scuba diving, snorkeling, tennis, bonefishing, and offshore fishing. This is a private club whose members have bought property; nonmembers can stay in the hotel-style cabanas and cottages and use all facilities one time while evaluating membership and real-estate options. ✉ *Cherokee Sound turnoff, Cherokee Sound* ☎ *844/442–2226, 242/367–0077* ⊕ *www.theabacoclub.com.*

Fodor's Choice ★ **Abaco National Park.** Established in 1994 as a sanctuary for the endangered Abaco parrot, many other birds call the park home, including the Bahama yellowthroat and pine warbler. Walk through 20,500 protected acres and end at the Hole-in-the-Wall lighthouse overlooking the ocean. ⊠ *South end of Great Abaco* ✛ *The turnoff for park is just before you make final turn on main road leading to Sandy Point* ☎ *242/367–6310 Bahamas National Trust Abaco Office* ⊕ *www.bnt.bs.*

Hole-in-the-Wall. Off the Great Abaco Highway at the turn in the road that takes you to Sandy Point, a rugged, single-lane dirt track leads you to this navigational lighthouse that stands on Great Abaco's southern tip. The lighthouse was constructed in 1838 against local opposition from islanders who depended on salvaging shipwrecks for their livelihood. Over the years the lighthouse has survived sabotage and hurricanes, and was automated in 1995 to continue serving maritime interests. The Bahamas Marine Mammal Research Organisation has leased the site to monitor whale movements and conduct other ocean studies. ⊠ *South of Sandy Point.*

Fodor's Choice ★ **Johnston Studios Art Gallery and Foundry.** Sculptor Pete Johnston and his sons and acolytes cast magnificent lifelike bronze figures using the age-old lost-wax method at the only bronze foundry in the Bahamas. You can purchase the art in the gallery. Tours are available by appointment for $50 per person. ⊠ *Little Harbour, Little Harbour* ☎ *242/577–5487* ⊕ *www.petespubandgallery.com* ✉ *$50 for tours.*

Sawmill Sink Blue Hole. A half-hour drive south of Marsh Harbour is a crudely marked electric pole directing you to turn right onto an old logging trail. A short drive down this road takes you to an incredible blue hole. It was featured by *National Geographic* in 2010 for the fossils found deep within it. Though you cannot dive this hole, you can swim in it. ⊠ *Great Abaco Hwy.*

BEACHES

Pelican Cay Beach. In a protected park, this is a great spot for snorkeling and diving on nearby Sandy Cay reef. The cay is small and between two ocean cuts, so the water drops off quickly but its location is also what nurtures the pure white sand. If you get restless, ruins of an old house are hidden in overgrowth at the top of the cay, and offer fantastic views of the park. **Amenities:** none. **Best for:** snorkeling. ⊠ *8 miles north of Cherokee Sound, Cherokee Sound.*

Sandy Point Beach. If shelling and solitude are your thing, venture 50 miles southwest of Marsh Harbour to the sleepy fishing village of Sandy Point. Large shells wash up on the sandy beaches, making it great for a stroll and shelling. The best spot for picking up one of nature's souvenirs is between the picnic site and Rocky Point. Well offshore is the private island Castaway Cay, where Disney Cruise Line guests spend a day. **Amenities:** none. **Best for:** solitude; walking. ⊠ *Sandy Point.*

WHERE TO EAT

$$ BAHAMIAN Fodor's Choice ★ ✕ **Pete's Pub.** Next door to Pete's Gallery is an outdoor tiki hut restaurant and bar where you can wiggle your toes in the sand while you chow down on fresh seafood, burgers, and cold tropical drinks. Try the mango-glazed grouper, lemon-pepper mahimahi, or coconut cracked

conch while you kick back and enjoy the view of the harbor. **Known for:** refreshing cocktails; pig roasts. $ *Average main: $20* ✉ *Little Harbour* ☎ *242/577–5487* ⊕ *www.petespubandgallery.com.*

WHERE TO STAY

$$$$
B&B/INN
Fodor'sChoice
★

Black Fly Lodge. Make your reservations well in advance if you want to stay at what has very quickly become one of the most popular bonefishing lodges around. **Pros:** world-class fishing lodge; meals, drinks, fishing, and airport transfer included in room rate; lovely location. **Cons:** often booked far in advance; not on the beach; not many activities for nonfishing guests. $ *Rooms from: $1000* ✉ *Bay St.* ☎ *242/376–0321* ⊕ *www.blackflylodge.com* ☉ *Closed mid-Aug.– early Sept. and Christmas Eve until just after New Year's* ⤳ *10 rooms* ⍥ *All-inclusive.*

$$$$
B&B/INN
Fodor'sChoice
★

Delphi Club. Although Delphi Club is billed as a bonefishing lodge, it's a great middle-of-nowhere bed-and-breakfast perfect for anyone looking to get away from it all but not willing to give up style or comfort. **Pros:** private and secluded; great bonefishing; situated on a beautiful private beach. **Cons:** very remote; lots of stairs; dinner is always family style. $ *Rooms from: $1000* ✛ *Leaving Marsh Harbour, head south 24 miles along Great Abaco Hwy.; turn left when you see large white rock on right-hand side, and follow signs to Delphi Club along unpaved road* ☎ *242/366–2222* ⊕ *www.delphi-bahamas. com* ⤳ *8 rooms.*

$$$$
B&B/INN

Rickmon Bonefish Lodge. Well-regarded fishing guide Ricardo Burrows operates this comfortable waterside lodge at the end of the road in Sandy Point. **Pros:** perfect location for bonefishing; some of the best professional fly-fishing guides in the Abacos; private guides, meals, and accommodations included with fishing packages. **Cons:** average restaurant; intermittent Internet; three-night minimum. $ *Rooms from: $650* ✉ *Sandy Point* ☎ *800/628–1447* ⊕ *www.angleradventures.com/ rickmon* ⤳ *11 rooms* ⍥ *All-inclusive.*

$$
B&B/INN
Fodor'sChoice
★

Sandpiper Inn. With harbor views, luxuriously decorated rooms and suites, and the only restaurant and swimming pool in Schooner Bay right downstairs, this quaint bed-and-breakfast inn is the perfect spot for visitors who want to be taken care of. **Pros:** personalized service; public pool; small and intimate. **Cons:** no organized activities; limited dining options. $ *Rooms from: $200* ☎ *242/376–9858* ⊕ *www.sand-piperabaco.com* ⤳ *7 rooms.*

$$
RENTAL
FAMILY

Schooner Bay. Many of the homes and cottages in this designer community are available for rent. **Pros:** homes are completely turnkey; a selection of beaches; sense of community. **Cons:** no organized activities; just one full restaurant in the village; long way from other communities. $ *Rooms from: $300* ☎ *954/246–3792, 888/275–1639* ⊕ *schoonerbay-vacations.com* ⤳ *7 homes* ⍥ *No meals.*

SHOPPING

Johnston Studios Art Gallery. The gallery displays original bronzes by the Johnstons, as well as unique gold jewelry, prints, and gifts. ✉ *Little Harbour* ☎ *242/577–5487* ⊕ *www.petespubandgallery.com.*

ELBOW CAY

Five-mile-long Elbow Cay's main attraction is the charming village of **Hope Town.** The saltbox cottages—painted in bright colors—with their white picket fences, flowering gardens, and porches and sills decorated with conch shells, will remind you of a New England seaside community, Bahamian style. Most of the 300-odd residents' families have lived here for several generations. For an interesting walking or bicycling tour of Hope Town, follow the two narrow lanes that circle the village and harbor. (Most of the village is closed to motor vehicles.)

Although modern conveniences like Wi-Fi and cell service are found throughout the island, most residents remember the day the island first got telephone service—back in 1988. Before that, everyone called each other the way many still do here and in the other Out Islands: by VHF, the party line for boaters. If you are boating, want to communicate with the locals, or would like to make a dinner reservation on one of the cays, you should carry a VHF radio and have it tuned to channel 16.

GETTING HERE AND AROUND

FERRY TRAVEL

Elbow Cay is 4 miles southeast of Marsh Harbour. Every day except Sunday and holidays, **Albury's Ferry Service** (☎ *242/367–0290* ⊕ *www. alburysferry.com*) leaves Marsh Harbour for the 20-minute ride to Hope Town at 7:15, 9, 10:30, 12:15 (unavailable August–October), 2, 4, and 5:45; ferries make the return trip at 8, 9:45, 11:30 (unavailable August–October), 1:30, 3, 4, 5, and 6:30. They also offer nighttime ferry service between Marsh Harbour and Hope Town and the Seaspray Marina with the last boat departing for the mainland at 1 am. A same-day round-trip costs $27. One-way tickets cost $17. Tickets are half-price for children ages 6–11, and free for children 5 and under.

GOLF CART TRAVEL

Once in Hope Town you can walk everywhere. In fact, only local work vehicles are permitted through town. To visit other areas you can rent a bicycle or a golf cart.

Contacts Hope Town Cart Rentals. ✉ *Hope Town* ☎ *242/366-0064* ⊕ *www. hopetowncartrental.com.* **Island Cart Rentals.** ✉ *Hope Town* ☎ *242/366-0448* ⊕ *www.islandcartrentals.com.* **T&N Cart Rentals.** ✉ *Hope Town* ☎ *242/366-0069* ⊕ *www.tandncarts.com.*

EXPLORING

Hope Town Lighthouse. Upon arrival in Hope Town Harbour you'll first see a much-photographed Bahamas landmark, an 89-foot-tall, candy-striped lighthouse built in 1864. The light's construction was delayed for several years by acts of vandalism; then-residents feared it would end their profitable wrecking practice. Today the lighthouse is the last hand-turned, kerosene-fueled beacon in operation anywhere in the world. Monday through Saturday from 9 to 5 you can climb up the spiral staircase to the top for a superb view of the sea and the nearby cays. There are 101 steps in all and there is no graceful way for an adult to crawl through the small door onto the viewing platform that goes all the way around the top. The lighthouse keepers and their families live in the small cottages at its base, so keep noise to a minimum as one of them is resting up for his night shift. There's no road between the lighthouse and the town proper. You can use your own boat to cross the harbor or take a ferry to the dock and explore the lighthouse; the ferry does not run very frequently, so expect to spend at least an hour here before the next one comes along, either to head back to Marsh Harbour or continue on to Hope Town. There's a small gift shop at the base of the lighthouse and proceeds support the efforts to keep the lighthouse maintained and operational. ⊠ *Elbow Cay* 🕮 *Free* ☉ *Closed Sun.*

Wyannie Malone Historical Museum. This volunteer-run museum houses Hope Town memorabilia and photographs. Exhibits highlight Lucayan and pirate artifacts found on the island. Many descendants of Mrs. Malone, who settled here with her children in 1875, still live on Elbow Cay. ⊠ *Queen's Hwy., Hope Town* 🕮 *242/366–0293* ⊕ *www.hope-townmuseum.com* 🕮 *$5.*

BEACHES

Tahiti Beach. This small beach at the southern tip of Elbow Cay is a popular boater's stop. The soft white sand is well protected from the close ocean cut by thick vegetation, a few barrier cays, and shallow water. This shallow area is popular for shelling, and, of course, simply relaxing and watching the tide rise. At low tide, the true beauty of this beach is revealed when a long sand spit emerges, perfect for picnics. It's great for young children, as the water on one side of the spit is ankle deep, stays calm, and remains warm. During peak season the beach can become a bit crowded. **Amenities:** none. **Best for:** surfing; swimming. ⊠ *Elbow Cay.*

WHERE TO EAT

$$$
BAHAMIAN
Fodor'sChoice
★

✕ **Abaco Inn Restaurant.** Set in the country-club-style main lodge splashed with lively Bahamian colors and floor-to-ceiling windows that provide an incredible view of the ocean, the restaurant serves breakfast, lunch, and dinner to guests and visitors in classic island style. Fresh-baked bread, fruit, and egg dishes are breakfast highlights. **Known for:** views of the Sea of Abaco and the Atlantic Ocean; fresh ahi tuna; largest wine selection on island. $ *Average main: $38* ⊠ *2 miles south of Hope Town, Hope Town* 🕮 *242/366–0133* ⊕ *www.abacoinn.com.*

$$$
CARIBBEAN

✕ **Bridget's Rum Bar.** Catch the Hope Town Inn & Marina's free boat shuttle from any of the docks across the harbor in Hope Town and pull up a chair under the open octagonal restaurant or hop in and place your order at the swim-up bar. The Caribbean-inspired menu features lots of seafood for lunch and dinner as well as some fun twists on Bahamian staples like the Bahamian cheese sticks—fried macaroni and cheese. **Known for:** cool swim-up bar; Friday night dancing under the stars; Parmesan-crusted lobster. $ *Average main: $32* ⊠ *Across the harbor, Hope Town* 🕮 *242/366–0003* ⊕ *www.hopetownmarina.com.*

$ BAHAMIAN 🍴 **Cap'n Jack's Restaurant and Bar.** There are a handful of booths and a small rowdy bar, but most of this casual eatery's seating is out on the pink-and-white-striped dock–patio. Locals, boat people, and land-based tourists gather here every day for value-priced eats and drinks. **Known for:** Monday night bingo; taco Thursday with two-for-one margaritas; grilled or blackened catch-of-the-day Reuben. [$] *Average main: $17* ✉ *Hope Town* ☎ *242/366–0247* 🌐 *www.capnjackshopetown.com* 🕒 *Closed weekends and mid-Aug.–Sept.*

$$ BAHAMIAN Fodor's Choice ★ 🍴 **Firefly Bar & Grill.** Ask anyone in the Abacos where you must eat during your stay and they are likely to recommend Firefly Bar & Grill. Whether you pull in by golf cart or tie up by boat, it's worth the trip. **Known for:** Firefly Vodka cocktails; best food for miles around; sushi Tuesday. [$] *Average main: $30* ✉ *Hope Town* ☎ *242/366–0145* 🌐 *www.fireflysunsetresort.com.*

$$$ BAHAMIAN 🍴 **Gaffer's Dockside Bar & Grille.** The bar is huge, the drink specials are flowing, and the music plays all night long. As if that weren't enough reason to check out the most remote restaurant on island, they also serve dinner long after all other kitchens have closed. **Known for:** late-night bites; $5 margaritas all day, every day; karaoke and live entertainment. [$] *Average main: $35* ✉ *Sea Spray Resort* ☎ *242/366–0065* 🌐 *www.seasprayresort.com.*

$$$ BAHAMIAN Fodor's Choice ★ 🍴 **Great Harbour Room.** While casual attire is fine, this restaurant overlooking the harbor feels like an upscale establishment with dimmed lighting, quiet music, and especially attentive service. Start off with a creamy white conch chowder. **Known for:** casual elegance; prime rib Sunday (reservation required); excellent seafood. [$] *Average main: $34* ✉ *Upper Rd., Hope Town* ☎ *242/366–0095* 🌐 *www.hopetownlodge.com* 🕒 *No lunch.*

$$$ BAHAMIAN 🍴 **Harbour's Edge.** Hope Town's happening hangout for locals and tourists, this bar and restaurant's deck is the best place to watch the goings-on in the busy harbor; you can tie your boat up right in front. The bar opens at 10:30 am, so kick back and have an icy Kalik or the Scattered Shower or Dark & Stormy cocktails. **Known for:** early first call at the bar; tasty bar food menu; lots of action. [$] *Average main: $35* ✉ *Lower Rd., Hope Town* ☎ *242/366–0087* 🌐 *www.harboursedge.net* 🕒 *Closed Tues.*

$ BAKERY 🍴 **Hope Town Coffee House.** Overlooking Hope Town Harbour, this upscale coffeehouse, bakery, boutique, and hot-spot café features coffee roasted right in the historic settlement, the first roastery in the Bahamas. It's a must for java drinks, smoothies, homemade pastries, quiches, and tapas-size savories. **Known for:** divine homemade roasted coconut popsicles; casual meeting spot; best coffee on the island. [$] *Average main: $8* ✉ *Queen's Hwy., Hope Town* ☎ *242/366–0760* 🌐 *hopetowncoffeehouse.com* 🕒 *Closed Sun. and late-Aug.–early-Nov.*

$ BAHAMIAN 🍴 **On Da Beach Bar and Grill.** Burgers, grilled kebabs, sandwiches, conch, fish, and icy rum drinks are served up with a terrific Atlantic view at this open-air bar and grill perched high on the beach dunes across the road from the small Turtle Hill resort. It closes at sunset because all seating is open to the elements, and a gully washer of a storm can shut the place down. **Known for:** jerk fish melt; one of the few spots for beachside dining; cool ocean breezes. $ *Average main: $11* ⊠ *Queens Hwy. between Hope Town and White Sound, Hope Town* ☎ *242/366–0557* ⊕ *www.turtlehill.com* ⊘ *Closed Mon.*

$

BAHAMIAN

✕ **The Reef Bar & Grill.** Pull up a chair by the pool or on the open-air deck overlooking the beach and enjoy salads, burgers, and wraps all served up with signature dressings and sauces like Pineapple Ginger Aioli, Creamy Caribbean Petal Dressing, and Guava BBQ Sauce. Try a classic Bahamian Chicken or Conch in a Bag—fried and served with french fries and smothered in ketchup and hot sauce. **Known for:** light and hearty lunches; poolside dining; Sunday brunch with free mimosas. $ *Average main: $18* ⊠ *Hope Town Harbour Lodge, Hope Town* ☎ *242/366–0095* ⊕ *www.hopetownlodge.com.*

WHERE TO STAY

PRIVATE VILLA RENTALS

Elbow Cay Properties. Besides being the most cost-efficient way for a family to stay a week or longer on Elbow Cay, a private house or villa is also likely to be the most comfortable. This long-standing rental agency handles a variety of properties, from cozy two-bedroom, one-bath cottages, to a six-bedroom, six-bath villa better described as a mansion. Many of the rental homes are on the water, with a dock or a sandy beach right out front. The owners are set on finding you a place to match your wishes and budget and can arrange any extra services—from boat rental to a personal chef or yoga classes. There are no Sunday check-ins as the agency is closed, and a three-night minimum is required most weeks; a full week is required during peak holiday seasons. ⊠ *Western Harborfront, Hope Town* ☎ *242/366–0569* ⊕ *www.elbowcayrentals.com.*

Hope Town Hideaways. This property-management company rents more than 75 private cottages and houses, including spectacular beachfront retreats at Tahiti Beach on the south end of the cay. Most of these units sleep four or more, and some of the more upscale properties can accurately be described as mansions. The management can also arrange for everything from kayak, boat, and golf-cart rentals to island excursions and fishing guides. All rentals have a four-night minimum stay. ⊠ *Hope Town* ☎ *242/366–0224* ⊕ *www.hopetown.com.*

HOTELS AND RESORTS

$$

HOTEL

⛱ **Abaco Inn.** The motto here is "Tan your toes in the Abacos," making this beachfront resort the ideal place for a getaway. **Pros:** self-contained resort with the best restaurant on the island; easy access to beaches, surfing, and fishing; hypnotic ocean views. **Cons:** 10-minute golf-cart or boat ride to Hope Town; nothing else around; accommodations are basic. $ *Rooms from: $265* ⊠ *2 miles south of Hope Town, Hope Town* ☎ *242/366–0133* ⊕ *www.abacoinn.com* ⇆ *14 rooms* ⦿ *No meals.*

$$$$

HOTEL

Fodor's Choice

★

⛱ **Firefly Sunset Resort.** Each of these fully equipped, beautifully appointed two-, three-, and four-bedroom cottages boasts a stunning view of the Sea of Abaco and all are situated on the vast property in a way that creates privacy and a sense of true exclusivity. **Pros:** beautiful settings; large, beautifully decorated accommodations; fantastic restaurant

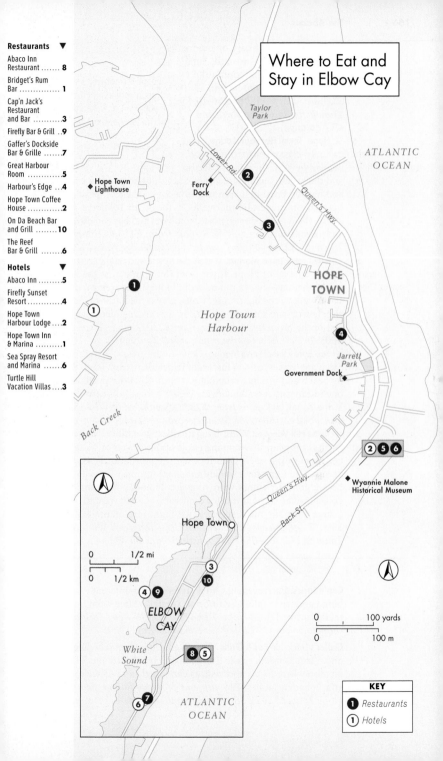

Where to Eat and Stay in Elbow Cay

ATLANTIC OCEAN

Taylor Park

Lower Rd.

Ferry Dock

Queen's Hwy.

◆ Hope Town Lighthouse

HOPE TOWN

Hope Town Harbour

Jarrett Park

Government Dock ◆

◆ Wyannie Malone Historical Museum

Queen's Hwy.

Back St.

Back Creek

Hope Town ○

0   1/2 mi

0   1/2 km

ELBOW CAY

White Sound

ATLANTIC OCEAN

0   100 yards

0   100 m

KEY

❶ *Restaurants*

① *Hotels*

on site. **Cons:** golf cart or boat is a must for getting around; small man-made beach; minimum three-night stay. $ *Rooms from: $450* ✉ *Hope Town* ☎ 242/366–0145 ⊕ *www.fireflysunsetresort.com* ↩ *7 cottages.*

$
HOTEL
Fodor's Choice
★

Hope Town Harbour Lodge. This casually classy resort offers spectacular views of the Atlantic Ocean and the beach, quality amenities, and is just steps away from the town and harbor. **Pros:** best spot in Elbow Cay for views, beach, and access to town; on-site restaurant overlooks the ocean; romantic. **Cons:** rooms are small; Wi-Fi is spotty; noise from pool and bar can disturb poolside and oceanfront cottages. $ *Rooms from: $175* ✉ *Upper Rd., Hope Town* ☎ 242/366–0095 ⊕ *www.hopetownlodge.com* ↩ *25 rooms.*

$$
RESORT
Fodor's Choice
★

Hope Town Inn & Marina. Watch the hustle and bustle (relatively speaking, of course) of Hope Town from this spot across the harbor. **Pros:** complimentary shuttle to and from Hope Town; removed from town; short walk to the lighthouse. **Cons:** across the harbor from everything else; few on-site activities; some cottages are remotely located from the rest of the property. $ *Rooms from: $220* ✉ *Hope Town* ☎ 242/366–0003 ⊕ *www.hopetownmarina.com* ↩ *20 rooms.*

$$
RESORT

Sea Spray Resort and Marina. Consider this resort if you're planning to catch any waves, or you just want to get away from it all. **Pros:** flanked by beach and marina; relaxing retreat; full-service marina. **Cons:** only one restaurant in walking distance; 10-minute golf-cart or boat ride to Hope Town. $ *Rooms from: $235* ✉ *South end of White Sound, Hope Town* ☎ 242/366–0065 ⊕ *www.seasprayresort.com* ↩ *5 villas.*

$$
HOTEL

Turtle Hill Vacation Villas. Bougainvillea- and hibiscus-lined walkways encircle the central swimming pools of this cluster of six one- and two-bedroom villas, each with its own private patio. **Pros:** comfortable accommodations for families and small groups; steps away from the beach; golf cart comes with your accommodation. **Cons:** you have to golf cart out to restaurants for dinner if you don't want to cook in; extra charge for daily maid service; two-night minimum. $ *Rooms from: $300* ✉ *Off Queens Hwy. between Hope Town and White Sound, Hope Town* ☎ 242/366–0557 ⊕ *www.turtlehill.com* ↩ *6 villas.*

> ### SURFING ELBOW CAY
>
> Though it's not well known, there is good surfing off Elbow Cay. If you want to wake up to the waves, stay at the Abaco Inn or at the Sea Spray Resort, or rent a house at Tahiti Beach.

NIGHTLIFE

Cap'n Jack's. Each evening Cap'n Jack's offers a different event, including bingo and trivia, along with drink specials. After 9 pm on Wednesday there's a live DJ. ✉ *Hope Town* ☎ 242/366–0247 ⊕ *www.capnjack-shopetown.com* ☾ *Closed Sun. and mid-Aug.–Sept.*

Gaffer's Dockside Bar & Grille. There's entertainment scheduled here every night, from smooth sax to lively Junkanoo and karaoke. This is a popular stop where locals and visitors can mingle and dance to classic rock and Bahamian tunes. ✉ *South end of White Sound, Seaspray Resort, Hope Town* ☎ 242/366–0065 ⊕ *www.seasprayresort.com.*

Tahiti Beach on Elbow Cay is a family favorite.

Harbour's Edge. After 9 pm every Saturday and on Thursday nights during peak seasons, Harbour's Edge has local bands playing Bahamian and reggae music. This is a favorite spot among locals. ⊠ *Lower Rd., Hope Town* ☎ *242/366–0087* ⊕ *www.harboursedge.net* ☾ *Closed Tues.*

Wine Down and Sip Sip. Featuring a selection of 50 properly cellared wines, Wine Down and Sip Sip is a classy hangout with a high-end liquor bar, draft beer, and weekly flights and pairings. The aura is sophisticated, and complimented by a lend-and-exchange selection of books. ⊠ *Queen's Hwy., Hope Town* ☎ *242/366–0399.*

SHOPPING

Da Crazy Crab. Here you'll find a wide selection of souvenirs, beach wraps, T-shirts, arts and crafts, and Cuban cigars. ⊠ *Front Rd., Hope Town* ☎ *242/366–0537.*

Ebbtide. This shop is on the upper-path road in a renovated Loyalist home. Come here for such Bahamian gifts as batik clothes, original driftwood carvings and prints, and nautical jewelry. They even sell the brightly colored Androsia fabric by the yard. Browse through the extensive Bahamian book collection. ⊠ *Hope Town* ☎ *242/366–0088.*

Hope Town Canvas. Bags of all sizes are made by hand out of sails in the upstairs workshop. Some of the sails are new, others are recycled. Sailors consider an old sail from their boat a fair trade for one of the stylish duffel bags, purses, or totes. ⊠ *Studio 1 Bldg., Lower Rd., Hope Town* ⊕ *www.hopetowncanvas.com.*

Iggy Biggy. This is the only shop in Hope Town that carries the lovely Abaco ceramics handmade in Treasure Cay. It also sells home decorations, handmade dishware and glasses, wind chimes, sandals, resort wear, jewelry, and island music. ⌂ *Front Rd., Hope Town* ☎ *242/366–0354.*

SPORTS AND THE OUTDOORS

BOATING

Hope Town Inn & Marina. If you want to get away from the hustle and bustle of Hope Town proper, consider docking your boat at this 50-slip marina that can accommodate up to 120-foot vessels. You'll have access to the standard amenities plus two pools, a restaurant and bar, free boat shuttle across the harbor to Hope Town, and pump-out service. ⌂ *Hope Town Inn* ☎ *242/866–0008* ⊕ *www.hopetownmarina.com.*

Lighthouse Marina. This marina situated at the base of the Hope Town Lighthouse is relatively small with just six transient slips that accommodate vessels up to 60 feet, but it has all the expected amenities and more. There's laundry, fuel, bait and tackle, a gift shop, and a liquor store. ⌂ *Hope Town* ☎ *242/366–0154* ⊕ *www.htlighthousemarina.com.*

Sea Spray Resort and Marina. This full-service marina has 62 slips accommodating vessels up to 120 feet and all the amenities in a very well-protected area. Stock up on beer and liquor and even bait for a day out fishing. This marina is the closest you'll get to the best fishing grounds offshore. ⌂ *Hope Town* ☎ *242/366–0065* ⊕ *www.seasprayresort.com.*

BOAT RENTALS

Island Marine. Island Marine rents 17- to 27-foot boats ideal for exploring the Abaco cays. It's closed early August to mid-October. ⌂ *Hope Town* ☎ *242/366–0282* ⊕ *www.islandmarine.com.*

Sea Horse Boat Rentals. Captain one of the Albury brothers' boats, which are handcrafted in nearby Man O'War Cay as you explore the islands. Sea Horse also has other makes ranging from 17 feet up to a 26-foot Paramount that can seat up to 10 people. ⌂ *Hope Town* ☎ *242/366–0023* ⊕ *www.seahorseboatrentals.com.*

FISHING

A Salt Weapon. This company offers deep-sea-fishing charters at the best price in Hope Town. ⌂ *Hope Town* ☎ *242/366–0245* ⊕ *www.asaltweaponcharters.com.*

Local Boy. Deep-sea charters are available with Local Boy Justin Russell—an eighth-generation Bahamian who has been fishing these waters for more than 20 years. ⌂ *Hope Town* ☎ *242/366–0528* ⊕ *www.hopetownfishing.com.*

Maitland Lowe. Book well in advance to have "Bonefish Dundee" Maitland Lowe guide you around Snake Cay or Little Harbour. ⌂ *Hope Town* ☎ *242/366–0234* ⊕ *www.wildpigeoncharters.com.*

Seagull Charters. This charter company sets up guided deep-sea excursions with Captain Robert Lowe, who has more than 40 years' experience in local waters. ⌂ *Hope Town* ☎ *242/366–0266* ⊕ *www.seagullcottages.com/fishing.*

KAYAKING

Abaco Eco. This company offers kayaking tours and rentals of the local area and Snake Cay. ⊠ *Hope Town* ☎ *242/475–9616* ⊕ *www. abacoeco.com.*

PADDLEBOARDING

Abaco Paddle Board. Rent a paddle- or surfboard by the hour or by the day or go on a guided nature tour. If you're new to the sports, sign up for private lessons or the three-day surf clinic. Based in Green Turtle Cay but will deliver rentals anywhere in the Abacos. ⊠ *Located at Pineapples Bar & Grill, Green Turtle Cay* ☎ *242/475–0954, 242/365–4226* ⊕ *www.abacopaddleboard.com.*

4

MAN-O-WAR CAY

Fewer than 300 people live on skinny, 2½-mile-long Man-O-War Cay, many of them descendants of early Loyalist settlers who started the tradition of handcrafting boats more than two centuries ago. These residents remain proud of their heritage and continue to build their famous fiberglass boats today. The island is secluded, and the old-fashioned, family-oriented roots show in the local policy toward liquor: it isn't sold anywhere on the island. (But most folks won't mind if you bring your own.) Three churches, a one-room schoolhouse, several boutique shops, small grocery stores, and just one restaurant round out the tiny island's offerings.

A mile north of the island you can dive to the wreck of the USS *Adirondack,* which sank after hitting a reef in 1862. It lies among a host of cannons in 20 feet of water.

GETTING HERE AND AROUND

FERRY TRAVEL

Man-O-War Cay is an easy 20-minute ride from Marsh Harbour by water taxi or aboard a small rented outboard runabout. The island has a 28-slip marina. No cars are allowed on the island, but you'll have no problem walking it, or you can rent a golf cart. The two main roads, Queen's Highway and Sea Road, run parallel.

Water Ways Rentals. Rent a golf cart to explore the island for $50 a day. ⊠ *Man-O-War Cay* ☎ *242/365–6143* ⊕ *www.waterwaysrentals.com.*

EXPLORING

Man-O-War Heritage Museum. Historic artifacts from the boat-building industry are on display in this small museum. Built in the 1800s, the quaint white wooden building is the former "Church Corner House" commissioned by the patriarch of one of the island's best-known boat-building families. ⊠ *Queen's Hwy. and Pappy Ben Hill* 🍴 *Free.*

WHERE TO EAT

$
BAHAMIAN

✕**Dock & Dine.** Not only is this one of the few places to get a meal in Man-O-War, but it's the only place to get a glass of beer or wine. The granting of a limited liquor license caused quite a controversy among locals proud of their history and tradition as the only dry island. **Known for:** only place serving alcohol on the island; daily lunch and dinner specials; relaxed atmosphere. Ⓢ *Average main: $18* ✉ *Waterfront, Sea Rd.* ☎ *242/365–6380* ▭ *No credit cards.*

$$
BAHAMIAN

✕**Hibiscus Cafe.** This small restaurant doubled the number of eateries on the island when it opened. Locals, upset that the competition started serving beer and wine on what used to be a dry island, flocked to Hibiscus where the food is simple but good, and the drinks are all nonalcoholic. **Known for:** upholding the island's teetotaling tradition; ice cream selection; simple but yummy food. Ⓢ *Average main: $20* ✉ *Waterfront* ☎ *242/365–6380.*

WHERE TO STAY

Waterways Boat and Cottage Rentals. With no hotels on the island, the only way to stay in this quaint settlement is to rent a condo or a home. Available accommodations range from a tiny dockside cottage at the entrance, to the sheltered harbor to Loyalist-era houses nestled among the locals, to newly constructed beachfront homes that sleep 10 comfortably and offer all the amenities of home. Most require a week's rental agreement. The company also rents boats and golf carts. ✉ *Sea Rd. and Pappy Ben Hill* ☎ *242/365–6143, 242/357–6540* ⊕ *www. waterwaysrentals.com* ⋗ *18 homes.*

SHOPPING

Fodor's Choice
★

Albury's Sail Shop. This shop is popular with boaters, who stock up on duffel bags, briefcases, hats, and purses, all made from duck, a colorful, sturdy canvas fabric traditionally used for sails. ✉ *Lover's La. at Sea Rd.* ☎ *242/365–6014.*

Joe's Studio. This store sells paintings by local artists, books, clothing, and other nautically oriented gifts, but the most interesting souvenirs are the half models of sailing dinghies. These mahogany models, which are cut in half and mounted on boards, are meant to be displayed as wall hangings. Artist Joe Albury, one of the store's owners, also crafts full, 3-D boat models. ✉ *Sea Rd.* ☎ *242/365–6082* ⊕ *www. joesstudioabaco.com.*

Sally's Seaside Boutique. Ladies sit in the back of this small shop and sew Bahamian-made Androsia fabric into original shirts, dresses, blouses, and linens for the home. You can also pick up a locally made wooden handicrafts or books about the Abacos. ✉ *Sea Rd.* ☎ *242/365–6044.*

SPORTS AND THE OUTDOORS

BOATING

Man-O-War Marina. This marina has 28 slips and also rents golf carts. Enjoy the pool, grill, cable TV, and Wi-Fi. For people coming from Marsh Harbour or other cays, the Albury Ferry dock is adjacent. ⊠ *Front Rd.* ☎ *242/365–6008* ⊕ *www.manowarmarina.com.*

SCUBA DIVING

DiveTime. Learn to scuba dive in some of the most beautiful waters around. Seasoned divers can join one of the daily two-tank dives, rent equipment, or book a private charter for a maximum of six divers. Half-day snorkeling trips are also available. ⊠ *Abaco Beach Resort and Boat Harbour Marina, Marsh Harbour* ☎ *242/365–6235* ⊕ *www. divetimeabaco.com.*

4

GREAT GUANA CAY

The essence of Great Guana Cay can be summed up by its unofficial motto, painted on a hand-lettered sign: "It's better in the Bahamas, but it's gooder in Guana." This sliver of an islet just off Great Abaco, accessible by ferry from Marsh Harbour or by private boat, has both alluring deserted beaches and grassy dunes. Only 100 full-time residents live on 7-mile-long Great Guana Cay, where you're more likely to run into a rooster than a car during your stroll around the tranquil village. Still, there are just enough luxuries here to make your stay comfortable, including a couple of small, laid-back resorts and a restaurant–bar with one of the best party scenes in the Abacos. The island also has easy access to bonefishing flats you can explore on your own.

GETTING HERE AND AROUND

The ferry to Great Guana Cay leaves from the Conch Inn Marina in Marsh Harbour. The ride is about 30 minutes. Golf carts are available for rent in Great Guana Cay, though most places are within walking distance.

WHERE TO EAT

$$
BAHAMIAN

✕ **Captain Kidd's Cove Seafood Bar & Grill.** Perch on a bar stool around the tiki bar or take a seat on one of the rocking chairs on the porch and enjoy the comings and goings of Guana Cay's harbor and main road. While they boast the "conchiest" conch fritters around, it's the sushi that keeps folks coming back. **Known for:** great spot for people-watching; sushi; friendly hosts. $ *Average main: $20* ⊠ *Front St.* ☎ *242/475–3701.*

$$
BAHAMIAN
Fodor'sChoice
★

✕ **Nippers Beach Bar & Grill.** With awesome ocean views and a snorkeling reef just 10 yards off its perfect beach, this cool bar and restaurant is a must-visit hangout. Linger over a lunch of burgers and sandwiches or a dinner of steak and lobster, then chill out in the two-tiered pool. **Known for:** Sunday pig roast; best pool and beach party spot in the Abacos; beautiful beach. $ *Average main: $30* ⊠ *Great Guana Cay* ☎ *242/365–5111* ⊕ *www.nippersbar.com.*

Nippers Beach Bar & Grill is the best restaurant on Great Guana Cay.

$$ ✕ **Sunsetters.** Sit indoors to soak up the cool air-conditioning or outdoors
BAHAMIAN on the open deck overlooking the Sea of Abaco while enjoying a cool
beverage and enjoying some of the best Bahamian food available on
island. The conch and fresh fish are always a hit, and Thursday night's
wings special is only beat by the one pound of ribs for $10 on Satur-
day nights. **Known for:** amazing Sea of Abaco views; Thursday night
wings; only indoor dining option on Guana Cay. $ *Average main: $30*
✉ *Orchid Bay Yacht Club* ☎ *242/365–5175* ⊗ *Closed Mon.*

WHERE TO STAY

$$ 🏨 **Flip Flops on the Beach.** Reserve one of the four one- or two-bedroom
HOTEL beachside bungalows at this casually elegant boutique resort and you
can melt into the island lifestyle of sun, sand, serenity, and ocean breezes
on arrival. **Pros:** beachfront location; the essence of tranquillity; quality
accommodations and in-room amenities. **Cons:** remote location means
there is no nightlife, shopping, or larger resort-style activities; no Internet; no daily housekeeping. $ *Rooms from: $220* ✉ *Great Guana Cay*
☎ *800/222–2646, 242/365–5137* ⊕ *www.flipflopsonthebeach.com*
⊗ *Closed mid-Aug.–mid-Oct.* ⇥ *4 bungalows* ⦿ *No meals.*

$$ 🏨 **Grabber's Bed, Bar & Grill.** The only hotel on Guana Cay is simple but
HOTEL ideally located: just a short walk from the ferry dock and marina, and
Fodor's Choice steps away from an idyllic calm beach. **Pros:** open year-round; best
★ sunsets in the Abacos; restaurant right on property. **Cons:** not much
else to do on island; need a boat to explore; no breakfast served in on-
site restaurant. $ *Rooms from: $225* ✉ *Guana Cay* ☎ *242/365–5133*
⊕ *www.grabbersatsunset.com* ⇥ *14 rooms* ⦿ *No meals.*

NIGHTLIFE

Grabbers Bar and Grill. This is a popular local spot on weekend nights. There's music, cornhole in the sand, and the Guana Grabber, a potent frozen drink designed to lighten any mood. If you're not staying here and want to keep the party going after the last ferry leaves, ask the staff about catching a ride back to Marsh Harbour with them. ⊠ *Great Guana Cay* ☎ *242/365–5133* ⊕ *www.grabbersatsunset.com.*

Nippers. Not only is this the best spot on a Sunday, but weekend nights Nippers continues to rock. ⊠ *Great Guana Cay* ☎ *242/365–5143* ⊕ *www.nippersbar.com.*

SHOPPING

Gone Conchin'. Pick up some island-appropriate outfits for your vacation in this small yellow store right at the foot of the ferry dock. They also sell sea glass jewelry and other trinkets. It's the only place in Abaco that carries the full line of Bahama Hand Prints clothing. ⊠ *Great Guana Cay* ☎ *242/365–5215.*

SPORTS AND THE OUTDOORS

BOATING

Baker's Bay Golf & Ocean Club. At the northwestern end of the island, Baker's Bay Golf & Ocean Club has 158 slips. ⊠ *Great Guana Cay* ☎ *242/557–0635* ⊕ *www.bakersbayclub.com.*

Orchid Bay Yacht Club and Marina. Orchid Bay Yacht Club and Marina has 66 deep-water slips and full services for boaters at the entrance to the main settlement bay, across from the public docks. The club office rents luxury apartments, cottages, and homes, and prime real estate is for sale. There's also a swimming pool and a restaurant that serves fresh seafood, steaks, and healthy salads on an outdoor deck overlooking the marina. ⊠ *Great Guana Cay* ☎ *242/365–5175* ⊕ *www.orchid-bay-marina.com.*

SCUBA DIVING

Dive Guana. This dive shop organizes scuba and snorkeling trips and island-hopping boat tours. The shop also rents boats, kayaks, and bicycles. Renting a boat, at least for a day, is the best way to get around and enjoy other nearby cays. ⊠ *Great Guana Cay* ☎ *242/365–5178* ⊕ *www.diveguana.com.*

GREEN TURTLE CAY

This tiny 3-mile-by-½-mile island is steeped in Loyalist history; some residents can trace their heritage back more than 200 years. Dotted with ancestral New England–style cottage homes, the cay is surrounded by several deep bays, sounds, bonefish flats, and irresistible beaches. **New Plymouth,** first settled in 1783, is Green Turtle's main community. Many of its approximately 550 residents earn a living by diving for conch or selling lobster and fish.

GETTING HERE AND AROUND

FERRY TRAVEL

Many hotels provide an occasional shuttle from the main ferry dock in Green Turtle Cay to their property, and there are a couple of taxis on the island. Most people travel via golf cart or boat. Don't worry, you won't miss having a car; even in the slowest golf cart you can get from one end of the island to the other in 20 minutes or less.

The **Green Turtle Cay Ferry** (☎ *242/365–4166*) leaves the Treasure Cay airport dock at 8:30, 10:30, 11:30, 1:30, 2:30, 3:30, 4:30, and 5, and returns from Green Turtle Cay at 8, 9, 11, 12:15, 1:30, 3, and 4:30 (from New Plymouth dock only). The trip takes 10 minutes, and one-way fares are $12, same-day round-trip fare is $17. The ferry makes several stops in Green Turtle, including New Plymouth, the Green Turtle Club, and the Bluff House Beach Hotel.

GOLF CART TRAVEL

Contacts D & P Golf Cart Rentals. ☎ *242/365–4655.* **Island Roadrunner.** ☎ *242/365–4160.* **KoolKart Rentals.** ☎ *242/356–4176* 🌐 *www.koolkartrentals.com.* **Seaside Cart Rentals.** ☎ *242/365–4147* 🌐 *www.seasidecartrentals.com.*

EXPLORING

Albert Lowe Museum. This is the Bahamas' oldest historical museum, dedicated to a model-ship builder and direct descendant of the island's original European-American settlers. ✉ *Parliament St.* ☎ *242/365–4094* 🌐 *www.albertlowemuseum.com* 🎟 *$5.*

Memorial Sculpture Garden. The past is present in this garden across the street from the New Plymouth Inn (note that it's laid out in the pattern of the British flag). Immortalized in busts perched on pedestals are local residents who have made important contributions to the Bahamas. Plaques detail the accomplishments of British Loyalists, their descendants, and the descendants of those brought as slaves, such as Jeanne I. Thompson, a contemporary playwright and the country's second woman to practice law. This is an open garden, free to the public. ✉ *Parliament St.*

WHERE TO EAT

$$ AMERICAN 🍴 **Ballyhoo Bar & Grill.** This casual eatery on the water in the Bluff House Marina offers tasty meals for breakfast and dinner. Sitting under an umbrella on the deck is the best way to enjoy the view of the sailboat-filled harbor, but you can also eat in the air-conditioned pub-style dining room. **Known for:** live music on Tuesday night; fresh local catch; romantic evenings overlooking White Sound. [$] *Average main: $25* ✉ *Between Abaco Sea and White Sound, at Bluff House Beach Hotel Marina* ☎ *242/365–4247* 🌐 *www.bluffhouse.com.*

$$ EUROPEAN Fodor's Choice ★ 🍴 **The Club Restaurant at Green Turtle Club Resort.** Breakfast and lunch are served harborside on a covered, screened-in patio, while dinner takes place in the elegant dining room. At lunch, treat yourself to a lobster salad, lobster corn chowder, cheeseburger, or grilled grouper sandwich. **Known for:** upscale dining; lobster ravioli; great service. [$] *Average*

main: $30 ✉ *Green Turtle Club, north end of White Sound* ☎ *242/365–4271* 🌐 *www.greenturtleclub.com* 🕒 *Closed mid-Sept.–Oct.*

$ BAHAMIAN Fodor's Choice ★ 🍴 **Eddie The Rock's World Famous Conch Salad.** Starting around 11 am, locals and tourists in the know gather round this wooden mobile stand at the start of the Government Dock to see if Eddie has begun slicing and dicing fresh conch and vegetables for his conch salad. His spicy lobster salad is also made to order. **Known for:** only made-to-order conch salad on island; spot to stop and chat; authentic Bahamian takeout. [$] *Average main: $10* ✉ *Government Dock* ☎ *242/365–4069* 💳 *No credit cards.*

$$ BAHAMIAN 🍴 **Harvey's Island Grill.** Sit inside and enjoy the cool air-conditioning, or grab one of the brightly painted blue and pink picnic tables on the harborside beach across the street to enjoy your lunch or dinner. The menu is a simple mix of American and Bahamian fare. **Known for:** homemade ice cream; Friday night fish fry; views of Green Turtle Cay. [$] *Average main: $20* ✉ *Bay St.* ☎ *242/365–4389* 💳 *No credit cards.*

$ ASIAN 🍴 **Laure's Kitchen.** The kitchen of this very basic restaurant is a converted food truck that no longer goes anywhere. The only place to get Asian food on the island serves up a mix of standard Chinese and Filipino dishes, but makes use of the abundant seafood found in the Abacos. **Known for:** only Asian restaurant on island; chicken wings done 11 different ways; delicious lobster spring rolls. [$] *Average main: $10* ✉ *Crown St.* ☎ *242/425–6107.*

$$ BAHAMIAN 🍴 **Lizard Bar & Grill.** Dine poolside overlooking the Leeward Yacht Club marina at this casual bar and grill. The grilled lobster or fresh catch (which can be jerked, blackened, grilled, or fried) are popular menu choices, as are the conch burger and the grilled conch fritters. **Known for:** decadent lobster-and-truffle mac and cheese; happy hour in the pool; deconstructed key lime pie. [$] *Average main: $20* ✉ *Leeward Yacht Club* ☎ *242/365–4191* 🌐 *www.leewardyachtclub.com.*

$$ BAHAMIAN 🍴 **McIntosh Restaurant and Bakery.** At this simple diner-style restaurant, lunch means excellent renditions of local favorites, such as fried grouper and cracked conch, and sandwiches made with thick slices of a slightly sweet Bahamian bun. At dinner, large portions of pork chops, lobster, fish, and shrimp are served with rib-sticking sides like baked macaroni and cheese, peas 'n' rice, and coleslaw. **Known for:** moist coconut bread; island hospitality. [$] *Average main: $25* ✉ *Parliament St.* ☎ *242/365–4625.*

$$ BAHAMIAN 🍴 **Pineapples Bar & Grill.** Hang out, take a dip in the saltwater pool, and enjoy Bahamian fare with a flair. In Black Sound, at the entrance to the Other Shore Club and Marina, you'll find this simple open-air restaurant with a canopy-shaded bar and picnic tables next to the pool. **Known for:** tropical drinks in the pool; best sunset views; world-famous piña coladas. [$] *Average main: $20* ✉ *Black Sound* ☎ *242/365–4039.*

$ BAHAMIAN 🍴 **The Wrecking Tree.** The wooden deck at this casual restaurant was built around the wrecking tree, a place where 19th-century wrecking vessels brought their salvage. Today it's a cool place to linger over a cold Kalik and a hearty lunch of cracked conch, fish-and-chips, or zesty conch salad. **Known for:** tender cracked conch; interesting history. [$] *Average main: $16* ✉ *Bay St.* ☎ *242/365–4263* 🕒 *No dinner Sun.–Thurs.*

WHERE TO STAY

PRIVATE VILLA RENTALS

Island Property Management. Choose from a five-bedroom oceanfront mansion with wraparound verandah, full-time staff, and a marble fireplace, or rent a two-bedroom cottage in the heart of New Plymouth. This agency has more than 50 cottages and houses for rent to meet different budgets and needs. It can also help arrange excursions and boat and golf-cart rentals. Most homes have water views, and some have docks for your rental boat. The offices in New Plymouth are in a blue two-story building just down from the ferry dock. ✉ *Various Green Turtle Cay locations* ☎ *242/365–4047, 888/405–6054 reservations* 🌐 *www.abacoislandrentals.com.*

HOTELS AND RESORTS

$$ HOTEL Fodor's Choice ★ 🏨 **Bluff House Beach Resort & Marina.** Full of old-world charm, the first stage of this property's restoration includes eight beautifully appointed suites overlooking the Sea of Abaco. **Pros:** secluded and private; great views; beautiful decor. **Cons:** golf cart or boat required to get into New Plymouth; lots of steps up to all suites; crowds at on-site bar/restaurant make private beach less secluded. [$] *Rooms from: $250* ✉ *Green Turtle Cay* ☎ *242/365–4247* 🌐 *www.bluffhouse.com* ⏲ *Closed early Sept.–late Oct.* 🛏 *8 rooms* 🍴 *No meals.*

$$ RENTAL 🏨 **Coco Bay Cottages.** Sandwiched between one beach on the Atlantic and another calmer, sandy stretch on the bay are six spacious cottages—including two three-bedroom cottages and a four-bedroom cottage—all with views of the water. **Pros:** spacious accommodations; great beaches; Wi-Fi. **Cons:** renting a boat and/or golf cart is essential; four-night minimum stay; not well lighted at night. [$] *Rooms from: $250* ✉ *Coco Bay, north of Green Turtle Club* ☎ *561/202–8149, 561/202–8149* 🌐 *www.cocobaycottages.com* 🛏 *6 cottages* 🍴 *No meals.*

$$ RESORT 🏨 **Green Turtle Club.** The long-standing colonial tradition and tone of casual refinement continues at this well-known resort. **Pros:** excellent on-site restaurants for casual or fine dining; easy access to great beaches; personalized service. **Cons:** if you're looking for Bahamian casual, this isn't it; golf cart or boat is essential to explore the island; some rooms are a long walk from the hotel amenities. [$] *Rooms from: $239* ✉ *North end of White Sound* ☎ *242/365–4271, 866/528–0539* 🌐 *www.greenturtleclub.com* ⏲ *Closed mid-Aug.–late Oct.* 🛏 *34 rooms.*

$$ RENTAL 🏨 **Linton's Beach and Harbour Cottages.** These three classic Bahamian-style cottages are ideally placed on 22 private acres between Long Bay and Black Sound. **Pros:** stocked libraries and fully equipped kitchens; great value for families and groups; private access to beautiful Long Bay beach. **Cons:** gathering groceries and supplies can be an adventure; no phones or TV in some beach cottages; no swimming pool on property. [$] *Rooms from: $230* ✉ *S. Loyalist Rd., Black Sound* ☎ *772/538–4680* 🌐 *www.lintoncottages.com* 🛏 *3 cottages* 🍴 *No meals.*

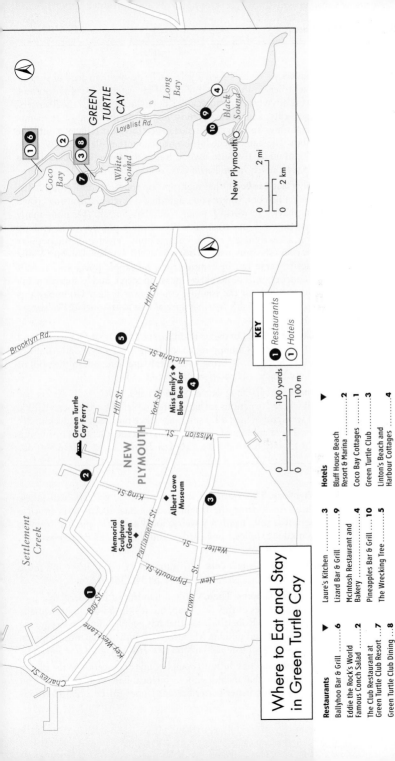

Where to Eat and Stay
in Green Turtle Cay

Restaurants   ▼

Ballyhoo Bar & Grill **6**
Eddie the Rock's World
Famous Conch Salad **2**
The Club Restaurant at
Green Turtle Club Resort ...**7**
Green Turtle Club Dining ...**8**
Harvey's Island Grill **1**

Laure's Kitchen **3**
Lizard Bar & Grill **9**
McIntosh Restaurant and
Bakery **4**
Pineapples Bar & Grill **10**
The Wrecking Tree **5**

Hotels

Bluff House Beach
Resort & Marina **2**
Coco Bay Cottages **1**
Green Turtle Club **3**
Linton's Beach and
Harbour Cottages **4**

KEY

1 Restaurants
① Hotels

NIGHTLIFE

Gully Roosters. At night, Green Turtle can be deader than dead or surprisingly lively. Bet on the latter if the local favorites, the Gully Roosters, are playing anywhere on the island. Known locally as just the Roosters, this reggae-calypso band is the most popular in the Abacos. Their mix of original tunes and covers can coax even the most reluctant onto the dance floor. The band's schedule is erratic, but they play every Wednesday at 9 pm under the Buttonwood tree at the **Green Turtle Club** during the high season. ⊠ *Green Turtle Cay.*

Fodor's Choice
★

Miss Emily's Blue Bee Bar. Other nighttime options include a visit to Miss Emily's Blue Bee Bar, where you might find a singing, carousing crowd knocking back the world-famous Goombay Smash. (Or not—many Goombay novices underestimate the drink's potency, and end up making it an early night.) Mrs. Emily Cooper, creator of the popular Goombay Smash drink, passed away in 1997, but her daughter Violet continues to serve up the famous rum, pineapple juice, and apricot brandy concoction. The actual recipe is top secret, and in spite of many imitators throughout the islands, you'll never taste a Goombay this good anywhere else. It's worth a special trip to try one. ⊠ *Parliament St.* ☎ *242/365–4181.*

Pineapples Bar & Grill. On the water in front of the Other Shore Club and Marina, this bar has a hopping happy hour from 4 to 6 daily and live music every Friday at 7. Bring your bikini and hang out in the pool or the shallow beach. ⊠ *Brooklyn Rd.* ☎ *242/365–4039.*

Sundowner's. Locals hang out at Sundowner's, a waterside sports bar and grill where attractions include a pool table, lots of big-screen TVs, and, on weekend nights, a DJ spinning dance music on the deck under the stars. There are lots of drink specials and the kitchen is open until midnight for late-night snacks. ⊠ *Green Turtle Cay* ☎ *242/365–4060.*

SHOPPING

Native Creations. This is one of the few places to get a bolt of fabric or clothing made from the bright and whimsical Androsia fabrics. The shop also sells beaded jewelry, local artwork, picture frames, locally made candles, postcards, and books. ⊠ *Parliament St.* ☎ *242/365–4206.*

Plymouth Rock Liquors and Café. This shop sells Cuban cigars and more than 60 kinds of rum. ⊠ *Parliament St.* ☎ *242/365–4234.*

Robertha's Faith Grocery. There's only a handful of nonperishable groceries on the shelves of this tiny shop, but it's the $3-a-cup homemade ice cream made by Robertha's son that has people lining up to squeeze inside the tiny green building. Mango or coconut are the most popular, with chunks of fresh fruit. ⊠ *Victoria and Hill Sts.* ☎ *242/365–4284.*

Sid's Food Store. Sid's has the most complete line of groceries on the island, plus a gift section that includes books on local Bahamian subjects. You can also buy conch fritter batter here. ⊠ *Upper Rd.* ☎ *242/365–4055.*

SPORTS AND THE OUTDOORS

BOATING

It's highly recommended that you reserve your boat rental at the same time you book your hotel or cottage. If you're unable to rent a boat on Green Turtle Cay, try nearby Treasure Cay or Marsh Harbour.

BOAT RENTALS

Donny's Boat Rentals and Marina. The best way to spend your Abaco vacation is by exploring the cays by boat. Rent a 17-, or 19-foot Whaler, a 20-foot Wellcraft, or a 23-foot Angler for the day or week and find your own deserted beach or island. Bonefishing and deep-sea fishing excursions are also offered. ⊠ *Green Turtle Cay* ☎ *242/365–4119* ⊕ *www. donnysboatrentalsgtc.com.*

Reef Boat Rentals. A 17-foot Keywest with a bimini top and 90-hp engine is perfect for up to four people, but you can rent boats in varying sizes, all the way up to the 26-foot Panga with 150 hp, which is perfect for shallow seas and accommodates up to eight people comfortably. ⊠ *Green Turtle Cay* ☎ *242/365–4145* ⊕ *www.reefboatrentals.com.*

FISHING

Captain Rick Sawyer. The top recommendation on Green Turtle Cay, Captain Rick Sawyer is one of the best guides in the Abacos. Rick's company, Abaco Flyfish Connection and Charters, offers bonefishing on 17-foot Maverick flats skiffs, and reef and offshore fishing aboard his 33-foot Tiara sportfisher. Book as far in advance as you can. ⊠ *Green Turtle Cay* ☎ *242/365–4261* ⊕ *www.abacoflyfish.com.*

Ronnie Sawyer. Considered one of the best in the business, Ronnie Sawyer has been fishing the Abaco flats professionally for more than 30 years so knows all the best spots. ⊠ *Green Turtle Cay* ☎ *242/365–4070.*

SCUBA DIVING AND SNORKELING

FAMILY

Fodor's Choice

★

Brendal's Dive Center. This dive center leads snorkeling and scuba trips, plus wild-dolphin encounters, fun- and rum-filled day excursions, and more. Personable owner Brendal Stevens has been featured on the Discovery Channel and CNN, and he knows the surrounding reefs so well that he's named some of the groupers, stingrays, and moray eels that you'll have a chance to hand-feed. Trips can include a seafood lunch, grilled on the beach, and complimentary rum punch. A visit to the swimming pigs on nearby No Name Cay has become one of the most popular adventures. ⊠ *Green Turtle Cay* ☎ *242/365–4411* ⊕ *www.brendal.com.*

Lincoln Jones. Rent some snorkel gear or bring your own, and call Lincoln Jones, known affectionately as "the Daniel Boone of the Bahamas," for an unforgettable snorkeling adventure. Lincoln will dive for conch and lobster (in season) or catch fish, then grill a sumptuous lunch on a deserted beach. ⊠ *Green Turtle Cay* ☎ *242/365–4223.*

ANDROS, BIMINI, AND THE BERRY ISLANDS

WELCOME TO ANDROS, BIMINI, AND THE BERRY ISLANDS

TOP REASONS TO GO

★ **Bonefish:** Andros, Bimini, and the Berry Islands have world-class reputations for bonefishing. Hire a guide to show you how to fly-fish, then hunt the bights of Andros or the shallow flats of Bimini and the Berries in pursuit of the elusive "gray ghost."

★ **Casino cruise:** From Miami, catch the Bimini Superfast cruise ship to Resorts World Bimini for gaming, beaching, and a menu of fun shore excursions.

★ **Dive Andros or Bimini:** Go with the diving experts at Small Hope Bay or Kamalame Cay and drop "over the Andros wall" or at Neal Watson's Bimini Scuba Center to explore magnificent wrecks and reefs.

★ **Fish for big game:** Charter a boat and experience the thrill of catching deep-sea prizes such as marlin, mahimahi, tuna, and wahoo.

The northwestern islands of Andros, Bimini, and Berry lie just off the east coast of Florida. Bimini is 50 miles from Miami; the Berry Islands are a 30-cay chain 100 miles east of Bimini. Andros comprises the Bahamas' largest landmass (about half of all the Bahamas' land in total), and is split into three islands: North and Central Andros, Mangrove Cay, and South Andros. Two tidal estuaries called Northern and Middle Bight separate North and Central Andros from Mangrove Cay, and the Southern Bight splits Mangrove Cay and South Andros. Remote beaches and small settlements stretch along the eastern shores while a vast wilderness of mangrove estuaries and swamps characterize their western leeward coasts.

1 Andros. Vast fishing flats, blue holes, vibrant reefs (including the third-largest barrier reef in the world), and the Tongue of the Ocean wall make fishing, diving, and snorkeling the main reasons adventurers travel to Andros. The island is mostly flat, lush with pine forests and mangroves, rimmed with white-sand beaches, and

Alice Town North Bimini

South Bimini

Turtle Rocks

Bimini

Holm Cay **2**

North Cat Cay
South Cat Cay

Ocean Cay

laced with miles of creeks and lakes. Explore North and Central Andros by car to see gorgeous beaches and quaint settlements.

2 Bimini. Year-round, boaters and tourists from Florida cross the Gulf Stream seeking fish and fun. Many visit North Bimini via the Bimini fast ferry to enjoy Resorts World Bimini with its new Hilton hotel, casino, dining, and fun excursions. Fishing and yachting fans frequent Alice Town's quaint hotels, bars, and Bahamian food shacks. South Bimini, with the islands' only airport and the Bimini Sands Resort & Marina, appeals more to the nature-minded visitor.

3 The Berry Islands. For the ultimate remote island getaway, fly and stay on the small capital of Great Harbour Cay in the north or on semiprivate Chub Cay in the south. In between lies a necklace of beautiful island gems accessible only by boat. Both hubs have clubs, affordable villas, and full-service marinas, and both are celebrated for bone-, deep-sea, and bottom-fishing. On every Berry Island, the beaches and reefs are breathtaking.

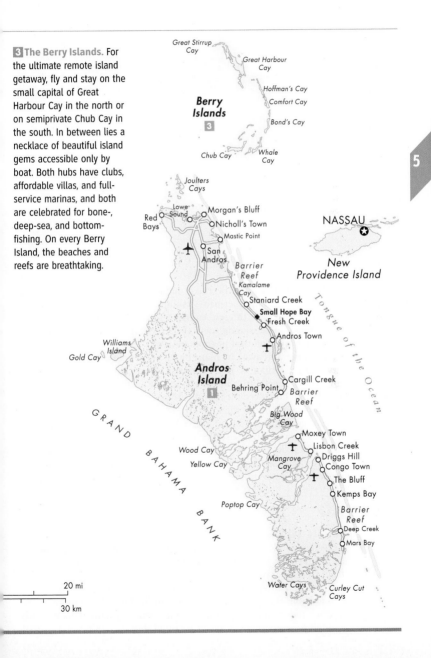

Great Stirrup Cay

Great Harbour Cay

Hoffman's Cay

Comfort Cay

Berry Islands **3**

Bond's Cay

Chub Cay

Whale Cay

Joulters Cays

Lowe Sound

Red Bays

Morgan's Bluff

Nicholl's Town

Mastic Point

San Andros

Barrier Reef

Kamalame Cay

Staniard Creek

Small Hope Bay

Fresh Creek

Andros Town

NASSAU

New Providence Island

Williams Island

Gold Cay

Andros Island **1**

Behring Point

Cargill Creek

Barrier Reef

Big Wood Cay

Moxey Town

Wood Cay

Yellow Cay

Mangrove Cay

Lisbon Creek

Driggs Hill

Congo Town

The Bluff

Kemps Bay

Poptop Cay

Barrier Reef

Deep Creek

Mars Bay

Tongue of the Ocean

GRAND BAHAMA BANK

20 mi

30 km

Water Cays

Curley Cut Cays

5

Updated by
Bob Bower

Legends loom large (and small) on these northwestern Bahamas islands. On Bimini, you'll hear about the lost underwater city of Atlantis, Ernest Hemingway's visits, and the Fountain of Youth. Tiny birdlike creatures known as chickcharnies are said to inhabit the pine forests of Andros Island. On both islands, along with the Berry Islands, bone-fishing has made legends of mere men.

Andros, Bimini, and the Berries remain a secret mostly known to avid divers, boaters, and fishermen—fishing and commercial diving sustain the economies here, though Andros also thrives on farming fruit and vegetables. These islands stash their reputation for superlative blue holes and other natural phenomena away from the glamour of Nassau, just minutes away by plane but a world apart, yet you'll still find some of the Bahamas' most admired resorts here. North Bimini has been transformed into a busier island by Resorts World; its casino and new Hilton hotel feed the island with hundreds of golf-carting tourists that buy packages on the fast ferry from Miami. Although Andros is the largest Bahamas island and a favorite of nature-lovers, most of its land is far from any settlement and hardly habitable. All resorts, inns, and lodges lie on a narrow east-coast strip, adjoining beautiful beaches and the barrier reef. The 30-some cays of the Berry Islands are lesser known still.

PLANNING

WHEN TO GO
Traveling to all islands by boat is easiest in summer when seas are calmer. Fishing and diving are good year-round, although cold fronts from December to February can cause rough seas. November, March, and April are often the most pleasant months. Temperatures are more comfortable in winter and spring and, during these drier months, mosquitoes and sand flies are fewer. Temperatures usually remain steady enough to enjoy the beaches year-round, but they occasionally drop

into the 60s in cold fronts. Hurricane season runs from June through November. August and September, the most likely months for hurricanes, can be hot and steamy, and many resorts and restaurants are closed. Among Andros, Bimini, and the Berries, it seems each hotel or lodge has its own high, low, and shoulder seasons and respective rates. Some hotels, such as the Hilton at Resorts World Bimini peak in summer, while others such as bonefish lodges, peak in winter. Highest rates are invariably in the holiday seasons between late December and early January, around Easter in March and April, and U.S. Labor Day in early September. Bargains can be found in late January, February, October, and early December.

TOP FESTIVALS

WINTER **Junkanoo Celebrations** occur all over the islands on **Boxing Day** (December 26) and **New Year's Day,** with festivities that include traditional People's Rush mini-Junkanoo parades, music, dancing, and food. They take place in Fresh Creek, Central Andros; Nicholl's Town, North Andros; Moxey Town, Mangrove Cay; Driggs Hill, South Andros; Alice Town, North Bimini; and Bullock's Harbour Park in Great Harbour Cay, Berry Islands. In February, Resorts World Bimini hosts its annual **Wahoo Challenge** fishing tournament.

SPRING In Andros, though bonefishing is the name of the game, in May the town of Red Bays, North Andros, hosts a Snapper Tournament. Mangrove Cay in mid-May comes alive with its own local Mother's Day Homecoming and Regatta with islander sloop sailing races, food, drinks, and entertainment.

SUMMER During the second weekend in June, three days of crab races, cook-offs, live Rake 'n' Scrape music, and national musical artists comprise the **All Andros CrabFest** in Fresh Creek, held at Queen's Park. Expect wild street parties across the Bahamas on July 10, **Independence Day.** The Regattas are often the Bahamas Out Islands' most attended festivals featuring passionate rivalry and multiple races of one or more of the A, B, and C class Bahamian sailing sloops. Around Labour Day in early June, South Andros holds its regatta at The Bluff. The largest sailing festival in the region is the **All Andros & Berry Islands Regatta,** on Morgan's Bluff Beach on the second weekend in July. In Nicholl's Town, at the end of July you can also catch the **Junkanoo Summer Festival.** Every Saturday in July Fresh Creek's Queen's Park hosts **Andros Nights** where locals and visitors gather until midnight to dance and enjoy Bahamian food prepared by women in the community. In Andros, on the third weekend in July, the **Goombay Summer Festival** is held on Friday (noon to midnight) at Morgan's Bluff in North Andros and on Saturday night (6 pm to midnight) at Cargill Creek, south Central Andros. Both feature live local bands, Junkanoo, food, drinks, and fun contests such as onion-peeling, watermelon-eating, and sack races. Every Saturday in July, the Berry Island's Great Harbour Cay Marina hosts the **Junkanoo Summer Fest** with a Junkanoo miniparade, and on the second August weekend, it hosts the **Lobster & Lionfish Derby,** a fishing tournament with prizes and entertainment including Junkanoo, limbo, fire-dancing, and a lobster cook-off contest. In June and July, Bimini hosts the **Bahamas Boating Flings,** guided flotillas of motor yachts wishing to cross the Gulfstream with piloting help organized by the Bahamas Ministry of Tourism's Boating Department. Participating boats gather at a marina in Fort Lauderdale. (See Boating Flings at ⊕ *www.bahamas.com*)

FALL   In mid-October, South Andros hosts the three-day **Andros ConchFest** on Mars Bay Blue Hole Beach and Community Center where locals and a few lucky visitors are entertained with myriad ways to cook and eat conch amid fun contests including dancing and crack-conching. In November, the famous deep-sea fishing resort Bimini Big Game Club hosts its **Annual Wahoo Smackdown** fishing tournament. Conviviality abounds when the boats arrive back at the dock and at the evening parties. All are welcome to enter.

HOTELS AND LODGING

Find everything from luxury properties to boutique hotels, rentals on private cays (pronounced "keys"), and simple fishing lodges. Comfortable lodge and motel-style accommodations are most common, and usually have a restaurant and bar. Some lodges don't have in-room telephones, TVs, or Internet. Most have a phone for guest use on the property, and some will have a computer with Internet in the lounge or lobby. Almost all take credit cards, though very small lodges and non-hotel restaurants may accept cash only. Although places advertise Internet services, connection can be spotty. Rates typically vary between high and low seasons. In the smaller Out Islands, rates are often expressed per cabin, room, or cottage (usually with double occupancy).

Hotel prices are for two people in a standard double room in low season, excluding service and 6%–12% tax and 7.5% VAT. Some establishments are by law too small to charge VAT and some, especially in the smaller Out Islands, don't charge gratuities either. The highest rates and busiest times vary with each resort, usually occurring around the Thanksgiving, Christmas, and Easter holidays and from February to June. High season is usually February to April, but these islands can also be busy through June.

RESTAURANTS

With a few notable exceptions, dining here is a casual experience. Most restaurants, lodges, and inns serve traditional Bahamian fare. Call ahead to make sure a restaurant is open. Except for roadside and seaside conch shacks, almost all require you to order dinner ahead of time. Resort restaurants have à la carte sit-down meals. Some lodges have all-inclusive meal plans with stays and offer day or night passes for dining nonguests. Many of the favored Bahamian food outlets are take-out places with picnic tables. A common practice is to take food back to your room to enjoy air-conditioned and fly- and mosquito-less comfort. Thatched conch stands and colorful roadside bars are a great way to mingle with the locals.

Restaurant prices are based on the median main course price at dinner, excluding gratuity, typically 10% to 15%, coupled with the new Bahamas Valued Added Tax (VAT) of 7.5% (on food but not gratuities)—which are usually automatically added to the bill.

WHAT IT COSTS IN DOLLARS			
	$	**$$**	**$$$**	**$$$$**
Restaurants	under $20	$20–$30	$31–$40	over $40
Hotels	under $200	$200–$300	$301–$400	over $400

VISITOR INFORMATION

Contacts Andros Tourist Offices. ☎ 242/368–2286 Central Andros, 242/369–1688 South Andros, 242/368–2286 North Andros ⊕ www.bahamas.com/islands/andros. **Association Of Bahamas Marinas.** ☎ 844/556–5290 toll-free, 954/462–4591 U.S. and Canada ⊕ www.bahamasmarinas.com. **Bahamas Out Islands Promotion Board.** ☎ 954/740–8740 U.S. and Canada, 242/322–1140 Nassau office ⊕ www.myoutislands.com. **Berry Islands Tourism Administrator.** ✉ Great Harbour Cay Airport, Great Harbour Cay ☎ 242/367–8291 office, 242/451–0404 cell, 242/225–2563 toll-free within Bahamas ⊕ www.bahamas.com/islands/berry. **Bimini Tourist Office.** ✉ Alice Town ☎ 242/347–3528 or 29 ⊕ www.bahamas.com/islands/bimini.

GETTING HERE AND AROUND

AIR TRAVEL

Scheduled nonstop and direct flights from the United States to the Bahamas' northwestern islands are growing in frequency with small, reliable operators from Miami International Airport (MIA), Miami's Watson Island Seaplane Base (XX4), Fort Lauderdale-Hollywood International (FLL), and Fort Lauderdale Executive (FXE) airports. Relative newcomer, Elite Airways, flies into South Bimini (BIM) from New York Newark Liberty (EWR) and Melbourne-Cocoa Beach (MLB) airports.

From Nassau Flamingo Air. ☎ 242/377–0354 ⊕ flamingoairbah.com. **GlenAir.** ☎ 242/368–2116, 242/471–1860. **LeAir.** ☎ 242/377–2356 ⊕ www.flyleair.com. **Randolph Holdings.** ☎ 242/368–2922, 242/477–1335 ⊕ www.flycharterbahamas.com.

From Fort Lauderdale and Miami Air Flight Charters. ☎ 954/359–0320 ⊕ www.airflightcharters.com. **Silver Airways.** ☎ 801/401–9100 ⊕ www.silverairways.com. **Tropic Ocean Airways.** ☎ 800/767–0897 ⊕ www.flytropic.com. **Watermakers Air.** ☎ 954/771–0330 ⊕ www.watermakersair.com.

From New York (Newark) and Melbourne, FL Elite Airways. ☎ 877/393–2510 ⊕ www.eliteairways.com.

BOAT AND FERRY TRAVEL

Visiting private boaters must clear Bahamas Customs and Immigration at the nearest port-of-entry, found in Bimini on both South and North Bimini, in the Berry Islands on Great Harbour Cay and Chub Cay, and in Andros at Nicholl's Town (Morgan's Bluff Harbour) in North Andros, Fresh Creek Harbour and Drigg's Hill Harbour in South Andros. Customs officers are stationed at the nearest airport—San Andros, Andros Town, and Congo Town airports, respectively—so call the airports ahead of time to inform them you are coming in. Once cleared, you can explore other islands, marinas, and anchorages. You can also clear at gorgeous private island and marina Cat Cay

Yacht Club, a few miles south of Bimini. Except for Morgan's Bluff, all ports-of-entry have full-service marinas with amenities, lodging, dining, beaches, and fun activities. From Florida, North Bimini is the only island reachable by ferry. From the Port of Miami, FRS Caribbean has a fast ferry that speeds in two hours to Resorts World Bimini's pier, costing from $130 to $200 round-trip. From Nassau's Potter Cay Dock, each main island is served weekly or three times a month by ferry or mail boat. Note that mail boats may make several stops, and due to weather, you may be marooned on your chosen island for days until the next mail boat arrives. Between South and North Bimini a ferry runs the 15-minute harbor ride every half hour or so and even until 11 pm. Boating between other islands requires a boat rental or charter. *See Boat and Ferry Travel for each island.*

Contacts Bahamas Customs. ☎ *242/347–3100 Alice Town, North Bimini, 242/347–3101 South Bimini airport, 242/325–5788 Chub Cay airport, 242/367–8116 Great Harbour Cay airport, 242/329–2140 San Andros airport (for Nicholl's Town, Morgan's Bluff), 242/368–2030 Andros Town airport (for Fresh Creek), 242/369–2640 Congo Town airport (for Drigg's Hill and Kemp's Bay), 242/377–7030 Nassau Airport customs, answers call all hrs, 242/326–4401 through 6 Customs HQ Nassau, business hrs only ⊕ www.bahamas.gov.bs/customs.* **Bahamas Ferries.** ✉ *From Potter's Cay Dock, Nassau* ☎ *242/323–2166* ⊕ *www.bahamasferries.com.* **FRS Caribbean Fast Bimini Shuttle.** ☎ *877/286–7220 toll-free* ⊕ *www.frs-caribbean.com.* **Potter's Cay Dockmaster's Office.** ☎ *242/393–1064.*

CAR TRAVEL

Blessedly devoid of rental cars, most of Bimini is accessed on foot or by golf cart. Car rentals are available on Andros and on Great Harbour Cay in the Berry Islands. Don't expect major companies; rentals are done through microenterprises and are usually arranged directly by the hotel or lodge. Most take credit cards but cash is handy. Rates range between $60 and $120 per day and average $85 per day. Especially in Andros, make sure to call in advance to have a rental car waiting upon arrival. Some Andros hotels and lodges offer free airport transfers.

TAXI TRAVEL

Taxis are readily available at airports to meet incoming flights and for sightseeing. On Andros's larger islands, most mail boats and ferries are greeted with one or two taxis. If not, you can often hitch a ride with a friendly islander going your way.

ANDROS

The Bahamas' largest island (100 miles long and 40 miles wide) and one of the least explored, Andros's landmass is carved up by myriad channels, creeks, lakes, and mangrove-covered cays. The natural **Northern, Middle,** and **South bights** cut through the width of the island, creating shallow boating access between both coasts. Andros is best known for its bonefishing and diving, and is also a glorious ecotourism spot with snorkeling, blue-hole exploration, sea kayaking, and nature hikes.

The Spaniards who came here in the 16th century called Andros *La Isla del Espíritu Santo*—the Island of the Holy Spirit—and it has retained its eerie mystique. The descendants of Seminole Indians and runaway slaves who left Florida in the mid-19th century settled in the North Andros settlement of **Red Bays** and remained hidden until a few decades ago. They continue to live as a tribal society, making a living by weaving straw goods. The Seminoles originated the myth of the island's legendary (and elusive) chickcharnies—red-eyed, bearded, green-feathered creatures with three fingers and three toes that hang upside down by their tails from pine trees. These mythical characters supposedly wait deep in the forests to wish good luck to the friendly passersby and vent their mischief on the hostile trespasser. The rest of Andros's roughly 8,000 residents live in a dozen settlements on the eastern shore. Farming and commercial fishing sustain the economy, and the island is the country's largest source of freshwater.

Andros's undeveloped **West Side** adjoins the Great Bahama Bank, a vast shallow-water haven for lobster, bonefish, and tarpon. Wild orchids and dense pine and mahogany forests cover the island's lush green interior. The marine life–rich **Andros Barrier Reef**—the world's third largest—is within a mile of the eastern shore and runs for 140 miles. Sheltered waters within the reef average 6 to 15 feet, but on the other side ("over the wall") they plunge to more than 6,000 feet at the **Tongue of the Ocean.**

GETTING HERE AND AROUND

AIR TRAVEL
Consult your hotel to figure out which airport to fly into. From north to south: serving North Andros is the **San Andros Airport (SAQ)**, serving Central Andros and Fresh Creek is **Andros Town Airport (ASD); Mangrove Cay Airport (MAY)** serves the island of the same name, and serving South Andros is **Congo Town Airport (TZN)**. All except Mangrove Cay are ports-of-entry, enabling customs clearance for private flights or charters directly from the United States. San Andros (SAQ) is best for hotels between Nicholl's Town to Stafford Creek, and is reachable from the United States via Watermakers Air four times a week and from Nassau via Western Air twice daily. Best for all other hotels in North and Central Andros is Andros Town airport, which sees the most traffic and is reachable from the United States by Watermakers Air four times a week. Le Air operates a twice daily service from Nassau's domestic terminal and Randolph Holdings Air Charters usually flies twice a day from Nassau Airport's General Aviation base, a short taxi ride from the main Nassau airport. Mangrove Cay Airport is reachable from Nassau twice daily via Le Air and Flamingo Air. Congo Town in South Andros is served by Watermakers Air from Fort Lauderdale Executive and Western Air from Nassau twice daily.

For groups and families, private charters from Miami, Fort Lauderdale, or Nassau can be an affordable, convenient option. From the United States are numerous charter services to all Andros airports including Watermakers Air and Air Flight Charters. If you're willing to splash out on luxurious travel, a float plane via Tropic Ocean Airways or a helicopter from Florida can be an exotic highlight.

Contacts Andros Town Airport. ☏ *242/368–2134.* **Congo Town Airport.** ☏ *242/369–2270.* **Mangrove Cay Airport.** ☏ *242/369–0270.* **San Andros Airport.** ☏ *242/329–4401.*

CAR RENTAL

All airports have jeeps or cars for rent from $70 to $120 a day, plus gas, depending on size and vehicle condition. Note that some resorts or lodges may also offer cars-plus-stay packages and free transfers to and from the airport. Lodges will often offer you a ride to wherever you want to go.

FERRY TRAVEL

Andros is divided by water into three parts: North and Central Andros, Mangrove Cay, and South Andros. Each is serviced by either a ferry or mail boat from Potter's Cay Dock in Nassau. Mail boats are good options for budgeting backpackers, adventurous students, or groups carrying lots of luggage such as film crews. Passage costs vary between mail boats from $35 to $65 one-way and may include a meal. The journey is often overnight and each vessel sails three or four times a month. Nicholl's Town and The Bluff in North Andros is served by M/V *Lady Rosalind*; Fresh Creek by Bahamas Ferries and the M/V *KCT*, Mangrove Cay and South Andros by the M/V *Capt. Moxey* and M/V *Lady Katherine*. Note that mail boats may make several stops, and due to their infrequency you may be marooned on your chosen island for days, if not weeks, until the next mail boat arrives. For the most up-to-date information on mail boat schedules, passengers should always consult the dockmaster in Potter's Cay in Nassau, weekdays 9 to 5. Once on North and Central Andros you have to fly or charter a boat to reach its southerly sister islands, but you can take the *Capt. Moxey* mail boat or the free twice-daily government ferry between Mangrove Cay and South Andros. The ferry is run by Frederick Major in a 30-foot outboard from Driggs Hill on South Andros to Lisbon Creek on Mangrove Cay, at 8 am and 4 pm. The journey takes around six minutes.

Contacts Frederick Major's Ferry Service. ☏ *242/376–8533, 242/395–3864* ⊕ *www.bahamas.com/andros.* **Potter's Cay Dockmaster's Office.** ☏ *242/393–1064.* **South Andros Tourist Office.** ☏ *242/369–1688* ⊕ *www.bahamas.com/andros.*

TAXI TRAVEL

Confirm with the hotel to see if your taxi will meet airplanes and ferries. Rates run around $1.50 per mile, though most fares are set and generally known. In North or South Andros fares can be quite a surprise; always ask your hotel and always agree on a fare before you set foot in a taxi. Taxis are also available for touring around the islands and, because of their friendliness, local knowledge, and insight, they often become vacation highlights. Tours will take you to shops, farms, restaurants, beaches, historic ruins, and blue holes—giving you a sense of the scene and recommendations on where to dine and more. Tour rates vary: for five passengers and up they start from $50 per person for a half day and $100 per person for a full day.

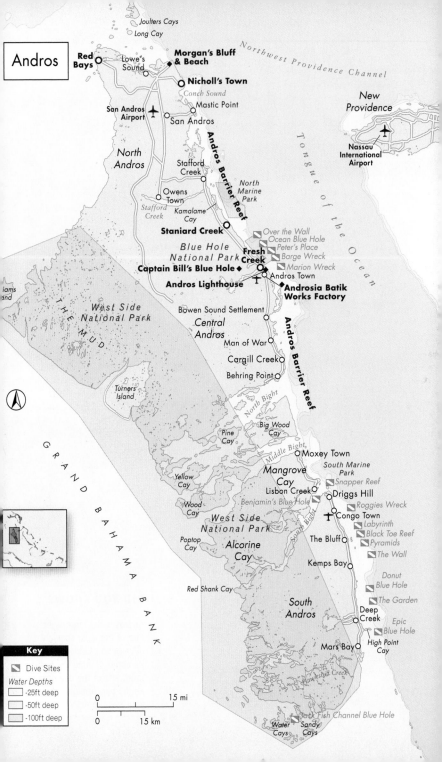

NORTH ANDROS

The northern part of Andros spreads from the settlements of **Morgan's Bluff, Nicholl's Town, Lowe's Sound,** and **Red Bays,** and ends at **Stafford Creek.** North Andros consists of long stretches of pine forests, limestone bluffs, and fields and gardens of ground crops. Seminole Indians, American slaves, and Mennonites settled this land along with the West Indian population. White-sand beaches, mostly deserted, line the island's eastern face, interrupted by creeks, inlets, and rock outcroppings. Logging supported North Andros in the 1940s and 1950s, and laid the foundation for its roads. Tourism, farming, and commercial fishing, especially in the west and the northernmost Joulters Cays, drives the economy today.

San Andros is home to North Andros's airport, but **Nicholl's Town** is the port and largest settlement here and in all of Andros. Once home to a vogue resort in the 1960s (Andros Beach Hotel), today it is mostly residential, inhabited in part by snowbirds who own the adorable Bahamian-style, brightly painted cottages that were once part of the iconic resort. Although recent repaving has improved the main highway, you'll often encounter potholes. Near the airport, road conditions are good; don't worry about traffic—you'll be lucky if you see more than 20 vehicles on the highway in a single day.

GETTING HERE AND AROUND

The San Andros airport (SAQ) has flights from Nassau through SkyBahamas and Western Air. Taxis meet incoming flights. You can get around on foot in Nicholl's Town; car rentals are available for exploring the island's 65 miles of Queen's Highway and feeder roads in the north. They run about $70 to $120 a day. Main roads in Central Andros are in good shape, but watch out for potholes in North Andros. If you're renting a car, call in advance to make sure your car is available at the airport.

Car Rentals CJ's Car Rental. ☎ 242/417–3386, 242/329–2080. **Executive Car Rentals.** ☎ 242/471–5259, 242/329–4081. **Gaitor's Car Rental.** ☎ 242/471–1550, 242/464–3151 ✉ andreadaphne@yahoo.com. **Tropical Car Rentals.** ☎ 242/329–2515.

EXPLORING

Morgan's Bluff & Beach. Three miles north of Nicholl's Town is a crescent beach, a headland known as Morgan's Bluff, and a set of caves named after the 17th-century pirate Captain Henry Morgan, who allegedly dropped off some of his stolen loot in the area. The beach and park is the site of Regatta Village, a colorful collection of stands and stalls used in July when the big event, the All Andros & Berry Islands Regatta, takes place. Adjacent is the Government Dock and a safe harbor, with a small, popular island bar and restaurant. ⊠ *Nicholl's Town.*

Nicholl's Town. Nicholl's Town, on Andros's northeastern corner, is a spread-out settlement with its eastern shore lying on a beautiful beach and its northern shore on Morgan's Bluff beach. It is the island's largest settlement, with a population of about 600. (Interestingly, the name used to be spelled Nicoll's Town, without the h.) This friendly community, with its agriculture- and fishing-based economy, has grocery and supplies stores, a few motels, a public medical clinic, government offices, and more. Adorable cottages, a throwback from the town's big resort era of the 1960s, house the island's wintering population from the United States, Canada, and Europe. ⊠ *Nicholl's Town.*

Red Bays. Fourteen miles west of Nicholl's Town, Red Bays is the sole west-coast settlement in all of Andros. The town was settled by Seminole Indians and runaway African slaves escaping Florida pre–Civil War and was cut off from the rest of Andros until a highway connected it to Nicholl's Town in the 1980s. Residents are known for their craftsmanship, particularly straw basketry and wood carving. Tightly plaited baskets, some woven with scraps of colorful Androsia batik, have become a signature craft of Andros. Artisans have their wares on display in front of their homes (with fixed prices). Despite opening their homes to buyers, Red Bays locals don't seem very used to visitors. Expect a lot of curious stares and occasional smiles. ⊠ *Red Bay Settlement.*

Uncle Charlie's Blue Hole. Mystical and mesmerizing, blue holes pock Andros's marine landscape in greater concentration than anywhere else on Earth—an estimated 160-plus—and provide entry into the islands' network of coral-rock caves. Offshore, some holes drop off to 200 feet or more. Inland blue holes reach depths of 120 feet, layered with fresh, brackish, and salt water. Uncle Charlie's Blue Hole is one of Andros's most popular with a 40-feet diameter, lined with picnic benches and a ladder. ⊠ *North Andros, north of San Andros airport, 300 yards off main highway after turnoff for Owen Town.*

BEACHES

If solitude is what you're searching for, you'll definitely find it on the beaches of North Andros. Long and secluded, you might find each beach with just one small resort or bar close by—and a few reefs for snorkeling.

Conch Sound & Ocean Hole. South of Nicholl's Town's eastern shore, Conch Sound is a wide bay with strands of white sand and tranquil waters where you can also find Conch Sound Ocean Hole, a sea-filled blue hole where you can snorkel around and see the rich marine life. The flats are a convenient wading spot for bonefishermen who can wade for hours. Commercial fishermen bring their catches to a little beach park nearby. You can buy fresh catch and dine at a couple of shacks. **Amenities:** only at nearby restaurants. **Best for:** solitude; fishing; snorkeling. ⊠ *Nicholl's Town.*

Nicholl's Town Beach. Two-and-a-half miles east of Nicholl's Town commercial center, the settlement reaches the east-facing coast along beautiful and long Nicholl's Town Beach, which catches the easterly breezes and is by far the preferred beach in this area. It adjoins Conch Sound to the south. You might be on your own except for guests at the renovated Andros Island Beach Resort with its tiki bar and restaurant, where you can rent kayaks or snorkeling gear. **Amenities:** resort nearby. **Best for:** solitude; swimming; walking. ⊠ *Nicholl's Town.*

WHERE TO STAY

$ RESORT FAMILY 🏨 **Andros Island Beach Resort.** Facing east on long, pristine Nicholl's Town Beach, this palm tree–festooned property offers three secluded beachfront cottages, four villas, and a beachside tiki bar and restaurant with beautiful views. **Pros:** gorgeous beach and water activities; on-site restaurant and bar; spacious villas with kitchens; gym and car rentals. **Cons:** breakfast usually self-catered; bug spray in summer and fall; rental car necessary. [$] *Rooms from: $185* ✉ *Nicholl's Town* ☎ *242/329–1009* 🌐 *www.androsislandbeachresorts.com* 🛏 *4 villas and 3 suites from 1 to 3 bedrooms* 🍴 *No meals.*

$ B&B/INN 🏨 **Love at First Sight.** At the mouth of Stafford Creek, self-sufficient anglers and do-it-yourself vacationers can sit on the sundeck or at the bar, sip a cold local beer or a cocktail, and contemplate the superb fishing and diving in Central Andros. **Pros:** restaurant and bar overlooking creek; quiet and clean. **Cons:** rental car necessary; basic rooms with amenities; not on beach. [$] *Rooms from: $130* ✉ *On main highway at mouth of Stafford Creek* ☎ *242/368–6082* 🌐 *www.loveatfirstsights.com* 🛏 *10 rooms.*

$ B&B/INN 🏨 **Pineville Motel.** This truly one-of-a-kind, eye-popping plot of land fits in 16 rooms, a petting zoo, a small disco, a movie theater, a bar, and a DIY gift shop—made mostly of recycled materials such as tires, reclaimed wood, and seashells. **Pros:** unique experience; cheap rates; enthusiastic owner. **Cons:** not near beach; basic accommodations; overcrowded petting zoo. [$] *Rooms from: $80* ✉ *Nicholl's Town* ☎ *242/329–2788, 242/557–4354* 🌐 *www.pinevillemotelandlodge.com* 🛏 *16 rooms* 🍴 *No meals.*

DINING AND NIGHTLIFE

Da Big Shop. Overlooking Nicholl's Town Beach, Da Big Shop is as local as it gets. The 200-year-old building used to be Andros's only trading post for the sponge harvesters; unfortunately, the building has not aged well, but the interior bar, open daily from noon until late, is a good time. On the weekends it has DJs and on some holidays, a live band. For lunch or dinner, try Da Big Shop's island dinners, sandwiches, burgers, and pastas. It tends to attract local anglers and North Andros's younger demographic. You might be the only tourists here. ✉ *Nicholl's Town* ☎ *242/225–2947, 242/329–2047* 🎟 *Free.*

$ BAHAMIAN ✕ **F&H Take Away.** This tiny shack on the water in Lowe's Sound is the quintessential Bahamian conch shack experience where owner will wade out in the water, select, and hammer out the conch before your eyes. Ask him to eat the extraneous pistile or bibby for a laugh. **Known for:** authentic Bahamian experience; extremely fresh catches; delicious seafood. [$] *Average main: $10* ✉ *Nicholl's Town* ✥ *Lowes Sound, 2 miles north of Nicholl's Town* ☎ *242/329–7143* 💳 *No credit cards.*

$ BAHAMIAN ✕ **Lil' Anchor Restaurant.** On the water at Conch Sound this cute shack of a restaurant is a great place for island-fresh fish, conch, and lobster in season. View the fishermen come in with their catches. **Known for:** local patronage; fresh fish and conch. [$] *Average main: $12* ✉ *Nicholl's Town* ☎ *242/464–3049, 242/429–4387* 💳 *No credit cards.*

Sweet Mahogany Lounge. This speakeasy-type indoor bar and lounge, which caters mostly to professional locals, is relaxing with its low lights, soft music, air conditioner, and auto-massaging chairs. Island and American dishes and sandwiches are available. Open Tuesday through Sunday, from 6 pm until late. ✚ *North of San Andros airport on Queen's Hwy.* 🕾 *242/329–5557* 💰 *Free.*

SPORTS AND THE OUTDOORS

Bonefishing. North Andros' north coast and the string of Joulter Cays lying 5 to 10 miles offshore, are among the country's richest fly-fishing grounds for bonefish and permit. Conch Sound and Lowes Sound are reachable by car and good for DIY fishing by wading, but to have full scope of the best fishing spots and to learn about this tricky craft of catching spooky bonefish, hire a skiff and Bahamian guide. Some of the country's leading guides operate in North Andros, and visiting enthusiasts flock to the local lodges to fish with them. They can also arrange diving and snorkeling tours. ✉ *North Andros* 🕾 *242/471–5299 Elias Griffin, 242/471–1535 Keith Russell, 242/357–2781 Phillip Rolle, 242/329–2661 North Andros Flyfishing* ⊕ *www.NorthAndrosFlyfishing.com.*

Deep Sea and Bottom Fishing. From Morgan's Bluff Harbour, Craig Curry takes out fishing charters to the reefs and shelfs for grouper and snapper bottom fishing and to the deep ocean Tongue of the Ocean for bill- and game fish. His 35-foot open fisherman comfortably accommodates 6; the larger 55-foot yacht can fit 10. Craig can also arrange snorkeling and scuba- diving tours. Call for rates. ✉ *North Andros* 🕾 *242/558–3799, 242/471–3339.*

Wild Boar Hunting. Perhaps oddly for such a passionate animal-lover, Eugene Campbell of Pineville Hotel offers sometimes thrilling guided wild boar hunting in the scrub forests of mid-west North Andros. With a vast National Park to escape to and live in, they have a similarly vast non-park habitat. They are not endangered and often hard to track down. Eugene closely guides up to three hunters and, because hunting the tusk-bearing boars is dangerous, he gives a mandatory safety lecture. Prices include hunting gear, transportation, and lunch. ✉ *North Andros* 🕾 *242/329–2788, 242/557–4354* ⊕ *www.pineville-motelandlodge.com* 💰 *$350 for half day and $600 for full day, with gear, transportation, and lunch included.*

CENTRAL ANDROS

Those arriving in **Central Andros** by Bahamas Ferries from Nassau will arrive in the village of **Fresh Creek**; those arriving by plane will arrive in neighboring **Andros Town** (the petite transportation and governmental hub). Both Fresh Creek and Andros Town, joined by a small bridge over the creek, are found midisland, on the east coast of North and Central Andros.

Heading north from Andros Town and Fresh Creek, Central Andros extends as far north as Stafford Creek, near Kamalame Cay, where the land officially becomes North Andros (though it's debated exactly where Central ends). As you head south from Andros Town airport, scrub pine forests and brush give way to mangroves and hardwood coppice. Long beaches scallop the eastern shoreline and the sole road, Queen's Highway, will bring you to the bonefishing villages of **Cargill Creek** and **Behring Point.** Here, along the bonefish sweet spot of **Northern Bight,** you'll find nice homes with flowering gardens, palm trees, and sea grapes that overlook the ocean or the wide estuary.

Central Andros accounts for 60% of Andros's entire hotel inventory. Those expecting the glitz and glamour of the Bahamas' megaresorts and more touristy islands should look elsewhere. Here the glamour is the romantic, natural type with open vistas of the beaches, tidal estuaries, pine forests, and distant barrier reef. However rustic it may seem, you'll find pockets of extraordinary excellence and success, notably the award-winning, luxurious private island resort **Kamalame Cay,** as well as the more homey, family-friendly, all-inclusive **Small Hope Bay Lodge,** and private villa **KettleStone.** This part of Andros has many simpler home rentals and bonefishing lodges with lodging, dining, and fishing packages. All lodging types attract many repeat visitors who come year after year (or a couple times every year) to savor Andros's beautiful beaches, reefs, and world-class diving and fishing.

Central Andros's famed and remote **West Side** is a national park that teems with mangrove estuaries, rich with marine life, including conch, lobster, bonefish barracuda, and small sharks. However, this uninhabited region is accessible only by private boat. Central Andros has several national parks, two marine parks offshore, Blue Hole National Park north of Fresh Creek and a Crab Reserve south of it.

GETTING HERE AND AROUND

Fly into Andros Town airport (ASD) with LeAir from Nassau, with Watermakers Air from Fort Lauderdale Executive (FXE) or Tropic Ocean Airways from Miami's Seaplane base at Watson Island or Fort Lauderdale International Airport (FLL). Randolph Holdings and Glen Air fly here regularly, even a couple times a day. Alternatively, take the three-hour Sealink ferry with Bahamas Ferries from Nassau to Fresh Creek. Taxis meet airplanes and ferries. The fare from the airport to Fresh Creek is $15; to Cargill Creek area, some 20 miles south of the airport, it costs about $40.

A number of car-rental operators are available (rentals start at $70 a day), but if you're staying in the Cargill Creek area, you'll probably be doing most of your traveling by boat. Many lodges will pick you up at the airport. In Andros Town and Fresh Creek you can easily get around to the local restaurants, beaches, and blue holes by bike and on foot. Good advice is to take a taxi tour early in your stay to get the lay of the land and meet a well-informed local. They know all the places to go, and where to shop and dine.

Car Rental Contacts Adderley's Car Rental. ⊠ *Fresh Creek* ☎ *242/357–2149.* **Rooney's Auto Car Rental.** ☎ *242/471–0346, 242/368–2255.* **Shorr's Car Rental.**

EXPLORING

Androsia Batik Works Factory. The Androsia Batik Works Factory in Andros Town is home to the famous Androsia batik that has been declared the official fabric of the Bahamas. Small Hope Bay Lodge's Birch family established it in 1973 to boost employment in Andros. The brightly colored hand-dyed cotton batik has designs inspired by Andros's flora, fauna, and culture. You can prearrange a batik lesson ($25) and make your own design on a choice of fabric, garment, or bag. Self-tours are free. The unique brand is seen and sold throughout the Bahamas, the Caribbean, and online. The outlet store (with different opening times) offers bargains on shirts, skirts, wraps, fabric, jewelry, books, crafts, and souvenirs. ⊠ *Andros Town* ☎ *242/368–2020* ⊕ *www.androsia.com.*

Andros Lighthouse. As you enter Fresh Creek Harbour, you'll see this historical lighthouse built circa 1892 to navigate boats into the southern entrance of Fresh Creek Channel. No longer in use, the lighthouse and a brace of rusty cannon near a delightful small beach is an island landmark and a picturesque view including a large, rusty old shipwreck. ⊠ *Andros Town* ⌇ *Free.*

Captain Bill's Blue Hole. One famous Andros sight that nature lovers should catch is Captain Bill's Blue Hole, one of hundreds in Andros and in the Bahamas National Trust's Blue Hole National Park. Blue holes are the top of extensive water-filled underground cave systems formed in the ice age. Located northwest of Small Hope Bay, the National Trust has made Captain Bill's popular and comfortable with a boardwalk and a shady gazebo. Steps allow you to jump 30 feet down to cool off and there's a nature trail around the hole's 400-foot diameter. Accessible by car or bike, Captain Bill's is included on most guided tours. ⊠ *Fresh Creek* ✛ *Go 2 miles north from Small Hope Bay, turn left (west) in Love Hill, and take white road 2.7 miles west* ☎ *242/368–2882 Steven Smith, national park warden* ⊕ *www.bnt.bs/parks/andros* ⌇ *Free.*

Fresh Creek. Fresh Creek is an estuary, a hamlet, and a harbor, forming the north side of Andros Town and the south side of Fresh Creek settlement, both joined by a small bridge. The north Fresh Creek side is more built up with a few docks, stores, churches, motels, and restaurants, including Hank's Place, a local hotspot. On the south Andros Town side, the ferry and mail boats offload at the dock next to the closed Andros Lighthouse Beach Club & Marina. You can still walk around the resort's point to get close to the lighthouse, small beach, and shipwreck. The Andros Tourist Office and some shops are a short walk away. The creek itself cuts over 16 miles into the island, creating tranquil bonefishing flats and welcoming mangrove-lined bays that boaters and sea kayakers can explore. Upstream, there's even a remote Sunset Point houseboat where you can stay surrounded by the flowing water and scintillating views. ⊠ *Fresh Creek* ⊕ *www.bahamas.com/andros* ⌇ *Free.*

Staniard Creek. Sand banks that turn gold at low tide lie off the northern tip of Staniard Creek, a small island settlement 9 miles north of Fresh Creek, accessed by a bridge off the main highway. Coconut palms and casuarinas shade the ocean-side beaches, and offshore breezes are pleasantly cooling. Kamalame Cove, part of nearby luxurious resort and private Kamalame Cay, are at the northern end of the settlement. Three creeks snake into the mainland, forming extensive mangrove-lined back bays and flats, good for wading and bonefishing. ✉ *Staniard Creek.*

BEACHES

Because they're famous for their off-the-chart fishing and diving, the islands of Andros often get shorted when talk turns to beaches. This is a great injustice, especially in the case of the long, deserted beaches defining Central Andros's east coast and the abandoned white-sand beaches of Central Andros's outlying cays.

Kamalame and The Saddleback Cays. East of Staniard Creek lies a series of serene cays, idyllic for beach drops or consummating the ultimate Robinson Crusoe fantasies. The first is Kamalame Cay, home to the luxurious resort of the same name. Just past Kamalame, uninhabited Big and Little Saddleback Cay boast sparkling, white-sand beaches and crystal-clear waters. You'll need a small, private boat to reach either (note that these cays are a regular drop point for guests of Kamalame Cay). Little Saddleback is tiny with no shade; so bring plenty of sunblock. Big Saddleback has a wider crescent beach, and plenty of shade from the pine trees. Also nearby is Rat Cay, which offers excellent snorkeling especially around the adjacent blue hole. **Amenities:** none. **Best for:** solitude; snorkeling; swimming; walking. ✉ *Staniard Creek.*

5

Small Hope Bay Beach. Small Hope Bay Lodge is planted squarely on this long, coved beach where the near-shore snorkeling is excellent and the sand is white. Sign up for a resort course, a dive excursion, or simply enjoy a $55 beachside lunch buffet (with advance notice). A full day of beach fun with breakfast, lunch, and dinner, and all drinks and water sports included, is $199. Nonguests can also enjoy dinner buffet with its open bar and music. **Amenities:** food and drink; showers; toilets; water sports. **Best for:** snorkeling; swimming; walking. ✉ *Small Hope Bay Lodge* ☎ *855/841–6966 toll-free U.S. and Canada, 242/368–2014 office* 🌐 *www.smallhope.com.*

Somerset Beach. Two miles south of Andros Town airport, off a long beaten-up bare road through an arch of Australia pines, is Somerset Beach, a stunning, long, and wide beach with offshore sandbars that let you walk offshore for half a mile. The pines offer shade and there's a picnic table built by the workers from AUTEC, the nearby U.S. Navy's submarine testing base. Bring a camera as this is one of the most beautiful beach sights in the Bahamas. **Amenities:** none. **Best for:** photography; shelling; swimming; walking.

WHERE TO EAT

$ BAHAMIAN 🍴 **Hank's Place Restaurant and Bar.** On the north side of Fresh Creek, near the bridge, this restaurant and bar juts out into the harbor and is graced with sweeping views. Locals, visitors, and workers from the nearby naval base enjoy Hank's for decent Bahamian dinners (chicken, fish, lobster, and pork), and for the popular dance parties on Saturday nights. **Known for:** Hanky Panky frozen cocktail; dance parties. [$] *Average main: $18* ✉ *Fresh Creek* ☎ *242/368–2447* 🌐 *www.hanksplace2.com* 🕒 *Closed Sun. and Mon.*

$$$ CARIBBEAN Fodor's Choice ★ 🍴 **Kamalame Cay.** If you're not a guest on Kamalame Cay's private island resort you might have to travel miles to enjoy this casual but luxurious dining experience, which is every bit worthwhile. Set on one of the Bahamas' most beautiful beaches, Kamalame's guests gather to enjoy cocktails at the poolside Tiki Bar then spread out in the Big House to enjoy Andros's top cuisine. **Known for:** romantic setting; fixed menu; innovative dishes. [$] *Average main: $33* ✉ *Kamalame Cay Resort, Staniard Creek.*

$$$$ BAHAMIAN 🍴 **Small Hope Bay Lodge.** Unless you're a lucky all-inclusive guest at this resort famous for its diving and fishing, the best way to enjoy it is to buy an all-inclusive $199 day pass allowing you breakfast, lunch, dinner, and bar drinks (starting at lunchtime). From 7 am to 10 pm you can enjoy all the facilities and equipment on Small Hope's gorgeous beach: kayaks, windsurfers, sailboats, snorkeling, paddleboards, and the fresh whirlpool on the gorgeous beach. Just dinner and wine is $90 per person, and does not include bar drinks. [$] *Average main: $99* ✉ *Small Hope Bay* ☎ *242/368–2014* 🌐 *www.smallhope.com.*

WHERE TO STAY

$$$$ B&B/INN 🏨 **Andros Island Bonefish Club** (*AIBC*). If you're a dedicated bonefisher, AIBC is the place for you. **Pros:** outdoor deck and bar idyllic for fishing stories; prime location on Cargill Creek; waterslide. **Cons:** not much for nonanglers; basic accommodations. [$] *Rooms from: $485* ✉ *Cargill Creek* ☎ *242/368–5167* 🌐 *www.androsbonefishing.com* 🛏 *12 rooms* 🍽 *All meals.*

$$$$ B&B/INN 🏨 **Big Charlie's & Fatiha's Fishing Lodge.** On the banks of Cargill Creek, this small and charming bonefishing lodge is run by Charlie Neymour, a bonefishing legend, and his wife, Fatiha, who serves deliciously aromatic Moroccan and Mediterranean cuisine in the dining room—with tasty fresh seafood Bahamian-style as well. **Pros:** pristine facilities; fridges, satellite TV, and Wi-Fi in rooms; unusually good cuisine for a lodge. **Cons:** beach is some distance; only for fishing fans. [$] *Rooms from: $500* ✉ *Cargill Creek* ☎ *242/368–4297* 🌐 *www.bigcharlieandros.net* 🛏 *4 rooms, 8 guests maximum* 🍽 *All-inclusive.*

$$$$ B&B/INN 🏨 **Hank's Place & Boat Rentals.** Hank's Place, with its restaurant and bar next door, offers four spacious, comfy rooms on the water for $95 double occupancy. **Pros:** central convenience; on the water; seven-night package with meals and boat; on-site restaurant. **Cons:** basic but clean; loud music Saturday night. [$] *Rooms from: $1105* ✉ *Fresh Creek* ☎ *242/357–2214 cell, 242/368–2447* 🛏 *4 standard rooms* 🍽 *All meals.*

$$ RESORT Fodor's Choice ★ 🏨 **Kamalame Cay.** An all-inclusive resort with individual villas spaced along a 3-mile beach, the breathtaking and private 96-acre Kamalame Cay occupies a Bahamian pinnacle in luxury island retreats—and is surprisingly affordable. **Pros:** private white-sand beaches; quiet, remote location; discreet pampering; delicious, innovative food; on-site overwater spa. **Cons:** Wi-Fi only in reception area; eye mask needed for sleeping past sunrise; round-trip airport transfers are costly. [$] *Rooms from: $250* ✉ *Staniard Creek* ✥ *At north end of Staniard Creek* ☎ *242/368–6281, 800/768–9423* 🌐 *www.kamalame.com* ⏲ *Closed Aug. 10–Oct. 7* 🛏 *5 cottages, 5 villas, 9 rooms* 🍽 *All-inclusive.*

DID YOU KNOW?

In the Bahamas, mail is still delivered by mail boats, and has been for decades. Mail boats leave Nassau's Potter's Cay carrying mail, cars, produce, consumer goods, and passengers on trips to more than 30 Bahamian islands, including Andros, a four-hour cruise.

$$$$ RENTAL FAMILY Fodor's Choice ★ **KettleStone Luxury Villa.** Perched on a small bluff overlooking Andros's Barrier Reef, this dreamy newly constructed luxury villa provides a consummate private getaway. **Pros:** oceanfront luxury; very private; near town; freshwater pool and free snorkeling. **Cons:** must drive to beach; self-catered or hired chef; not a resort. [$] *Rooms from: $857* ✉ *Fresh Creek* ☎ *242/357–2746 cell, 800/827–7048 toll-free in U.S. and Canada* 🌐 *www.kettlestoneluxuryvilla.com* 🛏 *3 bedrooms sleeping 8 maximum* 🍴 *No meals.*

$$$$ HOTEL FAMILY Fodor's Choice ★ **Small Hope Bay Lodge.** This casual, lusciously palm-shaded beach and oceanfront property is more than 50 years strong and offers 17 private cottages, a main dining clubhouse, lounge, and waterfront terrace and bar. **Pros:** best dive operation on Andros; air-conditioning; free Wi-Fi in public areas; all-inclusive options; camaraderie; friendly service. **Cons:** in summer you'll need insect repellent; hot tub instead of pool. [$] *Rooms from: $572* ✉ *Small Hope Bay* ☎ *242/368–2014 resort, 800/223–6961 toll-free* 🌐 *www.smallhope.com* 🛏 *17 cottages* 🍴 *All-inclusive.*

$$$ B&B/INN **Sunset Point House Boat.** If you're into nature and relaxation, this B&B on Fresh Creek lets you snorkel under your lodge and view birds, fish, rays, and maybe even dolphins passing mere feet away. **Pros:** private, serene, and ecoimmersed; self-catered or cook for hire; expert Andros tourism guide. **Cons:** too quiet for some; children must be eight years or older and able to swim; car rental often needed. [$] *Rooms from: $375* ✉ *Fresh Creek* ✥ *1¼ miles west of Fresh Creek Bridge, on southern side of estuary* ☎ *242/357–2061 cell* 🌐 *www.sunsetpointhouseboat.com* 🛏 *3 beds, 3 baths, available for 2 to 6 persons* 🍴 *No meals.*

NIGHTLIFE

Hank's Place. The over-water bar at Hank's Place Restaurant and Bar is *the* place to be on Saturday and some Fridays. Sunset is more of a relaxed scene; but come late night the music gets louder, people get "happier," and the dancing begins! It's also enjoyed by mostly young workers from the nearby AUTEC U.S. Navy base. It's open from 2 pm to 10 pm Tuesday to Friday, and until 3 am on Saturday. ✉ *Fresh Creek* ☎ *242/368–2447, 242/357–2214 cell* 🌐 *hanksplace2.com.*

SHOPPING

Fodor's Choice ★ **Androsia Store.** Adjacent to the Androsia Batik Works Factory is the Androsia Store, where you can buy original fabrics, clothing, bags, souvenirs, and stuffed toys. Designed with island-inspired natural and cultural motifs, Androsia is popular nationwide and is the official fabric of the Bahamas. ✉ *Andros Town* ☎ *242/368–2080* 🌐 *www.androsia.com* 🕒 *Closed Sun.*

5

SPORTS AND THE OUTDOORS
BOATING AND FISHING

Andros fishermen claim the island is the world's best bonefishing location, and legends at Central Andros's south end are famed for pioneering the field of fly-fishing and island fishing lodges. The four main fishing regions are the hard-to-reach West Side flats, the creeks (Stafford, Staniard, and Fresh), the Joulters Cays north of Andros, and the bights between Central and South Andros. Fishermen will find a wealth of knowledgeable bonefishing guides in the **Cargill Creek–Behring Point** area who will take you into the Northern Bight and West Side for some of the world's best bonefishing. Full-day fishing excursions cost about $500 to $600 for two. Better value are the lodges' guided bonefishing, lodging, and dining packages that work out to range from $400 to $660 per person per day at the half dozen lodges in the area.

Reef and deep-sea fishing excursions are secondary although you can catch snapper, and in season, grouper, along with game fish mahimahi, wahoo, and tuna.

Andra "Andy" Smith. Andy is a living legend and highly recommended for guiding anglers through Andros's bights and to the bonefish-rich West Side, for both novices and professionals. Andy now has his own exclusive fishing lodge at Broad Shad Cay, located in the middle of North Bight, accessible from either Andros Town airport with a 25-mile taxi ride (about $60) to the dock and a further 25-minute boat ride with Andy, or from Mangrove Cay's Moxey Town airport, with a 5-minute taxi ride and 25-minute boat ride. ⊠ *Behring Point* ☎ *242/368–4261, 242/225–0082.*

Charlie Neymour. Legend and expert guide Charlie Neymour is popular for guided fishing expeditions; now he and his wife Fatiha own a cute new bonefishing lodge with excellent island and Moroccan cuisine, plus fishing, dining, and lodging packages. The lodge is in Behring Point near the expansive flats. ⊠ *Behring Point* ☎ *242/368–4297* ⊕ *www.bigcharlieandros.net.*

Rupert Leadon. Led by owner Rupert, expert fishing guides have modern flats skiffs to whisk you to nearby or distant fishing grounds in the North Bight, the famed West Side for bonefish and permit, or to the barrier reef and the shelf off Tongue of the Ocean for grouper, snapper, marlin, sailfish, mahimahi, or wahoo, with all the gear you need. The Leadon family operate the Andros Island Bonefish Club one of Andros's best specialty lodges where prices include all meals and guided fishing on skiffs. ⊠ *Cargill Creek* ☎ *242/368–5167* ⊕ *www.androsbonefishing.com.*

Fodor'sChoice
★
Small Hope Bay Lodge. A famous and popular Andros diving and bonefishing resort, Small Hope Bay Lodge has bone-, deep-sea, fly-, and reef-fishing, as well as vast flats rich in bonefish and tarpon in the 20-mile-long Fresh Creek and more on the West Side. Small Hope offers more variety than regular fishing lodges: a fabulous beach with free kayaks, paddleboards, and bikes, superb diving, sumptuous buffets, open bar, and a strong sense of camaraderie. Rates for bonefishing in Fresh Creek and reef-fishing are $385 for a hal f day and $550 for a full day. Deep-sea rates are $500 for half a day and $700 for a full day

(with all gear and lunch). Small Hope books seven of the top bonefishing guides in Andros including Glaister Wallace, known for his magical casting skills. Book in advance. ⊠ *Small Hope Bay* ☎ *242/368–2014* ⊕ *www.smallhope.com.*

SCUBA DIVING AND SNORKELING

Divers can't get enough of the sprawling **Andros Barrier Reef,** the world's third largest, stretching the length of the island's east coast, ½ to 3 miles offshore. Boats from local lodges and resorts bring guests to beautiful parts of the reef to relish in underwater rapture. Snorkelers can explore such reefs as the Trumpet Reef, where visibility is clear 15 feet to the sandy floor and jungles of elkhorn coral snake up to the surface. Divers can delve into the 60-foot-deep coral caves of the Black Forest, beyond which the wall slopes down to depths of 6,000 feet. Anglers can charter boats to fish offshore or over the reef, and bonefishers can wade the flats on their own. While the marine life is not as rich nor as diverse as one would expect from such a vibrant, healthy reef, the assemblies of coral are breathtaking.

Fodor's Choice ★ **Kamalame Cay.** The luxury, all-inclusive resort on private Kamamale Cay offers bespoke diving, dive certification, and snorkeling tours on top of its all-inclusive rates. For the four- to five-day PADI Open Water Certification with nine dives you can do theory at home or, with the cay's instructors, either online or at the resort starting from $740 (with multiple divers). Two-hour resort courses are from $197 to $292 depending on group size. Fabulous snorkeling tours are also available from $140 for the first hour and $80 for additional. With all that it offers on the cay and the barrier reef, it's probably one of the nicest places in the world to gain certification. ⊠ *Central Andros* ☎ *876/632–3213, 800/790–7971* ⊕ *www.kamalame.com.*

Fodor's Choice ★ **Small Hope Bay Lodge.** Andros's top dive center is full-service with resort dives, PADI certification courses, one- and two-tank dives, specialty dives such as shark and night, and snorkeling. One-tank dives are $90, two-tanks are $110, and a day with three dives is $140. Rental equipment is available for Small Hope Bay Lodge excursions only. Lodging dive packages are offered. Hot showers await after long days at sea. ⊠ *Small Hope Bay* ☎ *242/368–2014, 800/223–6961* ⊕ *www. smallhope.com.*

MANGROVE CAY

Home to 800 resilient, friendly locals, remote Mangrove Cay is sandwiched between two sea-green bights, separating it from Central and South Andros and creating an island of shorelines strewn with washed-up black coral, gleaming deserted beaches, and dense pine forests. **Moxey Town,** known locally as Little Harbour, is historically based on commercial fishing and conch and sponge harvesting and rests on the northeast corner in a coconut grove. Pink piles of conch shells and mounds of porous sponges dot the small harbor. Anglers come on a mission, in search of giant bonefish on flats called "the promised land" and "land of the giants." A five-minute boat ride takes fly-fishers to Gibson Cay to wade hard sand flats sprinkled with starfish.

GETTING HERE AND AROUND

From Nassau twice daily, Flamingo Air and LeAir fly a scheduled service to Mangrove Cay Airport (MAY), located in Moxey Town. Through many services you can charter from Nassau or from Fort Lauderdale with Tropic Ocean Airways's float planes or Watermakers Air. Taxis meet airplanes and mail boats from Nassau, and taxi tours are a great way to get to know the island with all its shops, restaurants, and attractions.

Rent a car from Gaitor's or PB's car rentals at the airport from $80 to $100 a day. The cay's main road runs south from Moxey Town, past the airport, then along coconut-tree-shaded beaches to the settlement of Lisbon Creek.

Frederick Major runs the free government ferry linking Mangrove Cay with South Andros. In his 30-foot outboard, it takes a few minutes to run from Lisson Creek to Drigg's Hill—or a few more minutes to reach Tiamo Resort and a lodge along the Southern Bight's north shore. The ferry leaves Drigg's Hill twice a day at 8 am and 4 pm. The proposed ferry link from Mangrove Cay to Central Andros Island (Behring Point) has been put on hold.

Transport Contacts Frederick Major Ferry Services. ☎ 242/376–8533, 242/395–3864. **Gaitor's Car Rental.** ☎ 242/329–3655, 242/464–3151. **Henson "Harry" Saunders Taxi & Tours.** ☎ 242/369–0312. **Patrick King Taxi & Tours. PB's Car Rental.** ☎ 242/471–1126.

EXPLORING

With its beautiful wildlife along its coastline, tidal flats, and limestone caves, Mangrove Cay offers days of adventuresome exploring and sightseeing. Ask your local lodge about guided tours. Patrick King or Harry Saunders will take you around the cay's 8 miles to see Little Harbour and the fisherman's dock with its fresh catches of lobster, conch, grouper, and snapper. You can also explore caves, myriad churches, and small souvenir stalls replete with Mangrove Cay sponges. Ask to visit Ralph Moxey, another kind of Andros legend, in his case, in the crafts of boat-building and carving. Ralph has built many island sloops, won many races, and, today, carves miniatures out of local woods like Andros Mahogany and Sapodilla along with shell crafts. He can also teach you about bush medicine and the healing qualities of local plants such as Noni, Naked Wood, Strongback, and more. Visit Diane Cash's souvenir and craft store to browse her raffia-and-shell-decorated straw dolls, hats, bags, billfolds, and fish- and star-shaped bags. Dine and sample tropical homemade breads from Rosa Bullard's Four Kid's Bakery & Restaurant.

Victoria Point Blue Hole. On an island known for magical blue holes, the Victoria Point Blue Hole is Mangrove Cay's superb ocean hole for snorkeling and diving. Just ask the folks at Swain's Cay Lodge or Seascape Inn—or any local—to point out where to find it. ⊠ *Mangrove Cay*.

WHERE TO EAT

If you stay at one of Mangrove Cay's lodges, you're sure to be served fresh, delicious island fare, usually as part of your lodging and fishing package. You can, however, also explore other lodges. It's a great way to get to know them, so long as you book a day ahead. Swain's Cay Lodge is a wonderful dining spot on the beach, 3 miles south of the airport on the main road. Enjoy fresh catches, conch, lobster, and more island dishes either alfresco on the beachfront porch or in the cool inside. The island's famous conch stand is Shine's One-Stop Conch Shack north and then west of the airport road, sitting on the edge of Middle Bight. Here, enclosed in air-conditioning and away from flies, enjoy conch and fresh fish myriad ways. Some snowbirds and second-home owners treat themselves to Tiamo Resort's finer dining by taking the Tiamo's free ferry from Lisbon Creek (south Mangrove Cay) to the resort on South Andros. Explore other eateries as you bike, drive, or walk around other settlements on the 7-mile-long cay.

$$ BAHAMIAN 🍴 **Seascape Inn's Barefoot Bar and Grill.** Every table has a nice ocean view at this warm and friendly beachfront restaurant and bar at the Seascape Inn. Owners Mickey and Joan McGowan do the baking and cooking themselves. **Known for:** homemade ice cream; chocolate ganache; fresh catch of the day. [$] *Average main: $24* ✉ *Seascape Inn* ☎ *242/369–0342* 🌐 *www.seascapeinn.com.*

$$ BAHAMIAN 🍴 **Shine's One-Stop Conch Shack.** Also known as Greene's after its owner Ornald "Shine" Greene, this waterfront spot on Little Harbour is as close to nightlife as you'll get on Mangrove Cay—live music is rare (certainly there during homecoming and regatta festivals) but if the island's busy or a big group requests it, they'll arrange a live band. Dominoes and backgammon with reggae and calypso tunes add to the upbeat ambience as you view the harbor, sip a beer of Goombay Smash, and tuck into the daily catch of fish, conch, and lobster. **Known for:** lively ambience; outstanding hospitality; excellent fresh ceviche. [$] *Average main:* ✉ *Mangrove Cay* ☎ *242/369–0078* 🎫 *Free* 💳 *No credit cards.*

$$ BAHAMIAN 🍴 **Swain's Cay Reefside Restaurant.** Swain's Cay Lodge's beachside Reefside Restaurant & Bar is a local dining and cocktail-sipping hotspot serving delicious authentic Bahamian cuisine for B, L & D, supported with a well-stocked bar. (Nonguests are welcome, but book in advance.) The decor is modern contemporary and big windows and glass doors give it a bright ambience. Dine inside in air-conditioned comfort or on the beachside deck. **Known for:** extensive drinks menu; warm hospitality; authentic cuisine. [$] *Average main: $22* ✉ *Mangrove Cay* ☎ *242/422–5018 cell* 🌐 *www.swainscaylodge.com.*

WHERE TO STAY

$ B&B/INN 🏨 **Seascape Inn.** One of Andros's few lodging options catering to more than fishermen, Seascape Inn is a small, rustic beachfront gem; five individual, well-maintained cottages with private decks overlook the glass-clear ocean. **Pros:** quiet beachfront location; outstanding food; great snorkeling, kayaking, and bird-watching on-site. **Cons:** no air-conditioning; no TV; insect repellent a must. [$] *Rooms from: $159* ✉ *Mangrove Cay* ☎ *242/369–0342* 🌐 *www.seascapeinn.com* 🛏 *5 cottages* 🍽 *Breakfast.*

$ B&B/INN 🏨 **Swain's Cay Lodge.** This petite, beachfront resort is a gem for bonefishing fans and escape artists who want to enjoy Andros's natural beauty in peace and quiet. **Pros:** beachfront; excellent island food; free transfers to airport and tours. **Cons:** sleeps only 22; beach is shallow for swimming. [$] *Rooms from: $170* ✉ *Mangrove Cay* ☎ *242/422–5018* 🌐 *www.swainscaylodge.com* 🛏 *3 rooms and 1 3-bed apartment with kitchenette* 🍽 *Breakfast.*

Undersea Adventures in Andros

Andros probably has the largest number of dive sites in the country. With the third-longest barrier reef in the world (behind those of Australia and Belize), the island offers about 100 miles of drop-off diving into the Tongue of the Ocean.

Uncounted numbers of **blue holes** are forming in the area. In some places these constitute vast submarine networks that can extend more than 200 feet down into the coral (Fresh Creek, 40–100 feet; North Andros, 40–200-plus feet; South Bight, 40–200 feet). Blue holes are named for their inky-blue aura when viewed from above and for the light-blue filtered sunlight that is visible from many feet below. Some of the holes have vast cathedral-like interior chambers with stalactites and stalagmites, offshoot tunnels, and seemingly endless corridors. Others have distinct thermoclines (temperature changes) between layers of water and are subject to tidal flow.

The dramatic Fresh Creek site provides an insight into the complex Andros cave system. There isn't much coral growth, but there are plenty of midnight parrot fish, big southern stingrays, and some blacktip sharks. Similar blue holes are all along the barrier reef, including several at Mastic Point in the north and the ones explored and filmed off South Bight.

Undersea adventurers also have the opportunity to investigate wrecks such as the *Potomac*, a steel-hulled freighter that sank in 1952 and lies in 40 feet of water off Nicholl's Town. And off the waters of Fresh Creek, at 70 feet, lies the deteriorated 56-foot-long World War II LCM (landing craft mechanized) known only as the

Barge Wreck, which was sunk in 1963 to create an artificial reef. Newer and more intact, the *Marian* wreck lies in 70 feet. Both are encrusted with coral and are home to a school of groupers and a blizzard of tiny silverfish. You'll find fish-cleaning stations where miniature cleaning shrimp and yellow gobies clean grouper and rockfish by swimming into their mouths and out their gills, picking up food particles. It's an excellent subject matter for close-up photography.

The multilevel **Over the Wall** dive at Fresh Creek takes novices to depths of 65–80 feet and experienced divers to 120–185 feet. The wall is covered with black coral and all kinds of tube sponges. **Small Hope Bay Lodge** is the most long-respected dive resort on Andros. It's a friendly, informal place where the only thing taken seriously is diving and fishing. There's a fully equipped dive center with a wide variety of specialty dives, including customized family-dive trips with a private dive boat and dive master. If you're not certified, check out the lodge's morning resort course and be ready to explore the depths by afternoon. If you are certified, don't forget to bring your C card.

If you are leery of diving but want to view the spectacular undersea world, try a snorkeling excursion. Shallow reefs, beginning in 6 feet of water, and extending down to 60 feet or more, are ideal locations for spotting myriad brightly colored fish, sea urchins, and starfish. Don't forget your underwater camera.

Winter water temperatures average about 74°F. In summer, water temperatures average about 84°F.

Tiamo Resort is the most luxurious resort in South Andros.

SOUTH ANDROS

South Andros's road stretches 25 miles from **Drigg's Hill**—a small settlement of pastel houses, a tiny church, a grocery store, the government dock, and the Emerald Palms Resort—to Mars Bay. Eight miles farther south, the Bluff settlement sprawls atop a hill overlooking miles of golden beaches, lush cays, and the Tongue of the Ocean. Here skeletons of Arawak peoples were found huddled together. A local resident attests that another skeleton was found—this one of a 4-foot-tall, one-eyed owl, which may have given rise to the legend of the mythical, elf-like chickcharnie. South Andros is laced with an almost continuous set of beaches on the northwest and east coast, and more than 15 boutique resorts, bonefishing lodges, inns, and rentals are scattered along the island's many small settlements. It's a magnet for serious anglers and divers alike.

GETTING HERE AND AROUND

The Congo Town Airport (TZN) is 4 miles south of Drigg's Hill and receives flights four times a week from Fort Lauderdale Executive Airport (FXE) via Watermakers Air and daily flights from Nassau (NAS) via Western Air. Nassau-based Golden Wings Charters is a respected charter company that can be used to reach South Andros. For the ultimate thrill and the convenience of flying direct to your resort's beach or dock, charter a seaplane either with Miami Seaplane Tours & Charters or Safari Seaplanes from Nassau. Taxis and many lodges and hotels meet incoming flights and ferries.

A free government ferry operated by Frederick Major's Ferry Services makes the quick trip between Mangrove Cay and South Andros twice daily. It departs from South Andros at 8 am and 5 pm and from Mangrove Cay soon after. Schedules (and weather) are subject to change.

Transport Contacts Frederick Major Ferry Services. ☎ 242/376–8533, 242/395–3864. **Lee Meadows Taxi Service.** ☎ 242/369–5029. **Lenglo Car Rental.** ✉ South Andros, Congo Town ☎ 242/369–1702. **Rahming's Rental Car.** ☎ 242/369–1608. **Shirley Forbes Taxi Service.** ☎ 242/369–2930.

WHERE TO STAY

$$$$
ALL-INCLUSIVE
🖼 **Andros Beach Club.** In Kemp's Bay, 10 miles south of Congo Town Airport, Andros Beach Club lies on a beach of powder soft sand that stretches uninterrupted for almost 4 miles north. **Pros:** on fabulous beach; excellent diving and instructing; includes delicious meals; safe and secluded. **Cons:** remote and petite; fairly basic. $ *Rooms from: $542* ✉ *Deep Creek* ✛ *10 miles south of Congo Town Airport* ☎ *954/681–4818, 242/369–1454 resort* ⊕ *www.androsbeachclub.com* ✑ *7 rooms* ⦿ *All meals.*

$$
HOTEL
🖼 **The Pointe Resort & Marina.** This modern, smart, two-story resort with six suites, a restaurant, bar, and small marina makes great use of the views on a breathtaking point south of Kemp's Bay. Favoring bonefishing and diving fans, the rooms all have air-conditioning, fans, kitchenettes, free Wi-Fi, and DirectTV. **Pros:** clean and modern ambience; gorgeous views; popular on-site restaurant good for groups. **Cons:** long taxi ride from airport; call in advance for dining; not on beach. $ *Rooms from: $262* ✉ *Deep Creek* ⊕ *www.thepointeresortsouthandros.com* ✑ *4 rooms with kitchettes* ⦿ *No meals.*

$$$$
RESORT
Fodor'sChoice
★
🖼 **Tiamo Resort & Spa.** At this chic hideaway for jetsetters in-the-know you might feel like you're in French Polynesia, yet it is one of the Atlantic's last great secrets. **Pros:** 1½-to-1 staff-to-guest ratio; spectacular private beachfront location; great cuisine and water sports. **Cons:** alcohol not included in rates; insect repellent a must; only accessible by resort's ferry. $ *Rooms from: $900* ✉ *South Bight, Driggs Hill* ✛ *3-mile boat ride from Driggs Hill or Lisbon Creek (Mangrove Cay)* ☎ *242/225–6871 within Bahamas, 786/374–2442 in U.S. and Canada* ⊕ *www.tiamoresorts.com* ⊙ *Closed Sept. and Oct.* ✑ *2 small rooms, 11 villas (3 large, 8 medium; 9 with pools, 2 without)* ⦿ *All meals.*

SPORTS AND THE OUTDOORS

FISHING

Reel Tight Charters. Usually operated by Jesse from Abaco Beach Club, an experienced diving instructor, this renowned charter company is often hired by other resorts and lodges on South Andros. With its 25-foot 300HP catamaran and 14-foot skiff, they offer a variety of excursions, mostly in South Andros but also farther afield such as Green Cay on the other side of Tongue of the Ocean. Tours, including deep-sea, reef, and spearfishing, plus diving, snorkeling, private island picnics, and blue hole exploring tours. They also rent water-sports gear and kayaks. ✉ *Drigg's Hill Marina, Driggs Hill* ☎ *242/369–1454 Bahamas, 954/681–4818 in U.S. and Canada.*

BIMINI

Bimini has long been known as the Bahamas' big game-fishing capital. Bimini's strong tourist season falls from spring through summer, when calmer seas mean the arrival of fishing and pleasure boats from South Florida. The nearest of the Bahamian islands to the U.S. mainland, Bimini consists of two main islands and a few cays just 50 miles east of Miami, across the Gulf Stream that sweeps the area's western shores. Most visitors spend their time on bustling North Bimini; South Bimini is quieter and more ecooriented. Except for the vast new Resorts World Bimini development that occupies the island's northern third, most of the hotels, restaurants, churches, and stores in Bimini are in capital **Alice Town** and neighboring **Bailey Town** and **Porgy Bay,** along North Bimini's King's and Queen's highways. Along the east coast of North Bimini are long beaches; on the west, the protected harbor, docks, and marinas. Most of the islands' 2,500 inhabitants reside in the southern 2-mile southern built-up area. Although Alice Town is walkable, the preferred (and fun) way to scoot around is by golf cart. Resorts World Bimini has increased North Bimini's bustle and economy. Three times a week, the FRS Caribbean Fast Ferry takes up to 427 passengers to Bimini in two hours from Miami, who spread around the island enjoying its beaches, eateries, bars, nightclubs, and casino.

Sparsely populated **South Bimini** is where Juan Ponce de León allegedly looked for the Fountain of Youth in 1513, and a site with a well and natural trail memorialize it. More engaging, however, is the island's biological field station, known as the Sharklab for its study of lemon-, hammerhead-, and nurse-shark behavior and tracking, among other things. The main resort on this island is the modern, marina-based, Bimini Sands Resort & Marina that sits atop of a gorgeous mile-long beach. South Bimini is much more low key than North Bimini, a slower pace loved by hundreds of visiting residents (and some visiting boating partiers) who have built nearly 80 homes in Port Royal on the island's southern tip.

Salvagers, gunrunners, rum-runners, and the legendary Ernest Hemingway peopled the history of Bimini. Hemingway wrote much of *To Have and Have Not* and *Islands in the Stream* here between fishing forays and street brawls.

GETTING HERE AND AROUND
AIR TRAVEL
South Bimini's teensy airport (BIM) was enlarged and improved in 2015 thanks to help from Resorts World Bimini, to cope with the extra traffic it brings. South Bimini Airport receives flights via Elite Airways twice a week from Orlando Airport (MLB), and a jet service from Newark Liberty (EWR). Silver Airways, with its feeder network of many Florida cities, flies in from Fort Lauderdale (FLL) twice a day. Tropic Ocean Airways with its float planes fly from Miami's Watson Island Seaplane base (MPB) and Fort Lauderdale International (FLL) straight to North Bimini Harbour (NSB), docking at Resort World. From Nassau, Western Air and Flamingo Air fly to South Bimini daily and Flamingo also has a daily schedule from Grand Bahama

Airport (FPO). Numerous operators from Florida and Nassau fly into South Bimini. More than six charter airlines fly from Fort Lauderdale: Apollo Jets from FLL, Island Air Charters, and Watermakers Air and Bahamas Express from FXE. To reach North Bimini (Alice Town) from South Bimini Airport, you take a short taxi ride ($3) from the airport and a five-minute ferry ($2). The ferry runs until 10 pm or so for staff and guests who live on South Bimini.

Contacts Bimini Airport. ☎ *242/347–4111.*

BOAT AND FERRY TRAVEL

Three times a week (Wednesday, Friday, and Sunday) FRS Caribbean's fast ferry whisks visitors and day-trippers to North Bimini, docking at Resorts World's new ocean-side pier. Accommodating more than 400 passengers in relative spacious comfort, the high-speed catamaran *San Gwann* departs Terminal H in The Port Of Miami and covers the 49 nautical miles in only two hours. Business Class includes everything in Economy Class but adds a light lunch and snack and discounts at the duty-free store. You can choose day trips from $70 plus taxes, giving you seven hours on Bimini. (Oddly, if you book a ferry ticket for longer, such as three days, the price rises to $198 per person.) You can book a ferry-and-stay at the Hilton, which, for the lodging, works to be around $235 per night, double occupancy. RWB's website, however, usually offers great ferry-and-stay specials as well as exciting party weekends with live bands and more. Of course, with a ferry-only ticket, you don't have to stay at the Hilton; you can choose any of Bimini's hotels or inns.

Although rarely chosen, you can also sail to Bimini by old-fashioned mail boat. Contact the Dockmaster in Potter's Cay in Nassau at or the Bimini mail boat office at ☎ *242/347–3203* for an up-to-date schedule. M/V *Sherice M* usually leaves Potter's Cay, Nassau, on Thursday afternoon for Chub Cay, North Bimini, and Cat Cay, and returns on Monday morning. The one-way trip takes about 12 hours and costs $50. Going between North and South Bimini requires a five-minute ferry crossing, managed by the local government ($2 each way but, combined with the airport taxis' $3, totals $5). It runs from early morning to fairly late at night.

Bimini's eight marinas accommodate private yachts and fishing boats in droves with most crossing the Gulf Stream from Florida, a distance of around 48 nautical miles. As you enter port, fly the yellow quarantine flag. Coming into North Bimini, you have to clear Customs and Immigration in Alice Town at the Bimini Big Game Club or at the government buildings in Bailey Town. Coming into South Bimini, dock at Bimini Sands Resort & Marina and take a taxi to clear at Customs and Immigration at the airport, 2 miles away.

Once docked, only the captain can leave the boat in order to clear with local Customs and Immigration. All crew are required to remain on board until the captain returns having cleared. The clearance fee is $150 for boats up to 30 feet in length and $300 for boats over 30 feet, and covers the cruising permit, fishing permit, Customs and Immigration charges, and the $25-per-person departure tax for up to three persons. Additional persons over the age of six are charged a $25 departure tax.

Sunsets in Bimini can be otherworldly.

Contacts Bimini Big Game Resort & Marina. ✉ *Alice Town* ☎ *242/347–3391*
⊕ *www.biggameclubbimini.com.* **Bimini Customs Office.** ✉ *Alice Town*
☎ *242/347–3100.* **FRS Caribbean Bimini Fast Ferry.** ☎ *877/286–7220*
⊕ *www.frs-caribbean.com.* **Nassau Dockmaster's Office.** ☎ *242/393–1064.*
Resorts World Bimini. ☎ *888/930–8688 toll-free* ⊕ *www.rwbimini.com.*

VISITOR INFORMATION

Contacts Bimini Tourist Office. ✉ *Alice Town* ☎ *242/347–3528, 242/347–
3529* ⊕ *www.bahamas.com/bimini.*

NORTH BIMINI

Bimini's capital, **Alice Town,** is at North Bimini's southern end. It's colorful, painted in happy Caribbean pastels, and by night and day is buzzing
with golf-carting visitors from Resorts World and the marinas along the
main road of King's Highway. In a prominent location stand the ruins of
the Compleat Angler Hotel, Ernest Hemingway's famous haunt, which
burned down in 2006. A short walk away on the west coast is Radio
Beach (aka Alice Town Beach) and in the center of town is the Bimini
Native Straw and Craft Market, the tourist office, the government dock,
the marinas, and many restaurants and bars.

In quick succession, Alice Town turns into **Bailey Town,** then **Porgy Bay**.
Going north you'll see conch stands, restaurants, and the pink-color
government center and clinic. The beaches here are less frequented.
Beyond Porgy Town, the north third of the island is the expansive
Resorts World Bimini development.

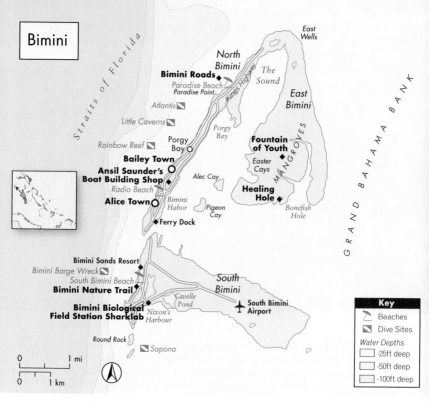

GETTING HERE AND AROUND

If arriving by plane, catch a taxi ($3) at the South Bimini Airport and a ferry ($2) to the new government dock in Alice Town. The entire process costs $5. You can walk, take a taxi, or hire a golf cart to reach your accommodations. From Resorts World you can hire a golf cart or taxi, or take the free hourly tram into Alice Town.

Most people get around North Bimini on gas-powered golf carts, available for rent from various vendors from $70 to $100 per day. At smaller rental companies, try bargaining. Note that the speed limit is 25 mph and that the roads follow the British system—driving on the left.

Golf Cart Rental Contacts ABC Rentals. ⊠ *King's Hwy., Alice Town* ☎ *242/473–0286 cell* ⊕ *www.biminigolfcarts.com.* **Elite Golf Carts At Resorts World.** ☎ *242/464–5025.* **Sue & Joys Rentals.** ⊠ *Alice Town* ☎ *242/347–6081.*

EXPLORING

Ansil Saunder's Boat Building Shop. In Bailey Town, near the government park, is Ansil Saunder's boat-building shop where you can see his beautiful flats fishing boat called the *Bimini Bonefisher*, handcrafted from oak, mahogany, and island horseflesh. Ansil is firstly a bonefisherman of some repute, having scared up a 16-pound, 3-ounce bonefish for Jerry Lavenstein in 1971—the still-standing bonefish world record. Ansil is equally famous for taking Dr. Martin Luther

King Jr. on a guided boat tour to the East Bimini wilderness. Dr. King wanted inspiration for an upcoming speech to be given for striking sanitation workers in Memphis. He found it in the mangroves, so rich in life and full of God's Creation, says Ansil, who recited his Creation Psalm to King. Three days after the Memphis speech, Dr. King was killed. At the time, with some foreboding, Ansil says that Dr. King mentioned to him that he didn't think he would live very long. To those who inquire, Ansil proudly shows memorabilia from Dr. King's wife and various VIPs. Saunders became an active member of the Bahamas independence movement, and met Margaret Thatcher and the Queen Elizabeth of England twice. Saunders is regarded as one of the Bahamas' living legends—and a consummate ambassador. You probably can't find, in all the country, a more historically rich guide to take you fishing or to the Healing Hole in one of the boats he crafted. ⊠ *Bailey Town, on harbor front, Alice Town* ☎ *242/347–2178 shop* ✆ *Donations accepted.*

Bailey Town. Most of the island's residents live in Bailey Town in small, pastel-color concrete houses, just off King's Highway, north of the Bimini Big Game Club and before Porgy Bay. Bailey Town has two of Bimini's biggest grocery stores, where goods and produce come in by mail boat usually on Thursday, Friday is the best day to shop. It's also a good place to find a home-cooked meal or conch salad from shacks along the waterfront. Don't miss a bite at Joe's Conch Stand; it's a local institution. ⊠ *North Bimini.*

Bimini Museum. The Bimini Museum, sheltered in the restored (1921) two-story original post office and jail—a two-minute walk from the ferry dock, across from the island straw market—showcases varied artifacts, including Adam Clayton Powell's domino set and photos, a fishing log, and rare fishing films of Ernest Hemingway with artifacts from the old Rod & Gun Club. Also view photos from Bimini's Prohibition rum-running era, rum kegs, old cannonballs, and Martin Luther King Jr.'s immigration card from 1964. The exhibit includes films shot on the island as early as 1922. The museum is privately managed. ⊠ *King's Hwy., Alice Town* ☎ *242/347–3038, 242/473–1252 cell* ✆ *$2 donation requested.*

Bimini Roads. Avid divers shouldn't miss a trip to underwater Bimini Roads, aka the Road to Atlantis. This curious rock formation under about 20 feet of water, 500 yards offshore at Bimini Bay, is shaped like a backward letter J, some 600 feet long at the longest end. It's the shorter 300-foot extension that piques the interest of scientists and visitors. The precision patchwork of large, curved-edge stones forms a perfect rectangle measuring about 30 feet across. A few of the stones are 16 feet square. It's purported to be the "lost city" whose discovery was predicted by Edgar Cayce (1877–1945), a psychic with an interest in prehistoric civilizations. Archaeologists estimate the formation to be between 5,000 and 10,000 years old. Carvings in the rock appear to some scientists to resemble a network of highways. ⊠ *North Bimini.*

You can kayak in North Bimini's mangrove flats.

Dolphin House. Bimini historian and poet laureate Mr. Ashley Saunders has spent decades constructing this eclectic home and guesthouse from materials salvaged from local construction sites and the sea, and writing a two-volume set on Bimini's history. Mr. Saunders offers walking tours of Alice Town, which begin with a tour of his structure—named for the 27 mosaic, sculpted, and painted dolphins throughout—then continues through Alice Town to tell the island's history. His books on the history of Bimini make for a fascinating read and souvenir. You'll see intricate conch shell and coconut crafts for sale. ⊠ *Alice Town between King's and Queen's Hwys., Alice Town* ☎ *242/347–3201* 🕐 *Tours $20 hr.*

OFF THE BEATEN PATH

Healing Hole. Hidden in the west coast mangroves of East Bimini is the Healing Hole—a cold spring of freshwater amid the hot sea saltwater with, some say, real, and others, mythical, healing powers. Hard to get to and find, it's best to hire a guide in a shallow boat, or, if you want exercise, in a kayak. You can only get there in mid-to-high tide, and make sure to take insect repellent. You'll see much life above and below water. For ecolovers and adventure-seekers only. ⊠ *North Bimini.*

BEACHES

Luna Beach at Resorts World. On Resorts World's long Paradise Beach, Luna Beach brings chic luxury to fun-in-the-sun and beach parties at night. Upscale food, exquisite cocktails, mod music, and beach toys are all part of the mix, centered on the open-air clubhouse. The solar-powered private cabanas even have phone charging ports. For more action jump on a Jet Ski, paddleboard, or kayak, or simply sun bake on a float. You can even book stingray and snorkeling tours here. During Sunset Sessions Happy Hour DJ Arlette reverbs the beach with danceable tunes. On special full-moon weekends, Luna Beach imports live bands for its moonlight beach parties, also featuring Bahamian bands and mini-Junkanoo breakouts. Cocktails are half price from 8 to 9 pm. Open Sunday to Wednesday noon–7 pm; Friday and Saturday, noon–11 pm. **Amenities:** food and drink; lifeguards. **Best for:** partiers; snorkeling; swimming ✉ *Resort World* 🌐 *www.rwbimini.com.*

Radio Beach/ Blister Bay. Alice Town's Radio Beach and Bailey Town's Blister Bay form a continuous stretch of beach off Queen's Highway, easily accessible in many places. Also called Alice Town Beach, its southern part is often busier and where spring breakers and the young like to party together. CJ's bar and grill, among other stands, is the default HQ, serving affordable beers, drinks, burgers, and island dinners. Eat inside (away from the flies), on the deck, or on the beach. **Amenities:** food and drink. **Best for:** partiers; swimming. ✉ *Alice Town.*

South Bimini Beach. Many would say Bimini's finest beach is on South Bimini, stretching about a mile from Bimini Sands Resort & Marina to South Bimini Beach Club (now closed) at Port Royal where the sand loops round the point and collects in a wide crescent—a favorite of spring breakers and Florida boaters. At South Bimini Beach Club is a protected anchorage and docks, but if you have a boat it's best to slide into the marina at the north end of the beach. There you have amenities and an infinity pool with a bar serving food and drinks. From North Bimini, take a $5 ferry plus taxi to reach the resort—it's well worth the trip to get away from it all. ✉ *South Bimini* ☎ *242/347–3500* 🌐 *www.thebiminisands.com.*

Spook Hill Beach. North of Radio Beach and named for its proximity to the local cemetery and Bimini's memorial park, Spook Hill Beach is quieter than Radio and Blister Bay beaches and caters mostly to families looking for quiet sands and calm waters. Shallow shores are ideal for wading and the crystal-clear waters make for great snorkeling. There is a permanent snack bar here and usually a few pop-up beach bars add to the fun. The beach is heavily lined with pine trees and is narrow at high tide. **Amenities:** food and drink. **Best for:** solitude; snorkeling; swimming. ✉ *North Bimini.*

5

WHERE TO EAT

$$ BAHAMIAN 🍴 **Bimini Big Game Bar & Grill.** A favorite place for boaters and anglers, this popular restaurant has a large, cool (and insect-free) interior and patio deck with excellent second-story views of the marina, boats passing in the harbor, and shimmering flats beyond. Enjoy beers, cocktails, and island and American fare at reasonable prices. **Known for:** great place to watch sports; great views; camaraderie and atmosphere. [$] *Average main: $26* ✉ *Alice Town* ☎ *242/347–3391* 🌐 *biggameclubbimini.com.*

$ BAHAMIAN 🍴 **Captain Bob's.** Across from the Sea Crest Marina, centrally located in Alice Town, this casual cafeteria-style joint starts serving rib-sticking American and Bahamian breakfasts at 7 am (try the conch or lobster omelet), seven days a week. Bob's is now serving lunches and dinners, closing at 4 pm on Monday and Tuesday and at 11 pm other days. **Known for:** family-owned; people-watching; hearty dinners in summer. [$] *Average main: $15* ✉ *King's Hwy., Alice Town* ☎ *242/347–3260, 242/473–4665* 💳 *No credit cards* 🕒 *No dinner fall–spring.*

$ BAHAMIAN **Joe's Conch Shack.** This small island-style open-air conch stand lies on a tiny beach between Bailey Town and Resorts World. Both locals and visitors swear the salad has more conch and is more tender here and his fritters and lobster salad are favorites. Joe personally extracts conch (with his eyes on you) while serving with a big smile. **Known for:** genuine Bahamian experience; fresh conch; harbor views. *Average main: $12 ✉ North Bailey Town ☎ 242/554–5183 No credit cards.*

WHERE TO STAY

$$ HOTEL **Bimini Big Game Club Resort & Marina** (*BBGC*). This king of Alice Town's marina-based resorts has an illustrious fishing history since 1936, and in 2015 enjoyed a $10 million upgrade. **Pros:** spacious rooms; excellent marina for fishing boats; great base with good restaurant. **Cons:** only fishing and diving oriented; most rooms ground level; not on the beach. *Rooms from: $211 ✉ King's Hwy., Alice Town ☎ 242/347–3391 resort, 800/867–4764 reservations www.biggameclubbimini.com 35 rooms, 12 cottages, 4 penthouses No meals ☞ On-site is Bimini Scuba Center, a top Bahamas dive operator. Also on-site are Bahamas Customs & Immigration for quick clearing for yachts.*

$$ RESORT FAMILY Fodor's Choice ★ **Resorts World Bimini Hilton & Marina.** This pastel-splashed luxury resort now boasts a boutique casino and a stunning new Hilton hotel with a rooftop infinity pool, a luxury spa, and a fitness center. **Pros:** top-quality marinas with all services; children's activity center; shuttle service around the property. **Cons:** restaurant opening times irregular; north-end units are long walk from town; beach can get crowded. *Rooms from: $239 ✉ King's Hwy., north of Bailey Town ☎ 888/930–8688 reservations, 242/347–8000 Hilton, 242/347–2900 front desk, 305/374–6664 marina rwbimini.com 374 units with 200 rooms and suites at the Hilton No meals.*

$ HOTEL **Sea Crest Hotel & Marina.** Near Radio Beach, this small marina has two buildings: one with three stories down a little lane leading to the beach and one with two stories on the marina. **Pros:** free Wi-Fi; central location; welcoming service. **Cons:** rooms are motel style; rooms lack decor; no restaurant. *Rooms from: $120 ✉ King's Hwy., Alice Town ☎ 242/347–3071 www.seacrestbimini.com 25 rooms, 2 suites.*

NIGHTLIFE

Big John's Bar & Grill. This waterside sports bar, restaurant, and tiny marina, patronized by the younger set, is one of the most popular places on-island to party, dance, and grab a cold beer, burger, or island snack. It's open from 11:30 am until late. It now sports a snazzy humidor with authentic Cuban cigars. Come nightfall Thursday to Saturday, a fabulous local Bimini band plays live music combining pop, Bahamian hits, reggae, and soca. At midnight, a local DJ takes over and spins until 3 am. If you want to book a room in the boutique hotel upstairs be mindful of the loud vibes. *✉ King's Hwy., Alice Town ☎ 239/347–3117 $10 cover for live music.*

SHOPPING

Bimini Craft Centre & Straw Market. Near the Government Public Dock in Alice Town, this craft center features the original straw, wood carving, and craft works of myriad islanders. Products are showcased over 17 stalls. A great place for tie-dye resort wear and T-shirts, there's also some amazing food to be had. Make sure to stop at Nathalie's Thompson's Bread stand to try a loaf of decadent Bimini Bread. Think hot challah with sugar glaze. ⊠ *Next to a big pink government building and government dock, Alice Town* ☎ *242/347–3529.*

Fisherman's Village Marina. This 136-slip full-service marina, one of two marinas at Resorts World Resort & Marina, doubles as North Bimini's main touristic shopping village. Adjacent to the reception area, the "village" houses Bimini Undersea dive shop, a liquor and grocery store, an ice-cream shop, a gourmet pizzeria, a café and deli, a clothing boutique, and the surprisingly affordable and good-value Healing Hole Rum Bar & Grill (only open 11 am–4 pm, Monday, Wednesday, and Friday). ⊠ *North Bimini* ☎ *242/347–2900, 242/347–2941 Bimini Undersea Tours* ⊕ *rwbimini.com/dining/on-island-dining.*

Trev Inn Marketplace. Trev Inn has probably the largest selection of groceries and produce on North Bimini. It's located four buildings south of the pink-color Bimini Clinic in Porgy Bay, a short distance from Resorts World. (Also, Brown's is nearby and farther south is Roberts' Grocery Store near the big power station in Bailey Town, and Jontra's near the Bimini Big Game Club.) The mail boat comes in Thursday, so best to shop for fresh produce Thursday evening, Friday, and Saturday. Exploring local grocery stores is quaint and amusing except when you get to the cash register: with costly freight, import duties, and 7.5% VAT tax, expect to pay about double. To save money, bring coolers packed with fresh and frozen food. ⊠ *King's Hwy., Porgy Town, Alice Town* ☎ *242/347–2452* ✉ *patricia-roberts@hotmail.com.*

SPORTS AND THE OUTDOORS

BOATING AND FISHING

Bimini is not only one of the big game fishing capitals of the world, it also holds six bonefishing world records. Hire one of the island's famous guides—and great characters—to hunt for the spooky "gray ghost." Full-day fishing excursions cost upwards of $600. Reef and deep-sea fishing excursions are also available from $400 for a half day. The best bonefishing guides must be booked well in advance.

Bimini Big Game Club Resort & Marina. Bimini Big Game Club Resort & Marina is a great base for fishing, diving, and snorkeling charters. They book the island's top bonefish guides and bottom and deep-sea fishing captains. You can also rent a small boat here, as well as kayaks, paddleboards, and snorkeling gear, and you can buy bait. There's a convenience store on property for mid-dive and mid-tour snacks (and liquor)—along with a Bahama Customs and Immigration office for port-of-entry clearance for boats. It's also the new home of the famous Neal Watson's PADI Bimini Scuba Center. At this writing, BBGC offers $250 credit off your airline or ferry tickets with a stay of four nights or more. ⊠ *Alice Town* ☎ *800/867–4764 toll-free, 954/615–1011 Florida, 242/473–8816 dive center.*

"Bonefish" Ebbie David. With his personality-plus, you'll get more laughs out of Ebbie David than fish—or will you? He's one of Bimini's most famous and highly recommended bonefishing guides. In 2015 he won a coveted Ministry of Tourism Cacique Award for his excellence in the sport and in hospitality. Ebbie now runs his own bonefishing lodge. ⊠ *Alice Town* ☎ *242/347–2053, 242/359–8273 cell* ⊕ *www.bahamas.com.*

"Bonefish" Tommy Sewell. Renowned bonefishing guide Tommy Sewell has over 26 years' experience leading bonefishing expeditions. Although sometimes quiet and thoughtful, Tommy calls himself "the friendly guide" and is, indeed, very obliging and pleasing. Known for delivering excellent customer service, he's proud of the big catches he can hunt down for his guests. ⊠ *Alice Town* ☎ *242/347–3234, 242/473–1089 cell.*

Captain Carson Saunders. For snorkeling and sightseeing tours in relatively calm weather, Captain Carson, based at Bimini Big Game Club, is a great choice for his value. Half days are $400 and full days are $800 in his 25-foot Proline center console. Although it lacks the luxury of bigger cabin cruisers, you'll save time and money. Bring a hat and sunblock. ⊠ *Bimini Big Game Club Resort & Marina, Alice Town* ☎ *242/464–5810.*

Captain Jerome Stuart. For deep-sea fishing in Bimini, Captain Jerome Stuart is your man. He is (or was) a Metropolitan Miami Fishing Tournament registered captain. Stuart charges from $1,400 per day, and from $800 per half day for deep-sea fishing, with captain, mate, and gear included. Depending on the season, expect to catch wahoo, yellowfin, marlin, bluefin tuna, and swordfish. ⊠ *Alice Town* ☎ *242/347–2081.*

Golden Dream Charters. Ex-commercial fisherman and island-born Captain Stephen Knowles has a special insight when and where the fish are biting. His Ocean Yachts 46-foot Convertible *Golden Dream* is purpose-made for comfortable, fun fishing. Stephen heads to the Gulf Stream, trolling for big game: blue marlin, sailfish, mahimahi, wahoo, and tuna. Bimini abounds with bottom-fishing spots where he'll set you on groupers, snappers, porgies, and yellowtails. In his 46-foot luxury sportfishing cabin cruiser it's $1,000 for a half day, and $1,800 for a full day. ⊠ *Alice Town* ☎ *242/727–8144 cell, 242/347–3391 Bimini Big Game Club marina* ✉ *stephenknowles57@hotmail.com.*

SCUBA DIVING AND SNORKELING

The **Bimini Barge Wreck** (a World War II landing craft) rests in 100 feet of water. **Little Caverns** is a medium-depth dive with scattered coral heads, small tunnels, and swim-throughs. **Rainbow Reef** is a shallow dive popular for fish gazing. **Moray Alley** teems with captivating moray eels and **Bull Run** is famous for its profusion of sharks. And, of course, there's **Bimini Road (aka, Road to Atlantis)**, thought to be the famous "lost city." Dive packages are available through most Bimini hotels. You can also check out the best diving options through the **Bahamas Diving Association** (☎ *954/236–9292 or 800/866–3483* ⊕ *www.bahamasdiving.com*).

Bimini Undersea. Headquartered in Fisherman's Village at Resorts World, the highly rated Bimini Undersea tour operator offers myriad excursions and experiences, including scuba diving, shark dives and stingray adventures, scuba, nature boat tours, fishing, and snorkeling

This large bonefish was caught on Bimini's shallow flats.

with wild spotted dolphins. They run Sunset Celebration Cruises, and near the marina and on Paradise Beach at the new Luna Beach Club they offer Jet Skis, kayaks, and paddleboards. You can also rent or buy snorkel and diving gear. They offer two, two-tank dives a day and introductory scuba lessons. Dive packages with accommodations at Resorts World are available, and day-trippers are also welcome to join. ☒ *Resorts World Bimini & Marina* ☎ *242/347–2941, 786/462–4641 in U.S. and Canada* ⊕ *www.biminiundersea.net.*

Neal Watson's PADI Bimini Scuba Center. The PADI-certified Bimini Scuba Center, located at Bimini Big Game Club Resort & Marina, offers two-tank dives in the morning and one-tank dives in the afternoon. Besides exciting Great Hammerhead Shark dives (from October to March), Bull Shark dives near Cat Cay, and Caribbean Reef and Lemon Shark dives, BSC also offers Wild-Spotted Dolphin snorkeling excursions. (You may need patience and understanding; after all, these are free and wild creatures.) The operator visits all of Bimini's popular dive spots: the Sapona Wreck, the Bimini Barge, Atlantis Road, Tuna Alley, Victory Reef, the Nodules, the Strip, Rainbow Reef, and much more. They offer full range of rentals and tank fills, as well as kayaks and paddleboards for exploring the harbor and flats beyond. You can also arrange for small boat rentals and all types of fishing charters. Novices can safely train in the resort's pool, then grab a quick bite and drink. With everything so convenient, Bimini Scuba Center is an excellent choice for a diving or fishing vacation. ☒ *Alice Town* ☎ *242/347–3391 resort, 800/867–4764 toll-free in U.S. and Canada.*

SOUTH BIMINI

Bigger, with nicer beaches and higher elevation than low-lying North Bimini, South Bimini is nonetheless the quieter of the two islands. Home to the island's only airport, it has a smattering of shops near the ferry landing where boats make regular crossings between the two islands, a short five-minute ride. Bimini Sands Resort is the biggest property on the island with its safe-harbor marina, condos, and nature trail. South of the main resort in Port Royal are 80-plus vacation homes, some docks, and a scalloped beach that's a favorite of visiting boaters. The resort also helps preserve the island's ecofocus by staying low-key and keeping much of its land undeveloped. It helps maintain the little Fountain of Youth Park, the Sharklab, and beautiful beaches.

GETTING AROUND

Visitors do not need a car on Bimini, and there are no car-rental agencies. A taxi from the airport to Bimini Sands Resort is $3. Hitching a ride is common.

EXPLORING

Bimini Biological Field Station Sharklab. The Bimini Biological Field Station Foundation's Sharklab was founded more than 25 years ago by Dr. Samuel Gruber, a shark biologist at the University of Miami. Visitors can tour the lab at low tide. The highlight is wading into the bay where the lab keeps several lemon sharks. The hands-on presentation, done by the research assistants or researchers themselves, is entertaining and educational. Tours are offered daily but visitors must call in advance. ⊠ *South Bimini* ✣ *End of long road to south of island, turn left* ☎ *242/347–4538* ⊕ *www.biminisharklab.com* ✉ *$10 donation desirable.*

FAMILY **Bimini Nature Trail.** Developed by Bimini Sands Resort on undeveloped property, this mile-loop trail is one of the best of its kind in the Bahamas. Its slight rise in elevation means a lovely shaded walk under hardwood trees such as gumbo-limbos, poisonwood (marked with "Don't Touch" signs), and buttonwood. Check out the ruins of the historic Conch House, a great place for sunset-gazing. There is also a pirate's well exhibit devoted to the island's swashbuckling history. Excellent signage guides you through the island's fauna and flora if you prefer doing a self-guided tour. However, for the best interpretation and learning experience, book a guided tour through Bimini Sand's front desk. Kids always love petting the indigenous Bimini boa on the guided tour. The trail was recently improved by Bahamian bird-watchers such as Erika Gates of Freeport's famous Garden of the Groves reserve. ⊠ *South Bimini* ☎ *242/347–3500 resort* ✉ *Free. Guided tours $12.*

Fountain of Youth. Famous explorer Juan Ponce de León heard from Indians about a Fountain of Youth possibly located in Bimini, so in 1513, on his way to discovering Florida and the Gulf Stream, he landed on Bimini but never found the fountain. The historical result? Somehow Biminites adopted a freshwater natural well that was carved out of limestone by groundwater thousands of years ago and used it to commemorate Ponce de León's search. Now there's a plaque to celebrate the myth. So, nonetheless, go there and make a wish (without casting a penny—this is an ecoisland). You'll find the Fountain of Youth on the road to the airport. ✉ *South Bimini* ☎ *242/347–3500 Bimini Sands Resort & Marina* 🎫 *Free.*

BEACHES

South Bimini claims Bimini's prettiest beaches, with a pristine, mile-long stretch on the western side and near Port Royal, a sandy cove and point on the southern side, with some of the best from-shore snorkeling around. In the far south, the South Bimini Beach Club was closed after a hurricane in 2016, but the point's gorgeous beach is there to enjoy for all and sundry. It's a favorite beach for boaters, with a couple of docks and safe anchorages from northerly or easterly winds. The partiers tend to congregate here leaving the northern beaches relatively secluded. At the north of the long beach is Bimini Sands Resort & Marina. Dock there and you can use their infinity pool and other amenities (and a fuel dock, too). The Pool Bar with its refreshments and food, is welcome to all beach walkers.

5

Bimini Sands Beach. Patrons of Bimini Sands Resort & Marina are not the only ones who love Bimini Sands's mile-long beach. This gorgeous stretch of white-sand powder, with its offshore snorkeling, is so enticing that vacationers from North Bimini and even Floridians often take the quick ferry over or boat cross the Gulf Stream for the day. The southern cove and point once had facilities which are, at press time, closed, but the beach and beautiful waters are still a magnet for boaters. To clear Bahamas Customs, who are stationed at the airport, it's best to slide into Bimini Sands's marina where you have access to amenities including the Pool Bar and freshwater pool. The southern beach gets particularly busy during spring break but the northern stretch stays relatively secluded. ✉ *South Bimini* ☎ *242/347–3500 Bimini Sands Resort & Marina* 🌐 *www.thebiminisands.com* 🎫 *Free. Ferry plus taxi from North Bimini $5.*

WHERE TO EAT

$ BAHAMIAN 🍴 **The Petite Conch.** This second-story cozy little diner/café overlooks Bimini Sands Marina, and although they don't serve fancy cuisine, it does have excellent and comforting Bahamian dishes at a reasonable cost. Very convenient for the resort's and marina's guests, The Petite Conch serves breakfast, lunch, and dinner with American and local favorites. **Known for:** cozy ambience; convenient for resort and marina guests; fast and friendly service. [$] *Average main: $10* ✉ *South Bimini* ☎ *242/347–3500* 🌐 *www.thebiminisands.com.*

WHERE TO STAY

$$ RESORT FAMILY 🏨 **Bimini Sands Resort & Marina.** Overlooking the Straits of Florida on a stunning beach, this well-designed property rents one- to three-bedroom condominiums with direct marina access. **Pros:** self-catering condos; full-service marina with customs nearby; small restaurant with pool bar and café; good tour operations. **Cons:** limited nightlife on South Bimini (party is daytime here); sometimes shortage of lounge chairs; somewhat remote. [$] *Rooms from: $250* ✉ *South Bimini* ☎ *242/347–3500 resort, 888/588–2464 in U.S. and Canada* 🌐 *www.thebiminisands.com* 🛏 *206 condominiums* 🍽 *No meals.*

SPORTS AND THE OUTDOORS

BOATING, FISHING, AND DIVING

Bimini Sands Resort & Marina. Bimini Sands Resort & Marina arranges and has access to all the tours and excursions offered by the excursion and dive operators in North Bimini including the shark, stingray, wreck, reef, and wild spotted dolphin tours offered by Neal Watson's Bimini Scuba Center. You can join those tours either by taking the $5 ferry plus taxi to Alice Town or by asking the tour boat to pick you up at the Bimini Sands Marina. The resort itself offers kayaks, snorkeling gear, and boat rentals so you can go and discover Bimini's many reefs and wrecks on your own. ⊠ *Bimini Sands Resort & Marina* ☎ *242/347–3500* ⊕ *www.thebiminisands.com.*

SCUBA DIVING AND SNORKELING

Bimini has excellent diving opportunities, particularly for watching marine life. Off the shore of South Bimini the concrete wreck of the SS *Sapona* attracts snorkelers as well as partiers.

THE BERRY ISLANDS

The Berry Islands consist of more than two dozen small islands and almost a hundred tiny cays stretching in a thin crescent to the north of Andros and Nassau. Although a few of the islands are privately owned, most of them are uninhabited—except by rare birds who use the territory as their nesting grounds, or by visiting yachters dropping anchor in secluded havens. The Berry Islands start in the north at **Great Stirrup Cay** and **Coco Cay** where thousands of cruise passengers enjoy Bahama-island experiences and the Stingray City Bahamas attraction on neighboring Goat Cay. The Berries end in the south at **Chub Cay,** only 35 miles north of Nassau.

Most of the islands' 700 residents live on the tranquil, 10-mile-long **Great Harbour Cay,** the largest of the Berry Islands. Its main settlement, **Bullock's Harbour,** aka "the Village," has a couple of good restaurants, grocery and liquor stores, and small shops. A mile west, the Great Harbour Cay's beach area was developed in the early 1970s. More homes, condos, and villas have been built or remodeled since. The 65-slip protected marina has also been renovated and is once again popular with yachties. There are no big resorts on Great Harbour; instead, there's a delightful, world-class boutique hotel called Carriearl, a former house of a famous Hollywood star matchmaker who invited his guests here to party within their tight circle. There's a small hotel at the marina, and homes and villas for rent on the marina and beaches. The GHC Property Owners Association is active and provides many fun activities and events, including the partial upkeep of 9 holes of the original golf course. Many private pilots have homes and fly in here. The Berries are reputed to have one of the world's highest concentrations of millionaires per square mile, but, surprisingly, there are no banks or ATMs, so make sure you bring some cash with your credit cards.

In recent years, family, wedding, honeymoon, and beach-seeking vacations and bonefishing have become more popular. In the south, Chub

Cay is close to a deep-sea pocket where the Tongue of the Ocean meets the North West Providence Channel—a junction that traps big game fish. Remote flats south of Great Harbour, from Anderson Cay to Money Cay, are excellent bonefish habitats, as are the flats around Chub Cay. Deeper-water flats hold permit and tarpon.

Chub Cay, a popular halfway point for boaters crossing to and from Florida, is also experiencing a comeback with millions having been recently invested in the Chub Cay Resort & Marina, which is soon to become private, catering more to investors who own or build homes on the island. On Chub, you'll certainly connect with your friends and young ones but make sure you have a boat to give you freedom to explore, dive, and fish. Bring food, drinks, and snacks for your stay. The luxury-looking new clubhouse has a well-stocked convenience store. Most rental units come with kitchens.

AIR TRAVEL

In the Berry Islands, Great Harbour Cay (GHC) Airport receives regular flights from Fort Lauderdale airport (FLL) through Tropic Ocean Airways, with their land-capable float planes, on Friday and Sunday. Four times weekly Watermakers Air flies to Chub Cay (CCZ) and GHC from Fort Lauderdale Executive Airport (FXE). From Nassau (NAS), two flights a day come in via LeAir. Many other charter operators with props, jets, and helicopters fly in from Florida.

Chub Cay is served from Nassau every Friday and Sunday by Captain Bill Munroe's Bill Air (⊕ *http://billair.com/index.html*, who can vary the aircraft's size according to passenger numbers. It's $75 one-way.

On Great Harbour Cay, one of the few taxis will take you to your resort or villa. After that, renting an SUV, golf cart, or at least a bike is sensible, although walking around the Bullock's Harbour village itself is a nice 40-minute stroll. On 6-mile-long Chub Cay, it's only a mile from the marina resort to the airport.

BOAT TRAVEL

Great Harbour Cay and Chub Cay are popular yachting destinations and stop-offs for boats going farther afield. Both are ports-of-entry with friendly service by Customs and Immigration for entry clearance and gaining the mandatory cruising permits. Both have excellent marinas with fuel and full services. From Nassau, the mail boat M/V *Capt. Gurth Dean* sets sail twice or three time a month from Potter's Cay Dock on Wednesday night, arriving Thursday morning to supply the GHC with groceries, supplies, and general cargo. Some weeks, although not all, the mail boat *Sherice M* leaves Nassau on Wednesday afternoon to arrive in Chub Cay the next morning. For $40 each way you can secure passage—an authentic island adventure if somewhat bare-boned. Fuel for boaters is also available at Alder Cay and Little Whale Cay, halfway down the chain.

Take a boat or hire a guide and island hop to explore the cays' splendid turquoise serenity and wildlife on land and undersea. The Berries are favored among bone- and deep-sea fishermen in-the-know and who want to get away from crowds. World-class fishing tournaments used to be held here and at the start of the crawfish season on August 1, many boats from Nassau chose to spearfish here for its westerly lee-side shelters, its proximity, and the lucrative bounty. On Little Harbour Cay, 16 miles southeast of Great Harbour, is the famous outpost Flo's Conch Bar, now run by Flo's family. Visit the Stingray City Bahamas' tour to snorkel with stingrays off Goat Cay by catching the company's staff boat from Great Harbour Cay.

Contacts Chub Cay Resort & Marina. ☎ *242/325–1490 resort and marina, 786/209–0025 in U.S. and Canada* ⊕ *www.chubcayresortandmarina.com.* **Great Harbour Cay Marina.** ☎ *242/367–8005 marina* ⊕ *www.greatharbourcay.com.*

ISLAND TRANSPORTATION

On Great Harbour Cay, you can get most places on foot, but you can also rent a bike, car, or golf cart. Golf-cart rentals start at $60 a day, rattle-trap SUVs from $60, and better cars from $75 up to $90. On Chub Cay you can rent golf carts at the marina and elsewhere. On both islands, transport maybe included in your villa rental. Hopefully you'll get on to the water and sightsee some Berry magic by renting a small boat or doing some fishing. Make sure you have a good VHF radio and plot your course on a good chart that you can buy at the marinas: these islands have many hazardous reefs and sandbars. Gas is around $5 a gallon.

Contacts Happy People Rentals. ✉ *Great Harbour Cay Marina, Great Harbour Cay* ☎ *242/367–8117 shop, 242/359–9052 cell.* **Krum's Rentals.** ☎ *242/367–8370, 242/451–0579 cell.*

BEACHES

Off these always secluded, immaculate beaches, the clarity of Bahamian waters is especially evident when you reach the Berry Islands. Starfish abound, and you can often catch a glimpse of a gliding stingray, eagle ray, barracuda, and needle fish. You'll find ocean beaches with gentle lapping waves, sultry beaches with sandbar flats where you can walk half a mile, and private coves enclosed by cliffs for ultraprivate experiences.

Chub Cay Beach. As well as the 400-yard beach right at the marina, Chub Cay has a splendid 1¼-mile strand with great swimming and nearby snorkeling. The Club House with its pool is a mere 400 yards away for refreshments. **Amenities:** none. **Best for:** swimming; snorkeling. ✉ *Chub Cay's southern coast* ☎ *242/325–1490 clubhouse and marina office.*

Great Harbour Cay Beach. Two crescents scoop Great Harbour Cay's east coast with 5 miles of almost unbroken powder. Travel north to discover Sugar Beach with its bluff-surrounding romantic private coves. Progressing south, the beach becomes Lover's Beach, thinning out until Hotel Point Beach where the strand widens and you can see waves clash from two directions. Farther south still is famous Great

Harbour Beach itself, where you'll encounter the fabulous boutique hotel Carriearl and its fine pool, restaurant, and bar. On the south end of Great Harbour Beach near the airport, you'll find The Beach Club, a popular daytime bar and grill with a gift shop. Play beach volleyball, or take a yoga class. (They may ask for a small donation.) At the extreme south are the shallow, simmering sandbars of Shelling Beach that let you wade out for yards. At low tide, you can cross the tidal Shark Beach Creek to the pristine Haines Cay that, hidden from the north by a hill, offers an even more splendid, long beach. Along Great Harbour Cay's powdery 5-mile stretch, nearby reefs beckon snorkelers and gin-clear waters invite kayakers and paddleboarders. **Amenities:** food and drink. **Best for:** shelling; swimming; walking, snorkeling. ⊠ *Great Harbour Cay* ✛ *5 miles long with varying names* ☎ *242/367–8005 marina and resort* ⊕ *www.greatharbourcay.com.*

Haines Cay Beach. At low tide, walk across from Shelling Beach estuary, round the point, and walk south a half mile and you'll discover one of the Bahamas' most unspoiled, beautiful beaches. It's 2 miles long with excellent snorkeling on its north end and swimming all along. Wear some sturdy footwear for the land walk. It's also reachable by kayak. There are no trees for shade, so an umbrella, lots of fluids, and sunscreen are advisable. **Amenities:** none. **Best for:** swimming; walking; snorkeling; solitude. ⊠ *Great Harbour Cay* ✛ *½ mile west of Shelling Beach.*

Sugar Beach. Sugar Beach is the northernmost of the island's beaches, where rock bluffs divide the sand into romantic "private" coves of various lengths. Explore the caves or snorkel in calm waters. On top of one of the hills are the ghostly remains of the Sugar Beach Hotel, a 1950s lair built by the Hollywood Rat Pack—Sammy Davis Jr., Dean Martin, Frank Sinatra, Peter Lawford, and Joey Bishop. Female stars invited there included Marilyn Monroe, Shirley MacLaine, Lauren Bacall, Angie Dickinson, and Judy Garland. This was their scenic escape from paparazzi. The hilltop ruins are decrepit and surrounded by bush and cliffs, so explore with caution. ⊠ *Great Harbour Cay.*

WHERE TO EAT

$ | ✕ **The Beach Club.** This is the island's cool locale for breakfast and lunch,
BAHAMIAN | across the road from the airport, overlooking the beach and turquoise water. At breakfast, go for the eggs and ham with home grits, and at lunch, have a grilled cheeseburger or whatever fresh fish is on the menu for the day. **Known for:** group dinners available on request; yoga and volleyball at club; fresh fish. Ⓢ *Average main: $14* ⊠ *On Great Harbour Cay Beach, near airport, Great Harbour Cay* ☎ *242/367–8108* ▭ *No credit cards* ⊗ *No dinner unless requested by group.*

$$ | ✕ **Carriearl Restaurant.** Guests who discover Carriearl Restaurant are
BAHAMIAN | pleasantly stunned that a restaurant of such charm and caliber just
Fodor'sChoice | happens to be on their tiny island. The warm and capable couple
★ | from Manchester, restaurateur Martin "Dronzi" Dronsfield and former British Airways flight attendant Angie Jackson, have managed to fashion one of the Bahamas' most illustrious beachside mansions

into a gem of culinary and visual delight. **Known for:** opulent atmosphere; outstanding pizzas. $ *Average main: $28* ⊠ *Great Harbour Cay Beach, Great Harbour Cay* ☎ *242/367–8785, 242/451–8785 cell* ⊕ *www.carriearl.com* ⊗ *For nonguests: closed Mon. and Tues., no lunch Wed., no dinner Sun.* ☞ *Breakfast, lunch, and dinner daily for hotel guests.*

$$ ✕ **Coolie Mae's Sunset Restaurant.** In
BAHAMIAN   the island food category, expats, locals, and visitors rate Mae's food as true-true excellent. Her bright sign makes the casual 60-seat restaurant, on Bullock's Harbour's central seafront, easy to find. **Known for:** conch salad; Bahamian specialties; reservations recommended. $ *Average main: $22* ⊠ *In middle of Bullock's Harbour's west peninsula, Great Harbour Cay* ☎ *242/367–8730* ▤ *No credit cards* ⊗ *Closed Sun.*

$$ ✕ **The Tamboo Club.** A tradition at the Great Harbour Marina, this grand
BAHAMIAN   supper club—once a private club for the likes of Cary Grant, Brigitte Bardot, and Walter Cronkite—now holds fun dinner events on weekends when the island is busy. Thursday night is Pizza Night with prices ranging from $25 to $40 for lobster pizza. **Known for:** fun happy hour and theme nights; lobster pizza; former Hollywood hangout. $ *Average main: $25* ⊠ *Great Harbour Marina, Great Harbour Cay* ☎ *242/367–8203, 242/451–0251* ▤ *No credit cards.*

WHERE TO STAY

$$ 🏨 **Carriearl Boutique Hotel.** An unassuming front entrance hides what
B&B/INN   many say is one of the Bahamas' top small vacation retreats, and
Fodor'sChoice guests love having 7 miles of powdery beach to themselves. **Pros:** right
★   on 7 miles of silky sand beach; superb restaurant and bar; excellent, attentive, and friendly service. **Cons:** only four rooms; rooms only for 18 years or older. $ *Rooms from: $255* ⊠ *Great Harbour Cay* ☎ *242/367–8785 hotel, 242/451–8785 cell* ⊕ *www.carriearl.com* ⤳ *4 rooms en suite.*

$$$$ 🏨 **Chub Cay Resort & Marina.** Chub Cay Resort & Marina has been
HOTEL   speedily and most beautifully restored to what is a luxury oasis on
Fodor'sChoice an otherwise rustic cay. **Pros:** excellent location for flats and offshore
★   fishing; quality bar and restaurant serves three meals; luxury-style clubhouse and well-appointed rooms with balconies. **Cons:** construction may occur but away from hotel; not much to do on land but plenty on the sea. $ *Rooms from: $425* ⊠ *Chub Cay* ☎ *242/325–1490 hotel, 786/209–0025 in U.S. and Canada* ⊕ *www.chubcay.com* ⤳ *11 rooms and suites, 8 1-bedroom beach cabanas, 12 villas with 2–4 bedrooms, largest sleeps 10* ⊚ *All meals.*

Kayaks line the beach at Little Stirrup Cay in the Berry Islands.

SPORTS AND THE OUTDOORS

BOATING

The water's depth is seldom more than 20 feet here. Grass patches and an occasional coral head or flat coral patch dot the light-sand bottom. You might spot the odd turtle, and if you care to jump over the boat's side with a mask, you might also pick up a conch or two in the grass. Good snorkeling and bonefishing, and peaceful anchorages, can be found on the lee shores of the Hoffmans and Little Harbour cays. **Flo's Conch Bar**, at the southern end of Little Harbour Cay serves fresh conch prepared every way.

Great Harbour Cay Marina. In the upper Berry Islands, the full-service Great Harbour Cay Marina has 65 slips for yachts up to 150 feet. This is the island's touristic nerve center where you can book fishing and snorkeling charters and arrange boat rentals. Accessed through an 80-foot-wide channel from the west, the marina has almost no motion even in rough weather: it's a top hurricane hole. (Matthew in 2016 went right over it.) This sleepy and crime-free island on a gorgeous beach still has plenty to do: join a game of petanque in the street with free rum punch on Wednesday evenings or the Chill 'N' Grill ($10–$15) get-together on Friday night, or weekly yoga, fitness classes, and beach volleyball at The Beach Club. You can even play nine holes of golf on the rather weedy course. The marina is a great base for boating, snorkeling, and fishing. HeuBoo's Deli on the dock is a good place for ice cream and pastries. Fuel is at a separate dock west of the marina. The marina's management company also rents out town houses. ⊠ *Great Harbour Cay* ☎ *242/367–8005 dock, 242/457–4216 cell* ⊕ *www.greatharbourcay.com.*

Happy People Boat Rental. At Great Harbour Cay Marina, Elon Rolle, located in a small convenience store on the dock, hires for the day, half day, or hour, an unsinkable 20-foot Boston Outrage with 200HP for $200 a day plus gas (using about $150 for 30 gallons for a day). Snorkeling, spear, and fishing gear are extra. It also comes with VHF radio. ✉ *Great Harbour Cay Marina, Great Harbour Cay* ☎ *242/367–8117, 242/367–8761 cell.*

FISHING

Percy Darville's Five Hearts Charters. Percy Darville and his family and crew know the flats of the Berries better than anyone. The fleet comprises four skiffs. Percy has a speedy 26-foot Mako with 400HP, speedy and ideal for bottom and deep-sea fishing and taking tours to highlights such as Hoffman's Cay Blue Hole. From GHC, Five Hearts also travels the 1½ hours to Chub Cay when clients request them, or anywhere in the Berries. Worldly fishermen say the Berries have a higher percentage of larger fish. A half day with Five Hearts is $400 and a full day is $600, with gas included; you only pay extra for gas on longer trips. Contact this top crew well in advance as they are much in demand. In 2007, Capt. Percy was awarded the Cacique Award for Sports and Leisure, the Bahamas' prestigious award for hospitality, and for his contribution to tourism. ✉ *Great Harbour Cay* ☎ *242/464–4149 cell, 242/367–8119 home, 242/225–9104 toll-free in Bahamas.*

SNORKELING

FAMILY   **Stingray City.** A snorkel trip by boat to this spot on Goat Island is a favorite experience of both cruise passengers and anyone staying in Great Harbour Cay. Visitors interact in the pristine, sparkling, and shallow water with southern rays. It's by far the most popular attraction in the region. ✉ *Great Harbour Cay* ☎ *242/364–1032 Nassau office, 242/477–0261 excursion manager; call at night* ⊕ *stingray-bahamas.com.*

6

ELEUTHERA AND HARBOUR ISLAND

WELCOME TO ELEUTHERA AND HARBOUR ISLAND

TOP REASONS TO GO

★ **Play in pink sand:** Glorious, soft pink sand, the ethereal shade of the first blush of dawn, draws beach connoisseurs to Harbour Island. Plenty of pretty pink beaches also dot Eleuthera's east and north coasts.

★ **Ogle island architecture:** Historic homes with storybook gables and gingerbread verandahs are the norm on Harbour Island and Spanish Wells. Picturesque Victorian houses overlook Governor's Harbour in Eleuthera.

★ **Savor soulful sounds:** Nights here rock with the Bahamian group Afro Band, the hip-hop of TaDa, the traditional sound of Jaynell Ingraham, and the calypso of Dr. Sea Breeze.

★ **Indulge in alfresco dining:** Harbour Island's intimate restaurants have reinvented regional cuisine. On Eleuthera, Governor's Harbour has a number of laid-back spots with memorable menus and magnificent views.

Eleuthera, at the center of the Bahamas chain, is a narrow, 110-mile island. The fierce, deep-blue Atlantic is to the east, and the usually placid azure and teal shallows of the Bight of Eleuthera and Great Bahama Bank are to the west. Eleuthera's mainland holds the majority of the island's residents, about 8,000. The rest of the 3,000 residents are split between 3-mile Harbour Island, 1 mile off Eleuthera's northeast coast, and 2-mile Spanish Wells, 1 mile off Eleuthera's northern coast. The island is 200 miles east of Florida and 50 miles east of Nassau.

1 Gregory Town and North Eleuthera. Eleuthera's undeveloped, serene north holds some of the island's most iconic natural wonders: the Glass Window Bridge, a heart-racing span between 80-foot cliffs often buffeted by a raging Atlantic; the 17th-century Preacher's Cave; and the thrilling waves of Surfer's Beach.

2 Hatchet Bay. "The Country's Safest Harbour" is Hatchet Bay's claim to fame. The naturally protected harbor is a popular place to anchor sailboats and fishing vessels.

3 Governor's Harbour. The administrative capital of Governor's Harbour is a pretty, Victorian town, with a lively harbor that's a frequent stop for mail boats, ferries, and yachts. The town offers upscale restaurants and down-home conch cafés, boutique inns, and inexpensive apartments.

4 Rock Sound and South Eleuthera. Rock Sound, the original capital of Eleuthera, is a quaint seaside settlement with 19th-century homes. Thirty miles away, yachties stop at Cape Eleuthera peninsula for a few nights of luxury in elegant town houses. Environmentalists also come here from around the world to learn about the self-sustaining Island School.

5 Harbour Island. Dunmore Town, the first capital of the Bahamas, has historic Loyalists' houses, fronted by white picket fences, some with cutouts of pineapples and boats, and festooned with red bougainvillea and tumbling purple morning glories. Luxurious inns, renowned restaurants, and the magnificent pink beach attract celebrities.

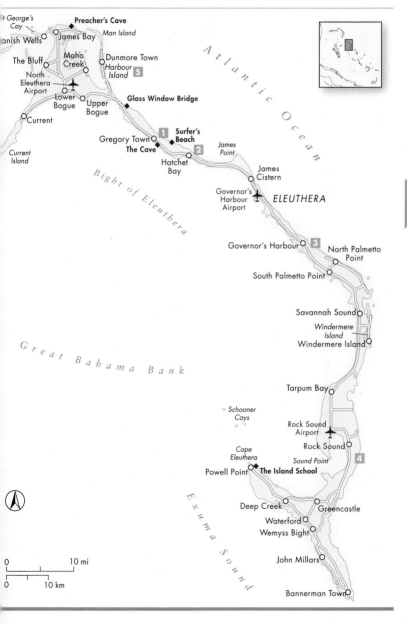

Preacher's Cave

James Bay

Man Island

anish Wells

St George's
Cay

The Bluff

Maho
Creek

Dunmore Town

Harbour
Island **5**

North
Eleuthera
Airport

Lower
Bogue

Upper
Bogue

Glass Window Bridge

Current

Current
Island

Bight of Eleuthera

Gregory Town

The Cave

Hatchet
Bay

**Surfer's
Beach**

James
Point

James
Cistern

Atlantic Ocean

ELEUTHERA

Governor's
Harbour
Airport

Governor's Harbour

North Palmetto
Point

South Palmetto Point

Savannah Sound

Windermere
Island

Windermere Island

Great Bahama Bank

Tarpum Bay

Schooner
Cays

Rock Sound
Airport

Rock Sound

Cape
Eleuthera

Powell Point

The Island School

Sound Point

Deep Creek

Waterford

Wemyss Bight

Greencastle

John Millars

Exuma Sound

Bannerman Town

0   10 mi

0   10 km

6

Updated by Sheri-kae McLeod

You haven't experienced a real escape until you've vacationed in Eleuthera. Simple luxury resorts are the norm, deserted expanses of white- or pink-sand beaches are your playground, and islanders are genuinely friendly. Seclusion, sun, and starry skies are abundant here.

Eleuthera was founded in 1648 by a British group fleeing religious persecution; the name is taken from the Greek word for freedom. These settlers, who called themselves the Eleutheran Adventurers, gave the Bahamas its first written constitution. "Adventurers" has taken on new meaning as a clarion call to sailors, tourists, and, more recently, retirees looking for adventures of their own.

Largely undeveloped rolling green hills and untrammeled sandy coves, along with sleepy 19th-century towns, offer an authentic Bahamas experience that is quickly disappearing. Try not to notice the ubiquitous HG Christie and Sotheby's "For Sale" signs unless, of course, you're so smitten you want to stay. Rent a car—or even better, an SUV—for washboard back roads, and explore the island's secluded beaches and sandy coves fringing turquoise and aqua water that rivals anything in the Caribbean. The island is among the prettiest in the Bahamas, with gentle hills, unspoiled "bush" (backwoods), and gardens of tumbling purple lantana and sky-blue plumbago. Hotels and inns are painted in the shades of Bahamian bays and sunset, which is best watched from the comfort of inviting verandahs and seaside decks.

If you're looking for all of this and a bit more action, ferry over to Harbour Island, Eleuthera's chic neighbor. With its uninterrupted 3-mile pink-sand beach, top-notch dining, and sumptuous inns, the island has long been a favorite hideaway for jet-setters and celebrities. For splendid beaches with few, if any, tourists, head to Spanish Wells, a quiet, secluded island, located approximately 500 meters off the northern tip of Eleuthera island. Eleuthera and Harbour Island beaches are some of the best in the world, thanks to their pristine beauty and dazzling variety.

PLANNING

WHEN TO GO

High tourist season in Eleuthera runs December through April. Low temperatures might dip into the 60s, and the water can be chilly. Bring a sweater and a jacket, especially if you plan on boating. Expect to pay higher rates for rooms, boat rentals, and airfare during this time. For the cheapest hotel rates and some of the best deals on water-sports packages, visit in summer or fall when the ocean is generally calm and warm. Be aware, however, that hurricane season runs June through November, with the highest risk of storms from August to October. During this time weather can be steamy and rainy.

The liveliest times to visit Eleuthera are when island-wide festivals and celebrations are held like the annual Junkanoo celebration during Christmas, the Pineapple Festival and Conch Fest in June, the Rock Sound Homecoming during Easter, and the North Eleuthera Sailing Regatta in October. Reserve hotel rooms early.

TOP FESTIVALS

FALL AND WINTER **The North Eleuthera/Harbour Island Sailing Regatta** in October is an exciting five-day boat competition, with onshore activities like live Bahamian bands plus food and drink. **Junkanoo** is celebrated in Rock Sound and Harbour Island on December 26. Celebrations start around 7 pm.

SUMMER **The Eleuthera Pineapple Festival** is celebrated at the beginning of June in Gregory Town. If you like a little competition during your vacation, time your trip around the Pineappleman Sprint Triathalon. **Conch Fest** with live Rake 'n' Scrape promoting Deep Creek's cultural heritage takes place in June in Rock Sound.

HOTELS

Harbour Island, more than any other Out Island, is where the cognoscenti come to bask in ultraluxurious inns and atmospheric small resorts. Follow the celebrities to $600-a-night cottages with views of the beach, or to elegant rooms in Dunmore Town. Eleuthera offers elegant intimate, beach-adjacent resorts pleasantly empty of crowds. You'll also find plenty of friendly, tidy, and affordable inns, a few on the beach, for around $200 a night. For urbanites who want all-out American luxury, there are modern town houses with stainless-steel appliances and granite in the kitchens, and bedrooms for the entire family. Whether you spend a lot or a little, the staff on this friendly island will know your name after a day. Many hotels are closed in September and October.

RESTAURANTS

Don't let the outdoor dining on rustic wood tables fool you—Harbour Island and Eleuthera offer sophisticated cuisine that rivals that of any restaurants in Nassau. Although the place is usually casual and you never have to wear a tie, food is taken seriously. Island specialties such as cracked conch, barbecued pork, or chicken, and the succulent Bahamian lobster (known locally as crawfish) still abound, but you'll also find cappuccinos, steak, and lobster ravioli. Stop by Harbour Island's conch shacks on Bay Street north of Government Dock, where you can eat fresh conch salad on decks next to the water.

Most eateries are closed Sunday. Many restaurants have entertainment on regular nights so plan your dining schedule accordingly.

Restaurant prices are based on the median main course price at dinner, excluding gratuity, typically 15%, which is often automatically added to the bill. Hotel prices are for two people in a standard double room in high season, excluding service and 6%–12% tax.

WHAT IT COSTS IN DOLLARS			
$	$$	$$$	$$$$
Restaurants	under $20	$20–$30	$31–$40	over $40
Hotels	under $200	$200–$300	$301–$400	over $400

VISITOR INFORMATION

Contacts Eleuthera Tourist Office. ☎ *242/332–2145* ⊕ *www.bahamas.com.*
Harbour Island Tourist Office. ⊠ *Dunmore St.* ☎ *242/333–2621*
⊕ *www.bahamas.com.* **Out Islands Promotion Board.** ☎ *242/322–1140*
⊕ *www.myoutislands.com.*

GETTING HERE AND AROUND

AIR TRAVEL

Eleuthera has three airports: **North Eleuthera (ELH)**, midisland **Governor's Harbour (GHB)**, and **Rock Sound International (RSD)** in the south. Taxis usually wait for scheduled flights at the airports. Taxi service for two people from North Eleuthera Airport to the Cove is $35 ($60 from Governor's Harbour Airport); from Governor's Harbour to Pineapple Fields, $30; from Rock Sound airport to Cape Eleuthera, $70. Visitors going to Harbour Island and Spanish Wells should fly into North Eleuthera Airport.

Contacts Governor's Harbour Airport. ☎ *242/332–2321.* **North Eleuthera Airport.** ✣ *North Eleuthera* ☎ *242/335–1242.* **Rock Sound Airport.**
☎ *242/334–2177.*

BOAT AND FERRY TRAVEL

Mail boats leave from Nassau's Potter's Cay for the five-hour trip to Eleuthera. One-way tickets cost $30. M/V *Current Pride* sails to Current Island, Hatchet Bay, the Bluff, and James Cistern on Thursday, returning Tuesday to Nassau. M/V *Bahamas Daybreak III* leaves Nassau on Monday and Wednesday for Harbour Island, Rock Sound, and Davis Harbour, returning to Nassau Tuesday and Friday. The *Eleuthera Express* sails for Governor's Harbour, Rock Sound, Spanish Wells, and Harbour Island on Monday and Thursday, returning to Nassau on Tuesday and Sunday. Contact the **Dockmaster's Office. Bahamas Ferries,** high-speed catamarans, connect Nassau to Harbour Island, Governor's Harbour, and Spanish Wells. The trip takes three hours and costs $155 round-trip.

Contacts Dockmaster's Office. ☎ *242/393–1064.*

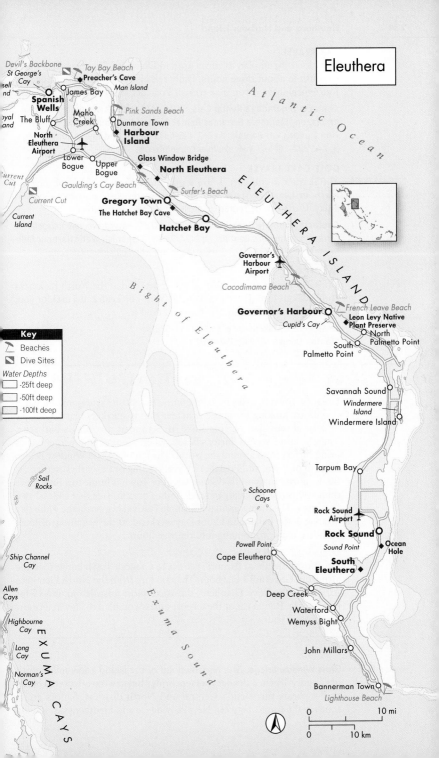

CAR TRAVEL

Rent a car if you plan to travel around Eleuthera. You can drive north to south in about three hours. Daily rentals run about $70. Request a four-wheel drive if you plan to visit Preacher's Cave or Surfer's Beach.

Contacts Big Daddy's Rental Cars. ☎ *242/470–9003* ⊕ *www.wcbigdaddyrentalcars.com.* **Eleuthera Bahamas Rental Car and Taxi Tour.** ☎ *242/359–7163.* **Fine Threads Car Rentals.** ☎ *242/436–5989.* **Taylor and Taylor Rent-A-Car.** ☎ *242/332–1665* ⊕ *www.eleutheracarrentals.com.*

GOLF CART TRAVEL

You'll want a golf cart if you spend more than a couple of days on Harbour Island or Spanish Wells. Four-seater carts start at about $60 a day. Carts can be rented at most hotels and at the docks.

Contacts Dunmore Rentals. ☎ *242/333–2372* ⊕ *www.dunmorerentalsgolfcarts.com.* **Johnson's Rentals.** ☎ *242/333–2376.* **Spanish Wells Harbour Side Rentals.** ☎ *242/333–5022* ⊕ *www.spanishwellsharboursiderentals.com.*

TAXI TRAVEL

Taxis are almost always waiting at airports and at the North Eleuthera and Harbour Island water taxi docks. Your hotel can call a taxi for you; let them know a half hour before you need it.

Contacts J.Q. Taxi Service. ☎ *242/553–6781.* **Stanton Cooper.** ☎ *242/359–7007.*

GREGORY TOWN AND NORTH ELEUTHERA

Gregory Town is a sleepy community, except on Friday nights when people are looking for music, whether that is speakers blasting reggae or a local musician playing Rake 'n' Scrape at a roadside barbecue. There's action, too, at Surfer's Beach, where summer and winter waves bring surfers from around the world. The famous Glass Window Bridge is north of town, and Preacher's Cave, landing of the earliest settlers, is on the northern tip of the island. Gregory Town is home to a little more than 400 people, residing in small houses on a hillside that slides down to the sea. The town's annual Pineapple Festival begins on the Thursday evening of the Bahamian Labor Day weekend, at the beginning of June, with live music continuing into the wee hours.

GETTING HERE AND AROUND

The North Eleuthera Airport is closer to Gregory Town hotels than the airport in Governor's Harbour. The taxi fare from the North Eleuthera Airport to the Cove Eleuthera, the area's most upscale inn, is $35 for two people. Rent a car at the airport unless you plan to stay at a resort for most of your visit.

EXPLORING

Fodor'sChoice
★   **Glass Window Bridge.** At a narrow point of the island a few miles north of Gregory Town, a slender concrete bridge links two sea-battered bluffs that separate the island's Central and North districts. Sailors going south in the waters between New Providence and Eleuthera supposedly

named this area the Glass Window because they could see through the natural limestone arch to the Atlantic on the other side. Stop to watch the northeasterly deep-azure Atlantic swirl together under the bridge with the southwesterly turquoise Bight of Eleuthera, producing a brilliant aquamarine froth. Artist Winslow Homer found the site stunning, and painted *Glass Window* in 1885. The original stone arch, created by Mother Nature, was destroyed by a combination of storms in the 1940s. Subsequent concrete bridges were destroyed by hurricanes in 1992 and 1999. Drive carefully, because there is frequent maintenance work going on. ⊠ *Queen's Hwy, North of Gregory Town, Gregory Town.*

> ### PINEAPPLE EXPRESS
>
> Pineapples remain Eleuthera's most famous product, even though the industry has been greatly reduced since the late 1800s, when the island dominated the world's pineapple market. These intensely sweet fruits are still grown on family farms, primarily in northern Eleuthera. Don't miss Gregory Town's Pineapple Festival in June.

Fodor'sChoice ★ **Preacher's Cave.** At the island's northern tip, this cave is where the Eleutheran Adventurers (the island's founders) took refuge and held services when their ship wrecked in 1648. Note the original stone altar inside the cave, done by Captain William Sayles in the 1600s. Across from the cave is a long succession of deserted pink-sand beaches. ⊠ *North Eleuthera* ⊹ *Follow Queen's Hwy. to T-intersection at north end of island. Turn right and follow signs to cave.*

BEACHES

Gaulding's Cay Beach. Snorkelers and divers will want to spend time at this beach, 3 miles north of Gregory Town. You'll most likely have the long stretch of white sand and shallow aqua water all to yourself, and it's great for shelling. At low tide, you can walk or swim to Gaulding's Cay, a tiny rock island with a few casuarina trees. There's great snorkeling around the island; you'll see a concentration of sea anemones so spectacular it dazzled even Jacques Cousteau's biologists. **Amenities:** none. **Best for:** snorkeling; sunset. ⊠ *Queen's Hwy., across from Daddy Joe's restaurant, Gregory Town* ☎ *242/332–2142.*

Surfer's Beach. This is Gregory Town's claim to fame and one of the few beaches in the Bahamas known for surfing. Serious surfers have gathered here since the 1960s for decent waves from December to April. If you don't have a jeep, you can walk the ¾ mile to this Atlantic-side beach—take a right onto the paved road past the Hatchet Bay silos, just south of Gregory Town. Look for a young crowd sitting around bonfires at night. **Amenities:** none. **Best for:** surfing. ⊠ *Queen's Hwy., Gregory Town.*

Tay Bay Beach. Steps from historical Preacher's Cave, this beach offers a long expanse of pink powdery sand. The area is remote, so you're likely to have the beach to yourself. There are plenty of palmetto trees to relax underneath for a quiet afternoon. Just offshore is Devil's Backbone, where the Eleutheran Adventurers shipwrecked and sought shelter in the cave. **Amenities:** parking. **Best for:** solitude; walking. ⊠ *North*

Eleuthera ✥ Follow Queen's Hwy. to T-intersection at north end of island. Turn right and follow signs to Preacher's Cave.

WHERE TO EAT

$$$ EUROPEAN Fodor's Choice ★ **The Cove Eleuthera Restaurant.** The spacious, window-lined dining room serves three meals a day, blending classic Continental with fresh Bahamian fare. An extensive cocktail list from the Freedom Bar includes the Glass Window Bridge—the exquisite landmark of the same name is just a short drive away. **Known for:** excellent sushi; stone crab; soy agave St. Louis ribs. *Average main: $33 ✉ Queen's Hwy., Gregory Town ☎ 242/335–5142, 888/776–3901 ⊕ www.thecoveeleuthera.com.*

$$ BAHAMIAN **Daddy Joe's.** Located just south of the Glass Window Bridge, this restaurant hosts live bands every Sunday. Order conch bites as a starter to complement the long list of tropical concoctions, including the aptly named "Da Glass Window." In addition to wings and wraps, Daddy Joe's also offers grilled options like fresh seafood and chicken. **Known for:** live music; in-season guava duff dessert; delicious chicken wings. *Average main: $21 ✉ Queen's Hwy., Gregory Town ☎ 242/335–5688 ▭ No credit cards.*

WHERE TO STAY

$$$ RESORT Fodor's Choice ★ **The Cove Eleuthera.** Forty secluded acres studded with scenic beach cottages set the tone for this relaxing island escape; a rocky promontory separates two coves, each with a sandy beach and calm water, perfect for snorkeling. **Pros:** sandy beaches; top-rated amenities; one of the most luxurious places to stay on the island. **Cons:** need a car if you want to do anything outside the property; resort is quiet and secluded; some lower-budget rooms lack the privacy of the bungalows and villas. *Rooms from: $395 ✉ Queen's Hwy., Gregory Town ✥ 1½ miles north of Gregory Town ☎ 242/335–5142, 888/776–3901 ⊕ www.thecoveeleuthera.com ⇨ 57 rooms ǀ◎ǀ No meals.*

NIGHTLIFE

The Sunset Lounge. The new Sunset Lounge formally known as Elvina's derives its name from the breathtaking views from the balcony at dusk. Guests can enjoy live sessions with local bands on a Friday night while dining indoors, outside on the porch, or up on the sunset deck. *✉ Gregory Town ✥ Queen's Hwy. ☎ 242/699–5598 ✉ Free.*

SHOPPING

Fodor's Choice ★ **Island Made Shop.** This shop, run by Pam and Greg Thompson, is a good place to shop for Bahamian arts and crafts, including Androsia batik (made on Andros Island), driftwood paintings, Abaco ceramics, Neem products and prints. Look for the old foam buoys which have been carved and painted into fun faces. *✉ Queen's Hwy., Gregory Town ☎ 242/335–5369 ⏲ Closed Sun.*

SPORTS AND THE OUTDOORS

ADVENTURE TOURS

Bahamas Out-Island Adventures. This tour operator offers day, half-day, and overnight kayaking, snorkeling, and surfing trips, and offers accommodations at its headquarters at Surfer's Beach. ⊠ *Gregory Town* ☎ *242/551–9635* ⊕ *www.bahamasadventures.com.*

ISLAND TOURS

Arthur Nixon Tours. The caretaker and keeper of the North Palmetto Sound Lighthouse offers tours of the lighthouse and the island. ☎ *242/359–7879.*

Eleuthera Adventure Tours. Eleuthera Adventure Tours provides a guided tour of southern Eleuthera, including quaint villages with pristine little churches, lush vegetation, and glimpses of the island's historical sites and beaches. The company also provides yacht and boat charters. ☎ *242/334–2356* ⊕ *www.eleutheraadventuretours.com* 🖃 *$99.*

Pineapple Tours. Pineapple Tours can help you experience the northern end of Eleuthera. The tour visits the Backyard Nature Trail, Ocean Hole landmark, and Rock Sound Cave, followed by lunch and lounging on a white sandy beach. ⊠ *Rock Sound* ☎ *242/551–0366.*

SCUBA DIVING AND SNORKELING

The **Current Cut,** a narrow passage between North Eleuthera and Current Island, is loaded with marine life and provides a roller-coaster ride on the currents. You'll want a boat and, most importantly, a guide, as the fast current can be dangerous. In North Eleuthera, **Devil's Backbone** offers a tricky reef area with a nearly infinite number of dive sites and a large number of wrecks. Contact a local dive shop to schedule a trip.

SURFING

Rebecca's Beach Shop. In Gregory Town, stop by Rebecca's Beach Shop, a general store, crafts shop, and, most important, a surf shop, where local surf guru "Ponytail Pete" rents surfboards, fishing and snorkel gear, and more. A chalkboard lists surf conditions and tidal reports. He also gives surf lessons. ⊠ *Queen's Hwy., Gregory Town* ☎ *242/335–5436.*

HATCHET BAY

"The Country's Safest Harbour," Hatchet Bay, which has one of mid-Eleuthera's few marinas, is a good place to find a fishing guide and friendly locals, or to anchor sailboats and fishing vessels when storms are coming. Take note of the town's side roads, which have such colorful names as Lazy Road, Happy Hill Road, and Smile Lane. Just south of town, the Rainbow Inn and restaurant is the hub of activity for this stretch of the island. Don't miss James Cistern, a seaside settlement to the south.

GETTING HERE AND AROUND

Hatchet Bay is equidistant between the Governor's Harbour and North Eleuthera airports. The taxi fare from either airport is about $50 for two people. Rent a car at the airport unless you plan to stay at a resort for most of your visit.

EXPLORING

The Hatchet Bay Cave. North of Hatchet Bay lies a subterranean, bat-populated tunnel complete with stalagmites and stalactites. Pirates supposedly once used it to hide their loot. An underground path leads for more than a mile to the sea, ending in a lofty, cathedral-like cavern. Within its depths, fish swim in total darkness. The adventurous may wish to explore this area with a flashlight (follow the length of guide string along the cavern's floor), but it's best to inquire first at one of the local stores or the Rainbow Inn for a guide. ✉ *Queen's Hwy.* ✣ *2 miles north of Hatchet Bay, turn left at sign for "Hatchet Bay Caves".*

WHERE TO EAT

$$ SEAFOOD 🍴 **The Front Porch.** This little roadside restaurant features a beautiful view of the bay, particularly at sunset when the orange horizon is freckled with the silhouettes of moored sailboats. The menu is island-inspired European cuisine and always includes fresh seafood. **Known for:** Caesar salad with a twist; sunset views; can arrange captains and tour guides. [$] *Average main: $24* ✉ *Queen's Hwy.* ☎ *242/335–0727.*

$$$ EUROPEAN 🍴 **The Rainbow Inn Steakhouse.** With a classy but no-fuss aura and exhibition windows that face gorgeous sunsets, this restaurant is well known for its steaks, which are flown in daily. Grouper, conch, mahimahi, and cobia are also fresh, caught daily. **Known for:** fresh fish; wood-fired pizzas; live music. [$] *Average main: $35* ✉ *Queen's Hwy.* ✣ *2½ miles south of Hatchet Bay* ☎ *242/335–0294* 🌐 *www.rainbowinn.com* ⏲ *Closed Tues. and end of Aug.–Oct.*

$$ BAHAMIAN 🍴 **Twin Brothers.** This brightly painted restaurant is famous for its frozen daiquiris. Icy mixes of strawberry and piña colada are swirled into a striking (and delicious) dessert cocktail. **Known for:** dessert cocktails; alfresco dining; Bahamian specialties. [$] *Average main: $25* ✉ *West off Queen's Hwy.* ☎ *242/335–0730* 🌐 *www.twinbrothersbahamas.com* 💳 *No credit cards* ⏲ *Closed Mon.*

WHERE TO STAY

$ RENTAL Fodor's Choice ★ 🏨 **Rainbow Inn.** Immaculate, generously sized cottages, some octagonal—all with large private porches—have sweeping views of the ocean. **Pros:** super-spacious cottages at reasonable prices; great water views; friendly service. **Cons:** not on the beach; not close to a town or shops; rustic accommodations. [$] *Rooms from: $135* ✉ *Queen's Hwy.* ✣ *2½ miles south of Hatchet Bay* ☎ *242/335–0294* 🌐 *www.rainbowinn.com* ⏲ *Closed end of Aug.–Oct.* 🛏 *4 cottages, 2 villas* 🍽 *Some meals.*

NIGHTLIFE

Dr. Sea Breeze. The debonair Cedric Bethel, better known as Dr. Sea Breeze, strums his acoustic guitar while singing island songs at the Rainbow Inn in Hatchet Bay and Sky Beach Club in Governor's Harbour. Call beforehand to confirm his schedule. ☎ *242/470–0504.*

GOVERNOR'S HARBOUR

Governor's Harbour, the capital of Eleuthera and home to government offices, is the largest town on the island and one of the prettiest. Victorian-era houses were built on Buccaneer Hill, which overlooks the harbor, bordered on the south by a narrow peninsula and Cupid's Cay at the tip. To fully understand its appeal, you have to settle in for a few days and explore on foot—if you don't mind the steep climb up the narrow lanes. The town is a step into a gentler, more genteel time. Everyone says hello, and entertainment means wading into the harbor to cast a line, or taking a painting class taught by Martha's Vineyard artist Donna Allen at the 19th-century pink library on Monday mornings. You can see a current movie at the balconied Globe Princess, the only theater on the island, which also serves the best hamburgers in town. Or, swim at the gorgeous beaches on either side of town, which stretch from the pink sands of the ocean to the white sands of the Bight of Eleuthera. There are three banks, a few grocery stores, and some of the island's wealthiest residents, who prefer the quiet of Eleuthera to the fashionable party scene of Harbour Island.

GETTING HERE AND AROUND

Fly into Governor's Harbour Airport north of town, or arrive by mail boat from Nassau. You will want to rent a car at the airport, even if you plan to stay in Governor's Harbour, to best explore the beaches and restaurants.

EXPLORING

Haynes Library. The heart of the community, this 19th-century building offers art classes and Tuesday-morning coffee hours for visitors and residents. The library has a wide selection of books and computers, with gorgeous views of the harbor. ⊠ *Cupid's Cay Rd.* ☎ *242/332–2877* ☉ *Closed weekends.*

Leon Levy Native Plant Preserve. Walk miles of scenic trails in this 25-acre nature preserve located on Banks Road. Funded by the Leon Levy Foundation and operated by the Bahamas National Trust, the preserve serves as an environmental education center with a focus on traditional bush medicine. Follow the boardwalk over a small waterfall and take the path to the Observation Tower to see hundreds of indigenous trees, plants, and wildlife such as mangroves, five-finger plants, and bullfinches. Group tours are available, or if you'd prefer to tour the preserve on your own, the welcome center will provide you with a map and a plant identification guide. ⊠ *Banks Rd.* ☎ *242/332–3831* ⊕ *www.levypreserve.org* 🖂 *$10.*

BEACHES

FAMILY **Cocodimama Beach.** Many necklaces and shell decorations come from Cocodimama, which, along with Ten Bay Beach at South Palmetto Point, is well known for perfect small shells. The water at this secluded beach, 6 miles north of Governor's Harbour, has the aqua and sky-blue

A Governor's Harbour home

shades you see on Bahamas posters, and is shallow and calm, perfect for children and sand castles. **Amenities:** parking. **Best for:** sunset. ⊠ *Queen's Hwy.* ✛ *Look for Cocodimama Charming Resort* ☏ *242/332–2142.*

French Leave Beach. This stretch of pink sand was Club Med's famed beach before the resort was destroyed by a hurricane in 1999, and is now home to the new French Leave Marina Village. The gorgeous Atlantic-side beach is anchored by fantastic bistros like the Beach House and Tippy's. The wide expanse, ringed by casuarina trees, is often deserted and makes a great outpost for romantics. **Amenities:** food and drink. **Best for:** solitude; swimming; walking. ⊠ *Banks Rd.* ⊕ *www. frenchleaveeleuthera.com.*

WHERE TO EAT

$ ✕ **Banks Road Deli.** For the perfect beach picnic, stop by Banks Road
DELI Deli to pick up freshly made sandwiches, chips, and homemade cookies. Located in the same building as Pineapple Field's Gift Store, the deli also serves pastries and coffee in the morning, which you can enjoy in their quiet outdoor seating area. **Known for:** picnic supplies; gourmet groceries; coffee and pastries. Ⓢ *Average main: $9* ⊠ *Banks Rd.* ☏ *242/332–2221* ☾ *Closed Sun.*

$ ✕ **Mate & Jenny's Restaurant & Bar.** A few miles south of Governor's
PIZZA Harbour, this casual neighborhood restaurant specializes in pizza; try one topped with conch. Sandwiches and Bahamian specialties are also served. **Known for:** conch-topped pizza; kitschy decor; dart games. Ⓢ *Average main: $14* ⊠ *S. Palmetto Point* ☏ *242/332–1504* ▭ *No credit cards* ☾ *Closed Tues.*

$$ ✕ **Pascal's Oceanfront Seafood Res-**
ECLECTIC **taurant.** In addition to ocean-view seating in its outdoor dining room, Pascal's also features a swim-up bar, perfect for a leisurely lunch. Relax in the infinity-edge pool while you savor a mango daiquiri and cheeseburger, and take in the magnificent view of the Atlantic. **Known for:** sophisticated atmosphere; fresh local seafood; pool and beachside dining. $ *Average main: $25* ✉ *Sky Beach Club, Queen's Hwy.* ☎ *242/332–3422* ⊕ *www.pascalsoceanfront.com.*

> **WHERE DOES PINK SAND COME FROM?**
>
> Contrary to popular belief, pink sand comes primarily from the crushed pink and red shells of microscopic insects called foraminifera, not coral. Foraminifer live on the underside of reefs and the sea floor. After the insects die, the waves smash the shells, which wash ashore along with sand and bits of pink coral. The intensity of the rosy hues depends on the slant of the sun.

$$ ✕ **1648 Bar and Grille.** Take in the
ECLECTIC sunset view as you enjoy a glass of wine and an island-inspired pizza at 1648 Bar and Grille. Located at French Leave Harbour Village, the restaurant boasts a sweeping view of the Bight of Eleuthera and its stunning turquoise water. **Known for:** seafood risotto; tropical cocktails; poolside dining. $ *Average main: $28* ✉ *French Leave Harbour Village, Queen's Hwy.* ☎ *242/332–3777* ⊕ *www.frenchleaveeleuthera.com.*

$$ ✕ **Tippy's.** Despite its barefoot-casual environment (old window shutters
ECLECTIC used as tabletops, sand in the floor's crevices), the menu at this open-air
Fodor's Choice beach bistro is a sophisticated mix of Bahamian and European cuisine, with
★ items that change daily based on the availability of fresh local products. Expect things like lobster salad, specialty pizzas, and fresh fish prepared with some sort of delectable twist. **Known for:** French chef; outdoor seating; live music on Saturday. $ *Average main: $25* ✉ *Banks Rd.* ☎ *242/332–3331* ⊕ *www.pineapplefields.com* ⊗ *Closed Mon. and Sept. and Oct.*

$$ ✕ **Unique Village Sea View Restaurant and Bar.** Bahamas home cooking is
BAHAMIAN the reason to come to this octagonal restaurant, with its pagoda-style natural-wood ceiling, wraparound covered deck, and panoramic view of the beach. The restaurant–bar is a popular spot for locals and visitors, especially for the live music on Tuesday. **Known for:** live music on Tuesday; chef's snapper special; homemade bread. $ *Average main: $27* ✉ *North Palmetto Point, Banks Rd.* ☎ *242/332–1830* ⊕ *www.uniquevillage.com.*

WHERE TO STAY

$$$$ ⬚ **French Leave Harbour Village.** This Governor's Harbour resort, which
RESORT welcomed its first guests in August 2013, offers gorgeous waterfront
Fodor's Choice bungalows, a harbor-view bar and grill, a freshwater pool, and doz-
★ ens of other luxurious amenities. **Pros:** relatively new resort; beautiful harbor views; luxurious amenities. **Cons:** you'll need a car if you want to explore the island; construction is ongoing; all accommodations are presently harbor-facing, not on the beach. $ *Rooms from: $450* ✉ *Queen's Hwy.* ☎ *239/482–8173* ⊕ *www.frenchleaveeleuthera.com* ⇆ *4 villas* ⦿ *No meals.*

6

Where to Eat and Stay in Governor's Harbour

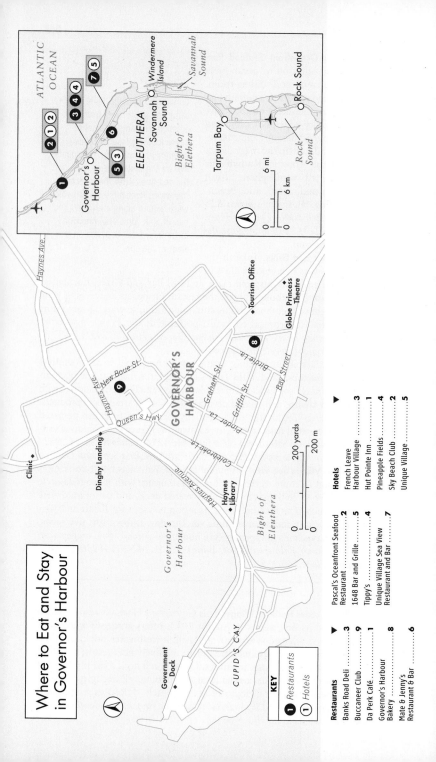

KEY
▸ Restaurants
① Hotels

Restaurants ▸

Banks Road Deli **3**
Buccaneer Club **9**
Da Perk Café **1**
Governor's Harbour
Bakery **8**
Mate & Jenny's
Restaurant & Bar **6**

Pascal's Oceanfront Seafood
Restaurant **2**
1648 Bar and Grille **5**
Tippy's **4**
Unique Village Sea View
Restaurant and Bar **7**

Hotels ▸

French Leave **3**
Harbour Village **1**
Hut Pointe Inn **1**
Pineapple Fields **4**
Sky Beach Club **2**
Unique Village **5**

$$ B&B/INN **Hut Pointe Inn.** Those looking for history and luxury will find much to like about this historic building constructed in 1944 by the first premier of the Bahamas, Sir Roland Symonette. **Pros:** historic building; wonderfully landscaped grounds; upscale amenities. **Cons:** within a few feet of the Queen's Highway; not on beach; 10 minutes from town. [$] *Rooms from: $255* ✉ *Queen's Hwy.* ☎ *760/908–6700* 🌐 *www.hutpointe.com* ⏲ *Closed Sept. and Oct.* 🛏 *5 suites* 🍴 *No meals.*

$$ RENTAL FAMILY Fodor's Choice ★ **Pineapple Fields.** Across the street from a pink-sand Atlantic beach and Tippy's oceanfront bistro, Pineapple Fields is the perfect base for a disappearing act. **Pros:** modern facilities and amenities; large units; secluded beach and Tippy's across the street. **Cons:** sterile American-style condo; will need to drive to town; not oceanfront. [$] *Rooms from: $220* ✉ *Banks Rd.* ☎ *242/332–2221* 🌐 *www.pineapplefields.com* ⏲ *Closed mid-Oct.–mid-Sept.* 🛏 *32 condo units* 🍴 *No meals.*

LEARNING IN PARADISE

The Island School is a pioneering 14-week program for high-school students that's a model of sustainability—students and teachers work together to run a campus where rainwater is captured for use, solar and wind energy are harnessed, food comes from its own small farm, wastewater is filtered and reused to irrigate landscaping, and biofuel is made from cruise ships' restaurant grease to power vehicles and generators. This "mind, body, and spirit experience" aims to inspire students to be responsible, caring global citizens. Occasional tours available by appointment. ☎ *242/334–8551*

$$$ RESORT **Sky Beach Club.** Perched on 22 acres of oceanfront property, this modern resort rents poolside bungalows and large four-bedroom houses. **Pros:** secluded pink-sand beach; restaurant on-property; close to airport. **Cons:** need a car to get to town; faces the less tranquil Atlantic. [$] *Rooms from: $325* ✉ *Queen's Hwy.* ☎ *242/422–9597* 🌐 *www.skybeachclub.com* 🛏 *3 bungalows, 4 houses.*

$ HOTEL **Unique Village.** Just south of Governor's Harbour near North Palmetto Point on marvelous pink Poponi Beach, this resort has large, refurbished rooms with French doors opening to private balconies. **Pros:** on a gorgeous pink beach; steps to large pool and restaurant. **Cons:** must go down many wood stairs to access beach; a 10-minute drive to Governor's Harbour. [$] *Rooms from: $180* ✉ *North Palmetto Point, Banks Rd.* ☎ *242/332–1830* 🌐 *www.uniquevillage.com* 🛏 *10 rooms, 4 villas* 🍴 *No meals.*

NIGHTLIFE

Dr. Sea Breeze. Dr. Sea Breeze plays calypso at Sky Beach Club in Governor's Harbour and at Rainbow Inn, south of Hatchet Bay. Be sure to call ahead to make sure he's scheduled. ☎ *242/470–0504.*

Globe Princess. The Globe Princess hosts a showing of one current film each night at 8:15 pm. Movies change weekly. The concession serves some of the best hamburgers in town and is open for lunch 11–3 weekdays. ✉ *Queen's Hwy.* ☎ 🎟 *$5.50* ⏲ *Closed Thurs.*

Ronnie's Hi-D-Way. With a pool table, outdoor basketball court, and large dance floor, Ronnie's is the most popular local hangout in Governor's Harbour. The scene really takes off on Friday and Saturday night, when the bar hosts a DJ. If you drop in for a drink on the weekend, expect to stay a while for dancing to popular reggae and hip-hop tunes. ⊠ *Cupid's Cay* ☎ *242/332–2307.*

SHOPPING

The Gift Shop at Pineapple Fields. You'll find Bahamian handcrafted art, locally made jewelry, and elegant beachwear in this gift shop, located in the same building as Pineapple Fields' office and Banks Road Deli. ⊠ *Bay St.* ☎ *242/332–2221* ⊕ *www.pineapplefields.com* ⊗ *Closed Sun. and Oct.*

SPORTS AND THE OUTDOORS

FISHING

Paul Petty. Paul is one of the best in the business for guiding anglers through the flats in Governor's Harbour. With his help, you're sure to hook a bonefish. He is also a knowledgeable reef-fishing and deep-sea-fishing guide. ⊠ *Governor's Harbour* ☎ *242/332–2963.*

ROCK SOUND AND SOUTH ELEUTHERA

One of Eleuthera's largest settlements, the village of **Rock Sound** has a small airport serving the island's southern part. Front Street, the main thoroughfare, runs along the seashore, where fishing boats are tied up. If you walk down the street, you'll eventually come to the whitewashed St. Luke's Anglican Church, a contrast to the deep-blue and green houses nearby with their colorful gardens full of poinsettia, hibiscus, and marigolds. If you pass the church on a Sunday, you'll surely hear fervent hymn singing through the open windows. Rock Sound has the island's largest supermarket shopping center, where locals stock up on groceries and supplies.

The tiny settlement of **Bannerman Town** (population 40) is 25 miles from Rock Sound at the island's southern tip, which is punctuated by an old cliff-top lighthouse. Rent an SUV if you plan to drive out to it; the rutted sand road is often barely passable. The pink-sand beach here is gorgeous, and on a clear day you can see the Bahamas' highest point, Mt. Alvernia (elevation 206 feet), on distant Cat Island. The town lies about 30 miles from the residential Cotton Bay Club, past the quiet little fishing villages of Wemyss Bight (named after Lord Gordon Wemyss, a 17th-century Scottish slave owner) and John Millars (population 15), barely touched over the years.

GETTING HERE AND AROUND

Fly into Rock Sound Airport and rent a car. The airport is just north of town, and The Island School is a 22-mile drive south. If you fly into Governor's Harbour, plan to rent a car at the airport—Rock Sound is about 34 miles south. Taxis are available at both airports, but can be expensive.

EXPLORING

Ocean Hole. A small inland saltwater lake a mile southeast of Rock Sound is connected by tunnels to the sea. Steps have been cut into the coral on the shore so visitors can climb down to the lake's edge. Bring a piece of bread or some fries and watch the fish emerge for their hors d'oeuvres, swimming their way in from the sea. A local diver estimates the hole is about 75 feet deep. He reports that there are a couple of cars at the bottom, too. Local children learn to swim here. ✉ *Queen's Hwy., Rock Sound* ✥ *A Bahamas Heritage sign, across street from church, marks path to Ocean Hole* ☎ *242/332–2142.*

St. Luke's Anglican Church. This idyllic seaside church on Front Street, which runs along the shore, has a belfry and a garden of poinsettia, hibiscus, and marigolds. ✉ *Queen's Hwy., Rock Sound* ☎ *242/334–2070.*

SOFTBALL: THE SPORT OF THE ISLAND

Fast-pitch softball is a ubiquitous sport in Eleuthera. The Eleuthera Twin City Destroyers were the men's champions of the 2006 Bahamas Softball Federation tournament. On most any weekend afternoon from March to November you can find the team playing at Rock Sound or Palmetto baseball parks on the island, known as the Softball Capital of the Bahamas. Eleuthera pitchers and brothers Edney and Edmond Bethel are both players for the Bahamas National Team, which has been consistently in the top 10 in the world.

BEACHES

Lighthouse Beach. You'll need an SUV to cross the rocky terrain to get to this beach, but the drive is well worth the breathtaking views. Lighthouse beach has it all: dramatic cliffs, a pink sand, plenty of shade beneath the trees—and you'll likely have it entirely to yourself. Reefs just off the beach make it a great place to spend the day snorkeling. Be aware that there can be a strong current. **Amenities:** none. **Best for:** solitude; snorkeling; walking. ✉ *Southern tip of Eleuthera, Bannerman Town.*

WHERE TO EAT

$$ CARIBBEAN 🍴 **Harbour Pointe at Cape Eleuthera.** Located at Cape Eleuthera Resort with a breathtaking sunset view, Harbour Pointe offers Caribbean cuisine in a casual setting. The restaurant features indoor and outdoor seating with panoramic views of the pool, marina, and ocean. **Known for:** burgers; beautiful views; chefs will cook what you catch. [$] *Average main: $25* ✉ *Cape Eleuthera Resort and Marina, Rock Sound* ☎ *242/334–8500* 🌐 *www.capeeleuthera.com* 🕓 *Closed Mon.*

$ BAHAMIAN FAMILY 🍴 **Northside Restaurant and Bar.** If you want an authentic Bahamian meal, look no further than Northside Restaurant & Bar, a Rock Sound establishment famous for its sweeping Atlantic views. Northside's menu varies based on available fresh seafood, but you can always find Bahamian specialties such as baked macaroni and cheese, plantains, and peas 'n' rice. **Known for:** made-to-order meals; authentic Bahamian cuisine; fresh seafood. $ *Average main: $18* ⊠ *Northside Cottages, Rock Sound* ☎ *242/334–2573* ⊕ *www.northsideinneleuthera.com.*

$ ✕ **Sammy's Place.** Owned by Sammy Culmer and managed by his
BAHAMIAN   friendly daughter Margarita, Sammy's serves conch fritters, fried chicken, lobster and fish, and peas 'n' rice. When it's in season, don't miss the guava duff dessert: sweet bread with swirls of creamy guava. **Known for:** guava duff dessert; great BLT; family owned and operated. $ *Average main: $19* ⊠ *Albury La., Rock Sound* ☎ *242/334–2121* ▭ *No credit cards.*

WHERE TO STAY

$$ ⛺ **Cape Eleuthera Resort and Marina.** Nestled between the aquamarine
RESORT   and emerald waters of Rock and Exuma sounds, gigantic townhomes
FAMILY   have two bright bedrooms, each with a full bath and a stainless-steel kitchen. **Pros:** handsome resort right on the water; professional and friendly staff; gear rental on-site for water and land excursions (some with fee). **Cons:** isolated from rest of island; need a car to leave resort; on-property restaurant is the only dining option nearby. $ *Rooms from: $299* ⊠ *Cape Eleuthera, Rock Sound* ☎ *242/334–8500* ⊕ *www.capeeleuthera.com* ⇴ *14 villas* ⦿ *No meals.*

$ ⛺ **Northside Cottages.** These quaint cottages are nestled into a hillside
RENTAL   with an extraordinary view of the Atlantic. **Pros:** beachfront; restaurant on-property; friendly staff. **Cons:** steep walk down to the beach; the area is remote; only three cottages on the property. $ *Rooms from: $140* ⊠ *Northshore Dr., Rock Sound* ⛿ *Turn off Queen's Hwy. in Rock Sound onto Fish St. Turn left at T-intersection onto Northshore Dr., then right at end of pavement* ☎ *242/334–2573* ⊕ *www.northsideinneleuthera.com* ⇴ *3 cottages* ⦿ *No meals.*

HARBOUR ISLAND

Harbour Island has often been called the Nantucket of the Caribbean and the most gorgeous of the Out Islands because of its powdery pink-sand beaches (3 miles' worth!) and its pastel-color clapboard houses with dormer windows, set among white picket fences, narrow lanes, cute shops, and tropical flowers.

The frequent parade of the fashionable and famous, and the chic small inns that accommodate them, have earned the island another name: the St. Bart's of the Bahamas. But residents have long called it Briland, their faster way of pronouncing "Harbour Island." These inhabitants include families who go back generations to the island's early settlement, as well as a growing number of celebrities, supermodels, and tycoons who feel that Briland is the perfect haven to bask in small-town charm against a stunning oceanscape. Some of the Bahamas' most handsome small hotels, each strikingly distinct, are tucked within the island's 2 square miles. Several are perched on a bluff above the shore, and you can fall asleep with the windows open and listen to the waves lapping the beach. Take a walking tour of the narrow streets of **Dunmore Town,** named after the 18th-century royal governor of the Bahamas, Lord Dunmore, who built a summer home here and laid out the town, which served as the first capital of the Bahamas. It's the only town on Harbour Island, and you can take in all its attractions during a 20-minute stroll.

GETTING HERE AND AROUND

Access Harbour Island via a 10-minute ferry ride from the North Eleuthera dock. Fares are $5 per person in a boat of two or more, plus an extra dollar to be dropped off at the private Romora Bay Club docks and for nighttime rides.

The best way to get around the island is to rent a golf cart or bike, or hire a taxi, since climbing the island's hills can be strenuous in the midday heat. Staying in Dunmore Town puts you within walking distance to everything you'll need.

EXPLORING

Lone Tree. If you stroll to the end of Bay Street and follow the curve to the western edge of the island, you'll find the Lone Tree, one of the most photographed icons of Harbour Island. This enormous piece of driftwood is said to have washed up on shore after a bad storm and anchored itself on the shallow sandbar in a picturesque upright position, providing the perfect photo op for countless tourists. ✉ *Bay St* ☎ *242/333–2621 Harbour Island Tourist Board.*

Straw Crafts. A row of straw-work stands are on Bay Street next to the water, including Pat's, Dorothy's, and Sarah's, where you'll find straw bags, hats, and T-shirts. Food stands sell conch salad, Kalik beer, coconut water, and fruit juices. ✉ *Bay St.*

6

BEACHES

Fodor's Choice ★ **Pink Sands Beach.** This is the fairest pink beach of them all: 3 miles of pale pink sand behind some of the most expensive and posh inns in the Bahamas. Its sand is of such a fine consistency that it's almost as soft as talcum powder, and the gentle slope of the shore makes small waves break hundreds of yards offshore; you have to walk out quite a distance to get past your waist. This is the place to see the rich and famous in designer resort wear or ride a horse bareback across the sand and into the sea. **Amenities:** food and drink; toilets. **Best for:** partiers; sunrise; swimming; walking.

WHERE TO EAT

Many Harbour Island hotels and restaurants are closed from September through mid- to late October.

$$ ITALIAN ✕ **Acquapazza.** Briland's only Italian restaurant offers a change of pace from the island's standard fare, and a change of scenery, too. It's located on the island's south end at the Harbour Island Marina, with a dockside terrace where you can take in the sunset while sipping one of its exclusively imported Italian wines. **Known for:** Italian wines; hearty portions; seafood. [$] *Average main: $30* ✉ *Harbour Island Marina, south end of island off Queens Hwy., Dunmore Town* ☎ *242/333–3240.*

DID YOU KNOW?

Deserted Island: It's not difficult to find an empty cay to call your own. Schooner Cays are just off the island's southern coast.

A stroll through Dunmore Town on Harbour Island is a must for any visitor.

$$ DELI

🍴 **Bahamas Coffee Roasters.** This charming café in the middle of Dunmore Town imports coffee beans from around the world and roasts them on-island to produce a number of special blends available to enjoy every morning. The vibe is decidedly surfer-chic, with modern artwork on the walls and picnic bench seating. Join them at brunch for a breakfast burrito with your fresh coffee; or during lunch for a sandwich, all made from local produce and organic meats. **Known for:** organic chicken sandwich; brunch; local produce. [$] *Average main: $20* ✉ *Dunmore St., Dunmore Town* ☎ *242/470–8015* 💳 *No credit cards.*

$$ ECLECTIC Fodor's Choice ★

🍴 **The Beach Bar at Coral Sands.** For lunch with a view, try Coral Sands' oceanfront bar and restaurant, just steps from the pink-sand beach. Executive Chef Ken Gomes creates delicious lunch options that go perfectly with a tropical cocktail or a glass of white wine. **Known for:** shrimp po'boy; gourmet pizzas; spicy fried calamari. [$] *Average main: $30* ✉ *Chapel St., Dunmore Town* ☎ *242/333–2350* 🌐 *www.coral-sands.com* 🕘 *Closed Sept. No dinner.*

$$ ECLECTIC

🍴 **The Blue Bar at Pink Sands.** Head to The Blue Bar for lunch outside overlooking the beach. You'll have an unbeatable view while sipping one of their signature cocktails and enjoying fish tacos, a grouper ciabatta, or any of the other island-inspired menu options. **Known for:** fish tacos; beachside dining; cracked conch. [$] *Average main: $20* ✉ *Pink Sands Resort, Chapel St., Dunmore Town* ☎ *242/333–2030* 🌐 *www.pinksandsresort.com* 🕘 *No dinner except in summer.*

$$$ CARIBBEAN

🍴 **The Dunmore.** Start with a signature cocktail at the handsome mahogany bar before enjoying dinner under the stars on the ocean-view porch at this recently renovated restaurant at The Dunmore. Executive Chef Philip Armbrister creates island-inspired dishes that

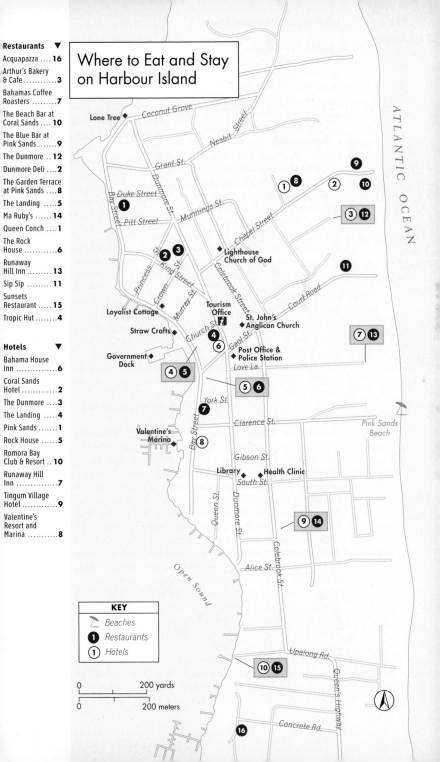

Where to Eat and Stay on Harbour Island

ATLANTIC OCEAN

Lone Tree ✦

Coconut Grove

Nesbit Street

Grant St.

Duke Street

Dunmore St.

Bay Street

Pitt Street

Munnings St.

Chapel Street

Princess St.

King Street

Crown St.

Murray St.

Lighthouse Church of God ✦

Catebrook Street

Court Road

Loyalist Cottage ✦

Tourism Office 🛈

Straw Crafts ✦

Church St.

Gaol St.

St. John's Anglican Church ✦

Post Office & Police Station ✦

Government Dock ✦

Love La.

York St.

Valentine's Marina ✦

Bay Street

Clarence St.

Pink Sands Beach

Gibson St.

Library ✦

Health Clinic ✦

South St.

Queen St.

Dunmore St.

Catebrook St.

Alice St.

Open Sound

Upalong Rd.

Queen's Highway

Concrete Rd.

KEY

☂ *Beaches*

● *Restaurants*

① *Hotels*

0 — 200 yards

0 — 200 meters

change seasonally. **Known for:** signature cocktails; charming interior; lobster ravioli. $ *Average main: $36* ⊠ *The Dunmore, Gaol La., Dunmore Town* ☎ *242/333–2200* ⊕ *www.dunmorebeach.com* ☺ *Closed mid-Aug.–mid-Nov.*

$ ✕**Dunmore Deli.** The Dunmore Deli
DELI   satisfies the epicurean demands of Briland's more finicky residents and visitors, while its shaded wooden porch, filled with hanging plants and bougainvillea, makes this the perfect spot for a lazy breakfast or lunch. Treat yourself to the Briland Bread Toast, the amazingly fluffy take on French toast, or pick up one of the inventive deli sandwiches for a picnic on the beach. **Known for:** excellent sandwiches; imported cheeses; fluffy French toast. $ *Average main: $15* ⊠ *King St., Dunmore Town* ☎ *242/333–2644* ☺ *Closed Sun.*

$$$$ ✕**The Landing.** You never know which actor or rock star you'll rub
ECLECTIC   elbows with—Richard Gere and Dave Matthews like to dine here—at
Fodor'sChoice   the Hemingway-esque bar, but none of it matters once you've moved on
★   to the dining room and are under the spell of Swedish chef Vincent Vitlock, whose dishes soar with a Southeast Asian flair. Standouts include the goat cheese ravioli with shrimp, walnut-crusted fresh fish, and banana upside-down cake. **Known for:** famous clientele; goat cheese ravioli; outdoor dining. $ *Average main: $45* ⊠ *The Landing, Bay St., Dunmore Town* ☎ *242/333–2707* ⊕ *www.harbourislandlanding.com* ☺ *Closed Wed. No lunch.*

$ ✕**Ma Ruby's.** Although you can sample local Bahamian fare at this
BAHAMIAN   famous eatery, the star of the menu is the cheeseburger, purportedly the inspiration for Jimmy Buffett's "Cheeseburger in Paradise" song. Maybe it's the rustic charm of the breezy patio, or the secret seasonings on the melt-in-your-mouth patty, but this burger served between thick slices of homemade Bahamian bread is definitely otherworldly. **Known for:** cheeseburgers; Ma's coconut tart; island charm. $ *Average main: $12* ⊠ *Tingum Village Hotel, Colebrooke St., Dunmore Town.*

$ ✕**Queen Conch.** Four blocks from the ferry dock on Bay Street, with a
BAHAMIAN   deck overlooking the water, this colorful snack stand—presided over by Lavaughn Percentie—is renowned for its freshly caught conch salad ($10), which is diced in front of you, mixed with fresh vegetables, and ready to eat right at the counter. On weekends, get there early to put in your order, as visitors from the world over place large orders to go. **Known for:** conch specialties; take-out; busy on weekends. $ *Average main: $10* ⊠ *Bay St., Dunmore Town* ☎ *242/333–3811* ⊟ *No credit cards* ☺ *Closed Sun.*

$$ ✕**Sip Sip.** Locals and travelers alike seek out this popular snow-cone-
BAHAMIAN   green house overlooking the beach for a little "sip sip" (Bahamian for
Fodor'sChoice   gossip) and delicious inspired food. Chef and owner Julie Lightbourn
★   uses whatever is fresh, local, and in season to create "Bahamian with

---

HEAVENLY MUSIC

The best live music on Harbour Island is at the Lighthouse Church of God on Chapel Street in Dunmore Town on Sunday mornings. Mick Jagger and Lenny Kravitz have dropped by to hear Pastor Samuel Higgs, drummer and bass player, and guitarist Rocky Sanders, both of whom played Europe's clubs for years before settling down on the island.

Harbour Island is a tranquil place to spend some time.

a twist" dishes; daily specials are listed on the blackboard. **Known for:** lobster quesadilla; carrot cake; conch chili. [$] *Average main: $25* ✉ *Court Rd., Dunmore Town* ☎ *242/333–3316* ⏲ *Closed Tues. and Wed. mid-Aug.–Nov. No dinner.*

WHERE TO STAY

$$$$ B&B/INN 🏨 **Bahama House Inn.** Originally deeded in 1796 and built by Thomas W. Johnson, Briland's first doctor and justice of the peace, this handsome seven-bedroom B&B, in a garden filled with bougainvillea, royal poincianas, and hibiscus, thrives thanks to the loving preservation work of genial innkeeper John Hersh. **Pros:** central location in the middle of Dunmore Town; historic house; peaceful garden. **Cons:** not on the beach; limited hotel services. [$] *Rooms from: $440* ✉ *Dunmore St., Dunmore Town* 🌐 *http://elevenexperience.com/experiences/hideouts/bahama-house/step-inside/* ⏲ *Closed July–Oct.* 🛏 *7 rooms* 🍴 *Breakfast.*

$$$ RESORT FAMILY 🏨 **Coral Sands Hotel.** An elegant yet energetic flair accents this 8-acre oceanfront resort, right on the beach. **Pros:** direct ocean access; trendy beach resort vibe; billiard room. **Cons:** rooms vary in quality and style; some rooms can be loud; complimentary breakfast menu has limited options. [$] *Rooms from: $365* ✉ *Chapel St.* ☎ *242/333–2350, 800/468–2799* 🌐 *www.coralsands.com* ⏲ *Closed Sept.* 🛏 *40 rooms* 🍴 *Breakfast.*

$$$$ RESORT 🏨 **The Dunmore.** This recently renovated hotel with private cottages evokes a 1940s club in the tropics—with its mahogany bar, casual yet elegant dining room, and faded paperbacks in the clubhouse library, it's a favorite with the New England yachting set. **Pros:** on the beach with ocean-side bar service; spacious bathrooms; private terraces and lawn chairs for every

cottage. **Cons:** cottages too close for real privacy; small clubhouse; not all cottages have a view of the ocean. [$] *Rooms from: $550* ✉ *Gaol La., Dunmore Town* ☎ *242/333–2200, 877/891–3100* 🌐 *www.dunmorebeach.com* ⏲ *Closed Aug. 15–Nov. 15* 🛏 *14 cottages* 🍴 *No meals.*

$$ B&B/INN 🏨 **The Landing.** Spare white walls and crisp white linens evoke a timeless, understated chic at The Landing, which is acclaimed as much for its singular style as for its superb cuisine. **Pros:** chic and comfortable rooms; glorious outdoor shower; acclaimed dining. **Cons:** 10 am checkout time; limited hotel services; not on the beach. [$] *Rooms from: $295* ✉ *Bay St., Dunmore Town* ☎ *242/333–2707* 🌐 *www.harbourislandlanding.com* ⏲ *Closed mid-Aug.–Oct.* 🛏 *13 rooms* 🍴 *No meals.*

$$$$ RESORT Fodor's Choice ★ 🏨 **Pink Sands.** Harbour Island's famed beachfront resort has long been praised by celebrities—Martha Stewart, Nicole Kidman, and Brooke Shields—and honeymooners alike for its 25 secluded acres of beautiful rambling gardens and private cottages. **Pros:** truly private cottages; state-of-the-art media room; discreet and well-trained staff. **Cons:** some cottages quite a walk from the main house and beach; need a golf cart to explore Dunmore Town; pool is small and needs updating. [$] *Rooms from: $510* ✉ *Chapel St., Dunmore Town* ☎ *242/333–2030* 🌐 *www.pinksandsresort.com* ⏲ *Closed Sept.* 🛏 *25 cottages* 🍴 *Breakfast.*

$$$ HOTEL Fodor's Choice ★ 🏨 **Rock House.** With a drawing room straight out of a villa on the Amalfi Coast, the Rock House is Harbour Island's most luxurious boutique hotel. **Pros:** heavenly beds; stellar service; best gym on the island. **Cons:** not on the beach; lack of views from some rooms; not ideal for families with young children. [$] *Rooms from: $315* ✉ *Bay St., Dunmore Town* ☎ *242/333–2053* 🌐 *www.rockhousebahamas.com* ⏲ *Closed Aug.–mid-Nov.* 🛏 *7 rooms, 4 suites* 🍴 *Breakfast.*

$$$$ RESORT FAMILY 🏨 **Romora Bay Club & Resort.** Three pink Adirondack chairs on the dock welcome you to this colorful and casual resort situated on the bay side of the island. **Pros:** friendly staff; water views from every room; private bay-side beach. **Cons:** sloping steps from dock to cottages are a hassle for luggage; main house has been converted into a resort showroom. [$] *Rooms from: $500* ✉ *South end of Dunmore St., Dunmore Town* ☎ *242/333–2325* 🌐 *www.romorabay.com* ⏲ *Closed Sept.* 🛏 *18 rooms* 🍴 *No meals.*

$$$$ B&B/INN 🏨 **Runaway Hill Inn.** This quiet seaside inn on gorgeous, rolling grounds feels far removed from the rest of the island, which is precisely the point. **Pros:** oceanfront location with direct beach access; well-stocked library; intimate character. **Cons:** limited service; not as chic a vibe as nearby resorts. [$] *Rooms from: $400* ✉ *Colebrooke St., Dunmore Town* ☎ *242/333–2150, 843/278–1724* 🌐 *www.runawayhill.com* ⏲ *Closed mid-Aug.–mid-Nov.* 🛏 *10 rooms, 1 cottage, 1 house* 🍴 *No meals.*

$$$$ RESORT FAMILY 🏨 **Valentine's Resort and Marina.** With the largest marina on Harbour Island, equipped with 50 slips capable of accommodating yachts up to 160 feet, this resort is ideal if you are a self-sufficient traveler or family that doesn't require many amenities but enjoys spacious condo-style rooms and water-focused activities. **Pros:** modern rooms; state-of-the-art marina; large swimming pool. **Cons:** not oceanfront; impersonal condo-style quality; lack of hotel service. [$] *Rooms from: $440* ✉ *Bay St., Dunmore Town* ☎ *242/333–2142* 🌐 *www.valentinesresort.com* 🛏 *41 rooms* 🍴 *No meals.*

NIGHTLIFE

Beyond the Reef. The party starts at this waterfront bar at sunset and extends well into the evening. Drink specials are available all day and you can find great Bahamian food at any one of its neighboring vendors. Live entertainment is provided by the Briland 123 on weekends. ⊠ *Bay St., Dunmore Town* ☏ *242/333–3478.*

Gusty's. Enjoy a brew on the wraparound patio of Gusty's, on Harbour Island's northern point. This lively hot spot has sand floors, a few tables, and patrons shooting pool. On weekends, holidays, and in high season, it's an extremely crowded and happening dance spot, especially after 10 pm. ⊠ *Coconut Grove Ave., Dunmore Town* ☏ *242/333–2165.*

Vic-Hum Club. Vic-Hum Club, owned by "Ma" Ruby Percentie's son Humphrey, occasionally hosts live Bahamian bands in a room decorated with classic record-album covers; otherwise, you'll find locals playing Ping-Pong and listening and dancing to loud recorded music, from calypso to American pop and R&B. Mick Jagger and other rock stars have dropped by. Look for the largest coconut ever grown in the Bahamas—33 inches in diameter—on the bar's top shelf. ⊠ *Barrack St., Dunmore Town* ☏ *242/333–2161.*

6

SHOPPING AND SPAS

Most small businesses on Harbour Island close for a lunch break between 1 and 3.

SHOPPING

ART GALLERIES

Princess Street Gallery. Princess Street Gallery displays original art by local and internationally renowned artists, as well as a diverse selection of illustrated books, home accessories, and locally made crafts. ⊠ *Princess St., Dunmore Town* ☏ *242/333–2788* ⊙ *Closed Sun.*

CLOTHING

Blue Rooster. This is the place to go for festive party dresses, sexy swimwear, fun accessories, and exotic gifts. ⊠ *King St., Dunmore Town* ☏ *242/333–2240* ⊙ *Closed Sun.*

Briland's Androsia. This shop has a unique selection of clothing, beachwear, bags, and home items handmade from the colorful batik fabric created on the island of Andros. ⊠ *Coconut Grove Ave., Dunmore Town* ⊙ *Closed weekends.*

Miss Mae's. Miss Mae's sells an exquisite and discerningly curated collection of fashion-forward clothing, accessories, and gifts from international designers and artisans. ⊠ *Dunmore St., Dunmore Town.*

Sugar Mill. Here you can find a glamorous selection of resort wear, accessories, and gifts from designers around the world. ⊠ *Bay St., Dunmore Town* ☏ *242/333–3558* ⊙ *Closed Sun.*

GIFTS AND SOUVENIRS

Bahamian Shells and Tings. This shop sells island wear, souvenirs, and crafts, many handmade on Harbour Island. ⊠ *Coconut Grove Ave., Dunmore Town* ☎ *242/333–2839.*

Dilly Dally. Here you can find Bahamian-made jewelry, maps, T-shirts, CDs, decorations, and other fun island souvenirs. ⊠ *Dunmore St., Dunmore Town* ☎ *242/333–3109* ⊙ *Closed Sun.*

Pink Sands Gift Shop. This shop offers a trendy selection of swimwear, accessories, casual clothing, and trinkets. ⊠ *Pink Sands Resort, Chapel St., Dunmore Town* ☎ *242/333–2030.*

The Shop at Sip Sip. The Shop at Sip Sip sells its own line of T-shirts and a small but stylish selection of handmade jewelry, custom-designed totes, Bahamian straw work, and gifts found by owner Julie Lightbourn on her far-flung travels. ⊠ *Court Rd., Dunmore Town* ☎ *242/333–3316.*

SPAS AND SPA SERVICES

The Island Spa. For romantic couples massages in the privacy of your own room, book Karen at The Island Spa. She makes in-room visits and offers evening beach massages, body scrubs, and aromatherapy. In addition to massages, The Island Spa can also do bridal hair and makeup, manicures, and pedicures—ideal for a destination wedding. ☎ *242/333–3326* ⊕ *www.theharbourislandspa.com* ☞ *Services: aromatherapy, massage, nail treatment, scrubs, wedding hair and makeup.*

SPORTS AND THE OUTDOORS

BIKING

Michael's Cycles. Bicycles are a popular way to explore Harbour Island; rent one—or golf carts, motorboats, Jet Skis, and kayaks—at Michael's Cycles. The cost is $15 a day per bike. ⊠ *Colebrooke St., Dunmore Town* ☎ *242/333–2384.*

BOATING AND FISHING

There's great bonefishing right off Dunmore Town at **Girl's Bank.** Charters cost about $350 for a half day. The Harbour Island Tourist Office can help organize bone- and bottom-fishing excursions, as can all of the major hotels.

Stuart Cleare. Bonefish Stuart is one of Harbour Island's best bonefishing guides. You'll want to call well in advance to arrange a trip with him. Trips start at $150. ☎ *242/464–0148.*

SCUBA DIVING AND SNORKELING

Valentine's Dive Center. This dive center rents and sells equipment and provides all levels of instruction, certification, and dive trips. ⊠ *Valentine's Resort and Marina, Bay St., Dunmore Town* ☎ *242/333–2080* ⊕ *www.valentinesdive.com.*

7

THE EXUMAS

WELCOME TO THE EXUMAS

TOP REASONS TO GO

★ **Party like a local:** Hot spots include the Fish Fry on weekends for conch salad and fresh fish and Chat 'N' Chill on Stocking Island for Sunday pig roasts.

★ **Island-hop:** Spend a couple of days boating through the 365 cays (one for every day of the year, as the locals say), and spot iguanas, swimming pigs, and giant starfish.

★ **Enjoy empty beaches:** Empty stretches of bleach-white sand are yours to explore.

★ **Explore the Land and Sea Park:** Snorkel in the 176-square-mile Exuma Cays Land and Sea Park and see queen conchs, starfish, and thriving coral reefs, as well as the endangered hawksbill and threatened green and loggerhead turtles.

Thirty-five miles southeast of Nassau, Allan's Cay sits at the top of the Exumas chain of 365 islands (most uninhabited) that skip like stones for 120 miles south across the Tropic of Cancer. Flanked by the Great Bahama Bank and Exuma Sound, the islands are at the center of the Bahamas. George Town, the Exumas' capital and hub of activity is on Great Exuma, the mainland and largest island, near the bottom of the Exumas' chain. Little Exuma is to the south and connected to the mainland by a bridge. Together, these two islands span 50 miles.

1 Great Exuma. George Town hosts the 12-day George Town Cruising Regatta and the Bahamian Music and Heritage Festival. Dazzling white beaches and fish fries offering cold Kaliks crop up along the coasts of the entire island. Visitors come to fish, dive, and snorkel. Luxurious resorts and inns offer solitude or hopping beach parties.

2 Little Exuma. The Tropic of Cancer runs through the chain's second-largest island, which is duly noted on the steps leading to Tropic of Cancer Beach, one of the most spectacular on the island.

3 The Exuma Cays. If you're looking for a true escape, boat over to the cays where celebrities like Johnny Depp own spectacular islands. The renowned Exuma Cays Land and Sea Park toward the chain's north end has gorgeous crystal-clear water and white sand.

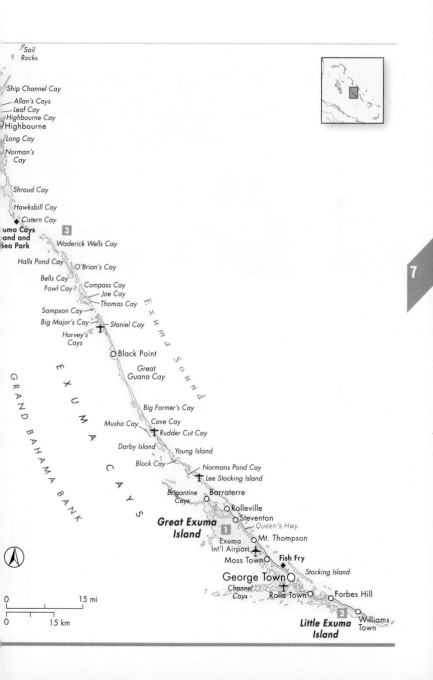

Sail
Rocks

Ship Channel Cay

Allan's Cays
Leaf Cay
Highbourne Cay
Highbourne

Long Cay

Norman's
Cay

Shroud Cay

Hawksbill Cay
Cistern Cay

uma Cays
and and
Sea Park   **3**

Waderick Wells Cay

Halls Pond Cay   O'Brian's Cay

Bells Cay
Fowl Cay   Compass Cay
Joe Cay
Thomas Cay

Sampson Cay
Big Major's Cay   Staniel Cay

Harvey's
Cays

Black Point

Great
Guana Cay

Exuma Sound

GRAND BAHAMA BANK

EXUMA CAYS

Big Farmer's Cay

Musha Cay   Cave Cay
Rudder Cut Cay

Darby Island   Young Island

Block Cay

Normans Pond Cay
Lee Stocking Island

Brigantine
Cays   Barraterre

Rolleville
Steventon
Queen's Hwy.

**Great Exuma
Island**   **1**

Exuma
Int'l Airport   Mt. Thompson

Moss Town   **Fish Fry**

George Town   *Stocking Island*

Channel
Cays   Rolle Town   Forbes Hill

2

**Little Exuma
Island**   Williams
Town

0 _____ 15 mi

0 _____ 15 km

EXUMA CAYS LAND AND SEA PARK

Created by the Bahamas National Trust in 1958, the 176-square-mile Exuma Cays Land and Sea Park was the first of its kind in the world—an enormous open aquarium with pristine reefs, an abundance of marine life, and sandy cays.

The park appeals to divers, who appreciate the vast underworld of limestone, reefs, drop-offs, blue holes, caves, and a multitude of exotic marine life including one of the Bahamas' most impressive stands of rare pillar coral. Since the park's waters have essentially never been fished, you can see what the ocean looked like before humanity. For landlubbers there are hiking trails and birding sites; stop in the main office for maps. More than 200 bird species have been spotted here. At Shroud Cay, jump into the strong current that creates a natural whirlpool whipping you around a rocky outcropping to a powdery beach. On top of the hill overlooking the beach is Camp Driftwood, made famous by a hermit who dug steps to the top, leaving behind pieces of driftwood. ⊠ *Between Conch Cut and Wax Cay Cut* ☎ *242/225–1791, VHF Channel 9 or 16* ⊕ *www.exumapark.info.*

BEST TIME TO GO

In summer the water is as warm as bathwater and usually just as calm. The park has vastly fewer boats than in the busy winter season, when the channel becomes a blue highway for a parade of sailing and motor vessels. Bring insect repellent in summer and fall.

BEST WAYS TO EXPLORE

By Boat. Boaters can explore the sandy cays and many islets that are little more than sandbars. The water is so clear it's hard to determine depths without a depth finder, so go slow and use your charts. Some routes are only passable at high tide. Get detailed directions before you go into the park, and be sure to stop by the park headquarters on Warderick Wells Cay for more information. Make sure you have a VHF marine radio on the boat or carry a handheld VHF radio so you can call for help or directions.

On Foot. The park headquarters has a map of hiking trails—most are on Warderick Wells Cay—that range from 2-mile walks to two-hour treks. Wear sturdy shoes, because trails are rocky. You'll see red, black, and white mangroves; limestone cliffs; and lots of birds—white-tail tropic birds, green herons, blue herons, black-bellied plovers, royal terns, and ospreys. Take sunscreen and water, and be aware that there's very little shade.

By Kayak. Visitors do sometimes take kayak trips from neighboring cays into the park and camp on the beach. The park has two kayaks that can be used free of charge by boaters moored in the park. As you paddle, look for sea turtles, which might pop up beside you.

Underwater. You have to go underwater to see the best part of the park—spiny lobsters walking on stilt legs on the sandy floor, sea grass waving in the currents, curious hawksbill turtles

(critically endangered), solemn-faced groupers, and the coral reefs that support an astonishing range of sea life. Bring your own equipment.

FUN FACT
The park has one native land mammal—the hutia, a critically endangered nocturnal rodent that looks similar to a gray squirrel.

MAKING A DIFFERENCE
How successful has the Exuma Cays Land and Sea Park been? About 74% of the grouper in the northern Exumas' cays come from the park. Crawfish tagged in the park have been found repopulating areas around Cat Island 70 miles away. The concentration of conch inside the park is 31 times higher than the concentration outside. This conservatively provides several million conchs outside the park for fishermen to harvest each year.

(above) Boats anchored in the bay at Warderick Wells Cay, the park's headquarters.

Updated by
Ashleigh Rolle

The Exumas are known for their gorgeous 365 cays. Get the wind and sea salt in your hair as you cruise through the pristine 120-mile chain. Combine the epic scenery with fresh seafood and friendly locals, and you have one of the best vacation destinations in the Bahamas.

There is not a casino or cruise ship in sight on the Exumas, and those who love the remote beauty of the windswept cays keep coming back.

In 1783 Englishman Denys Rolle sent 150 slaves to Great Exuma to build a cotton plantation. His son Lord John Rolle later gave all of his 5,000 acres to his freed slaves, and they took the Rolle name. On Great Exuma and Little Exuma you'll still find wild cotton, testaments from plantations first established by Loyalists after the Revolutionary War. Today the Exumas are known as the Bahamas' onion capital, although many of the 7,000 residents earn a living by fishing and farming, and, more recently, tourism.

The Exumas attract fishermen after bonefish, the feisty breed that prefers the shallow sandy flats that surround these islands. The healthiest coral reefs and fish populations in the country make for excellent diving and snorkeling.

Some cays are no bigger than a sandbar, but you won't stay on the sand long as Perrier-clear waters beckon. Beaches won't be hard to find on the tiny cays; on Great Exuma, look for "Beach Access" signs on the Queen's Highway.

PLANNING

WHEN TO GO

High season is December through April, when weather is in the 70s (lows can dip into the 60s). Hotels sell out for events such as the George Town Cruising Regatta and the Bahamian Music and Heritage Festival in March, and the National Family Islands Regatta in April.

Room rates are cheaper in summer, but fall (late August through November, the height of hurricane season) offers the best deals. Weather during this time can be rainy and hot. Some inns close for September and October.

TOP FESTIVALS

WINTER **Junkanoo.** The Exumas' Junkanoo Parade on Boxing Day (December 26) starts at 7 pm in Georgetown and normally ends around 10 pm at Regatta Park. Dancing, barbecues, and music happen before and after the parade. ⊠ *George Town.*

Annual New Year's Day Cruising Regatta. The Annual New Year's Day Cruising Regatta at the Staniel Cay Yacht Club marks the finale of a two-day celebration. ⊠ *Staniel Cay.*

George Town Cruising Regatta. The George Town Cruising Regatta in March is 12 days of festivities including sailing, a conch-blowing contest, dance, food and entertainment, and sports competitions. ⊠ *George Town.*

Bahamian Music and Heritage Festival. March's Bahamian Music and Heritage Festival brings local and nationally known musicians to George Town, along with arts and crafts, Bahamas sloop exhibitions, storytelling, singing, poetry reading, and gospel music. ⊠ *George Town.*

SPRING **National Family Islands Regatta.** In April the National Family Islands Regatta is the Bahamas' most important yachting event. Starting the race in Elizabeth Harbour in George Town, island-made wooden sloops compete for trophies. Onshore, the town is a weeklong riot of Junkanoo parades, Goombay music, and arts and crafts fairs. ⊠ *George Town.*

SUMMER **Junkanoo Summer Festival.** The Junkanoo Summer Festival in July and August is held beachside at the Fish Fry in George Town, and features local and visiting bands, kids' sunfish sailing, arts and crafts, and boat-building displays. It takes place Saturday at noon. ⊠ *George Town.*

HOTELS

Stay in simple stilt cottages, fabulous rooms with butler service, atmospheric old inns, modern condo rentals, all-inclusives, ecolodges, or bed-and-breakfasts—temporary homes-away-from-home for every taste and price point.

The mainland of Great Exuma has had an energetic growth spurt that includes some of the country's most luxurious hotels, including Sandals Emerald Bay, Grand Isle Resort, and Spa; and February Point Resort Estates.

RESTAURANTS

Exuma restaurants are known for terrific Bahamian home cooking—cracked conch, fried chicken served with peas 'n' rice, or macaroni baked with egg and loads of cheese. Try conch salad at the cluster of wooden shacks called the Fish Fry, just north of George Town. Pea soup and dumplings is a specialty here, and many local restaurants serve it as a weekly lunch special.

Restaurants at larger resorts have upscale dining, including Continental twists on local cuisine as well as imported steaks and gourmet pizzas.

Restaurant prices are based on the median main course price at dinner, excluding gratuity, typically 15%, which is often automatically added to the bill. Hotel prices are for two people in a standard double room in high season, excluding service and 6%–12% tax.

WHAT IT COSTS IN DOLLARS			
$	$$	$$$	$$$$
Restaurants	under $20	$20–$30	$31–$40	over $40
Hotels	under $200	$200–$300	$301–$400	over $400

VISITOR INFORMATION

Contacts Exuma Tourist Office. ⊠ *Queen's Hwy., George Town* ⊕ *Located in Turnquest Star Plaza* ☎ *242/336–2430* ⊕ *www.bahamas.com.* **Out Islands Promotion Board.** ⊕ *www.myoutisland.com.*

GETTING HERE AND AROUND

AIR TRAVEL

The airport is 10 miles north of George Town. Taxis wait at the airport for incoming flights; a trip to George Town costs $30 for two people; to Williams Town, $80; to February Point, $30; to Emerald Bay, $20; to Barraterre, $50. Each additional person is $3. Staniel Cay Airport accepts charter flights and private planes.

Contacts Exuma International Airport (GGT). ☎ *242/345–0002.*

BOAT AND FERRY TRAVEL

The Bahamas Ferries vessels *Seawind* and *Sealink* travel from Nassau to George Town on Monday and Wednesday, arriving in Exuma the next day (on Tuesday and Thursday). The trip takes 10 hours and costs $71 one-way, $130 round-trip.

The mail boat M/V *Grand Master* travels from Nassau to George Town on Tuesday and returns to Nassau on Thursday. The trip takes 14 hours and costs $45 each way. M/V *Captain "C"* leaves Nassau on Tuesday for Staniel Cay, Big Farmer's Cay, and Ragged Island, returning to Nassau on Friday. The trip is 14 hours and costs $45. Contact the Dockmaster's Office for more information.

Elvis Ferguson operates a boat taxi from Government Dock to Chat 'N' Chill on the hour throughout the day. If you plan on leaving the island after 6 pm, tell the captain in advance.

Contacts Dockmaster's Office. ☎ *242/393–1064.* **Elvis Ferguson.** ⊠ *Government Dock, George Town* ☎ *242/464–1558.*

CAR TRAVEL

If you want to explore Great Exuma and Little Exuma, you'll need to rent a car. Most hotels can arrange car rentals.

Contacts Airport Car Rentals. ⊠ *George Town Airport, George Town* ☎ *242/345–0090* ⊕ *www.exumacarrental.com.* **Thompson's Rentals.** ☎ *242/336–2442* ⊕ *www.exumacars.com.*

TAXI TRAVEL

Taxis are plentiful on Great Exuma, and most offer island tours. A half-day tour of George Town and Little Exuma is about $150 for two people.

Contacts Exuma Travel and Transportation Limited. ☎ 242/345–0232. **Kendal "Dr. K" Nixon.** ☎ 242/422–7399.

GREAT EXUMA

George Town is the capital and largest town on the mainland, a lovely seaside community with darling pink government buildings overlooking Elizabeth Harbour. The white-pillared, colonial-style Government Administration Building was modeled on Nassau's Government House and houses the commissioner's office, police headquarters, courts, and a jail. Atop a hill across from it is the whitewashed St. Andrew's Anglican Church, originally built around 1802. Behind the church is the small, saltwater Lake Victoria. It was once used for soaking sisal used for making baskets and ropes. The straw market, a half dozen outdoor shops shaded by a huge African fig tree, is a short walk from town. You can bargain with fishermen for some of the day's catch at the Government Dock, where the mail boat comes in.

Small settlements make up the rest of the island. **Rolle Town,** a typical Exuma village devoid of tourist trappings, sits atop a hill overlooking the ocean 5 miles south of George Town. Some of the buildings are over a century old. **Rolleville** overlooks a harbor 20 miles north of George Town. Its old slave quarters have been transformed into livable cottages. The Hilltop Tavern, a seafood restaurant and bar, is guarded by an ancient cannon.

GETTING AROUND

Dining and sightseeing beyond your resort may require you to rent a car, as taxis can get expensive if you're going long distances.

EXPLORING

Fish Fry. Fish Fry is the name given to a jumble of one-room beachside structures, such as Charlie's and Honeydew, about 2 miles north of George Town. They're favored by locals for made-to-order fish and barbecue. Some shacks are open weekends only, but most are open nightly until at least 11 pm. There's live Rake 'n' Scrape Monday nights and DJs on Friday and Saturday. Eat at picnic tables by the water and watch the fishing boats come into the harbor. This is a popular after-work meeting place on Friday night, and a sports bar attracts locals and expats for American basketball and football games. ⊠ *Queen's Hwy., George Town.*

Mt. Thompson. From the top of Mt. Thompson, rising from the Three Sisters Beach, there is a pleasing view of the **Three Sisters Rocks** jutting above the water just offshore. Legend has it that the rocks were formed when three sisters, all unwittingly in love with the same English sailor, waded out into deep water upon his departure, drowned, and turned into stone. If you look carefully next to each "sister," you'll see smaller boulders. These represent the "children" who the fickle sailors left with the three sisters. Mt. Thompson is about 12 miles north of George Town, past Moss Town. ⊠ *Queen's Hwy., Mount Thompson.*

Rolle Town Tombs. Seek out the three Rolle Town Tombs, which date back to Loyalists. The largest tomb bears this poignant inscription: "Within this tomb interred the body of Ann McKay, the wife of Alexander McKay who departed this life the 8th November 1792. Aged twenty-six years and their infant child." The tombs are off the main road; look for a sign. The settlement has brightly painted buildings, several more than a century old. ⊠ *Deep Creek.*

> **PEACOCKS**
>
> During your walks, you might glimpse peacocks on Great Exuma. Originally, a peacock and a peahen were brought to the island as pets by a man named Shorty Johnson, but when he left to work in Nassau he abandoned the birds, which gradually proliferated into a colony. The birds used to roam the streets, but development has forced them into the bush, so they are rarer sights these days.

Fodor's Choice ★ **Stocking Island.** Slightly more than a mile off George Town's shore lies Stocking Island. The 4-mile-long island has only 10 inhabitants, the upscale Hotel Higgins Landing, lots of walking trails, a gorgeous white beach rich in seashells and popular with surfers on the ocean side, and plenty of good snorkeling sites. Jacques Cousteau's team is said to have traveled some 1,700 feet into Mystery Cave, a blue-hole grotto 70 feet beneath the island. Stocking Island is the headquarters for the wildly popular George Town Cruising Regatta.

BEACHES

Jolly Hall Beach. A curve of sparkling white sand shaded by casuarina trees, this long beach is located just north of Palm Bay Beach Club. It's quiet and the shallow azure water makes it a great spot for families or romantics. When it's time for lunch, walk over to Palm Bay, Exuma Beach Resort, or Augusta Bay, three small nearby inns. Watch your bags when high tide comes in; much of the beach is swallowed by the sea. That's the signal for a cold Kalik and grouper sandwich. **Amenities:** none. **Best for:** solitude; sunrise; swimming; snorkeling. ⊠ *Queen's Hwy., George Town.*

WHERE TO EAT

$$
BAHAMIAN
Fodor's Choice ★

✕ **Blu on the Water Restaurant & Bar.** Located in the hustle and bustle of central George Town, Blu on the Water Restaurant & Bar at the Exuma Yacht Club has a magnificent view of the harbor. Enjoy the ocean breeze from the bar on the balcony, or dine in the chic indoor seating area. **Known for:** ocean views; cracked conch sushi; jerk chicken. $ *Average main: $29* ⊠ *Queen's Hwy., George Town* ☎ *242/336–2579* ⊕ *www. theexumayachtclub.com* ⊘ *Closed Sun.*

$$
ECLECTIC
✕ **Catch a Fire Bar and Grill.** Sip a tropical cocktail and enjoy the sunset at this waterfront bar and grill. Tastefully decorated with teak benches, a handsome bar, and infinity pool, Catch a Fire is a fun place to go for dinner and for dancing on Wednesday and Saturday night when the restaurant has live entertainment. **Known for:** sunset views; kebabs; live music. $ *Average main: $30* ⊠ *George Town* ☎ 242/636–7079 ▭ No credit cards ⊗ Closed Sun.

$
BAHAMIAN
Fodor's Choice
★
✕ **Chat 'N' Chill.** Yacht folks, locals, and visitors alike rub shoulders at Kenneth Bowe's funky open-air beach bar on the point at Stocking Island. All of the food is grilled over an open fire; awesome conch burgers with secret spices and grilled fish with onions and potatoes attract diners from all over Great Exuma. **Known for:** conch burger; grilled fish; BBQ. $ *Average main: $14* ⊠ *1 Stocking Island* ☎ 242/357–0926 ⊕ *www.chatnchill.com* ▭ No credit cards.

$
BAHAMIAN
✕ **Cheater's Restaurant and Bar.** Disregard the lack of ambience; this popular restaurant serves some of the best food on the island. Fresh fish and fried chicken dinners are the house specialties. **Known for:** cracked conch; personalized dining; fresh local seafood. $ *Average main: $15* ⊠ *George Town* ✛ *1½ miles south of Queen's Hwy.* ☎ 242/336–2535 ▭ No credit cards ⊗ Closed Sun. and Mon.

$$
EUROPEAN
✕ **Club Peace and Plenty.** The legendary hotel's restaurant has a fabulous view of the pool and harbor, along with traditional Bahamian specialties including conch fritters and grilled fish, and a 12-ounce New York strip steak. This is one of the nicer places to dine on the island, perfect for a romantic dinner or family celebration. **Known for:** friendly service; Thursday night BBQ; conch burger. $ *Average main: $29* ⊠ *Club Peace and Plenty, Queen's Hwy., George Town* ☎ 242/336–2551 ⊕ *www.peaceandplenty.com.*

$
DELI
✕ **Driftwood Café.** Located in central George Town just across from the Club Peace and Plenty, this café is a pleasant spot for a cup of coffee and hot breakfast sandwich in the morning. Driftwood Café also offers lunch, with specialties such as quiche, subs, and salads served with fresh lemonade or iced tea. **Known for:** basil pesto chicken salad; pancakes and waffles; all-day breakfast. $ *Average main: $10* ⊠ *Queen's Hwy., George Town* ☎ 242/336–3800 ▭ No credit cards ⊗ Closed Sun.

$
BAHAMIAN
✕ **Eddie's Edgewater.** Fried chicken, lobster, T-bone steak, and cracked conch are the delicious reasons people eat at this modest lakeside establishment. Stop by on Monday night for some authentic Bahamian Rake 'n' Scrape music. **Known for:** Monday night Rake 'n' Scrape; fresh seafood; fish burgers. $ *Average main: $15* ⊠ *Charlotte St., George Town* ☎ 242/336–2050 ⊗ Closed Sun. No dinner Tues. or Wed.

$$$
EUROPEAN
Fodor's Choice
★
✕ **Palappa Pool Bar and Grill at Grand Isle Resort.** This poolside restaurant serves three meals a day and offers a stunning view of the ocean. The extensive menu equally features American classics and Bahamian specialties. **Known for:** unique location; special house drinks; fish tacos. $ *Average main: $37* ⊠ *Grand Isle Resort, Queen's Hwy., Rokers Point Settlement* ☎ 242/358–5000 ⊕ *www.grandisleresort.com.*

$
BAHAMIAN
✕ **Splash Bar & Grill.** Restaurant highlights for lunch are fish burgers, conch burgers, and beef burgers. Dinner specialties include grilled grouper, cracked conch, and pizza. **Known for:** burgers; swing bar;

GEORGETOWN. 1 MILE

PUFF

Newburyport, MA 1180mi

OTTAWA · GATINEAU 1316mi

CANADA

LONDON · U.K.
3517 miles

COMPASS ROSE

PUT-IN-BAY OHIO 1,315mi

VERO BEACH FLORIDA

NJ. 5   015NM

WETHERSFIELD CT 1270

NEW BERN NC

PETERBOROUGH ONT 1087mi

ON. 1087mi

Paradise   nm

PITTSB

NEWFOUNDLAND

CH. 1037mi

RIO DE JANEIRO · BRASIL
1114 km

DID YOU KNOW?

The Tropic of Cancer cuts through Little Exuma. A helpful line marking the spot on the steps leading down to Tropic of Cancer Beach makes a great photo op.

beach access. $ *Average main: $13*
⊠ *Queen's Hwy., George Town*
☎ *242/336–3587* ⊕ *www.hideaway-
spalmbay.com.*

BAHAMIAN
$ ✕**Towne Café.** This George Town
restaurant serves breakfast (especially popular on Saturday)—consider trying the stew' fish or chicken
souse—and lunches of grilled fish
or seafood sandwiches with three
sides. It's open until 3 pm. **Known for:** Bahamian breakfast; cinnamon
rolls; fresh bread. $ *Average main: $14* ⊠ *Marshall Complex, Queen's
Hwy., George Town* ☎ *242/336–2194* ▭ *No credit cards* ⊘ *Closed Sun.*

WHERE TO STAY

$$
RESORT
Fodor'sChoice
★
▦ **Augusta Bay Bahamas.** The perfect balance of luxury and casual chic,
without the mega-resort feel, this 16-room resort on 300 feet of nar-
row beach is a mile north of George Town. **Pros:** luxurious rooms;
great water views; friendly service. **Cons:** beach almost disappears at
high tide; need a car to drive to town and shops. $ *Rooms from: $277*
⊠ *Queen's Hwy., George Town* ☎ *242/336–2250* ⊕ *www.augustabay-
bahamas.com* ↴ *16 rooms* ⦿ *Breakfast.*

$
HOTEL
▦ **Club Peace and Plenty.** The first Exumas hotel and granddaddy of
the island's omnipresent Peace and Plenty empire, this pink, two-story
lodge is in the heart of the action in George Town. **Pros:** in the middle
of George Town action; friendly staff; ocean-view balconies in some
rooms. **Cons:** no beach; have to take a water taxi to Stocking Island.
$ *Rooms from: $180* ⊠ *Queen's Hwy., George Town* ☎ *242/336–2551,
800/525–2210* ⊕ *www.peaceandplenty.com* ↴ *32 rooms* ⦿ *No meals.*

$
B&B/INN
▦ **Coral Gardens Bed and Breakfast.** Extremely popular with Brits and
Europeans, the sprawling two-story B&B, owned and run by British
expats Betty and Peter Oxley, is on a hilltop with an inviting veran-
dah. **Pros:** superb hilltop view of water in the distance; friendly hosts;
free Wi-Fi. **Cons:** not on the beach; need a car to go to George Town
and the beach. $ *Rooms from: $99* ⊠ *12 Garden Rd., off Queen's
Hwy., George Town* ✛ *3 miles north of George Town* ☎ *242/336–
2880* ⊕ *www.coralgardensbahamas.com* ⊘ *Closed Sept.–mid-Oct.* ↴ *3
rooms, 2 apartments* ⦿ *Breakfast.*

$
RESORT
▦ **Exuma Beach Resort.** This newly renovated beachfront resort just out-
side of George Town boasts eight guest rooms and one exceptional suite.
Pros: modern accommodations; centrally located. **Cons:** backs into main
road; resort can feel cramped. $ *Rooms from: $175* ⊠ *Queen's Hwy.,
George Town* ☎ *242/336–3100* ↴ *7 rooms, 2 suites* ⦿ *Breakfast.*

$$$$
RESORT
FAMILY
▦ **February Point Resort Estates.** This gated residential community and
resort is made up of 40 villas and privately owned homes—27 of the villas
are available as guest accommodations. **Pros:** elegant accommodations;
waterfront restaurant on-property. **Cons:** more like a gated community
than a resort; ongoing construction can be noisy. $ *Rooms from: $650*
⊠ *Queen's Hwy., George Town* ☎ *242/336–2695* ↴ *27 villas.*

Sandals Emerald Bay on Great Exuma has one of the island's best beaches.

$$
RESORT
FAMILY
Fodor'sChoice
★

Grand Isle Resort and Spa. This luxurious 78-villa complex boasts one of the island's few spas, an infinity pool overlooking the ocean, and a poolside patio restaurant. **Pros:** the ultimate in luxury accommodations; friendly staff; on-site spa and restaurant. **Cons:** 20-minute drive from George Town and not much to do near the resort; lacks local flavor. *$ Rooms from: $300 ⊠ Off Queens Hwy., Rokers Point Settlement ☎ 242/358–5000 ⊕ www.grandisleresort.com ↝ 78 villas ⊚ No meals.*

$$
RESORT
FAMILY

Hideaways at Palm Bay. Formerly called Palm Bay, one of George Town's most modern accommodations, is all about light and color. **Pros:** roomy accommodations; friendly young staff. **Cons:** beach all but disappears at high tide; accommodations are close together. *$ Rooms from: $250 ⊠ Queen's Hwy. ✛ 1 mile from George Town ☎ 888/396–0606, 242/336–2787 ⊕ www.hideawayspalmbay.com ↝ 43 rooms ⊚ No meals.*

$
HOTEL

Regatta Point. Soft pink with hunter-green shutters, this handsome two-story guesthouse overlooks Kidd Cove from its own petite island. **Pros:** private island feel; has its own beach; fantastic harbor views. **Cons:** water at the beach doesn't look clean; no restaurant; cash only. *$ Rooms from: $184 ⊠ Kidd Cove, George Town ☎ 242/336–2206, 800/561–7954 ⊕ www.regattapointbahamas.com ▤ No credit cards ↝ 6 suites ⊚ No meals.*

$$$$
RESORT

Sandals Emerald Bay. The former luxurious Four Seasons is now the even more luxurious Sandals Emerald Bay, an all-inclusive resort of pink and aqua buildings facing a 1-mile-long stretch of powdery white sand. **Pros:** spa and golf on-property; magnificent beach and swimming pools; great water sports. **Cons:** the resort is isolated; lacks Bahamian flavor. *$ Rooms from: $750 ⊠ Queen's Hwy., Rokers Point Settlement ☎ 242/336–6800, 800/726–3157 ⊕ www.sandals.com ↝ 245 suites ⊚ All-inclusive.*

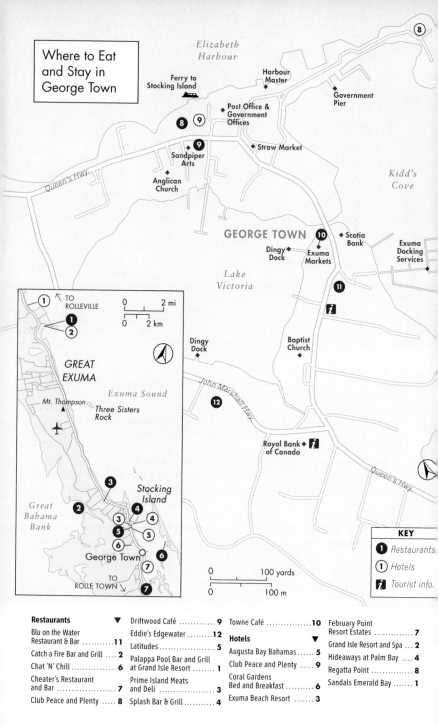

Where to Eat and Stay in George Town

Elizabeth Harbour

Ferry to Stocking Island

Harbour Master

Government Pier

Post Office & Government Offices

⑧ ⑨

Straw Market

Sandpiper Arts

⑨

Anglican Church

Queen's Hwy.

Kidd's Cove

GEORGE TOWN

⑩ Scotia Bank

Dingy Dock

Exuma Markets

Exuma Docking Services

Lake Victoria

⑪

ⓘ

Dingy Dock

Baptist Church

John Marshall Hwy.

⑫

Exuma Sound

Royal Bank of Canada ⓘ

Queen's Hwy.

GREAT EXUMA

↖ TO ROLLEVILLE

① ②

0   2 mi
0   2 km

Mt. Thompson ▲

Three Sisters Rock

Great Bahama Bank

③

②

③ ④ ④

⑤ ⑤

⑥ ⑥

George Town

⑦

TO ROLLE TOWN ↘

⑦

Stocking Island

0   100 yards
0   100 m

KEY

① *Restaurants*

① *Hotels*

ⓘ *Tourist info.*

Restaurants ▼		
Blu on the Water Restaurant & Bar **11**	Driftwood Café **9**	Towne Café **10**
Catch a Fire Bar and Grill **2**	Eddie's Edgewater **12**	**Hotels ▼**
Chat 'N' Chill **6**	Latitudes **5**	Augusta Bay Bahamas **5**
Cheater's Restaurant and Bar **7**	Palappa Pool Bar and Grill at Grand Isle Resort **1**	Club Peace and Plenty **9**
Club Peace and Plenty **8**	Prime Island Meats and Deli **3**	Coral Gardens Bed and Breakfast **6**
	Splash Bar & Grill **4**	Exuma Beach Resort **3**

February Point Resort Estates **7**	
Grand Isle Resort and Spa ... **2**	
Hideaways at Palm Bay **4**	
Regatta Point **8**	
Sandals Emerald Bay **1**	

The Straw Market in George Town features handmade crafts.

NIGHTLIFE

Club Peace and Plenty. In season, the Thursday-night poolside bashes at Club Peace and Plenty, fueled by live bands, keep Bahamians and vacationers on the dance floor. ⊠ *Queen's Hwy., George Town* ☎ *242/336–2551.*

Eddie's Edgewater. On Monday, head to Eddie's Edgewater for rousing Rake 'n' Scrape music. The front porch is a popular spot, where locals hang out all week long. ⊠ *Charlotte St., George Town* ☎ *242/336–2050.*

Fish Fry. There's always something going on at the Fish Fry, a cluster of shacks 2 miles north of George Town. A DJ is usually there on Friday and Sunday. ⊠ *Queen's Hwy., George Town.*

Two Turtles Inn. Two Turtles Inn is the other hot spot on Friday, when everyone comes to town to celebrate the end of the work week. 2T, as it's known, puts on a barbecue with live music. A week is too long to wait, so the celebration is repeated on Tuesday nights. ⊠ *George Town* ☎ *242/336–0009.*

SHOPPING AND SPAS

SHOPS

Exuma Markets. At this grocery store located in the center of George Town, yachties tie up at the skiff docks in the rear, on Lake Victoria. Boaters can also send emergency emails and faxes from this location. ⊠ *Across from Scotia Bank, Queen's Hwy., George Town* ☎ *242/336–2033.*

Sandpiper Arts & Crafts. Here you can find upscale souvenirs, from high-quality cards and books to batik clothing and art. ⊠ *Queen's Hwy., George Town* ☎ *242/336–2084* ⊘ *Closed Sun.*

Straw Market. The Straw Market offers a wide range of Bahamian straw bags, hats, and beachwear at a half dozen open-air shops under a huge African fig tree. Prices are negotiable. ⊠ *Queen's Hwy., George Town* ⊘ *Closed Sun.*

> ### CAPTURING WAVES
>
> Here are a few tips for capturing the water's incredible shades of blue: shoot early—before 9 am—on a sunny day, or late in the afternoon. Make sure the sun is behind you. Use a tripod, or hold the camera still. Find a contrasting color—a bright red umbrella or a yellow fishing boat.

SPAS

Red Lane Spa. Located on the Sandals Emerald Bay property, this elegant spa has 16 treatment rooms, a steam room, and a fitness center. Couples massages and "sun lover" relief are among the treatments offered. The spa is open to the public, but you'll need to call ahead to make your appointment. ⊠ *Sandals Emerald Bay, Queen's Hwy., Rokers Point Settlement* ☎ *242/336–6800* ⊕ *www.sandals.com* ☞ *Steam room. Gym with: cardiovascular machines, free weights, weight-training equipment. Services: body wraps, facials, massage, scrubs, nail treatment. Classes and programs: Pilates, yoga.*

SeaStar Spa. Seawater therapy, or the art of marine healing, is the philosophy at SeaStar Spa, located at Grand Isle Resort. Relax in one of three treatment rooms, including one designed especially for couples. The spa is open every day and offers a number of massages, scrubs, and wraps utilizing natural ingredients such as ginger, lime, coconut, and island spices. SeaStar also has a special "children's spa" menu, which includes shorter massages and pedicures as well as hair braiding. ⊠ *Grand Isle Resort, Rokers Point Settlement* ☎ *242/358–5000* ⊕ *www.grandisleresort.com* ☞ *Services: aromatherapy, massage, nail treatment, scrubs.*

SPORTS AND THE OUTDOORS

ADVENTURE TOURS

Island Boy Adventures. Floating down the lazy river at Moriah Harbor Park, boating through the Exuma Cays to swim with the pigs, and diving for lobster are just a few of the activities offered by experienced Captains Evvie and Tonio. If you're not sure what to choose, let Island Boy Adventures help you plan your day—you won't be disappointed. ⊠ *George Town* ☎ *242/357–0459* ⊕ *www.islandboyadventures.com.*

BOATING

Because of its wealth of safe harbors and regatta events, the Exumas are a favorite spot for yachtsmen. Renting a boat allows you to explore the cays near George Town and beyond, and a number of area hotels allow guests to tie up rental boats at their docks. For those who want to take a water jaunt through Stocking Island's hurricane holes, sailboats are ideal.

FISHING

In the shallow flats off Exuma's windward coast the elusive bonefish, the "ghosts of the sea," roam. Patient fishermen put featherweight, thumbnail-size flies on the lines, calculate the tides and currents, and cast out about 50 feet in hope of catching one. For sure success, avid fishermen pay guides about $300 a day to help them outsmart the skinny gray fish that streak through crystal water. Most hotels can arrange for expert locals guides, and a list is also available from the Exuma Tourist Office. The season is year-round and highly prized among fly-fishermen.

Exuma Bonefish Guides Association. These guides are all highly qualified to help you hook a bonefish. A full day on the flats costs $380. ⊕ *www.exumabonefish.com.*

Fish Rowe Charters. This charter company has a 40-foot Hatteras that holds up to four fishermen. Deep-water charters run $800 for a half day, $1,200 for ¾ day, and $1,600 for a full day. ☎ *242/357–0870* ⊕ *www.fishrowecharters.com.*

Steve Ferguson. Stevie is an experienced guide who will help you hook feisty bonefish. ☎ *242/422–7033* ⊕ *www.bonefishstevie.com.*

GOLF

Sandals Emerald Reef Golf Club. Golf legend Greg Norman designed the 18-hole, par-72 championship course, featuring six ocean-side holes, at Sandals Emerald Bay, the island's only golf course. There are preferred tee times for hotel guests. ⊠ *Sandals, Queen's Hwy., Rokers Point Settlement* ☎ *242/336–6800* ⊕ *www.sandals.com* ✉ *$175 for guests; $185 for nonguests. Admission includes golf cart* ⚑ *18 holes, 7000 yards, par 72.*

KAYAKING

Rolle's Sea Kayaking Adventures. Gully Rolle rents kayaks for $60/day for a single and $80/day for a double. Discounts are available for longer rentals. ☎ *242/524–4213.*

SCUBA DIVING

The popular **Angel Fish Blue Hole,** just minutes from George Town, is filled with angelfish, spotted rays, snapper, and the occasional reef shark. However, while it is full of mesmerizing schools of colorful fish, it is for experienced divers only.

Dive Exuma. This outfitter provides dive instruction, certification courses, scuba trips, and snorkel tours. Two-tank dives are $145; snorkel tours are $75. ⊠ *Government Dock, George Town* ☎ *242/357–0313, 242/336–2893* ⊕ *www.dive-exuma.com.*

SNORKELING

Minn's Water Sports. Minn's rents snorkeling gear for $10/day. ⊠ *Queen's Hwy., George Town* ☎ *242/336–2604* ⊕ *www.mwsboats.com.*

TENNIS

February Point. Nonguests can use the two Laykold cushion–surfaced courts and adjacent fitness center at February Point for $16 a day. ⊠ *February Point Resort, Queen's Hwy., George Town* ☎ *242/336–2661.*

You'll swim among multicolored tropical fish at Staniel Cay.

LITTLE EXUMA

Scenes from two *Pirates of the Caribbean* movies were filmed on the southern end of Little Exuma—only 12 square miles—and on one of the little cays just offshore. The movies' stars, Johnny Depp and Orlando Bloom, often roamed around the island and ate at Santana's open-air beach shack, the island's best-known restaurant. But that's just one of the many reasons people are drawn to this lovely island, which is connected to Great Exuma to the north by a narrow bridge. Rolling green hills, purple morning glories spilling over fences, small settlements with only a dozen houses, and glistening white beaches make this a romantic afternoon escape. Near **Williams Town** is an eerie salt lake, still and ghostly, where salt was once scooped up and shipped away. You can hike old footpaths and look for ruins of old plantation buildings built in the 1700s near the Hermitage, but you'll have to look beneath the bushes and vines to find them. Little Exuma's best beach is Tropic of Cancer Beach (also known as Pelican's Bay Beach); it is a thrill to stand on the line that marks the spot. You're officially in the tropics now.

GETTING HERE AND AROUND
Little Exuma is hot with little shade. It's possible to walk or bike, but a car or scooter is the best way to get around the island.

VISITOR INFORMATION
People-to-People Program. This group hosts a tea where visitors can learn about bush medicine and other aspects of local life, and get to know Exuma islanders. ☎ 242/356–0435, 242/336–2430 ⊕ *www.bahamas.com/people-to-people.*

EXPLORING

Hermitage. The Hermitage estate ruins are testaments to the cotton plantation days. The small settlement was built by the Ferguson family from the Carolinas who settled here after the American Revolutionary War. Visitors can see the foundations of the main house and tombs that date back to the 1700s. The tombs hold George Butler (1759–1822), Henderson Ferguson (1772–1825), and Constance McDonald (1755–59). A grave is believed to be that of an unnamed slave. ✉ *Williams Town.*

St. Christopher's Anglican. This is the island's smallest church, built in 1939 when the parish priest, Father Marshall, heard that a schooner loaded with timber from the Abacos had wrecked off Long Island. He visited the local Fitz-Gerald family and suggested they use the timber to build a church, which they did. Visitors can see the church and pews, all built of salvaged wood. ✉ *Queen's Hwy., Ferry.*

BEACHES

Fodor's Choice ★ **Tropic of Cancer Beach** (*Pelican's Bay Beach*). This is the beach most visitors come to the Exumas for, although don't be surprised if you're the only one here at noon on a Saturday. It's right on the Tropic of Cancer; a helpful line marking the spot on the steps leading down to the sand makes a great photo op. The beach is a white-sand crescent in a protected cove, where the water is usually as calm as a pond. A shady wooden cabana makes a comfortable place to admire the beach and water. *Pirates of the Caribbean* 2 and 3 were filmed on nearby Sandy Cay. Have lunch at the cast's favorite place, the open-air Santana's in Williams Town, a 10-minute drive from the beach. **Amenities:** none. **Best for:** solitude; snorkeling; swimming; walking. ✉ *Williams Town.*

WHERE TO EAT

$ BAHAMIAN Fodor's Choice ★ 🍴 **Santana's Grill Pit.** This seaside open-air restaurant—you can't miss the orange-and-yellow building—is the hot spot in Little Exuma, and the closest restaurant to the Tropic of Cancer Beach. Dinner highlights include cracked lobster, cracked conch, shrimp, and grilled grouper, all served with peas 'n' rice or baked macaroni and cheese. **Known for:** homemade rum cake; fried lobster; views. [$] *Average main: $16* ✉ *Queen's Hwy., George Town* ☎ *242/345–4102* 💳 *No credit cards* 🕒 *Closed Sun.*

THE EXUMA CAYS

A band of cays—with names like **Rudder Cut, Big Farmer's, Great Guana,** and **Leaf**—stretches northwest from Great Exuma. It will take you a full day to boat through all 365 cays, most uninhabited, some owned by celebrities. Along the way you'll find giant starfish, wild iguanas, swimming pigs, dolphins, sharks, and picture-perfect sandbars. The Land and Sea Park, toward the northern end of the chain, is world-renowned.

The famous swimming pigs of Big Major's Cay will be happy to meet you at your boat.

GETTING HERE AND AROUND

Most people visit the cays with their own boats; you'll need one to island-hop, although you can fly into Staniel Cay. The channels are confusing for inexperienced boaters, especially at low tide, and high tide can hide reefs and sandbars just underneath the surface. If this sounds intimidating, look into booking a boat tour. Once on a cay, most are small enough to walk. Golf carts are popular on Staniel Cay.

EXPLORING

Allan's Cay. Allan's Cay is at the Exumas' northernmost tip and home to the rare Bahamian iguana. Bring along some grapes and a stick to put them on, and these little guys will quickly become your new best friends.

FAMILY **Big Major's Cay.** Just north of Staniel Cay, Big Major's Cay is home to the famous swimming pigs. These guys aren't shy; as you pull up to the island they'll dive in and swim out to greet you. Don't forget to bring some scraps; Staniel Cay restaurant gives guests bags before they depart.

Compass Cay. Explore the many paths on the island, which is 1½ miles long and 1 mile wide, or sit on the dock and watch the sharks swim below—don't worry, they're harmless nurse sharks. There are four houses for rent on the island, all come with a 13-foot Boston Whaler. There's also a small convenience store stocked with snacks and beverages. ⊠ *Compass Cay.*

Fodor's Choice ★ **Exuma Cays Land and Sea Park.** Created by the Bahamas National Trust in 1958, the 176-square-mile Exuma Cays Land and Sea Park was the first of its kind in the world—an enormous open aquarium with pristine reefs, an abundance of marine life, and sandy cays. For land-lubbers there are hiking trails and birding sites. At Shroud Cay, jump into the strong current that creates a natural whirlpool whipping you around a rocky outcropping to a powdery beach. On top of the hill overlooking the beach is Camp Driftwood, made famous by a hermit who dug steps to the top, leaving behind pieces of driftwood. ⊠ *Park Headquarters* ☎ *242/225–1791* ⊕ *www.exumapark.org* ☞ *VHF Channel 9 or 16.*

Little Farmer's Cay. If you're looking for a little civilization, stop off at Little Farmer's Cay, the first inhabited cay in the chain, about 40 minutes (18 miles) from Great Exuma. The island has a restaurant and a small grocery store where locals gather to play dominoes. But don't expect too big of a party; just 70 people live on the island. A walk up the hill will reward you with fantastic island views.

Norman's Cay. North of the Exuma Cays Land and Sea Park is Norman's Cay, an island with 10 miles of rarely trod white beaches, which attracts the occasional yachter. It was once the private domain of Colombian drug smuggler Carlos Lehder. It's now owned by the Bahamian government. Stop by Norman's Cay Beach Club at MacDuff's for lunch or an early dinner and that it's-five-o'clock-somewhere beach cocktail. ⊠ *Norman's Cay.*

Pipe Creek. Boaters will want to explore the waterways known as Pipe Creek, a winding passage through the tiny islands between Staniel and Compass cays. There are great spots for shelling, snorkeling, diving, and bonefishing. Staniel Cay is a good place for lunch or dinner.

Staniel Cay. This is the hub of activity in the cays, and a favorite destination of yachters thanks to the Staniel Cay Yacht Club. Shack up in one of the cotton candy–color cottages and visit the club's restaurant for lunch, dinner, and nightlife. The island has an airstrip, one hotel, and paved roads, and everything is within walking distance. ⊠ *Staniel Cay.*

Starfish Reserve. Just off the mainland of Great Exuma, locals call the water surrounding the first few cays the Starfish Reserve, where tons of giant starfish dot the shallow ocean floor. Though it's not technically a protected area, starfish here are abundant. As long as you don't keep them out of the water for too long, it's okay to pick them up.

Thunderball Grotto. Just across the water from the Staniel Cay Yacht Club is one of the Bahamas' most unforgettable attractions: Thunderball Grotto, a lovely marine cave that snorkelers (at low tide) and experienced scuba divers can explore. In the central cavern, shimmering shafts of sunlight pour through holes in the soaring ceiling and illuminate the glass-clear water. You'll see right away why this cave was chosen as an exotic setting for such movies as 007's *Thunderball* and *Never Say Never Again,* and the mermaid tale *Splash.* ⊠ *Staniel Cay.*

Bahamian and continental cuisine is served at Staniel Cay Yacht Club's clubhouse restaurant.

WHERE TO EAT

$$$$ BAHAMIAN Fodor's Choice ★ 🍴 **Hill House Restaurant.** Housed in a charming British-style villa at the heart center of Fowl Cay Resort, this upscale restaurant serves fresh Bahamian-inspired modern cuisine. Located at one of the highest points on Fowl Cay, enjoy spectacular 360° views of the surrounding islands and sea while seated on the outdoor patio with a pool. **Known for:** open to nonguests; delectable hors d'oeuvres and innovative cuisine; lively cocktail hour. [$] *Average main: $50* ✉ *At Fowl Cay Resort* ☎ *242/355–2046 For reservations.*

$ BAHAMIAN 🍴 **Norman's Cay Beach Club at MacDuff's.** The outdoor patio strung with Christmas lights gives this beach bar a lost-island vibe. Inside the screened patio, at dinner you have a choice of three entrées: grilled chicken, grilled fish, or cracked conch. **Known for:** great cocktails; ocean views; call by 3 pm for dinner reservations. [$] *Average main: $16* ✉ *Norman's Cay* ☎ *242/357–8846* 🕐 *Closed Tues.*

$$ BAHAMIAN 🍴 **Staniel Cay Yacht Club.** Hand-painted tablecloths cover the tables in the dining room that serves Bahamian specialties such as cracked conch, fresh grouper, snapper, and grilled lobster with homemade bread. Many of the herbs come fresh from the restaurant's garden. **Known for:** tasty key lime pie; local fare; traditional Bahamian cuisine. [$] *Average main: $30* ✉ *Staniel Cay* ☎ *242/355–2024* 🌐 *www.stanielcay.com.*

WHERE TO STAY

$$$$
RENTAL
🏠 **Compass Cay.** Four spacious houses on the island, which is 1½ miles long and 1 mile wide, are so far apart and separated by lush palm and hardwood hammocks that you feel you have the island to yourself. **Pros:** remote tranquillity; boat included. **Cons:** expensive to get to. $ *Rooms from: $650* ✉ *Compass Cay, Compass Cay* 📞 *772/532–4793* ⊕ *www.compasscaymarina.com* 🛏 *4 villas* ⦿ *No meals.*

$$$$
RESORT
Fodor's Choice
★
🏠 **Fowl Cay Resort.** Simply speaking, the all-inclusive Fowl Cay Resort is a Caribbean paradise; set in the breathtaking turquoise waters of the central Exumas chain of little islands and cays in the Bahamas, it was originally used to keep chickens by the locals (hence the name). **Pros:** spacious and tasteful villas; fresh baked goods delivered to your door each morning; private pool at Birdcage Villa. **Cons:** Internet can be spotty on island. $ *Rooms from: $1,657* ⊕ *7-min boat ride from Staniel Cay airstrip* 📞 *877/845–5275* ⊕ *www.fowlcay.com* 🛏 *6 villas* ⦿ *All-inclusive.*

$$$$
RENTAL
🏠 **Norman's Cay Beach Club at MacDuff's.** There might be some rust on the refrigerator, but these three pastel villas are adorable, and just what you need for a true Out Island vacation. **Pros:** Out Island tranquillity; close to park; good restaurant on-site. **Cons:** expensive to get there; no Wi-Fi available. $ *Rooms from: $750* ✉ *Norman's Cay, Norman's Cay* 📞 *242/357–8846* 🛏 *3 villas* ⦿ *Breakfast.*

$
RENTAL
Fodor's Choice
★
🏠 **Staniel Cay Yacht Club.** The club once drew such luminaries as Malcolm Forbes and Robert Mitchum. **Pros:** great restaurant; authentic Bahamian experience. **Cons:** expensive to get to without a private boat or plane. $ *Rooms from: $185* ✉ *Staniel Cay* 📞 *242/355–2024, 954/467–6658* ⊕ *www.stanielcay.com* 🛏 *14 cottages* ⦿ *Some meals.*

NIGHTLIFE

Staniel Cay Yacht Club. Staniel Cay Yacht Club has a relatively busy bar, hopping with yachters from all over the world. ✉ *Staniel Cay* 📞 *242/355–2024.*

SPORTS AND THE OUTDOORS

BICYCLING

Staniel Cay Yacht Club rents beach cruisers if you want to pedal around the island.

BOATING AND FISHING

Staniel Cay Yacht Club. Rent a 13- or 17-foot Whaler and arrange for a fishing guide at Staniel Cay Yacht Club, a prime destination for serious bonefishers. Regular excursions can also be arranged for any resort guest. ✉ *Staniel Cay* 📞 *242/355–2024* ⊕ *www.stanielcay.com.*

GUIDED TOURS

BOAT TOURS

Fodor's Choice
★
Bahamas Revisited. Bahamas Revisited offers weeklong sailing excursions into the Exuma Cays aboard a 70-foot schooner. Guests can expect to feed iguanas, swim with pigs, snorkel with sharks, and lounge on sandbars all while giving to a great cause: a portion of each guest's payment funds free education excursions for underprivileged Bahamian youth. 📞 *242/544–6345* ⊕ *www.bahamasrevisited.com.*

Charter World. This company offers a variety of yacht charters. ☎ 954/603–7830 ⊕ *www.charterworld.com.*

Exuma Cays Adventures. This company offers several tour options, including a trip through the Exuma Cays, a snorkeling excursion to Long Island, and tours of Elizabeth Harbour in a glass-bottom boat. ☎ 242/357–0390 ⊕ *www.exumacaysadventures.com.*

Exuma Water Sports. Come here for guided Jet Ski tours through the Exuma Cays, as well as a scenic boat cruise that includes snorkeling at Thunderball Grotto. ☎ 242/357–0770, 242/357–0100 ⊕ *www.exumawatersports.com.*

Four C's Adventures. Various private and group charters are available through Four C's Adventures, including snorkeling, fishing, and sightseeing tours. ☎ 242/464–1720, 242/355–5077 ⊕ *www.exumawatertours.com.*

ISLAND TOURS

Exuma Travel and Transportation Limited. This company provides bus tours of Great Exuma and Little Exuma and can accommodate large parties. ☎ 242/345–0234.

Kendal "Dr. K" Nixon. Dr. K gives tours of Great Exuma and Little Exuma by car, for up to six passengers. ☎ 242/422–7399.

Luther Rolle. Luther's four-hour guided tour of the island by car is fully customizable, and can be split between days to best suit your vacation schedule. ☎ 242/357–0662.

SCUBA DIVING AND SNORKELING

Exuma Cays Land and Sea Park and **Thunderball Grotto** are excellent snorkeling and dive sites.

Minns Water Sports. ☎ 242/336–3483, 242/336–2604 ⊕ *www.mwsboats.com.*

THE SOUTHERN
OUT ISLANDS

WELCOME TO THE SOUTHERN OUT ISLANDS

TOP REASONS TO GO

★ **Stage a disappearing act:** Discover your inner castaway on islands way off the trampled tourist track. Pink or white sand, calm azure coves, or rolling ocean waves—you'll have your pick.

★ **Tell your own tall fishing tale:** Whether deep-sea fishing past the Wall off southern Inagua or bonefishing in the crystal-clear shallows on Cat Island's east coast, your fish-capades will be ones to remember.

★ **Explore historic lighthouses:** Surrounded by treacherous shoals and reefs, the Southern Out Islands have the country's most famous 19th-century lighthouses, most of which you can climb for stunning views.

★ **Feast on the reefs and walls:** Spectacular diving and snorkeling, and even specialty shark dives, are on the menu for nature lovers when visiting these secluded southern isles with their calmer, clearer waters undisturbed by cold fronts.

The southernmost Bahamas islands are remote, exposed to the open Atlantic, and ruggedly dramatic. One hundred thirty miles southeast of Nassau, Cat Island lies to the west of diminutive San Salvador, about the size of Manhattan. Long Island stretches 80 miles across the Tropic of Cancer, due south of Cat Island. Windswept Crooked and Acklins islands, with about 300 and 600 residents, respectively, are southeast of Long Island. And way down at the southernmost point of the country is Inagua, only 55 miles northeast of Cuba and 60 miles north of Haiti.

1 Cat Island. Stunning pink and white beaches, the highest hilltop in the country (the 206-foot Mt. Alvernia), 200-year-old deserted stone cottages, and superb diving and fishing attract loyal visitors. Less than a half dozen small resorts offer low-key luxury for those who want an Out Island experience with creature comforts.

2 San Salvador. Located on one of the largest reefs in the world, the tiny island's crystal-clear waters are a scuba diver's dream. The beach at Club Med is

gorgeous, with soft white sand and dazzling turquoise water.

3 Long Island. Ringed with stunning beaches that reach to the west out into the Bahamas Banks and string along the easterly reef-strewn Atlantic deep blue coast, this island is off the beaten path, yet offers comfortable resorts and inns with lots of amenities. Rich in history, it also has the world's deepest blue hole.

Arthur's Town

Cat Island
1

Port Howe

Exuma Sound

Great Exuma Island

Ragged Island Range

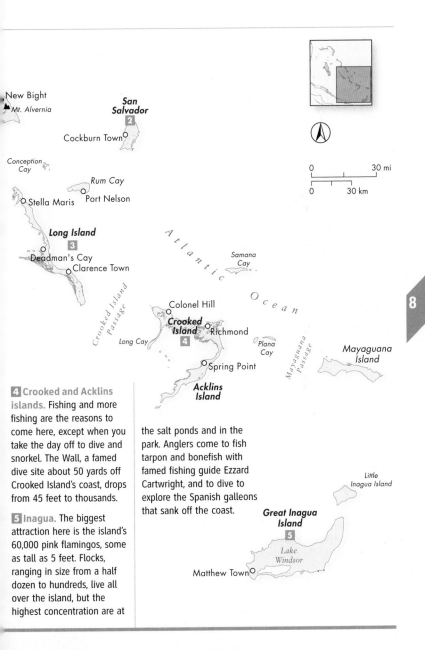

New Bight
▲ Mt. Alvernia

**San
Salvador**
2

Cockburn Town○

*Conception
Cay*

Rum Cay
○ Port Nelson

○ Stella Maris

Long Island
3

Deadman's Cay
○ Clarence Town

A t l a n t i c

Crooked Island passage

*Samana
Cay*

O c e a n

○ Colonel Hill

**Crooked
Island**
4
○ Richmond

Long Cay

*Plana
Cay*

Mayaguana passage

**Mayaguana
Island**

○ Spring Point

**Acklins
Island**

0   30 mi
0   30 km

8

4 **Crooked and Acklins
islands.** Fishing and more
fishing are the reasons to
come here, except when you
take the day off to dive and
snorkel. The Wall, a famed
dive site about 50 yards off
Crooked Island's coast, drops
from 45 feet to thousands.

the salt ponds and in the
park. Anglers come to fish
tarpon and bonefish with
famed fishing guide Ezzard
Cartwright, and to dive to
explore the Spanish galleons
that sank off the coast.

*Little
Inagua Island*

5 **Inagua.** The biggest
attraction here is the island's
60,000 pink flamingos, some
as tall as 5 feet. Flocks,
ranging in size from a half
dozen to hundreds, live all
over the island, but the
highest concentration are at

**Great Inagua
Island**
5

*Lake
Windsor*

Matthew Town○

INAGUA NATIONAL PARK

Nothing quite prepares you for your first glimpse of the West Indian flamingos that nest in Inagua National Park: brilliant crimson-pink, up to 5 feet tall, with black-tipped wings. A dozen flamingos suddenly fly across a pond, intermixed with fantastic pink roseate spoonbills.

It's a moving experience, and yet because of the island's remote location, as few as 100 people witness it every year. By 1952, Inagua's flamingos had dwindled to about 5,000. The gorgeous birds were hunted for their meat, especially the tongue, and for their feathers. The government established the 287-square-mile park in 1963, and today 60,000 flamingos nest on the island, the world's largest breeding colony of West Indian flamingos. The birds like the many salt ponds on Inagua that supply their favorite meal—brine shrimp.

You must contact the **Bahamas National Trust**'s Nassau office (☎ 242/393–1317 ⊕ *www.bnt.bs*) or **Wardens Henry Nixon or**

Randolph "Casper "Burrows (☎ 242/464–7618 or ☎ 242/395–0856) or the office ☎ 242/339–2125 to make reservations for your visit. All visits to the park are by special arrangement. *10 miles west of Matthew Town.*

BEST TIME TO GO

Flamingos are on the island year-round, but for the greatest concentration, visit during nesting season from late February through June. Around early March their courtship displays are an elaborate mass dance, and the chorus fills the air for miles around. They parade shoulder-to-shoulder, performing wing salutes, head wagging, and contorted preening with expanded wings. The courtship displays end around April and then the pairs build small volcano-like nest mounds from a few inches to 2 feet tall. Early morning and late afternoon are the best times to come. If you visit right after their hatching, the flocks of fuzzy, gray baby flamingos—they can't fly until they're older—are entertaining and the 50 shades of gray and pink are a photographer's delight.

BEST WAYS TO EXPLORE

With a guide. Senior Park Warden Henry Nixon or Deputy Randolph "Casper" Burrows leads all tours into the park and to Union Creek Reserve. They'll drive you past small flocks of flamingos in the salt ponds and answer questions. Nixon is difficult to reach by phone, but your best chance is in the early evening.

By kayak. You can't kayak in the park's salt ponds because they're too shallow, but you can in Lake Windsor, also called Lake Rosa (or locally as *The Pond*), a huge inland lake with its eastern half in the park. Because of badly washed-out dirt roads, you'll need a good 4x4 SUV or truck to reach the lake.

On foot. The best way to see flamingos up close is by parking the car and walking, or sitting quietly for a while in a thicket of mangroves. Flamingos are skittish and easily spooked. Although the ponds and mangroves look a lot

like the Florida Everglades, there are no alligators or poisonous snakes here. Make sure you have insect repellent on before you take off; the mosquitoes are in abundance.

FLAMINGO FACTS

Flamingos are the country's national bird, and they're protected from hunters by law.

Female flamingos lay one egg a year, and both parents take turns sitting on it for 28 days. Both parents also produce milk in the crop at the base of the neck for the chick for three months. The parents' feathers turn white while they feed the chick because they lose carotene.

Flamingos are monogamous and usually mate for life, but are extremely social birds that like to live in groups.

Their "knees," which seem to bend backward, are actually ankles (the knees are tucked under their feathers). What looks like the leg is actually the foot extending from the ankle.

Standing on one leg is the most comfortable position for a flamingo.

Brine shrimp, the flamingo's main source of food, is what gives the mature bird its brilliant deep pink.

8

RAKE 'N' SCRAPE

Rake 'n' Scrape music's contagious cadence, created by instruments made mostly from recycled objects, brings on a particularly strong urge to get up and shake it.

Most closely linked in sound, rhythm, and composition to zydeco music out of New Orleans, Rake 'n' Scrape is folk music at its best. It's unclear just where Rake 'n' Scrape originated, but most believe it has roots in Africa, made the voyage to the Bahamas with slaves, and was adapted over the years. Today's Rake 'n' Scrape was cultivated on remote Cat Island. Lacking money for and access to modern instruments, the resourceful locals made use of whatever supplies were available. Years later, many of these musicians could have their pick of shiny, finely tuned instruments, but they stick with what they know makes beautiful music.

HAVE A LISTEN

International recording artist and Cat Islander **Tony McKay,** who went by the stage name *Exuma,* incorporated Rake 'n' Scrape into his compositions. He paid homage to the style with the song "Goin' to Cat Island."

George Symonette's "Don't Touch Me Tomato" had a resurgence in a recent television commercial for Cable Bahamas. Symonette is associated with Goombay, a music style popular in Nassau in the 1950s. Goombay soon died out, giving way to closely related Rake 'n' Scrape.

Comprised of six Harbour Islanders, **The Brilanders** have toured with Jimmy Buffet. Their hit song "Backyard Party" is a sound track standard at just about any Bahamian party.

INSTRUMENTS

An authentic Rake 'n' Scrape band uses recycled objects to make music. An ordinary saw held in a musician's lap, then bent and scraped, becomes an instrument. A piece of wood, some fishing line, and a tin washtub is a good stand-in for the brass section. Plastic juice bottles are filled with pigeon peas, painted in bright colors, and turned into maracas. Add a goatskin drum, and you have all you need for a Rake 'n' Scrape ensemble, although many bands now add a concertina, guitar, or saxophone.

MAJOR PLAYERS

Authentic Rake 'n' Scrape is a dying art. The handful of groups scattered throughout the Bahamas are comprised of older men, as younger Bahamians prefer more modern sounds. Today **Ophie and the Websites, The Brilanders, Thomas Cartwright,** and **Bo Hogg** are among the few groups still performing old-style Rake 'n' Scrape. Other modern Bahamian musicians, such as **K.B., Phil Stubbs,** and **Ronnie Butler,** work the sound and rhythm into their own signature styles.

The popular four-day **Rake 'n' Scrape Festival** each June on Cat Island hosts dozens of bands from all over the Bahamas and the Caribbean.

On Harbour Island, **Gusty's** and **Vic-Hum Club** usually work at least one night of Rake 'n' Scrape into the weekly live music schedule. **The Brilanders** often play at **Seagrapes.**

DANCE LIKE A LOCAL

The Rake 'n' Scrape rhythm is so captivating that even the most rhythmically challenged will be hard-pressed to stand still. As the first beats are played, look around and see what the old folk do. It's not unusual to see a man stick his leg out (whether he's sitting or standing), lift his pants leg a bit, and let his footwork get fancy.

At festivals, schoolchildren usually dance the quadrille or heel-toe polka. If you ask a Bahamian to show you how to "mash de roach" or dance "the conch style," they may jump up and put on a show.

8

Updated by Bob Bower and Jessica Robertson

Wild and windswept, the southern Bahamian islands are idyllic Edens for those adventurers who want to battle a tarpon, dive a "wall" that drops thousands of feet, photograph the world's largest group of West Indian flamingos, or just sprawl on a sun-splashed beach with no sign of life—except maybe for a Bahama parrot pelting seeds from a guinep tree.

The quiet, simpler way of life on the Southern Out Islands is startlingly different from Nassau's fast-paced glitz and glamour, and even more secluded than the northern Out Islands. You won't find huge resorts, casinos, or fast-food restaurants here, not to mention stoplights. Instead, you'll be rewarded with a serene vacation that will make your blood pressure drop faster than a fisherman's hook and sinker.

Sportsmen are drawn to the Southern Islands to outsmart the swift bonefish, and fish for marlin, black and bluefin tuna, wahoo, and swordfish. Yachties roam these islands on their way to the Caribbean, and vacationers rent Hobie Cats and kayaks. On all these islands, divers and snorkelers come to see healthy reefs, abundant underwater wildlife, and even sharks. Romantics and honeymooners head south for the glorious sunsets viewed from the verandahs of beachside cottages, and for the lovely pink beaches. Bird-watchers arrive with binoculars in hand to see the green-and-red Bahama parrots, Bahama pintails, tricolor and crested night herons, and, of course, flamingos. They can also try to spot the Bahama woodstar hummingbird, which is very similar to one of the world's newest discovered species, the Inaguan lyretail hummingbird.

Hurricanes Joachin in 2015, Matthew in 2016, and Irma in 2017, damaged portions of the Southern Islands—yet only seemed to prove how resilient these hardy and community-minded folk are. Friends, families, and companies from neighboring islands and the United States and Canada poured in generous donations. While never fully complete, repairs to infrastructure and in the tourism sector were relatively quick.

The neighborliness and hospitality of the residents is well known, and visitors are often taken aback by their instant inclusion in the community. You can't walk 100 feet without someone offering a welcome ride on a hot day or a taxi driver offering you fresh fruit from his car trunk. Ask an islander where a certain restaurant is and they will walk with you until you see it. On Inagua, express any disappointment such as not seeing a flamingo up close, and the person standing behind you at the store will get on their cell phone. (There's a big flock now at the Town Pond.) The scenery is gorgeous, but this genuine rapport is what brings regulars back time and again to these tiny communities.

PLANNING

WHEN TO GO

Few visitors make it to these Southern Islands, but those who do, come at different times. Europeans tend to arrive in summer and stay for a month or longer. Sailors come through on their way to the Caribbean in fall and return to the Bahamas in spring or summer on trips back to North America. Fishermen arrive all year and divers prefer the calm seas in summer. Those looking for a winter warm-up visit from December to April, when temperatures are in the 70s. These months have the lowest rainfall of the year, but the ocean is chilly and, during cold fronts, are choppy for divers and boaters. Christmas, New Year's, and Easter are usually booked, so reserve rooms months in advance.

Many inns and resorts are closed in September and October for annual repairs, owners' vacations, and hurricane season, which technically runs from June through November. Mosquito repellent is usually needed year-round (except when string winds blow), but is imperative in summer and fall, especially after a period of rain when both mosquitoes and no-see-ums come out in full force, especially at sunset. Note that they remain in the sand on your feet and towels even after you leave the beach, so make sure to rinse or leave your towel outside your room.

The Southern Islands are generally a couple degrees warmer than Nassau, but farther south are more consistent trade winds in summer. You may need a windbreaker in winter, particularly on a boat. If possible, time your visit for Junkanoo on New Year's morning, sailing regattas in June and July, and special events such as the Cat Island's Rake 'n' Scrape Festival in early June.

TOP FESTIVALS

WINTER **Junkanoo.** Inagua puts on a spirited junkanoo parade on Boxing Day, December 26, and New Year's Day. Parades start at 4:30 am; you have to make the decision to stay up all night or get up early. There's food at the fish fry at Kiwanis Park in the center of town, where the parades end. ⊠ *Matthew Town.*

SUMMER **Long Island Sailing Regatta.** The annual Long Island Sailing Regatta, featuring Bahamian-made boats, is a three-day event the first weekend of June. Held in Salt Pond, the regatta is the island's biggest event and the Bahamas' second-largest regatta, attracting competitors from all over the islands. Booths featuring handmade crafts and Bahamian food and drink dot the site, and local bands provide lively entertainment beginning at sundown. Salt Pond is 10 miles south of Simms. ⊠ *Salt Pond* ⊕ *www.bahamas.com/event/long-island-regatta.*

Cat Island Rake 'n' Scrape Festival. The annual Cat Island Rake 'n' Scrape Festival celebrating the indigenous music is held in early June on the Bahamian Labour Day weekend. Each day the festivities begin with breakfast and lunch in the park with games of dominoes and checkers. At 7 pm the site is cleared for the Battle of the Rake 'n' Scrape Bands. You can also enjoy a gospel concert, cultural dance troupes, a children's corner with games, arts and crafts, and a fishermen and farmers' market. Nearby restaurants expand their menus for the after-parties. Between 1,000 and 2,000 people attend and fill local hotels, inns, and guesthouses, so book early. Two mail boats, Bahamasair, and private charters serve the festival, which takes place in the town square near Arthur's Town Airport. ⊠ *Arthur's Town Square, North Cat Island, Arthur's Town* 🖭 *$15.*

Cat Island Regatta. Growing in popularity (thanks to its Kalik Beer sponsorship), the annual Cat Island Regatta, held on the beach in New Bight over the Emancipation holiday weekend in early August, has parties, live music, games, dancing, and lots of island cooking. Some 30–40 island sloops compete in various classes over three days. Expect some Rake 'n' Scrape and party music from national and local live entertainers. Games can include dominoes, water relay races, ugliest man, water balloon toss, hula hoop relays, coconut races, and more. Book flights and lodging well in advance. ⊠ *New Bight* ⊕ *www.bahamas.com/event/ cat-island-regatta* 🖭 *Free.*

HOTELS

The inns in the Southern Out Islands are small and intimate, and usually cater to a specific crowd such as anglers, divers, or those who just want a quiet beach experience. Club Med Columbus Isle, an upscale resort on San Salvador, is an exception, with 236 rooms (and more being built) and a wide range of activities. Fernandez Bay Village in southern Cat Island is also more a full service resort with seven cottages, five villas, and a long menu of activities and dining.

Most inns are on the beach, and many have one- and two-bedroom cottages with private verandahs, offering three meals a day or self-catering along with free kayaks, paddleboards, and bikes. They'll either pick you up at the airport, ask you to get a taxi or arrange a car rental. Fishing guides, charters, dive trips, and sightseeing tours are just a call away, but you should book them in advance. If the hotel doesn't close in off-season, some of the best deals are available in September through early December. U.S. holidays and local holidays or festivals can quickly fill the islands' rooms. Club Med Columbus Isle offers early-bird booking bonuses and runs pricing promotions year-round.

RESTAURANTS

Out Island restaurants are often family-run and focus on home-style dishes. If you want to dine at a restaurant or another inn, it's crucial to call ahead. Dinner choices largely depend on what's planned or what fishermen and mail boats bring in; be prepared for limited choices. If you are renting, bring lots of food and snacks.

Anticipate tasty Bahamian fresh fish, lobster, conch, fresh-baked bread, and coconut tarts, along with a smattering of American and international dishes. Fish, lobster, and conch—which is served stewed, as a salad, or cracked (battered and deep fried)—is served at almost every restaurant for lunch and dinner. Chicken served many ways is a Bahamian staple and the skills of Bahamian cooks to prepare tasty chicken are legendary. These islands have breezy roadside conch stands—typically near a settlement or a beach or with sea views—that deserve a special trip from your hotel. On Friday and Saturday nights many restaurants and bars crank up the music and visitors and locals will drink and dance 'til late.

Restaurant prices are based on the median main course price at dinner, excluding gratuity, typically 15%, which is often automatically added to the bill as well as 7.5% VAT tax. Hotel prices are for two people in a standard double room in high season, excluding service and the 7.5% VAT tax. Some resorts can charge a 6% resort levy that goes to the Bahama Out Island Promotion Board. These BOIPB hotels typically offer a higher standard of service.

WHAT IT COSTS IN DOLLARS			
$	$$	$$$	$$$$
Restaurants	under $20	$20–$30	$31–$40	over $40
Hotels	under $200	$200–$300	$301–$400	over $400

8

VISITOR INFORMATION

Contacts Association of Bahamas Marinas. ☎ *844/556–5290 toll-free, 954/462–4591 Florida* ⊕ *www.bahamasmarinas.com.* **The Bahamas Ministry of Tourism.** ☎ *242/302–2000 in Nassau* ⊕ *www.bahamas.com.* **Bahamas Out Islands Promotion Board.** ☎ *242/322–1140 in Nassau* ⊕ *www.myoutislands.com.*

GETTING HERE AND AROUND

AIR TRAVEL

All of the Southern Out Islands have at least one airport, and several have multiple airports. Flights are primarily from the Nassau hub using local airlines and charter companies. San Salvador has scheduled flights from Montreal in Canada, Fort Lauderdale in Florida, and from Paris in France. *See individual island sections for more details.*

BOAT AND FERRY TRAVEL

Mail boats link all of these islands to Nassau, and, only for a popular festival, Bahamas Ferries may add a special service to supply the extra demand. *See individual island sections for more details.* If you plan to use the mail boat for transportation, check schedules by calling the Dockmaster's Office in Nassau. They change frequently.

CAR AND TAXI TRAVEL

You can rent a car on all of the islands. Taxi service is also available. Regardless, transportation tends to be expensive because of the isolation and cost of fuel.

CAT ISLAND

Cat Island is made up of exquisite pink-sand beaches and sparkling white-sand-ringed coves, as calm and clear as a spa pool. Largely undeveloped, the island has the tallest hill in the Bahamas, a dizzying 206 feet high, with an historic tiny stone abbey on top. The two-lane Queen's Highway runs the 48-mile length of the island from north to south, mostly along the western gorgeous sandy coastline, through quaint seaside settlements and past hundreds of abandoned stone cottages. Some are 200-year-old slave houses, crumbling testaments to cotton and sisal plantation days, while others, too old to have modern utilities, were abandoned. Trees and vines twist through spaces that used to be windows and roofs and the deep-blue ocean can be seen through missing walls. In 1938 the island had 5,000 residents and today only about 1,500. Many of the inhabitants left the cottages long ago out of necessity, to find work in Nassau and Florida, but the houses remain because they still mark family land.

Cat Island was named after a frequent visitor, the notorious pirate Arthur Catt, a contemporary of Edward "Blackbeard" Teach. Another famous islander is Sir Sidney Poitier, who grew up here before leaving to become a groundbreaking Academy Award–winning movie actor and director.

GETTING HERE AND AROUND

AIR TRAVEL

Cat Island has two airports: Arthur's Town (ATC) in the north and the New Bight (TBI) midisland. Two airlines fly in from Nassau to both airports: Southern Air four days a week, and SkyBahamas daily. (SkyBahamas has a connecting flight from Fort Lauderdale to Nassau in the early morning four days a week, providing convenient connections from Florida.) To reach these Southern Islands from Nassau, Stella Maris Air Service has a great reputation and, from Fort Lauderdale or Miami, you can arrange a charter through Eastern Air Express, Monarch Air Group, or Triton Airways to fly you direct, avoiding Nassau. For the best price, call around for a plane with the right number of seats. If you are going to Fernandez Bay Village or Hawk's Nest Resort, fly into the Bight. If you are going to Pigeon Cay, Orange Creek Inn, Shanna's Cove, or Tailwinds, fly to Arthur's Town. *For contact information of individual airlines, see also Air Travel in Travel Smart.*

Airport Contacts Arthur's Town Airport. ☎ *242/354–2236.* **New Bight Airport.** ☎ *242/342–2016.*

BOAT TRAVEL

Mail boats that bring supplies to the island each week make for an adventurous way to get around. You'll ride with groceries, large and small appliances, automobiles, and sometimes even livestock. All boats depart from Potter's Cay in Nassau. Schedules change frequently. The M/V *New G* sails to north and south Cat Island Wednesday at 5 pm, taking 10 hours and costing $60 each way.

Recent Hurricanes And Recovery

HURRICANES JOAQUIN, MATTHEW, AND IRMA

In October 2015, Category 4 Hurricane Joaquin passed over several of the Bahamas Southern Islands. The eye of the storm hit San Salvador, south Long Island and north Crooked Island, Rum Cay, and Samana Cay, and caused severe damage from wind, rains, and tidal surge. The hurricane resulted in a massive recovery effort from the populace in neighboring islands, the government, and the United States and Canada. In 2016, Hurricane Matthew's eye passed south and west of the Southern Islands, only giving the Southern Islands a strong tropical-force blow. In 2017, Hurricane Irma passed between north Inagua and south of the Turks & Caicos Islands and Acklins Island, and, again, submitted a large area with low hurricane force or tropical-force winds, only causing superficial damage with quick recoveries. The whole of Cat Island and the north of Long Island were never seriously affected and remained open for business. By late 2017, the islands had largely recovered. Hotels, restaurants, marinas, and amenities are renovated and repaired, with all essential facilities and infrastructure restored. Although recoveries are never fully complete, and evidence of past storms is noticeable, visitors' experience and enjoyment of the islands is practically back to normal. Building codes in the Bahamas, with requisite hotel inspections, are generally to a higher standard than in the United States, or equal to Florida's. Before booking vacations and tours, don't hesitate to ask the local Bahamas Tourism Offices or your resort questions to set your mind at ease.

CAR TRAVEL

The New Bight Service Station and Gilbert's New Bight Market rent cars on the southern end of Cat Island and will pick you up from the New Bight Airport. Robon Enterprises rents cars for the north (for those flying into Arthur's Town). It's important to rent a car from an agency that services the end of the island where you are staying because companies will not deliver cars to renters at the opposite end of the island. However, all inns and resorts can arrange rental cars for you upon arrival, and many people arrange their cars through their lodging. Rates depend on the number of days you're renting but are expensive, averaging $85 per day plus gas (which is also very expensive).

The best way to enjoy the overall Cat Island experience is to rent a car. Various settlements are not within walking distance. The two-lane, potholed Queen's Highway runs the 48-mile length of the island from north to south. You can also tour the island with a guide from Cat Island Experience.

Car Rental Contacts Gilbert's Car Rentals and Market. ⊠ *Across from Gilbert's Inn, New Bight* ☎ *242/342–3011.* **New Bight Car Rentals.** ☎ *242/342–3014.* **Robon Enterprises Car Rental.** ⊠ *In Bennett's Harbour, near Arthur's Town Airport, Arthur's Town* ☎ *242/354–6120, 242/359–9643.*

TAXI TRAVEL

Taxis wait for incoming flights at the New Bight and Arthur's Town airports, but be warned that fares can be expensive, starting at about $20 for the 10-minute trip from the New Bight Airport to the community of New Bight. Most inns and resorts will make arrangements for airport transfers, often complimentary.

ARTHUR'S TOWN AND BENNETT'S HARBOUR

Arthur's Town's claim to fame is that it was the boyhood home of actor Sidney Poitier, who wrote about growing up here in his autobiography. His parents and relatives were farmers. The village has a BTC Bahamas telephone station, a few stores, and Pat Rolle's **Cookie House Bakery** (☎ 242/354–2027)—an island institution that serves lunch and dinner by the order, so call ahead. Or just stop by to say hello, as Pat is a wealth of island knowledge and more than happy to bend your ear.

When you drive south from Arthur's Town, which is nearly at the island's northernmost tip, you'll wind along a road that passes through small villages and past bays where fishing boats are tied up. Fifteen miles south of Arthur's Town is Bennett's Harbour, one of the island's oldest settlements. Fresh-baked breads and fruit are sometimes sold at makeshift stands at the government dock, and there is good bonefishing in the creek.

WHERE TO EAT

$
BAHAMIAN
✕ **Da Smoke Pot.** Cold beer, Bahama Mama rum drinks, conch any way you want it, and the local Tough Skins live Rake 'n' Scrape music—Da Smoke Pot is an authentic Bahamian experience, named for the old local tradition of lighting green brush in the evening to keep the bugs at bay. Julian and the band will even let you take a turn playing on the saw with a screwdriver, while they sing and play along with you. You can't help but leave with a smile on your face. **Known for:** live Rake 'n' Scrape; rum drinks; conch specialties. $ *Average main: $15* ⊠ *Arthur's Town* ☎ 242/354–2094 ▤ *No credit cards* ☽ *Closed Mon.*

$$
BAHAMIAN
✕ **Sammy T's Restaurant and Bar.** Before sitting down to dinner on the wooden deck outside, grab a drink and take a stroll down the boardwalk bridge to the beach—a great place to see the sunset. The outside deck also has a pool table and darts for added entertainment. **Known for:** warm service; sunset views; Bahamian fare. $ *Average main: $25* ⊠ *Bennet's Harbour, north Cat Island, Bennett's Harbour* ☎ 242/354–6009 ⊕ *www.catislandbeachresort.com* ☽ *Closed Sept.*

$$$
EUROPEAN
Fodor'sChoice
★
✕ **Shannas Cove Restaurant.** This resort restaurant boasts a beautiful towering view above the sea and the north point of the island and offers three meals a day on the breezy verandah or in the cool interior. Owners Frank and Gabi, and chef Simon, take their European cuisine seriously and they please and surprise hotel guests and those from other resorts who drive far to dine here. **Known for:** homemade breads; extensive menu; reservations necessary. $ *Average main: $40* ⊠ *Shanna's Cove, north of Orange Creek, Bennett's Harbour* ☎ 242/354–4249 ⊕ *www. shannas-cove.com* ▤ *No credit cards* ☽ *Closed Sept.*

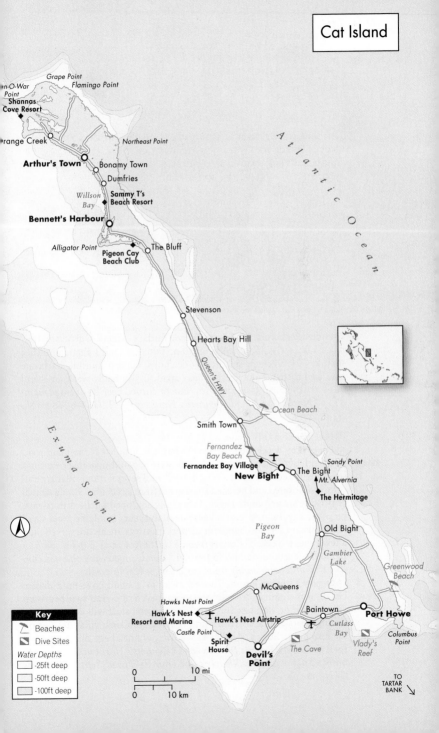

Cat Island

Atlantic Ocean

Exuma Sound

Grape Point
Flamingo Point
n-O-War Point
Shannas Cove Resort
range Creek
Northeast Point
Arthur's Town
Bonamy Town
Dumfries
Willson Bay
Sammy T's Beach Resort
Bennett's Harbour
Alligator Point
Pigeon Cay Beach Club
The Bluff

Stevenson

Hearts Bay Hill

Queen's HWY

Ocean Beach

Smith Town

Fernandez Bay Beach
Fernandez Bay Village
New Bight
The Bight
Sandy Point
Mt. Alvernia
The Hermitage

Pigeon Bay

Old Bight

Gambier Lake

Greenwood Beach

McQueens

Baintown
Port Howe

Hawks Nest Point
Hawk's Nest Resort and Marina
Hawk's Nest Airstrip
Castle Point
Spirit House
Devil's Point
Cutlass Bay
Vlady's Reef
The Cave
Columbus Point

TO TARTAR BANK

Key

- Beaches
- Dive Sites

Water Depths
- -25ft deep
- -50ft deep
- -100ft deep

0   10 mi

0   10 km

The Hermitage on Mt. Alvernia is Cat Island's most iconic sight.

$ JAMAICAN 🍴 **Yardie's Restaurant, Bar & Conch Stand.** Yardie's owners, Odette and Derrick Rolle, serve up large-size genuine Jamaican and Bahamian dishes such as jerk chicken, steamed pork chops, curried mutton, barbecue ribs, and their famous fresh conch salad. If you really want an island meal, try the breakfast grits with tuna or corned beef. [$] *Average main: $15* ✉ *North Cat Island, Bennett's Harbour* ☎ *242/354–6076* 💳 *No credit cards.*

WHERE TO STAY

$ RESORT 🏨 **Pigeon Cay Beach Club.** In a wide bay a half mile off the main road just south of Alligator Point, this family-owned-and-operated resort has seven deluxe cottages and a "big house" with several rooms that are colorfully decorated and perched steps away from a secluded 3-mile stretch of pristine sugary white beach. **Pros:** fully equipped kitchens in rooms; bicycles, kayaks, and snorkel gear available; cars available for a small fee. **Cons:** no TV; surcharge for airport transfers; meals are served only a few times a week. [$] *Rooms from: $180* ✉ *Rokers* ✥ *3 miles south of Bennetts Harbour* ☎ *242/354–5084* 🌐 *www.pigeoncaybahamas.com* 🛏 *11 rooms, some in big house or cottages* 🍽 *No meals.*

$ RESORT 🏨 **Sammy T's Beach Resort.** Tucked away in a small cove on a dream beach, this tranquil, friendly resort has seven one- and two-bedroom villas. **Pros:** private beach is great for sunsets; staff will arrange daily fishing/snorkeling excursions and rental cars. **Cons:** villas are not on the beach; facilities and villas are worn; pool has been filled in with a rock garden. [$] *Rooms from: $160* ✉ *Bennett's Harbour* ☎ *242/354–6009* 🌐 *www.catislandbeachresort.com* 🕒 *Closed Sept.* 🛏 *7 villas* 🍽 *No meals.*

$$ **Shannas Cove Resort.** This quiet and secluded owner-run beach resort
RESORT   is perched high on the hill on the northern tip of Cat Island, granting
sweeping views of the beautiful beach at Shanna's Cove and the north
of the island. **Pros:** stunning private beach; excellent on-site restaurant;
nicely designed, roomy cottages with air-conditioning. **Cons:** no TVs;
isolated from the rest of the island; no children under 18. $ *Rooms
from: $220* ⊠ *North of Orange Creek, Arthur's Town* ☎ *242/354–4249*
⊕ *www.shannas-cove.com* ☉ *Closed Sept.* ⌑ *5 villas* ❏ *No meals.*

NIGHTLIFE

The Hot Spot Restaurant & Karaoke Bar. Owners Ted and Melony (the latter
is also the fabulous cook here), entertain locals and visitors with great
indigenous food and karaoke. Noted for the Bahamian touches, like
coconut sky juice, the 46-ounce Como Hill cocktail, and other drinks
served in pea cans. Some claim Melony's food, served on palms and sea
grape leaves, is the best they've had. Spurred on by tuneful locals and
visitors pumping out a great selection of music, this place can rock until
3 am. If the music's too loud you can dine and drink on the deck. This
is the north's best nightlife spot. ⊠ *North Cat Island, Arthur's Town*
☎ *242/354–2076* ⌑ *Free.*

SPORTS AND THE OUTDOORS

SCUBA DIVING

Coral Reefs teeming with fish and mysterious shipwrecks make great
diving off the north end of the island, where visibility ranges from 165 to
200 feet thanks to a natural filtering system of limestone and rich fauna.

Diving with Shannas Cove Resort. This is not a certified dive shop, but
Frank, one of the owners of Shannas Cove, is a master diver and takes
only up to four divers at a time—making it very safe for beginners
and pros alike. Shannas offers north Cat Island's amazing range of
dives: from wrecks to walls, and reefs with amazing visibility, all from
the 22-foot catamaran. Diving spots can be reached within 5 to 30
minutes. Well-maintained equipment is available for rent. ⊠ *Shannas
Cove Resort, North of Orange Creek, Arthur's Town* ☎ *242/354–4249,
242/359–9668 cell* ⊕ *www.shannas-cove.com* ☉ *Closed Sept.*

8

NEW BIGHT

Yachts anchor off the coast of Regatta Beach, and boaters dingy in to
the Custom House amid a cluster of government buildings in this quaint
community, the largest town on the island. Houses face the Queen's
Highway, which twists through green hills. Yachties and visitors stock
up at the small grocery store and a bakery. The island's most iconic sight
is **Mt. Alvernia,** which is crowned with a historic little abbey. There's also
a colorful **Fish Fry,** a collection of fish shacks on Regatta Beach that's
a lively hangout at nights and on weekends, lovely old churches, and
eerie abandoned stone cottages, many of which are plantation ruins.
The town sits along a thin, Australian pine-lined white beach on the
west coast, and has peaceful saltwater estuaries which are nesting areas
for great blue herons, egrets, and pelicans.

EXPLORING

Fodor's Choice ★ **The Hermitage.** At the top of 206-foot Mt. Alvernia, the highest point in the Bahamas, the Hermitage is the final resting place of Father Jerome, an architect who traveled the world and eventually settled in the Bahamas. An Anglican who converted to Roman Catholicism, he built many structures including this hermitage on Mt. Alvernia, churches in Long Island, and a monastery in Nassau. He retired to Cat Island to live out his last dozen years as a hermit, and his final act of religious dedication was carving steps to the top of Mt. Alvernia. Along the way he also carved the Stations of the Cross. At the summit, he built an abbey with a small chapel, a conical bell tower, and living quarters comprising three closet-size rooms. He died in 1956 at the age of 80.

The pilgrimage to the Hermitage begins next to the commissioner's office at New Bight at a dirt path that leads to the foot of Mt. Alvernia. A caretaker clears the weeds around the tomb—islanders regard it as a shrine—and lights a candle in Father Jerome's memory. ✉ *New Bight.*

BEACHES

Fernandez Bay Beach. Imagine the perfect calm cove in the tropics—a 1-mile stretch of glistening, pristine white sand, inviting shade under coconut palms and sea grape trees, quaint resort cottages and verandahs facing the spectacular sand, and calm azure water. Two resorts (Fernandez Bay Village and Island HoppInn) have restaurants and bars built on decks overlooking the water and they each rent kayaks and paddleboards to guests. The beach is often deserted, so dinner for two might really mean just that. **Amenities:** food and drink; water sports. **Best for:** solitude; snorkeling; sunset; swimming; walking. ✉ *Just north of New Bight Airport* ☎ *242/342–3043.*

Ocean Beach. On the eastern Atlantic side, 4 miles from Queen's Highway at Smith's Bay is Ocean Beach, 1.8 miles of wide powdery white sand with a frequent breeze. There's no shade here and you should bring whatever water-sports toys you want. When conditions are right it's good for surfing and, when calm, paddleboarding, kayaking, and snorkeling on the nearby reefs. High on the dune crest is Ocean Dream Beach Resort, a quaint four-cottage inn, with a restaurant and bar serving Greek and Bahamian food. Bring water and snacks. Only reasonably accessed by car or bike. **Amenities:** food and drink. **Best for:** snorkeling ✉ *4 miles east of Smith's Bay* ☎ *242/342–2052 hotel.*

WHERE TO EAT

$$$$ INTERNATIONAL FAMILY 🍴 **Fernandez Bay Village Restaurant.** Fernandez Bay Village's Clubhouse serves delicious breakfasts buffet-style with seating on the beachfront terrace or inside—everywhere with splendid views of the beautiful bay. The breakfast buffet is loaded: pile on pastries, home-baked breads, croissants, bacon, sausage, grits, pancakes, cereals, yogurt, and fruit. **Known for:** exquisite dinner buffet; tiki hut bar; popular with pilots. [$] *Average main: $48* ✉ *Fernandez Bay Village* ✣ *1 mile northwest of New Bight Airport* ☎ *242/342–3043 resort, 954/474–4821 Fort Lauderdale, 800/940–1905 toll-free in U.S. and Canada* 🌐 *www.fernandezbayvillage.com* ⏲ *Closed mid-Aug.–Oct.*

$$ ✕ **Mermaid's Clubhouse.** A pleasant surprise for a remote Out Island, this
GREEK spacious, clean restaurant with a stunning location above Ocean Beach
serves down-home Bahamian food like grouper fingers, stew' fish, and
crab soup. Portions are generous, so bring your appetite. **Known for:**
local favorite; sea views; seating on deck. $ *Average main: $30* ⊠ *1½
miles east of Smith's Bay, along rugged white road* ☎ *242/342–2052*
⊕ *www.oceandreambeachresort.com* ▭ *No credit cards.*

WHERE TO STAY

$$ ⛱ **Fernandez Bay Village.** This owner-run resort is one of the Bahamas'
RESORT most famous and successful, and one of the best kick-back retreats
Fodor's Choice anywhere. **Pros:** private spacious accommodations; crescent-shape
★ white-sand beach in shade; lots of water sports there and activities off-
site. **Cons:** no TV; Wi-Fi in the main clubhouse only; insect repellent
needed outside in the evening. $ *Rooms from: $283* ⊠ *1 mile north of
New Bight Airport* ☎ *242/342–3043, 800/940–1905 toll-free* ⊕ *www.
fernandezbayvillage.com* ⇆ *17 rooms* ◯ *No meals.*

NIGHTLIFE

Regatta Beach Fish Fry. For an authentic Bahamian experience, don't
miss the Regatta Beach Fish Fry on Regatta Beach, just south of the
government buildings in the town center. On weekends, at least two
fish shacks open late in the afternoon and stay lively on into the
night. It's a great place for sunset watching and mingling with locals.
⊠ *Regatta Beach.*

SHOPPING

Pam's Boutique. This little shop at Fernandez Bay Village has reasonably
priced resort wear including sarongs, Havaiana flip-flops, logo hats,
and T-shirts. They also sell jewelry, bags, coffee cups, postcards, local
art, and books. This is one of your few chances to get a Cat Island
T-shirt. ⊠ *Fernandez Bay Village* ☎ *242/342–3043, 800/940–1905,
954/474–4821.*

SPORTS AND THE OUTDOORS

FISHING

Cat Island Fishing. On Cat Island you have myriad ways to fish: deep-
sea, bone-, fly-, and bottom-fishing. Several expert guides can do all
but each has his own specialty. Mark Keasler is great for bonefishing, Nathaniel Top Cat is great for deep-sea trolling, and Carl Pinder is great for reef fishing. Call Fernandez Bay to let them find out
who is available for which type of fishing. They also do snorkeling
tours and beach picnics. ⊠ *Fernandez Bay Village* ☎ *242/342–3043,
800/940–1905, 954/474–4821* ⊕ *www.fernandezbayvillage.com/
activities/#fishing.*

TOURS

The Cat Island Experience. C&O Tours, comprising Pastor Chris, son
Danny, and wife Olive King, have eight-seater air-conditioned vans
for guided tours of Cat Island. They have customizable tours, both
for the north and the south, which include much of the same sites.
The tour in the south includes beaches, Mt. Alvernia, the minimon-
astery on the Bahamas' highest point at 206 feet, a step-down well,

8

bat caves, cotton plantations and ruins, the old cotton railroad, an old lighthouse, churches, and also the modern structures and utilities. Chris and family can answer your many questions and give good, historical background. It's one of the most rewarding activities, giving you a lasting connection to the island. ⊠ *New Bight* ☎ *242/464–6181* 💵 *$175 for half day, $350 for full day.*

PORT HOWE

At the conch shell-lined traffic roundabout at the southernmost end of the Queen's Highway, head east out toward Port Howe, believed by many to be Cat Island's oldest settlement. Nearby lie the ruins of the **Deveaux Mansion,** a stark two-story, whitewashed building overrun with vegetation. Once it was a grand house on a cotton plantation, owned by Captain Andrew Deveaux of the British Navy, who was given thousands of acres of Cat Island property as a reward for his daring raid that recaptured Nassau from the Spaniards in 1783. Just beyond the mansion ruin is the entrance road to the Greenwood Beach Resort, which sits on an 8-mile stretch of unblemished, velvet pink-sand beach, but its fate as an operational hotel was up in the air at this writing.

BEACHES

Greenwood Beach. An 8-mile stretch of pink sand on the Atlantic Ocean makes this one of the most spectacular beaches on Cat Island. Hypnotized by the beauty, most visitors walk the entire beach, some even farther to an adjoining sandy cove accessible only by foot. After such a long walk, a dip in the shallows of the turquoise ocean is pure bliss. The beach is on the remote southeastern end of the island and is home to just one hotel, Greenwood Beach Resort, which is a good place for a bite and a drink. **Amenities:** none. **Best for:** solitude; snorkeling; swimming; walking. ⊠ *Greenwood Beach Resort, 3 miles northeast of Port Howe along a bumpy road* ⊕ *www.greenwoodbeachresort.com.*

DEVIL'S POINT

The small village of Devil's Point, with its bright-walled, thatch-roof houses, lies at the southern tip of the Queen's Highway 9 miles southwest of Old Bight. Beachcombers will find great shelling on the pristine beach; keep an eye out for dolphins, which are common in these waters. From Devil's Point, drive north through the arid southwest corner of the island to **McQueens,** then west to the area's biggest resort, Hawk's Nest Resort, which has an airstrip, marina, restaurant, and bar. This resort is well known to serious anglers and divers, who often fly in to the resort's private airstrip and stay a week to do little else but fish or dive. The southwest end of the island teems with great diving walls, reefs, and wrecks with an abundance of marine life and coral heads.

WHERE TO EAT AND STAY

$$

BAHAMIAN

✕ **Hawk's Nest Dining & Clubhouse.** High-beamed ceilings, tiled floors, blue-and-lime-green walls, and blue ceramic-topped tables create a cheerful vibe to go with the Bahamian comfort-food menu. If you have

Fernandez Bay Beach is a perfect, calm cove for swimming.

your heart set on a menu item, be sure to call your order in by 3 pm. **Known for:** fresh-squeezed juices; poolside dining; TVs showing sports and news. [$] *Average main: $25* ✉ *Hawk's Nest Resort* ✢ *7½ miles by road northwest of Devil's Point* ☎ *242/342–7050, 954/376–3865* 🌐 *www.hawks-nest.com* ⏲ *Closed mid-Sept.–Oct.*

8

$ RESORT 🏨 **Hawk's Nest Resort and Marina.** Catering to private pilots, yachters, and serious fishermen, this small laid-back resort at Cat Island's southwestern tip has its own 3,100-foot runway and a 28-slip full-service marina with a dive shop for guests. **Pros:** three meals served a day; fully stocked honor bar; PADI certified with great dive spots and shallow walls. **Cons:** long drive from other places on the island; good swimming beach a few yards from main clubhouse; afternoon shark feed can interrupt swimming at the dock. [$] *Rooms from: $175* ✉ *Devil's Point* ✢ *From Devil's Point village, go 4 miles north and 3½ miles west along white road* ☎ *242/342–7050 resort, 954/376–3865 in U.S. and Canada* 🌐 *www.hawks-nest.com* ⏲ *Clubhouse and hotel closed Sept. and Oct.* 🛏 *10 rooms* 🍴 *No meals.*

$ RENTAL 🏨 **Spirit House.** Three miles west of Devils Point, sitting on a 70-foot height and next to a stunning beach cove, Spirit House is an exotic and idyllic private house for rent for 8 or 10 people at $5,000/week. **Pros:** Freeda Major's incredible cooking; 20-foot Mako speedboat for fishing and snorkeling; TV/DVD and lots of games for fun. **Cons:** remote lodgings; miles to airport and bigger village. [$] *Rooms from: $179* ✉ *Devil's Point* ✢ *A mile down rough road, northwest of Devil's Point settlement* ☎ *242/424–6542* 🌐 *www.spirithousebahamas.com* 🛏 *5 bedrooms* 🍴 *No meals.*

SPORTS AND THE OUTDOORS

FISHING

Hawk's Nest Marina. Blue-water angling boat owners make a point of using Hawk's Nest Marina to access the dynamite offshore fishing. Look for wahoo, yellowfin tuna, dolphin, and white and blue marlin along the Exuma Sound drop-offs, Devil's Point, Tartar Bank, and Columbus Point. March through July is prime time, with multiple annual fishing tournaments on the books. Winter fishing from December through February is also good for wahoo. You can arrange bonefishing through the marina with a top guide. ⊠ *Hawks Nest Resort and Marina* ☎ *242/342–7050, 954/376–3865* ⊕ *www.hawks-nest.com.*

SCUBA DIVING

Cat Island's south coast offers some of the country's best diving. The walls start from very shallow depths, allowing long dive times and great photography. Some of the area's best dive sites, which are most easily reached from Hawk's Nest Marina, are: **Hole in The Wall** (12 miles, 50–100 feet); spectacular break in the wall and entrance to a small channel with lobster or spotted drums; impressive archway, black coral, stingray, sharks, dog snapper, barracudas, and groupers; all kinds of soft and hard coral. **The Oz** (7 miles, 55-100 feet): tunnels and canyons overgrown with soft corals, turtles, reef sharks, reef fish of any color, hogfish, Nassau and other grouper, and oceanic triggerfish. Spectacular when leading to the wall. **Tartar Bank** (6 miles, 40-60 feet): has strong currents, for pro divers only; offshore pinnacle, reef sharks, white-tip sharks, big turtles, and more. **Fish Bowls** (20-30 feet): from micro to macro, a photographer's paradise includes schools of goat fish, Atlantic spadefish, yellowtail, and mutton snapper. White-spotted eels are numerous, along with nurse sharks and lobster. See a spider crab refuge and cleaning station as you follow the reef's ledge. Dives at Hawk's Nest must be booked a month in advance.

Hawk's Nest Marina Dive Shop. Hawk's Nest at one time was the only PADI-certified dive operation on Cat Island. Today, certified diver Randy Holder conducts guided diving adventures (for guests only), rents diving and snorkeling gear, and has equipment and sundries for sale. The running time to dive sites off the southern tip of the island is 15 to 30 minutes in the shop's 43-foot custom dive boat, outfitted with VHF and GPS. Call ahead for bookings. Dives must be booked one month in advance; $250 minimum to take the dive boat out. Ask for package rates. ⊠ *Devil's Point* ⊹ *From Devil's Point, go 4 miles north and 3½ miles along white road* ☎ *242/342–7050, 954/376–3865* ⊕ *www.hawks-nest.com.*

SAN SALVADOR

On October 12, 1492, Christopher Columbus disrupted the lives of the peaceful Lucayan Indians when he landed on the island of Guanahani, which he renamed San Salvador. Apparently he knelt on the beach and claimed the land for Spain. (Skeptics of this story point to a study published in a 1986 *National Geographic* article in which Samana Cay, 60 miles southeast, is identified as the exact point of

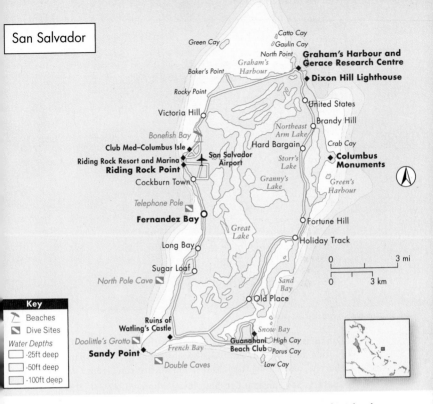

San Salvador

Green Cay
Catto Cay
Gaulin Cay
North Point
Graham's Harbour
Baker's Point
Rocky Point
Victoria Hill
Bonefish Bay
Club Med–Columbus Isle
Riding Rock Resort and Marina
Riding Rock Point
Cockburn Town
Telephone Pole
Fernandez Bay
Long Bay
Sugar Loaf
North Pole Cave
Ruins of Watling's Castle
Doolittle's Grotto
Sandy Point
French Bay
Double Caves

Graham's Harbour and Gerace Research Centre
♦ **Dixon Hill Lighthouse**
United States
Brandy Hill
Northeast Arm Lake
Hard Bargain
Crab Cay
Columbus Monuments
San Salvador Airport
Storr's Lake
Granny's Lake
Green's Harbour
Great Lake
Fortune Hill
Holiday Track
Sand Bay
Old Place
Snow Bay
High Cay
Guanahani Beach Club
Porus Cay
Low Cay

Key
↗ Beaches
◥ Dive Sites
Water Depths
▢ -25ft deep
▢ -50ft deep
▢ -100ft deep

0   3 mi
0   3 km

the weary explorer's landing.) Three monuments on the island commemorate Columbus's arrival, and the 500th anniversary of the event was officially celebrated here.

The island is 14 miles long—a little longer than Manhattan Island—and about 6 miles wide, with a lake-filled interior. Some of the most dazzling deserted beaches in the country are here. Most visitors come for Club Med's unique blend of fun and activities; others for the peaceful isolation and the diving. There are more than 50 dive sites and world-renowned offshore fishing and good bonefishing. The friendly locals have a lot to be proud of for their special island and their warmth shows it.

GETTING HERE AND AROUND

AIR TRAVEL

The island has one airport, in Cockburn Town (ZSA), which is modern, comfortable, and has a long runway. A new fuel depot and FBO by Odyssey Aviation means even more long-haul flights will commence and private aircraft can easily refuel here. XL, the French charter vacation company, flies from Paris on Wednesday, Air Canada from Montreal on Tuesday, and at least one carrier such as Spirit Airlines or American Eagle once a week from Fort Lauderdale or Miami. From Nassau, Southern Air has 13 flights each week in and out of San Sal, and

San Salvador has several popular diving sites.

Bahamasair has daily flights. A host of charter companies fly in from Florida and Nassau. Club Med's website has packages that include air charters, and Riding Rock Resort and Marina can arrange them as well.

Contacts San Salvador Cockburn Town Airport. ☎ 242/331-2131.

BOAT TRAVEL

Mail boats that bring supplies to the island each week make an adventurous mode of transportation. M/V *Tolyn* sails from Nassau on Tuesday at 1 pm with stops in Deadman's Cay, Long Island, and Rum Cay and arrives the next morning. You'll ride with groceries, large and small appliances, automobiles, and sometimes even livestock. All boats depart from Potter's Cay in Nassau. Schedules change frequently so best to call the Dockmaster's Office in Nassau to get the latest information.

BIKE TRAVEL

For a short visit to Columbus Cross or the lighthouse, a bike is a sufficient mode of transportation. Bike rentals are available at Club Med and Riding Rock Resort.

CAR TRAVEL

If you want to see the entire island, rent a car. Queen's Highway forms an oval that skirts the island's coastline, and road conditions are excellent. Car rentals are about $85 a day.

Contacts D&W Car Rental. ☎ 242/331-2484, 242/331-2488, 242/331-2184.

SCOOTER TRAVEL

Scooters are a fun, breezy, and convenient way to get around the entire island.

Contacts K's Scooter Rentals. ✉ *Cockburn Town Airport* ☎ *242/331–2125, 242/331–2651, 242/225–7392.*

TAXI TRAVEL

Club Med meets all guests at the airport. Riding Rock, five minutes away, provides complimentary transportation for guests. If you want to take your own taxi, it's approximately $10 to either resort.

Contacts Clifford "Snake Eyes" Fernander. ☎ *242/331–2676, 242/427–8198 cell.*

FERNANDEZ BAY TO RIDING ROCK POINT

In 1492 the inspiring sight that greeted Christopher Columbus by moonlight at 2 am was a terrain of gleaming beaches and far-reaching forest. The peripatetic traveler and his crews steered the *Niña, Pinta,* and *Santa María* warily among the coral reefs and anchored, so it is recorded, in **Fernandez Bay.** A cross erected in 1956 by Columbus scholar Ruth C. Durlacher Wolper Malvin stands at his approximate landing spot. An underwater monument marks the place where the *Santa María* anchored. Nearby, another monument commemorates the Olympic flame's passage on its journey from Greece to Mexico City in 1968.

Fernandez Bay is just south of what is now the main community of **Cockburn Town,** midisland on the western shore. This is where the airport is, and where the weekly mail boat docks. This small village's narrow streets contain two churches, a commissioner's office, a police station, a courthouse, a library, a clinic, a drugstore, and a telephone station.

8

From Cockburn Town to Club Med, you'll pass **Riding Rock Point.** All fish excursions leave from the marina. Riding Rock Resort makes a good spot to stop for a drink, meet locals and divers, and buy a local T-shirt.

BEACHES

Fodor's Choice ★ **Bonefish Bay.** The 3-mile beach in front of Club Med has bright white sand as fine as talcum powder, and water that is such a bright neon shade of turquoise, it appears to be glowing. There are activities such as waterskiing, snorkeling, sailing, kayaking, and paddleboarding in front of Club Med, but the beach is long enough that you'll be able to find an isolated spot. To join in all the fun activities and partying, buy a day pass at the front desk. **Amenities:** food and drink; showers; toilets; water sports. **Best for:** partiers; snorkeling; swimming; windsurfing. ✉ *Club Med—Columbus Isle, Cockburn Town.*

WHERE TO EAT

$$$$ ECLECTIC 🍴 **Christopher's at Club Med.** Christopher's open-air restaurant has buffets during breakfast, lunch, and dinner, with the latter changing themes nightly: Caribbean Night has local fare such as conch and fresh fish, and other themes include French, Mexican, and Mediterranean. Carving stations and European pastries and breads are impossible to skip, and simple pastas and pizzas are mainstays for the finicky eater. **Known for:** themed dinner buffets; dinner pass includes open bar; nightly entertainment. [$] *Average main: $64* ✉ *Club Med–Columbus Isle, Cockburn Town* ✣ *3 miles north of Riding Rock Point* ☎ *242/331–2000* 🌐 *www.clubmed.com.*

$$$$
ITALIAN
Fodor'sChoice
★

✕ **Guanahani Beach Club Restaurant.** At this resort restaurant, fresh fruit smoothies, panini on crusty French bread, fresh salads, and various authentic four-course Italian dinners, are all made to order by owner-chef Elena Sparta. Try the mille-feuille of smoked salmon and tomatoes; fettuccine with crab; shrimp with lime, basil, and herbs; lemon and rosemary risotto; or duck breast in Cointreau and orange sauce. **Known for:** nonguests should call ahead; outdoor patio over Snow Bay; cozy interior lounge. $ *Average main: $70* ⊠ *Snow Bay, Sunrise Rd., Cockburn Town* ☎ *242/452–0438* ⊕ *www.guanahanibeachclub.com* ▭ *No credit cards* ⊘ *Often closed June–Oct.*

$
BAHAMIAN

✕ **Paradis Restaurant and Bar.** A typical Bahamian enclosed restaurant, Paradis has a daily changing menu written on a chalkboard. Home-cooked Bahamian and American food such as burgers, conch, ribs, and the fresh catch of the day are tastily prepared. **Known for:** popular with locals; free Wi-Fi; fresh seafood. $ *Average main: $15* ⊠ *Cockburn Town* ⊕ *Just north of airport near Club Med* ☎ *242/331–2400.*

$$$$
CARIBBEAN

✕ **Riding Rock Seafront Restaurant.** This 100-seat restaurant offers seating indoors, by the pool, and on the back patio overlooking the ocean. During slower seasons or depending on resort guests, the restaurant is not always open, and each meal is set between certain hours—make sure to call ahead. **Known for:** tasty conch chowder; fresh catches grilled with lemon and butter; fresh-baked bread at breakfast. $ *Average main: $45* ⊠ *Riding Rock Resort and Marina, Cockburn Town* ☎ *242/331–2631, 954/453–5031* ⊕ *www.ridingrock.com* ⊘ *Sometimes closed during slow season.*

WHERE TO STAY

$$$$
RESORT
FAMILY

🏨 **Club Med–Columbus Isle.** This 89-acre oceanfront village is one of Club Med's most luxurious resorts, with state-of-the-art dive facilities and every water sport and activity imaginable. **Pros:** gorgeous beachfront location; revolving dinner themes; full-service dive shop. **Cons:** no children under age two; long walk to outlying rooms; fee for in-room Wi-Fi. $ *Rooms from: $500* ⊠ *Cockburn Town* ⊕ *½ mile by road from airport terminal* ☎ *888/932–2582, 242/331–2000* ⊕ *www.clubmed.com* ⇥ *256 rooms in 2-story bungalows* ⦿ *All-inclusive.*

$$$
RESORT
Fodor'sChoice
★

🏨 **Guanahani Beach Club.** This cozy, small, owner-operated resort is elegant and sophisticated, offering both quiet solitude on a stunning private beach and serious adventure for sports enthusiasts. **Pros:** excellent on-site restaurant; simple and chic villas; private beach adorned with loungers and hammocks. **Cons:** no children under 16; credit cards not accepted; far from other island amenities so you will probably want a rental car. $ *Rooms from: $365* ⊠ *Snow Bay, Sunrise Rd., Cockburn Town* ☎ *242/452–0438* ⊕ *www.guanahanibeachclub.com* ⊘ *Closed mid-June–late Oct.* ⇥ *3 villas* ⦿ *Some meals.*

$
HOTEL

🏨 **Riding Rock Resort and Marina.** Good for serious divers, this modest motel-style resort is a long-standing property on San Salvador and has a restaurant on-site serving breakfast, lunch, and dinner when enough guests warrant. **Pros:** budget-friendly alternative to other resorts; friendly, accommodating staff; rooms are standard but clean. **Cons:** no planned entertainment; diving is not daily and dependant on resort guests; rocky beachfront. $ *Rooms from: $162* ⊠ *Cockburn Town* ⊕ *½* *mile southwest of airport terminal* ☎ *800/272–1492, 242/331–2631* ⊕ *www.ridingrock.com* ⇋ *30 rooms* ⦶ *All meals.*

NIGHTLIFE

Club Med–Columbus Isle. Evening passes to Club Med cost $70 and include themed dinners, nightly entertainment, and all you can drink from 7 pm to 1 am. The predinner cocktail parties and beachside tiki hut parties are lively affairs with skilled DJs and rapid-fire, charming bartenders. This place is big enough to slink away to a romantic spot on your own. Entertainment gets going after dinner with staff shows in the open-air theater. ⊠ *Club Med, Cockburn Town* ☎ *888/932–2582, 242/331–2000.*

The Driftwood Bar at Riding Rock Resort. Driftwood decorated with messages, stickers, and accolades from regular visitors covers the walls and hangs from the ceilings of this little bar, giving it real character. Fishermen and scuba divers from all over the world gather frequently to tell tall tales, making it a favorite evening hangout. Try your luck at the ringtoss game, catch up on sports from home on the big-screen TV, or grab a cold Kalik or frozen piña colada (touted as the best on the island) and enjoy the sunset on the open-air back patio overlooking the sea. ⊠ *Riding Rock Resort, Cockburn Town* ☎ *242/331–2631, 800/272–1492, 954/453–5031* ⊕ *www.ridingrock.com.*

SHOPPING

Club Med – Columbus Isle. Club Med has a boutique that's clearly the best souvenir, swimsuit, resort-wear shop on the island. It's an independent French franchise chain that has excellent shopping. Browse 45 Club (Club Med's logo brand), Hip Way, Fila, Carrera, Le Mar, gorgeous Colombian swimwear, Havaiana flip-flops, sunglasses, hats, and souvenirs. Great gifts to return home with are the Bahamian-made John Waltlings Fine Rums and Red Turtle Vodka. ⊠ *Club Med, Cockburn Town* ☎ *242/331–2000.*

Simply Bahamian. A small local crafts and liquor store across the street from the airport sells locally made purses and sarongs featuring Andros batik. ⊠ *Cockburn Town.*

SPORTS AND THE OUTDOORS

SCUBA DIVING

San Salvador is famous for its vibrant wall dives and abundant marine life, including hammerhead sharks, sea turtles, Eagle rays, and more. The **Telephone Pole** is a stimulating wall dive where you can watch stingrays, grouper, snapper, and turtles in action.

Riding Rock Resort & Marina. The dive operation here (both SSI and PADI recognized) uses mostly buoyed sites to avoid damaging the marine environment by dropping anchor. The 42- and 46-foot dive boats are spacious and comfortable. Resort and certification courses are offered, and all new computerized dive gear is available for rent. Complete dive packages, including meals and accommodations, are available through Riding Rock Resort and Marina. However, dive trips are not offered daily so book well in advance. ⊠ *Riding Rock Resort and Marina, Cockburn Town* ☎ *800/272–1492, 242/331–2631, 954/453–5031* ⊕ *www.ridingrock.com.*

Fodor's Choice **Seafari Dive Center at Club Med Columbus Isle.** The diving operation at Club ★ Med is now run separately by Seafari International, and all dive trips and certifications (PADI and CMAS) are open to Club Med guests and other visitors to the island. This professional dive center consistently offers three dives a day except Thursday, in addition to a weekly night dive, to more than 35 dive sites with permanent moorings. Divers go out on one of two catamarans, 54 and 52 feet. A hyperbaric chamber is on-site, and the staff consists of 11 dive instructors and 4 dive masters. All necessary equipment is available for rent including udive computers, and Nitrox. ⊠ *Club Med, Cockburn Town* ☎ *242/331–2000, 242/331–2195* ⊕ *www.clubmed.us.*

TOURS

Fernander Tours. In addition to being a taxi driver and island tour guide extraordinaire, Mr. Clifford Fernander is friendly and full of information for the inquisitive tourist. He and son Bruno Fernander offer tours for all visitors. The 2½- to 3-hour tour includes a drive through all the settlements and stops at the best known historic monuments and even some few get to see. Afterward, you'll feel San Salvador is like a second home. ⊠ *Cockburn Town* ☎ *242/331–2676, 242/427–8198.*

FAMILY **Lagoon Tours.** Cruise through secluded Pigeon Creek on the island's beautiful southeast corner in a flat-bottom boat that maxes at five people to view baby sharks, sea turtles, and starfish, and top off the trip shell hunting on High Cay. Lagoon Tours caters to all interests from nature walks and historical tours to bird-watching and excursions through the quiet waters of the lagoons. This family-run company is very proud of San Salvador Island and they are happy to show you their favorite off-the-beaten-path spots, with a smile and a cooler full of refreshments. They also conduct kayaking, nature, and bird-watching tours. ⊠ *Cockburn Town* ☎ *242/452–0102 cell, 242/331–2459.*

Nat Walker's Island Adventures. As the island's former Warden for the Bahamas National Trust, Nat Walker has a unique understanding of the island's nature and history, and he will customize island tours to include visits to monuments, private beach picnics, islander restaurants, shopping, and the like. You can choose to see the archaeological site where its earliest inhabitants, the Lucayan Indians, lived; five monuments at Landfall Park commemorating Columbus's arrival in the Americas; a hand-operated Dixon Hill Lighthouse (one of three in the Bahamas); Watling's Estate 18th-century plantation ruins; and the Gerace Research Centre. Nathaniel also has 25-seat buses and rental cars and arranges private beach picnics, as well as snorkeling and reef tours. ☎ *242/331–2111, 242/464–9038.*

WATER SPORTS

Club Med – Columbus Isle. If you are not a guest at Club Med, you can buy a day pass for $150, which gives you access to water sports (including daily guided snorkeling trips, Hobie Cat sailing, paddleboards, kayaks, and windsurfing) and regular sports activities (including group power walks and jogging, beach volleyball, tennis, various aerobics classes, yoga, and tai chi). The day pass includes lunch, dinner, and all you can drink and is good from 10 am to 1 am. A $60 day pass inclusive of all the above except for dinner gets you access from 10 am to 6 pm. ⊠ *Club Med, Cockburn Town* ☎ *242/331–2000* ⊕ *www.clubmed.us.*

Guanahani Surf & Sail Center. San Salvador is one of the last "uncrowded kitesurfing paradises," with ideal wind conditions and year-round warm waters. Licensed by IKO (International Kiteboarding Organization), the Guanahani Surf & Sail Center offers in-depth kiteboarding instruction for every level. Led by qualified trainers with Cabrinha kites and boards, courses last anywhere from 3 to 10 hours, and are best done over the course of a few days. The flat, calm, shallow waters in Snow Bay offer the perfect practice and play area. ⊠ *Snow Bay, Sunrise Rd., Cockburn Town* ☎ *242/452-0438* ⊕ *www.guanahanibeachclub.com.*

> ### HISTORIC LIGHTHOUSES
>
> Since the 19th century, sailors' lives have depended on the lighthouse beacons that rotate over the Southern Islands and the treacherous reefs that surround them. But for landlubbers, these lighthouses also offer bird's-eye vantage points. Visit the 115-foot Bird Rock Lighthouse on Crooked Island, the Castle Island Lighthouse on Acklins Island, the Inagua Lighthouse, and San Salvador's Dixon Hill Lighthouse.

ELSEWHERE ON SAN SALVADOR

Sometimes you just don't want to stay put at the resort. San Salvador's off-the-beaten-path places require some work to get to, but make for interesting sightseeing. The Gerace Research Centre and the lighthouse are not difficult to reach, but the "other" Columbus monument requires a little more work and an adventurous spirit.

EXPLORING

Columbus Monuments. Christopher Columbus has more than one monument on San Salvador Island commemorating his first landfall in the New World on October 12, 1492. The simple white cross erected in 1956 at Landfall Park in Long Bay is the easiest to find, on Queen's Highway just outside Cockburn Town. (Also on the site is the Mexican Monument, which housed the Olympic flame in 1968 on its journey from Greece to Mexico City. The flame has not been lit since, but this location is popular for weekend family picnics and local gatherings.) The older and more difficult to find is the Chicago Herald Monument erected in 1891 to celebrate the 400th anniversary of the explorer's landing. No roads lead to this monument—a sphere hewn from limestone—so you'll have to trek through East Beach on Crab Cay by foot, which is fun for the more adventurous. ⊠ *Queen's Hwy., Cockburn Town* ⊕ *www.bahamas.com/islands/san-salvador.*

Dixon Hill Lighthouse. A couple of miles south of Graham's Harbour stands Dixon Hill Lighthouse. Built around 1856, it's the last hand-operated lighthouse in the Bahamas. The lighthouse keeper must wind the apparatus that projects the light, which beams out to sea every 15 seconds to a maximum distance of 19 miles, depending on visibility. A climb to the top of the 160-foot landmark provides a fabulous view of the island, which includes a series of inland lakes. The keeper is present 24 hours a day. Knock on his door and he'll take you up to the top and explain the machinery. Drop a dollar in the box when you sign the guest book on the way out. ⊠ *Cockburn Town ⊕ Northeast sector of the island.*

Graham's Harbour and Gerace Research Centre. Columbus describes Graham's Harbour in his diaries as large enough "to hold all the ships of Christendom." A former U.S. Navy base near the harbor houses the Gerace Research Centre, previously known as the Bahamian Field Station. The GRC is a center for academic research in archaeology, biology, geology, and marine sciences, backed by the University of the Bahamas and affiliated with many U.S. universities. It provides accommodations, meals, and air transportation arrangements for students and researchers from all over the world who come to study in this unique environment. ☎ 242/331–2520 ⊕ *www.geraceresearchcentre.com.*

Sandy Point. Sandy Point anchors the island's southwestern end, overlooking French Bay. Here, on a hill, you'll find the ruins of **Watling's Castle**, named after the 17th-century pirate. The ruins are more likely the remains of a Loyalist plantation house than a castle from buccaneering days. A 5- to 10-minute walk from Queen's Highway will take you to see what's left of the ruins, which are now engulfed in vegetation.

SPORTS AND THE OUTDOORS
SCUBA DIVING
For more information about these and other sites and for dive operators on the island, contact the Riding Rock Resort and Marina or Seafari at Club Med.

Doolittle's Grotto is a popular site featuring a sandy slope down to 140 feet. There are lots of tunnels and crevices for exploring, and usually a large school of horse-eye jacks to keep you company. As the name implies, **Double Caves** has two parallel caves leading out to a wall at 115 feet; there's typically quite a lot of fish activity along the top of the wall. **North Pole Cave** has a wall that drops sharply from 40 feet to more than 150 feet; coral growth is extensive, and you might see a hammerhead or two.

LONG ISLAND

Long Island lives up to its name—80 gorgeous miles are available for you to explore. The Queen's Highway traverses its length, through the Tropic of Cancer and many diverse settlements and farming communities. The island is 4 miles at its widest, so at hilly vantage points you can view both the white cliffs and the raging Atlantic on the east side, and the gentle surf on the Caribbean side.

Long Island was the third island discovered by Christopher Columbus, and a monument to him stands on the north end. Loyalist families came to the island in support of the Crown, and to this day there are Crown properties all over the island, deeded by the king of England. Fleeing the Revolution, their attempt at re-creating life in America was short-lived. The soil and lack of rainfall did not support their crops, cotton being their mainstay. Today you can see wild cotton growing in patches up and down the island, along with the ruins of the plantations.

8

Fishing and tourism support the 3,000 residents of Long Island. Farms growing bananas, mangoes, papaya, and limes also dot the landscape. Boat-building is a natural art here, and in the south you can always see a boat in progress as you travel the Queen's Highway.

Progress has come to the island slowly. There is now high-speed Internet and cell-phone service, but shops and modern forms of entertainment are still limited. People who come to Long Island don't seem to mind; they're here for the beauty, tranquillity, and the friendly people. Deep-sea fishing and diving are readily available, and bonefishing flats attract sportfishermen from all over the world. The beaches provide breathtaking views, shelling, exploring, and magnificent pieces of sea glass. The laid-back lifestyle is reminiscent of a slower, gentler time.

GETTING HERE AND AROUND

AIR TRAVEL

Long Island has two airports: Deadman's Cay (LGI) in the middle south and Stella Maris Airport (SML) in the far north. Bahamasair and Southern Air airlines provide daily service from Nassau to Stella Maris and Deadman's Cay airports. Pineapple Air flies daily from Nassau into Stella Maris and twice a week into Deadman's Cay. Stella Maris Resort has its own excellent air charter service to and from Nassau and between many Southern Islands including the Exumas. Other charter services are available from Nassau and Fort Lauderdale. Hawkline Aviation is an FBO at Stella Maris, a good fuel stop for private pilots going farther afield.

Guests staying at Cape Santa Maria or Stella Maris Resort should fly into Stella Maris Airport. Chez Pierre Bahamas' guests can fly into either airport, although the Stella Maris Airport is a bit closer. All others should fly into Deadman's Cay Airport midisland. Flying into the wrong airport will cost you not only an hour's drive, but also $100 or more in taxi fares. Listen carefully to the arrival announcement when you approach Long Island; most commercial airlines stop at both airports.

Contacts Deadman's Cay Airport. ☎ *242/337–1777, 242/337–7077.* **Stella Maris Airport.** ☎ *242/338–2006.*

BOAT TRAVEL

Mail boats that bring supplies to the island each week make an adventurous mode of transportation. You'll ride with groceries, large and small appliances, automobiles, and sometimes even livestock. All boats depart from Potter's Cay in Nassau. Schedules change frequently. M/V *Mia Dean* or its substitute ship the M/V *Sea Spirit II* (that also goes on to Acklins and Crooked islands) leaves Tuesday for Clarence Town in south Long Island and returns Thursday (18 hours; $60 one-way). The *Island Link,* a faster RORO boat, leaves Tuesday with stops in Salt Pond, Deadman's Cay, and Seymour's, returning Thursday (eight hours; $70 one-way). Bahamas Ferries, also a RORO that takes vehicles, and with its faster, more comfortable passenger lounge, leaves Nassau Monday and gets into Simms, north Long Island, having stopped in George Town, Exumas.

CAR TRAVEL

A car is absolutely necessary to explore the island or visit any place outside your resort. The Queen's Highway curls like a ribbon from north to south, ending abruptly at the ocean in the north and at a stop sign in the south. It's narrow, with no marked center line, which makes bikes and scooters dangerous modes of transportation. The highway is easily traversed, but some off-roads require four-wheel drive, such as the road to the Columbus Monument, which is rocky and treacherous. The roads to Adderley's Plantation and Chez Pierre's are rough, but a passable adventure.

Most hotels will arrange car rentals, and can have your car waiting on-site or at the airport. Rentals range from $60 to $85. Some include gas; all have a limited number of vehicles. It's best to go for an a SUV or compact SUV with all-wheel drive if you have a choice.

Keep your gas tank full; although there are service stations along the highway, hours can be irregular and some take only cash. Some gas stations are closed on Sunday, so if that's your departure day, be sure to fill up the night before so the tank will be full when you return the car. Gas is expensive in the Outer Islands.

Contacts Mr. T's Car Rental. ✉ *Mid–Long Island, Deadman's Cay* ☎ *242/337–1054, 242/357–1678.* **Omar's Rental Cars.** ✉ *Cape Santa Maria Resort* ☎ *242/357–1043.*

TAXI TRAVEL

Taxis meet incoming flights at both airports. From the Stella Maris Airport, the fare to Stella Maris Resort is $10 per couple; to Cape Santa Maria, the fare is $30 per couple. Guests staying at Chez Pierre Bahamas pay $40 from the Stella Maris Airport and $60 from Deadman's

Cay. Winter Haven provides free transportation from the Deadman's Cay Airport. A full-day tour of the island by taxi would cost about $350, and a half-day tour would be about $120. However, all taxis are privately owned, so rates can be negotiated. It is generally cheaper to rent a car for the duration of your trip than it is to pay taxi fares every time you want to go somewhere.

Contacts Jerry's Taxi Service. ⊠ *Alligator Bay, near Simms, north Long island, Stella Maris* ☎ *242/338–8592, 242/472–8065.* **Omar Daley.** ⊠ *North Long Island, Stella Maris* ☎ *242/357–1043, 242/338–2031.* **Scofield's Taxi Service.** ⊠ *Millers, mid-north Long Island* ☎ *242/338–8970.*

TOURS

Bahamas Discovery Quest. Discover the beauty of Long Island in a variety of adventures on land and sea: deep-sea, deep-drop, and reef fishing; snorkeling; sponging; crabbing for land crabs at night; sea life ecotours; hiking; beaching; shelling; and historical tours with Long Islander, Charles Knowles, who will take you off the beaten path to meet farmers and taste island dishes you wouldn't easily find on your own. ⊠ *Deadman's Cay* ☎ *242/472–2605, 242/337–6024* ⊕ *www.bahamasdiscoveryquest.com.*

Omar's Long Island Guided Tours. Now based at Cape Santa Maria Resort in the far north, Omar is more than just a tour guide. Raised on Long Island, he's fun and friendly and full of knowledge about the land and the people, and he will cater tours to your interests—from showing you the best spots to jump into Dean's Blue Hole, to introductions to local straw and seashell artisans. However, that's just the start of his long list of services: he's also a dive master and boat captain who will feed sharks and lead you through wrecks, a taxi driver who can transport you to and from the airport to your hotel, and the owner of Omar's Rental Cars if you want to explore the island on your own. ⊠ *Cape Santa Maria Resort* ☎ *242/357–1043 cell.*

VISITOR INFORMATION

Contacts Long Island Ministry of Tourism. ⊠ *Salt Pond, mid–Long Island* ☎ *242/338–8668.*

NORTH LONG ISLAND: CAPE SANTA MARIA TO GRAY'S

In the far north you will find two large resort communities: **Cape Santa Maria** and **Stella Maris**. Scattered between are the small settlements of **Seymour's, Glinton's,** and **Burnt Ground.** Columbus originally named the island's northern tip Cape Santa Maria after the largest of his three ships. The beach here is gorgeous, full of private homes and resort villas, and a restaurant, bar, and gift shop that are open to the public. North of the Cape Santa Maria Resort are the **Columbus Monument,** commemorating Columbus's landing on Long Island, and **Columbus Cove,** where he made landfall. Twelve miles south of the Cape, Stella Maris, which means Star of the Sea, is home to the so-named resort. The Stella Maris Airport sits on the property, along with private homes, restaurants, and bars, the magnificent **Love Beaches,** a full-service marina, and a tackle and gift shop—all open to the public. Just north of Stella Maris, off Queen's Highway, are the ruins of the 19th-century **Adderley's Plantation.**

Traveling south about 8 miles, you'll come to **Simms,** one of Long Island's oldest settlements. The Tropic of Cancer cuts through the island close to here, dividing the subtropics from the tropics.

Farther south are the idyllic communities of **Thompson Bay** and **Salt Pond,** both providing safe harbors for those who visit by sailboat. Salt Pond, a hilly bustling settlement so named for its many salt ponds, hosts the annual Long Island Regatta. Continuing south, you will pass the settlements of **the Bight** and **Gray's** before reaching **Deadman's Cay.**

EXPLORING

Adderley's Plantation. Just north of the Stella Maris Airport, west of the main road, are the ruins of 19th-century Adderley's Plantation, a cotton plantation that once occupied all of Stella Maris. Clearly marked, the road is marginally passable by car. It is about a 1-mile drive and then a fairly long walk. The walking path is marked by conch shells, and leads to the cotton plantation ruins. Seven buildings are practically intact up to roof level, but it is overgrown with vegetation. For historians, it is well worth the time. ⊠ *North of Stella Maris Airport, Stella Maris.*

Columbus Monument. Two miles north of Cape Santa Maria is the Columbus Monument, commemorating Columbus's landing on Long Island. The road to the monument is off the Queen's Highway, and while the sign is often not visible, any Long Islander will gladly give you directions. The 3-mile treacherous road is too rough for vehicles without four-wheel drive, and most rental car companies won't let you drive it without an SUV, yet it is an extremely long hike. At the end of the road is a steep hill, called Columbus Point, and a climb to the summit affords a spectacular vista. This is the highest point on Long Island, and the second highest in the Bahamas. Farther north on Queen's Highway is Columbus Harbour, on Newton's Cay. Columbus made landfall in this cove, protected by limestone outcroppings. The more adventurous can follow the beach to the left, where a rough walking path leads to three other coves; each one a delight. Two coves up you will find sea glass scattered on the beach like sparkling jewels, and by climbing through limestone formations, you will discover another cove perfect for snorkeling. ⊠ *North of Cape Santa Maria Resort.*

BEACHES

Cape Santa Maria Beach. Known as one of the Bahamas' top beaches, and located on the leeward side of the island at Cape Santa Maria Resort, the water colors here range from pale blue to aqua to shades of turquoise. The 4-mile stretch of soft white sand beckons you to stroll, build sand castles, sun worship, or wade into the calm shallow waters. In the early morning, you're likely to see a ray swimming along the shore. The resort has a beachside restaurant and lounge chairs for guests, in addition to kayak and paddleboard rentals, but there's also plenty of sand to find a secluded stretch all your own. **Amenities:** food and drink; water sports. **Best for:** solitude; snorkeling; sunset; swimming; walking. ⊠ *Cape Santa Maria Resort.*

WHERE TO EAT

After a period of rain, the mosquitoes and no-see-ums come out, so bring mosquito repellant with you when dining outdoors.

$$
SEAFOOD
FAMILY

✕ **Beach House Restaurant at Cape Santa Maria.** Upstairs in the Cape Santa Maria Beach House, guests enjoy sweeping vistas of the turquoise bay during the day, and bobbing boat lights in the evening along with the gentle sounds of the sea. Breakfast can be light with yogurt parfait and a seasonal fruit medley, or a splurge with banana bread French toast topped with caramelized plantains or Bahamian-style eggs Benedict. **Known for:** nightly happy hour with free conch fritters; oceanfront bar; banana bread French toast. $ *Average main: $30* ⊠ *Cape Santa Maria Resort* ☎ *242/338–5273, 800/926–9704* ⊕ *www.capesantamaria.com* ⊘ *Closed Sept. and Oct.* ☞ *Meal plans available.*

$$
ECLECTIC
Fodor's Choice
★

✕ **Chez Pierre Bahamas.** At this airy oceanfront restaurant a few steps from the beach, Chef Pierre has been serving sumptuous cuisine since 2002. This curmudgeonly chef serves the best food on the island, hands down. **Known for:** pasta and seafood dishes; delicious pizza; chef expects guests to be on time. $ *Average main: $28* ⊠ *Miller's Bay* ☎ *242/338–8809, 242/357–1374* ⊕ *www.chezpierrebahamas.com.*

$
BAHAMIAN
FAMILY

✕ **Moonshine Bar & Grill.** The views surrounding Stella Maris Resort Club's new poolside bar are as beautiful as the frozen fresh-fruit daiquiris they serve. Once a week, the delightful Bodo, legendary local guitarist and Rake 'n' Scrape musician, plucks your heartstrings with Bahamian and calypso songs. **Known for:** the Moonshine panini; weekly live music; coastal bluff views. $ *Average main: $15* ⊠ *Stella Maris Resort Club, Stella Maris* ☎ *242/338–2050* ⊕ *www.stellamarisresort.com.*

$$
SEAFOOD

✕ **Stella Maris Resort Club Restaurant & Bar.** Charming and experienced chef Bruno and his capable team do a superb job pleasing upmarket American and European palates. Dine in the cool inside or on the stone terrace. **Known for:** room-service pizza; delicious liqueur coffees; fresh fish. $ *Average main: $30* ⊠ *Stella Maris Resort Club, Stella Maris* ☎ *242/338–2050* ⊘ *Closed Sept.*

WHERE TO STAY

$
B&B/INN
FAMILY

🛏 **C Shells Guest Quarters.** These quaint, self-catering full-kitchen suites sit just steps away from a quiet private beach on Salt Pond, with a large grassy garden space—perfect for family picnics, naps in the hammock, and a vacation without the bustle of a busy resort. **Pros:** friendly, accommodating owners; cable TV, Wi-Fi, and DVD library; affordable. **Cons:** no maid service; no on-site restaurant; rental car is essential to explore the island. $ *Rooms from: $110* ⊠ *Salt Pond* ☎ *242/338–0103, 954/889–5075* ⊕ *www.cshellsguestquarters.com* ⊄ *4 suites* ⦿ *No meals.*

$$$
RESORT
FAMILY
Fodor's Choice
★

🛏 **Cape Santa Maria Beach Resort and Villas.** This stunning resort consists of spacious, new beachfront villas that sleep up to eight and beachfront one-bed and two-bed bungalows that each have a screened-in verandah—all overlooking serene turquoise waters on a gorgeous 4-mile-long white-sand beach. **Pros:** only 15 minutes from Stella Maris Airport; friendly staff arranges excursions; great swimming beach. **Cons:** secluded location means you'll need a rental car to explore; no TVs in rooms and no Wi-Fi in bungalows; seven-night stay required during Christmas holiday season. $ *Rooms from: $340* ⊠ *Galliot Cay,*

Cape Santa Maria Beach Resort is the best on the island.

off Seymour's ☎ 242/338–5273, 800/663–7090 toll-free in U.S. and Canada, 250/598–3366 free outside U.S. and Canada 🌐 www.capesantamaria.com ⏲ Closed Sept. and Oct. 🛏 20 bungalows, 18 luxury villas 🍴 No meals ☞ Kids 12 and under stay free.

8

$ B&B/INN **Chez Pierre Bahamas.** Lining lovely Miller's Bay beach, this rustic, remote resort has six simple cabins on stilts right on the beach, making it a real "get-away-from-it-all" place (guests should be self-sufficient and adventurous). **Pros:** screened-in porches; large private beach; excellent on-site restaurant serves three meals a day. **Cons:** must rent a car to explore the island; no air-conditioning; bathroom water is slightly salty. [$] *Rooms from: $175* ✉ *Miller's Bay* ☎ *242/338–8809, 242/357–1374 cell* 🌐 *www.chezpierrebahamas.com* 🛏 *6 cottages* 🍴 *Some meals.*

$ B&B/INN **Grotto Bay Bahamas.** In the settlement of Salt Pond is this small private hideaway, a labor of love for owners Kris and Jean who offer two lovely guest rooms with sweeping decks facing the ocean on the lower level of their home. **Pros:** centrally located for exploring north and south; personalized service; beautiful lush landscaping. **Cons:** no in-house restaurant, bar, or meals; you need to rent a car to explore the island; owners live right above the guest rooms. [$] *Rooms from: $120* ✉ *Salt Pond* ☎ *242/338–0011* 🌐 *www.grottobaybahamas.com* 💳 *No credit cards* 🛏 *2 rooms* 🍴 *No meals.*

$$ RESORT FAMILY Fodor's Choice ★ **Stella Maris Resort Club.** Stella Maris is more than a resort, it is a longstanding family-fun community that sits atop a hilly ridge offering many accommodations choices (including private homes), complemented by multiple pools, breathtaking views of the Atlantic, fun bars and restaurants, and activities for every interest—it's also in walking distance from Stella Maris Airport. **Pros:** all accommodations have an ocean

view or balcony; free activities like island tours and sailing; parties and events hosted by resort for guests. **Cons:** long walks between rooms, clubhouse, beach bar; rooms somewhat dated but clean and comfortable; not beachfront but free bus to other beaches. $ *Rooms from: $250* ⊠ *Stella Maris* ☎ *800/426–0466, 242/338–2050 resort* ⊕ *www. stellamarisresort.com* ⤴ *16 rooms, 4 cottages, 6 houses* ⏀ *No meals.*

NIGHTLIFE

Stella Maris Resort. This resort often has live music on the weekends, including Rake 'n' Scrape. Every Thursday night is their Rum Punch Party, which includes rum punch, conch fritters, and dinner. Cost is $55 for nonguests. The clubhouse bar has a pool table and foosball, plus a huge rum collection. The restaurant has an excellent selection of wines. Ask about the frequent (in winter) Cave Party where folks gather round and dine on barbecued treats in a cave. Call ahead to make reservations. ⊠ *Stella Maris Resort Club, Stella Maris* ☎ *242/338–2050.*

SHOPPING

Bonafide Bonefishing Fly Shop. This fly-and-tackle shop and souvenir boutique, usually open Monday, Wednesday, Friday, and Saturday 9 am to 5 pm, is located in Stella Maris on Queens Highway. In addition to fishing gear, they sell cold drinks and snacks, souvenirs, gifts, apparel, and jewelry. James "Docky" Smith is the fishing guru behind Bonafide Bonefishing. A Long Islander, he is a popular and knowledgeable bonefishing guide who "knows the flats." ⊠ *Queens Hwy., Stella Maris* ☎ *242/338–2035, 242/357–1417, 242/338–2025* ⊕ *www.bonafidebonefishing.com.*

Cape Santa Maria Resort. There is a small gift shop in the lobby with clothes, swimsuits, island straw works, island books, souvenirs, cold drinks, and sundries. ⊠ *Cape Santa Maria Resort's Beach House lobby* ☎ *242/338–5273, 800/926–9704* ⊕ *www.capesantamaria.com.*

Hillside Food Supply. Hillside is probably the largest store on Long Island and the ideal place to stock up if you're self-catering or want snacks in between mealtimes. Here you can find lots of fresh produce and dairy items (that you can't import into the Bahamas), dry foods, toiletries, and supplies. In the back of the store you will find just about anything, from snorkeling gear and ice chests to towels and assorted housewares. Hillside can also tell where and how to get fresh lobster, snapper, grouper, and more. There are seafood vendors living nearby. ⊠ *Salt Pond, mid–Long Island* ☎ *242/338–0022.*

Tingum's Boutique. *Tingums* is Bahamian for "I don't know what to call it." This cute gift shop sells clothing, jewelry, gifts, souvenirs, books, and toiletries. ⊠ *Stella Maris Resort Club, Stella Maris* ☎ *242/338–2050.*

SPORTS AND THE OUTDOORS

DIVING AND SNORKELING

Conception Island Wall is an excellent wall dive, with hard and soft coral, plus interesting sponge formations. The M/V *Comberbach,* a 103-foot British freighter built in 1948, sank off Cape Santa Maria in 1984, and was scuttled by the Stella Maris Resort in 1986 to create an artificial reef and excellent dive site. Take a guided diving excursion to **Shark's Reef** and watch a scuba master safely feed dozens of sharks.

Cape Santa Maria Resort. This resort uses expert divers and guides for myriad diving and snorkeling trips to various reefs, walls, and wrecks around Long Island as well as trips to Conception Island; dive and snorkel equipment is available for rent. In addition, visitors can rent stand-up paddleboards and Hobie Cat sailboats to explore the coast of Cape Santa Maria Beach and its surrounding bays. ⊠ *Cape Santa Maria Resort* ☎ *242/338–5273, 800/926–9704* ⊕ *www.capesanta-maria.com.*

Stella Maris Resort. This resort offers diving and snorkeling trips. In addition to daytime dives to some of Long Island's most interesting sites, including Dean's Blue Hole, you can do an overnight dive cruise. They also offer PADI Resort Dive and Open Water Certification courses and Advanced Open Water upon request. Equipment is available for rental. ☎ *242/338–2050.*

FISHING

Bonafide Bonefishing. James "Docky" Smith is highly regarded as one of the best bonefishing guides in the Bahamas. He does full- and half-day bonefishing excursions, as well as reef-fishing trips. He is also an expert fly-casting instructor. Book well in advance. His operation is based out of the Bonafide tackle shop in Stella Maris, open three days a week, which rents conventional and fly-fishing gear, prepares snacks and box lunches, and sells a range of tackle, clothing, and flies. Full days of bonefishing are $500 (maximum two anglers); reef, bottom, or deep-sea fishing are $1,200 (maximum six anglers). Call ahead. ⊠ *Near Stella Maris Resort, Queen's Hwy., Stella Maris* ☎ *242/338–2025, 242/357–1417.*

Stella Maris Resort. Stella Maris Resort arranges deep-sea fishing, bone-fishing and reef fishing trips with well-trained guides. The small fleet includes a 32-foot single engine inboard that can accommodate up to six fishermen and a 38-foot twin engine that can take up to eight for their deep-sea and reef fishing trips and a 16-foot Hells Bay or 17-foot Maverick with poling platforms for a half or full day of bone-fishing the flats. Rods and bait is available for rent and purchase. ☎ *242/338–2050.*

SOUTH LONG ISLAND: DEADMAN'S CAY TO GORDON'S

The most populated area on the island is **Deadman's Cay.** This umbrella central settlement covers all the communities stretching from **Gray's** to the north to **Scrub Hill,** and is the social, economic, and educational center of the island. The Deadman's Cay Airport is in Lower Deadman's Cay and the infamous Max's Conch Bar is only a short distance to the south. Shops, restaurants, and bars dot this area, along with amazing views of the Bahamas Banks.

Past Scrub Hill is **Dean's Blue Hole,** the deepest blue hole in the world. Free-diving contests, without use of any breathing apparatus, are held here each year, and divers come from all over the world to challenge the record. Fantastic snorkeling can be had around the blue hole's edges.

Clarence Town is the capital of Long Island and home to the Flying Fish Marina in one of the prettiest and safest harbors in the Out Islands. Situated at the top of the highest hills in town are the twin-towered Moorish style churches of **St. Paul's** and **St. Peter's,** designed by Father Jerome. Clarence Town is the last large settlement on the south end of the island.

South of Clarence Town you will find **Galloway Landing,** a long stretch of amazing beaches and saltwater canals dug into the limestone hills by the now defunct Diamond Salt Mine. From here to **Gordon's** is the most undeveloped stretch of the island. Plantation ruins are at **Dunmore's,** secluded beaches at **Ford's,** and the incredible pink flamingos at Gordon's along with the biggest assortment of sea glass.

EXPLORING

Some of the biggest changes on Long Island have taken place at **Flying Fish Marina** (⊕ *www.flyingfishmarina.com*) in Clarence Town. The full-service, 20-slip marina offers fuel, a new store, and a new, upscale restaurant.

Fodor'sChoice ★ **Dean's Blue Hole.** Known as the second deepest blue hole in the world with a depth of 663 feet, Dean's Blue Hole is the most amazing sight on the island and one of the most popular photo sites in the land. A blue hole is a term for a water-filled sinkhole with an entrance below the water level. Free divers from around the world gather here annually to take the plunge. In 2010 William Trubridge broke the world record for free immersion diving to 407 feet without fins. Dean's Blue Hole is surrounded by a pretty cliff and a superb beach. The shallows at the edge of the hole are perfect for snorkeling and swimming, and the more adventurous visitors can jump into the water from the cliffs above. To find the blue hole, watch for the well-marked sign on your left (going east on Queen's Highway) after passing through Scrub Hill. ⊠ *Just south of Scrub Hill on east coast, north of Clarence Town, Clarence Town.*

Hamilton's Cave. The largest cave system in the Bahamas, Hamilton's Cave features stalactites and stalagmites, and passages over 45 feet wide and 9 feet high. The Lucayan Indians were thought to have lived here about AD 500 and many Lucayan artifacts were discovered in 1936. Leonard Cartwright will take you on a guided tour, complete with flashlights, as you explore inside the dark depths of his childhood playground. For added excitement, plan to go closer to dusk when the resident bats are most active! ⊠ *Queen's Hwy., Deadman's Cay* ☏ *242/337–0235, 242/472–1796* 🖾 *$10.*

The Long Island Museum and Library. The Long Island Museum and Library is housed in a beautiful little pink cottage with island trees in front. Learn the history of Long Island and see artifacts collected by local Long Islanders in hopes of preserving their cultural heritage. It's a fascinating collection and exhibit, professionally designed by the Bahamas, Antiquities, Monuments and Museum Corporation. Island wares, homemade jellies, and other island goods are for sale, in addition to books on Long Island and a popular Bahamian calendar painted in watercolors by local artist Nick Maillis. ⊠ *Buckley's, near Scotia Bank, Queen's Hwy.* ☏ *242/337–0500* ⊕ *www.ammcbahamas.com* 🖾 *$3* ☉ *Closed Sun.*

A gray shark circles a boat off Long Island.

St. Paul's & St. Peter's Churches. The twin, towered Moorish churches of St. Paul's (Anglican) and St. Peter's (Catholic) are two of the island's most celebrated landmarks. Father Jerome, often referred to as the hermit of Cat Island, built St. Paul's when he was Anglican; later, after converting to Catholicism, he built St. Peter's. The architecture of the two churches is similar to the Spanish missions in California. The churches are open sporadically, but tours are available through the Ministry of Tourism. ⊠ *Atop of Clarence Town Hill, Clarence Town.*

BEACHES

Galloway Landing Beach. This remarkable beach on the southeast coast of the island, south of Clarence Town, is relatively unknown and visited mostly by the locals. Swim and sun at the first beach, or walk a short distance south to an even more wonderful and secluded stretch of sand. Here, canals carved into the limestone hills by the now defunct Diamond Salt Mine are filled with the palest blue ocean water and are home to small marine life. It's a wonderful area to kayak, snorkel and swim, and collect sea glass. A bit farther south, a narrow bridge leads to beyond-stunning lagoons and ocean flats. **Amenities:** none. **Best for:** solitude; snorkeling; swimming; walking. ⊠ *Clarence Town ⊹ 2.4 miles southwest of Clarence Town.*

WHERE TO EAT

$ ✕ **Forest Take-Away.** This family-owned and -operated takeout restaurant
BAHAMIAN   is a favorite with the locals for tasty, island food and value. It offers barbecued ribs, cracked conch, conch burgers, fish fingers, chicken snacks and dinners, and the ever-popular Forest Burger, a hamburger with boneless ribs and sautéed onions. **Known for:** cold beer while you

wait; shaded picnic table seating; local favorite. $ *Average main: $12* ⊠ *Just off Queen's Hwy., Deadman's Cay* ☎ 242/337–1246 ▤ *No credit cards* ⊙ *Closed Sun. and Mon.*

$ ✕ **Max's Conch Bar and Grill.** This island treasure and possibly the area's
BAHAMIAN   most-recommended dining spot, is praised up and down by locals and visitors alike. Quintessentially Bahamian, you can sit all day on a stool at the colorful roadside hexagonal gazebo or at a table in the garden patio amid chickens and a goat, enjoying beers and nibbling on excellent conch salad prepared right in front of you. **Known for:** warm hospitality; conch fritters; traditional Bahamian recipes. $ *Average main: $15* ⊠ *Deadman's Cay* ☎ 242/337–0056 ⊙ *Closed Sun.*

$ ✕ **Outer Edge Grill at Flying Fish Marina.** Outer Edge Grill is what local
BAHAMIAN   Long Islanders call a "poop deck," meaning a restaurant on the water. Open daily for lunch and dinner, Outer Edge serves up Bahamian favorites like conch fritters and fish fingers, along with sweet potato french fries, mozzarella sticks, and homemade desserts. **Known for:** open Sunday; Bahamian favorites; homemade desserts. $ *Average main: $12* ⊠ *Clarence Town Harbour, Flying Fish Marina, just down from Winter Haven Inn, Clarence Town* ☎ 242/337–3445 *restaurant, 954/654–7084 in U.S. and Canada, 242/337–3430 marina resort* ⊕ *www.flyingfish-marina.com* ▤ *No credit cards.*

$$ ✕ **Rowdy Boys Bar and Grill at Winter Haven Inn.** Don't let the name scare
BAHAMIAN   you—it's named after the Knowles family's well-known construction company and the owners' two sons. Breakfast, lunch, and dinner can be served in the cool inside or out, and feature authentic Bahamian and American fare. **Known for:** Friday pig roast; open Sunday; whirlpool and tiki bar. $ *Average main: $24* ⊠ *Winter Haven Inn, Clarence Town* ☎ 242/337–3062 ⊕ *www.winterhavenbahamas.com.*

$ ✕ **Seaside Village at Jerry Wells.** Located at the end of Jerry Wells Road,
BAHAMIAN   this charming, authentic conch shack stuck out on a dock in the water is truly local, offering friendly service, fun music, and good food. Sling back in the hammock, catch some tunes and breeze as you (if you're lucky) watch the almost-tame osprey, "Iron," snack on fish morsels. **Known for:** fresh-caught conch; grouper cooked to order; best conch salad. $ *Average main: $15* ⊠ *Jerry Wells Rd., on west coast just south of Deadman's Cay Airport, Deadman's Cay* ☎ 242/337–0119, 242/357–1080 *cell* ▤ *No credit cards.*

WHERE TO STAY

$ ⬚ **Gems at Paradise.** Situated on 16 acres of pink-sand beachfront prop-
HOTEL   erty, overlooking the low-lying Clem Cay and the Atlantic Ocean as far as the eye can see, this resort occupies a rare and superb site. **Pros:** gorgeous location and views; easy access to fishing and water sports; car rentals available on-site. **Cons:** many rooms have stairs; no on-site restaurant; car rental is essential. $ *Rooms from: $125* ⊠ *Clarence Town* ☎ 242/337–3016 ⊕ *www.gemsatparadise.com* ⤷ *8 rooms, 2 condos* ⦿〇 *All meals.*

$ ⬚ **Greenwich Creek Lodge.** One of Long Island's newest places is the
B&B/INN   tranquil Greenwich Creek Lodge on the west waters of Cartwright's—a simple two-story 11-room boutique inn with elevated views of the salt flats and the Exuma Sound, and each room opening onto a wraparound

porch or balcony. **Pros:** on the water with boat access; serves three meals a day and has a bar; free Wi-Fi and TV/DVD available; swimming pool and small gym. **Cons:** beach 2 miles away; no TVs in rooms; no private balcony space. [$] *Rooms from: $145* ✉ *Off Queen's Hwy., in Cartwright's, 3 miles south of Deadman's Cay Airport, Deadman's Cay* ☎ *242/337–6278 resort, 242/359–0980 cell* 🌐 *greenwichcreeklodge.com* 🛏 *11 rooms* 🍴 *Some meals.*

$$ RENTAL 🏨 **Harbor Breeze Villas.** Long Island's newest luxury villas are nestled among garden pathways atop a hillside, each with private balconies affording views of Clarence Town Harbour and the Atlantic Ocean. **Pros:** owner rents cars and will stock your villa with groceries ahead of your arrival; complimentary transfers to Arthur's Town Airport; laundry facilities on-site. **Cons:** no on-site restaurant or bar; not on beach; office can be hard to reach by phone. [$] *Rooms from: $270* ✉ *Lochabar, just south of Clarence Town, Clarence Town* ☎ *242/337–3088* 🌐 *www.harborbreezevillas.com* 🛏 *15 villas* 🍴 *No meals.*

$ HOTEL 🏨 **Winter Haven Inn.** In the heart of Clarence Town, this small, colorful inn has two-story houses with rooms overlooking the indigo waters of the Atlantic. **Pros:** complimentary airport transfers and Wi-Fi; good on-site restaurant serves three meals a day; family-owned. **Cons:** no kitchen facilities in-room; you must rent a car for exploring; rough, rocky beach not good for swimming. [$] *Rooms from: $150* ✉ *Clarence Town* ☎ *242/337–3062, 866/348–5935* 🌐 *www.winterhavenbahamas.com* 🛏 *15 rooms* 🍴 *No meals.*

NIGHTLIFE

Lloyd's Sporting Lounge & Entertainment Center. The long name is Lloyd's Sporting Lounge & Entertainment Center and, for Long Island, it has quite a bit. This new, comfortable, and smartly designed sports bar and lounge has big-screen TVs for sports, and five pool tables. In a separate room they also have a dance/disco to the live tunes of the D Changes Band and DJs every Friday and Saturday night. Lloyd's hosts frequent pool tournaments and people flock to enjoy happy hour from 5 to 7 pm weekdays when beer buckets are four for $12. Other times, beers and rum and Cokes are a reasonable $4.25. Their food is also good and affordable: Long Island mutton, chicken, steaks, seafood, and various fettuccine main courses average $11 for chicken to $32 for T-bone steak. Lloyd's is well thought out and rather luxurious for the Out Islands—very enjoyable especially for big-group entertainment and dining, to catch sports on TV, or to dance to some live music. ✉ *Queen's Hwy., opposite Turtle Cove Rd. that leads to Dean's Blue Hole, Clarence Town* ☎ *242/337–5762.*

Midway Bar and Restaurant. Stop by here on Friday for happy hour from 6 to 8, or come on Saturday for karaoke that starts at 10 pm. Lunch and dinner are available with Caribbean choices like various curries and otherwise it's Bahamian fare all the way. The kitchen is open from noon until 10 pm but bar is open until midnight and later on karaoke night, but the restaurant is generally open Tuesday through Saturday. ✉ *Off Queen's Hwy.* ☎ *242/337–7345* 🕒 *Usually closed Sun. and Mon.*

SHOPPING

It's All Under the Sun. As the name suggests, this "department store" has everything from a café with used books and Wi-Fi to office supplies, toys, baby stuff, souvenirs, beach bags, hats, and snorkeling and fishing gear. Owner Cathy Darville also sells fruit smoothies, deli sandwiches, and homemade ice cream. ⊠ *Off Queen's Hwy. in Mangrove Bush, near Cartwright's settlement* ☏ *242/337–0199* ⊙ *Closed Sun.*

SPORTS AND THE OUTDOORS

DIVING AND SNORKELING

Surrounded by a beautiful powder-beach cove, the area surrounding **Dean's Blue Hole** offers a great place for a beach picnic if it's not too windy. Visitors can jump into the blue hole from various locations on the overhanging cliff above, some at 25 feet above the water. Snorkelers will see a variety of tropical fish and marine life, and Stella Maris Water Sports at Stella Maris Marina offers guided dive trips; flashlights included and necessary. Although Dean's Blue Hole is safe for swimming, it is recommended that all swimmers be competent or wear life jackets.

FAMILY **Bahamas Discovery Quest.** This company, owned by Charles Knowles whose love for his island is obvious, offers full- and half-day snorkeling trips, along with many other unique island escapades including sponging, crabbing, beaching, and shelling, and different types of fishing. Charles also has two places to stay in Stella Maris and one in Salt Pond. ☏ *242/472–2605, 242/337–6024.*

FISHING

Deadman's Cay Bonefish Adventures. Since 2002, Samuel Knowles Bonefish Adventures has drawn a loyal following of saltwater anglers from around the globe, earning a reputation as one of the most popular bonefishing programs in the islands. The main attraction is their expert guides, who are Long Islanders, fourth- and fifth-generation bonefishermen, and champions of four of the five Bahamas bonefishing tournaments. Their location at the center of Long Island's pristine shoreline, with unique landlocked flats, creates an unforgettable fishing adventure for all ages and experience levels. They offer stay/fish/dine packages at Smith-Wells Bonefish Lodge: $2,195 for seven nights/six days fishing. ⊠ *Deadman's Cay* ☏ *242/337–0246, 242/357–1178* ⊕ *www.smith-wells.com.*

Long Island Bonefishing Lodge. This modern lodge offers all-inclusive stay/fish/dine packages for fly-fishermen. Packages include three meals and fishing from 8 am to 4 pm. LIBL specializes in and encourages DIY fishing where, although your guide is present, you're mostly in your own privacy, and he can boat you to other flats to find success. Most of Long Island's vast flats are wade-able shallows. The main clubhouse has gorgeous flats views. The two duplexes are modern and comfortable, and sleep a total of eight. ⊠ *Deadman's Cay* ☏ *242/472–2609* ⊕ *www.longislandbonefishinglodge.com* ⨝ *$1850 per person double occupancy. All-inclusive stay/fish/dine package Oct.–May. Visit must start or end on Sun.*

Winter Haven Inn. Winter Haven Inn organizes fishing and boating adventures through various local guides. ⊠ *Clarence Town* ☏ *242/337–3062* ⊕ *www.winterhavenbahamas.com.*

CROOKED AND ACKLINS ISLANDS

Crooked Island is 30 miles long and surrounded by 45 miles of barrier reefs that are ideal for diving and fishing. They slope from 4 feet to 50 feet, then plunge to 3,600 feet in the **Crooked Island Passage**, once one of the most important sea roads for ships following the southerly route from the West Indies to the Old World. If you drive up to **the Cove** settlement, you get an uninterrupted view of the region all the way to the narrow passage at **Lovely Bay** between Crooked Island and Acklins Island. Two lighthouses alert mariners that they are nearing the islands.

The tepid controversy continues today over whether Columbus actually set foot on Crooked Island and its southern neighbor, Acklins Island. What's known for sure is that Columbus sailed close enough to Crooked Island to get a whiff of its island herbs. Soon after, the two islands became known as the "Fragrant Islands." Today Crooked and Acklins islands are known as remote and unspoiled destinations for fishermen, divers, and sailors who value solitude. Here phone service can be intermittent, Internet access can be hard to find, and some residents depend on generators for electricity. Even credit-card use is a relatively new development. The first known settlers didn't arrive until the late 18th century, when Loyalists brought slaves from the United States to work on cotton plantations. About 400 people, mostly fishermen and farmers, live on each island today. Two plantation-era sites, preserved by the Bahamas National Trust, are on Crooked Island's northern end, which overlooks Crooked Island Passage that separates the cay from Long Island. Spanish guns have been discovered at one ruin, **Marine Farm**, which may have been used as a fortification. An old structure, **Hope Great House**, has orchards and gardens.

AIR TRAVEL

Crooked and Acklins have one airport each: Colonel Hill Airport (CRI) on Crooked Island and Spring Point Airport (AXP) on Acklins Island. Neither is open unless there's a flight expected. Bahamasair flies from Nassau to Crooked and Acklins islands twice a week and Pineapple Air flies into Acklins. The flights are quite early in the morning, making it hard to fly in from overseas without staying one night in Nassau. Many Crooked Island visitors have found a solution to that: fly in on a private aircraft direct from the United States. The private 3,500-foot airstrip at Crooked Island Lodge is complimentary for hotel guests. Nonguests pay landing and parking fees. This airstrip is most convenient for private and charter flights if you're staying in the area of Pittstown and Landrail Point. Ask your hotel to make arrangements for picking you up at the airport in case there are no taxis.

Hotels will arrange airport transportation. Generally someone from even the smallest hotel will meet you at the airport, despite the fact that taxis are usually waiting on flights.

Contacts Acklins Island Spring Point Airport. ⊠ *Midway along Acklins Island* ☎ *242/344–3169.* **Crooked Island Colonel Hill Airport.** ⊠ *On northeast side of Crooked Island* ☎ *242/344–2357.*

Crooked and Acklins islands both have a lighthouse. Bird Rock Lighthouse (pictured) is the newer of the two, built in 1872.

BOAT TRAVEL

Mail boats that bring supplies to the islands each week make an adventurous mode of transportation. You'll ride with groceries, large and small appliances, automobiles, and sometimes even livestock. All boats depart from Potter's Cay in Nassau. Schedules change frequently. M/V *Sea Spirit II* sails Tuesday at 3 pm to Acklins Island, Crooked Island, and Long Cay, returning Friday morning (30 hours; $90 one-way).

Ferry service between Cove Landing, Crooked Island, and Lovely Bay, Acklins Island, usually operates twice daily on varying schedules between 9 and 4.

Contacts Ferry Service. ☎ 242/344–2197 ferry, 242/344–2415 Island administrator's office.

CAR TRAVEL

There are many car-rental operators. To get a good vehicle, reserve a car through your hotel prior to your arrival; even if you have a reservation you should be prepared for the possibility of the car not being there when you arrive. Gas is also not always available on the islands, as it's delivered by mail boats, which are sometimes delayed. Fortunately, it's easy to get a ride to most places with locals, who are friendly and often willing to help.

EXPLORING

Bird Rock Lighthouse. The sparkling white Bird Rock Lighthouse (built in 1876) once guarded the Crooked Island Passage. The rotating flash from its 115-foot tower still welcomes pilots and sailors to the Crooked Island Lodge, currently the islands' best lodging facility. This lighthouse is located 1 mile offshore and can only be reached by boat. ✉ *Bird Rock* ✣ *On separate island off northwest point of Crooked Island.*

Castle Island Lighthouse. On a separate island on Acklins' southwest point, and only reachable by boat, is the Castle Island Lighthouse (built in 1867). It formerly served as a beacon for pirates who used to retreat there after attacking ships. ✉ *Castle Island.*

WHERE TO STAY

$$ HOTEL 🏨 **Crooked Island Lodge.** A true anglers' paradise, this is one of the best fishing destinations in the Bahamas and Caribbean for bone- and deep-sea fishing. **Pros:** mind-bending ocean and beachfront location; bar and restaurant serves three meals a day; private airstrip for easy access. **Cons:** insect repellent necessary in this area; might be too remote for some; not all rooms offer sea views. [$] *Rooms from: $195* ✉ *Pittstown Point Landing* ☎ *242/478–8989, 888/344–2507 toll-free in U.S. and Canada* 🌐 *www.crookedislandlodge.com* 🛏 *8 rooms* 🍴 *No meals.*

SPORTS AND THE OUTDOORS

FISHING

Crooked Island has a number of highly regarded bonefishing guides with quality boats and fly-fishing tackle. Most can be booked through Tranquillity on the Bay or the Crooked Island Lodge, but the guides also take direct bookings. Be aware that telephone service to and from Crooked and Acklins islands is not always operational.

You can stalk the elusive and swift bonefish in the shallows, or go deep-sea fishing for wahoo, sailfish, and amberjack.

Michael Carroll (☎ *242/344–2037*), **Derrick Ingraham** (☎ *242/344–2023*), **Elton "Bonefish Shakey" McKinney** (☎ *242/344–2038*), **Randy McKinney** (☎ *242/344–2326*), **Jeff Moss** (☎ *242/344–2029*), and **Clinton** and **Kenneth "The Earlybird" Scavalla** (☎ *242/344–2011 or 242/422–3596*) are all knowledgeable professional guides. **Captain Robbie Gibson** (☎ *242/344–2007*) has a 30-foot Century boat and is the most experienced reef and offshore fishing captain on Crooked Island, where astounding fishing in virgin waters is the rule. Many wahoo weighing more than 100 pounds are landed each season with his assistance. Robbie's personal-best wahoo is a whopping 180 pounds. He's also a skilled guide for anglers pursuing tuna, marlin, sharks, barracuda, jacks, snapper, and grouper.

SCUBA DIVING

Captain Robbie Gibson. In addition to fishing expeditions, Captain Robbie Gibson offers scuba diving of wreck sites and wall dives, snorkeling, and day tours to see flamingos or explore land caves. You can rent gear from him and a two tank dives with equipment runs about $100 per person. ☎ *242/344–2007, 242/422–4737.*

INAGUA

Inagua does indeed feel like the southernmost island in the Bahamas' 700-mile-long chain. Just 50 miles from Cuba, it's not easy to get to—there are only three flights a week from Nassau, and you must overnight there to catch the 9 am flight. At night the lonely beacon of the **Inagua Lighthouse** sweeps the sky over the southern part of the island and the only community, **Matthew Town**, as it has since 1870. The coastline is rocky and rugged, with little coves of golden sand. The terrain is mostly flat and covered with palmetto palms, wind-stunted buttonwoods, and mangroves ringing ponds and a huge inland saltwater lake. Parts of it look very much like the Florida Everglades, only without the alligators and poisonous snakes.

Matthew Town feels like the Wild West, with sun-faded wooden buildings and vintage and modern trucks usually parked in front. It's obviously not a tourist mecca, but those who do visit witness the great spectacles of the Western Hemisphere: the 60,000-some West Indian pink-scarlet flamingos that nest here alongside rare Bahama parrots and roseate spoonbills. If you're not a bird lover, there's extraordinary diving and fishing off the virgin reefs. Although there are few tourists, this remote island is prosperous. An unusual climate of little rainfall and continual trade winds creates rich salt ponds. The Morton Salt Company harvests a million tons of salt annually at its Matthew Town factory, where most of the 1,000 Inaguans work.

GETTING HERE AND AROUND

AIR TRAVEL

Inagua has one airport: Matthew Town Airport (IGA). Bahamasair has flights on Monday, Wednesday, and Friday from Nassau. Hotels will arrange airport transportation. Generally someone from even the smallest hotel will meet you at the airport, but taxis sometimes meet incoming flights.

Contacts Inagua Matthew Town Airport. ⊠ *Matthew Town* ☎ *242/339–1680 only answered Mon., Wed., and Fri. when a flight is expected, 242/339–1415 airport* ⊕ *www.bahamasair.com.*

BOAT TRAVEL

The M/V *Lady Mathilda* sails once a week or three times a month, first to Abraham's Bay, and then to Matthew Town, Inagua. Not only is the boat characteristically cluttered with all sorts of cargo, the service is sporadic—so, always call the captain on the scheduled sailing day, Thursday, or the Potter's Cay Dockmaster's Office in Nassau to check sailing times. She departs from Potter's Cay in Nassau and the journey in good seas takes 36 hours and costs $100 one-way. If bad weather is approaching, she may not even leave harbor, skipping a week and leaving you stranded. The whole process is an authentic Bahamian adventure. Take your camera!

Deep-sea fishing in the Southern Out Islands

CAR TRAVEL

You can rent a car for about $80 a day, but there are few rental cars on the island, so call in advance. If you are driving outside Matthew Town, you will need an SUV or truck to navigate dirt roads. If you plan to stay in Matthew Town, you can easily walk everywhere.

Contacts Ingraham Rent-A-Car. ☎ 242/225–3933, 242/339–1515.

TOURS

Great Inagua Tours. Colin Ingraham is a veteran tour guide who specializes in birding and island sightseeing. He can also arrange deep-sea fishing and snorkeling on the reefs. ✉ *Burnside St., Matthew Town* ⌖ *Southwest Inagua* ☎ *242/453–0429.*

EXPLORING

Erickson Museum and Library. The Erickson Museum and Library is a welcome part of the community, particularly the surprisingly well-stocked, well-equipped library. The Morton Company built the complex in the former home of the Erickson family, who came to Inagua in 1934 to run the salt giant. The museum displays the island's history to which the company is inextricably tied. The posted hours are not always that regular. The Bahamas National Trust office, and the office of the Inagua National Park, is also here, but hours are unpredictable. ✉ *Gregory St. on northern edge of town across from police station, Matthew Town* ☎ *242/339–1863* 🆓 *Free* ⊙ *Closed Sun.*

Inagua Lighthouse. From Southwest Point, a mile or so south of Matthew Town, you can see Cuba's coast—slightly more than 50 miles west—on a clear day from atop Inagua Lighthouse, built in 1870 in response to the number of shipwrecks on offshore reefs. It's a grueling climb—the last 10 feet are on a ladder—but the view of the rugged coastline and Matthew Town is worth the effort. Look to the west to see the hazy mountains of Cuba. Be sure to sign the guest book just inside the door to the lighthouse. ⊠ *Gregory St., 1 mile south of Matthew Town, Great Inagua Island.*

Fodor's Choice
★

Inagua National Park. Nothing quite prepares you for your first glimpse of the West Indian flamingos that nest in Inagua National Park: brilliant crimson-pink, up to 5 feet tall, with black-tipped wings. A dozen flamingos suddenly fly across a pond, intermixed with fantastic pink roseate spoonbills.

It's a moving experience, and yet because of the island's remote location, only about 50 people witnessed it in 2009. By 1952, Inagua's flamingos had dwindled to about 5,000. The gorgeous birds were hunted for their meat, especially the tongue, and for their feathers. The government established the 183,740-acre wildlife sanctuary and national park in 1963, and today more than 60,000 flamingos nest on the island, the world's largest breeding colony of West Indian flamingos. The birds thrive in the many salt ponds (owned by the Morton Salt Company) that supply their favorite meal—brine shrimp. Bird-watchers also flock here to spy gull-billed terns, egrets, herons, burrowing owls, pintail ducks, sandpipers, snowy plovers—more than 130 species in all. The Inaguan lyretail is one of the world's most recently announced species. Wild boar and feral donkeys who were left here after a brief French occupation in 1749 are harder to see.

To make reservations, you must contact the Bahamas National Trust's office (*242/393–1317*) or Warden Henry Nixon (*242/395–0856*). All visits to the park are by special arrangement. ⊠ *Matthew Town ✛ 10 miles west of Matthew Town* ⊕ *www.bnt.bs* ✆ *From: $25 per person. Rates include: park user fee and BNT warden's time. Not included: vehicle rental and fuel and park warden gratuity (optional).*

Morton Salt Company. Marveling at the salt process lures few visitors to Inagua, but the Morton Salt Company is omnipresent on the island: it has more than 47 square miles of crystallizing ponds and reservoirs. More than a million tons of salt are produced every year for such industrial uses as salting icy streets. (More is produced when the northeastern United States has a bad winter.) Even if you decide not to tour the facility, you can see the mountains of salt, locally called the Salt Alps, glistening in the sun from the plane. In an unusual case of industry assisting its environment, the crystallizers provide a feeding ground for the flamingos. As the water evaporates, the concentration of brine shrimp in the ponds increases, and the flamingos feed on these animals. Free tours are available by reservation at the salt plant in Matthew Town. ⊠ *Matthew Town* ☎ *242/339–1300, 242/457–6000* ⊕ *www.mortonsalt.com.*

BEACHES

Farquarson Beach. Ten-and-a-half miles north of Matthew Town is the island's nicest (at least the most accessible) beach where locals come out to chill. There's no shade; instead you'll have to keep cool in the mesmerizing turquoise waters. Bring sunscreen, bug spray, umbrellas or portable shade, lots of fluids in a cooler, and some beach toys and snorkeling gear. **Amenities:** none. **Best for:** solitude; snorkeling. ⊠ *Great Inagua Island* ☏ *242/339–1271 Evamae Palacious, Inagua's tourism representative.*

WHERE TO EAT

$
BAHAMIAN

✕**Cozy Corner.** Cheerful and loud, this lunch spot—locals just call it Cozy's—is the best on the island. It has a pool table and a large seating area with a bar. **Known for:** island-style dinners; local hangout; comfort food. **$** *Average main: $10* ⊠ *William and North Sts., Matthew Town* ☏ *242/339–1440* ▭ *No credit cards* ☉ *Closed Sun.*

$
BAHAMIAN
Fodor's Choice
★

✕**S sinn L Restaurant & Bar Lounge.** The best spot to dine and even party is at S sinn L in Matthew Town, which becomes Inagua's dance hot spot on the weekend. In a comfortable, smart, air-conditioned dining room, you can enjoy delicious fresh Bahamian breakfasts, lunches, and dinners with some American fare as well. **Known for:** live calypso and Bahamina Goombay; go-to spot for dancing; Bahama Mama cocktails. **$** *Average main: $15* ⊠ *East St., Matthew Town* ☏ *242/339–1677* ▭ *No credit cards.*

WHERE TO STAY

8

$$
B&B/INN

🏨 **The Great Inagua Outback Lodge.** The Great Inagua Outback Lodge is the dream of Inaguan Henry Hugh who wanted to relax in his own quiet island paradise. **Pros:** comfortable with modern amenities; right on water and close to beach and flats; full meals in stay/fish/dine packages. **Cons:** long and extremely bumpy road; remote; no pool. **$** *Rooms from: $284* ⊠ *Matthew Town* ✛ *15 miles from Matthew Town, along northern road and the beach road* ☏ *716/479–2327 in U.S. and Canada* ⊕ *www.ccoflyfishing.com/greatinagua.html* ➷ *2 rooms* ⦿*All meals.*

$
B&B/INN

🏨 **The Main House.** The Morton Salt Company operates this small, affordable guesthouse, with spotless and spacious guest rooms that have dark-wood furnishings, Masonite-paneled walls, and floral-print drapes and spreads. **Pros:** very inexpensive; clean; walking distance to a couple of bars and restaurants. **Cons:** no Internet service; power plant can be noisy; restaurant open for breakfast and lunch only. **$** *Rooms from: $110* ⊠ *Kortwright St., Matthew Town* ☏ *242/339–1267* ⊕ *www. inaguamainhouse.com* ▭ *No credit cards* ➷ *6 rooms.*

$
RENTAL

🏨 **Sunset Apartments.** These two spacious apartments seated on a rocky shoreline on Matthew Town's southern side are your only option for a room with a water view, and a great place to watch sunsets. **Pros:** great place for bonefishing; Ezzard is a wonderful host and a top fly-fishing guide; fully equipped kitchens. **Cons:** no Internet; little to do but fish and bird-watch; you need to pay in cash or wire transfer. **$** *Rooms from: $150* ⊠ *Matthew Town* ☏ *242/339–1362* ▭ *No credit cards* ➷ *2 apartments* ⦿*No meals.*

NIGHTLIFE

Da After Work Bar. This local bar on Gregory Street (the main street) next to Kiwanis Park is the most popular hangout in town and a good place to meet locals. It's also a nice spot for watching an animated Dominoes match. Typically they close on Sunday, but if you stop by they will still be happy to sell you a cold drink! ⊠ *Gregory St., Matthew Town* ☉ *Usually closed Sun.*

The Fish Fry. A collection of fish shacks next to the water is open on weekends, with DJs occasionally in the covered pavilion next door. ⊠ *Matthew Town.*

Super D Nightclub. On occasional weekends, this is one place you find some action and dancing. No food is served but drinks run aplenty. ⊠ *Matthew Town.*

SPORTS AND THE OUTDOORS

BIRD-WATCHING

Great Inagua Tours. Mr Colin Ingraham has been a tour guide for more than 22 years, and while he specializes in birding and island sightseeing, he can also take you fishing for tuna or wahoo, or snorkeling on the reefs. There is no scuba dive operator on the island despite Inagua's magnificent reefs. ⊠ *Matthew Town* ☎ *242/339–1336, 242/453–0429 cell.*

FISHING

Ezzard Cartwright. Inagua's only bonefishing and deep-sea fishing guide, Ezzard Cartwright has been featured in outdoors and fishing magazines, and on ESPN Outdoors shows. He is the only local with access to Lake Windsor, home to tarpon and snook as well as bonefish that can only be reached by boat. Call him if you're a serious fisher who wants to fish for eight hours a day. He's usually booked from January to July for bonefishing, so reserve early. He takes a well deserved vacation during July and August. ⊠ *Matthew Town* ☎ *242/339–1362, 242/453–1903 cell.*

TRAVEL SMART
BAHAMAS

GETTING HERE AND AROUND

■ AIR TRAVEL

Most international flights to the Bahamas connect through airports in Florida, New York, Charlotte, or Atlanta. The busiest airport in the Bahamas is in Nassau, which has the most connections to the more remote Out Islands. If you're traveling to these more remote islands, you might have to make a connection in both Florida and Nassau—and you still may have to take a ferry or a water taxi to your final destination.

A direct flight from New York City to Nassau takes approximately three hours. The flight from Charlotte to Nassau is two hours, and the flight from Miami to Nassau takes less than an hour. Most flights between the islands of the Bahamas also take less than an hour.

Airline Security Issues Transportation Security Administration. ⊕ www.tsa.gov.

AIRPORTS

The major gateways to the Bahamas include Lynden Pindling International Airport (NAS) on New Providence Island, and Freeport Grand Bahama International Airport (FPO) on Grand Bahama Island. There are no hotels near either airport. *For more airports, see individual chapters.*

Airport Information Grand Bahama International Airport. ☎ 242/352–2205. **Lynden Pindling International Airport.** ☎ 242/702–1010.

FLIGHTS

Air service to the Bahamas varies seasonally, with the biggest choice of flights usually available in the Christmas to Easter window.

Local carriers come and go, especially in the Out Islands, which are served mostly by smaller commuter and charter operations. Schedules change frequently. The smallest cays may have scheduled service only a few days a week. In the Out Islands, ask your hotel for flight recommendations, as they are likely to have the most up-to-date information on carriers and schedules; some can even help you book air travel.

Major Airlines American Airlines. ☎ 800/433–7300. **Delta Airlines.** ☎ 800/221–1212. **JetBlue.** ☎ 800/538–2583. **Southwest.** ☎ 800/435–9792. **United.** ☎ 800/864–8331.

Smaller Airlines Apollo Jets. ☎ 888/910–5387 ⊕ www.apollojets.com. **Bahamasair.** ☎ 242/702–4140, 800/222–4262. **Bahamas Express.** ☎ 754/200–0005 ⊕ flybahamasexpress.com. **Cherokee Air.** ☎ 242/367–1920 ⊕ www.cherokeeair.com. **Eastern Air Express.** ☎ 954/772–3363 ⊕ www.easternairexpress.com. **Flamingo Air.** ☎ 242/351–4963 ⊕ www.flamingoairbah.com. **Glen Air.** ☎ 242/368–2116. **Golden Wings Charter.** ☎ 242/377–0039 ⊕ www.goldenwingscharter.com. **Island Air.** ☎ 800/444–9904 ⊕ www.islandaircharters.com. **LeAir.** ☎ 242/377–2356 ⊕ www.flyleair.com. **Miami Seaplane.** ⊠ 3401 Rickenbacker Causeway, Key Biscayne ☎ 305/361–3909 ⊕ www.miamiseaplane.com. **Monarch Air Group.** ☎ 954/359–0059 ⊕ monarchairgroup.com. **Pineapple Air.** ☎ 242/328–1329 ⊕ www.pineappleair.com. **Silver Airlines.** ☎ 800/229–9990 in U.S. and Canada, 844/674–5837 toll-free from the Bahamas ⊕ www.silverairways.com. **Sky Bahamas.** ☎ 242/702–2600, 954/317–3751 ⊕ www.skybahamas.net. **Southern Air.** ☎ 242/323–7217 ⊕ www.southernaircharter.com. **Stella Maris Air Service.** ⊠ Stella Maris Airport ☎ 242/338–2050 reservations, 242/357–1182 pilot's cell phone ⊕ www.stellamarisresort.com/air-service. **Trans Island Airways.** ⊠ Odyssey Aviation, Lynden Pindling International Airport, Nassau ☎ 242/462–4006 in Nassau, 954/727–3377 in Fort Lauderdale ⊕ www.tia.aero. **Triton Airways.** ☎ 954/961–8485 ⊕ www.tritonairways.com. **Tropic Ocean Airways.** ⊠ Sheltair Aviation, 1100 Lee Wagener Blvd., Fort Lauderdale ☎ 954/210–5569, 800/767–0897 ⊕ flytropic.com. **Watermakers Air.** ⊠ 2331 N.W. 55th Court, Hangar 19, Fort Lauderdale ☎ 954/771–0330 ⊕ www.watermakersair.

com. **Western Air.** ☎ *242/329–4000* ⊕ *www. westernairbahamas.com.*

BOAT TRAVEL

BOATS AND FERRIES

If you're adventurous and have time to spare, take a ferry or one of the traditional mail boats that regularly leave Nassau from Potter's Cay, under the Paradise Island Bridge. Although faster air-conditioned boats now make some of the trips, certain remote destinations are still served by slow, old-fashioned craft. Especially if you choose the mail-boat route, you may find yourself sharing company with goats or chickens, or piles of lumber and crates of cargo; on these lumbering mail boats, expect to spend 5 to 12 or more hours slowly making your way between island outposts. These boats operate on Bahamian time, which is a casual unpredictable measure, and schedules can be thrown off by bad weather. Mail boats cannot generally be booked in advance, and services are limited. In Nassau, check details with the dockmaster's office at Potter's Cay. One-way trips can cost from $35 to $100.

Within the Bahamas, Bahamas Ferries has the most (and most comfortable) options for island-hopping, with air-conditioned boats that offer food and beverages served by cabin attendants. Schedules do change rather frequently; if you're planning to ferry back to an island to catch a flight, double-check the departure times and planned routes. Ferries serve most of the major tourist destinations from Nassau, including Spanish Wells, Governor's Harbour, Harbour Island, Abaco, Exuma, and Andros. The high-speed ferry that runs between Nassau and Spanish Wells, Governor's Harbour, and Harbour Island costs $81 one-way, and takes about two hours each way.

Local ferries in the Out Islands transport islanders and visitors from the main island to smaller cays. Usually, these ferries make several round-trips daily and

keep a more punctual schedule than the longer-haul ferry.

It's possible to get to Grand Bahama by ferry from Florida. Balearia Bahamas Express sails from Fort Lauderdale's Port Everglades (Terminal 1) and provides fast ferry service, making a day trip possible, while Bahamas Paradise Cruise Line sails from the Port of Palm Beach in Riviera Beach and is more like a small cruise ship. Some hotel packages include transportation to Grand Bahamas.

If you're setting sail yourself, note that cruising boats must clear customs at the nearest port of entry before beginning any diving or fishing. The fee is $150 for boats up to 35 feet and $300 for boats longer than 35 feet, which includes fishing permits and departure tax for up to three people. Each additional person above the age of three will be charged the $25 departure tax. Stays of longer than 12 months must be arranged with Bahamas customs and immigration officials.

Boat and Ferry Contacts Bahamas Ferries. ☎ *242/323–2166* ⊕ *www.bahamasferries. com.* **Bahamas Paradise Cruise Line.** ✉ *1 E. 11th St., Riviera Beach* ☎ *800/995–3201 reservations, 800/374–4363 customer service* ⊕ *www.bahamasparadisecruise.com.* **Balearia Bahamas Express.** ✉ *Port Everglades, Terminal 1, Fort Lauderdale* ☎ *866/699–6988* ⊕ *www.baleariacaribbean.com.* **FRS Caribbean.** ☎ *877/286–7220* ⊕ *www.frs-caribbean.com.* **Potter's Cay Dockmaster.** ☎ *242/393–1064.*

CAR TRAVEL

International rental agencies are generally in Nassau, and you will rent from privately owned companies on the small islands. Thoroughly check the vehicle before you leave as many are not in great condition. Bring your own car seats as companies do not often provide these.

To rent a car, you must be 21 years of age or older.

It's common to hire a driver with a van, and prices are negotiable. Most drivers charge by the half day or full day. Prices depend on the stops and distance, but the cost for a half-day tour is generally $50 to $100 for one to four people, and $100 to $200 for a full-day tour. It's customary to pay for the driver's lunch. All tour guides in the Bahamas are required to take a tourism course and pass an exam; they must also get a special license to operate a taxi.

GASOLINE

The cost of fuel in the Bahamas is usually at least twice that in the United States; be prepared to pay in cash. You can ask for a handwritten receipt if printed ones are not available. Stations are few and far between on the Out Islands, so keep the tank full. Gas stations may be closed on Sundays.

PARKING

There are few parking meters in the Bahamas, and none in downtown Nassau. Police are lenient with visitors' rental cars parked illegally and will generally just ask the driver to move it. Parking spaces are hard to find in Nassau, so be prepared to park on a side street and walk. Most hotels offer off-street parking for guests. There are few parking lots not associated with hotels.

ROADSIDE EMERGENCIES

In case of a road emergency, stay in your vehicle with your emergency flashers engaged and wait for help, especially after dark. If someone stops to help, relay information through a small opening in the window. If it's daylight and help does not arrive, walk to the nearest phone and call for help. In the Bahamas, motorists readily stop to help drivers in distress.

Ask for emergency numbers at the rental office when you pick up your car. These numbers vary from island to island. On smaller islands the owner of the company may want you to call them at their home.

RULES OF THE ROAD

Islanders drive on the left side of the road, though many cars here have a steering wheel on the left. Many streets in downtown Nassau are one-way. At roundabouts, keep left and yield to oncoming traffic as you enter the roundabout and at "Give Way" signs.

❙ TAXI TRAVEL

There are taxis waiting at every airport and outside all the main hotels and cruise-ship docks. Beware of "hackers," drivers who don't display their license (and may not have one). Sometimes you can negotiate a fare, but you must do so before you enter the taxi.

You'll find that Bahamian taxi drivers are more talkative than their U.S. counterparts. When you take a taxi to dinner or to town, it's common for the driver to wait there and take you back at no additional cost. A 15% tip is suggested.

ESSENTIALS

■ ACCOMMODATIONS

The lodgings we list are the top-rated in each price category. We always list the facilities that are available—but we don't specify whether they cost extra: when pricing accommodations, always ask what's included.

APARTMENT AND HOUSE RENTALS

Contacts Bahamas Home Rentals. ☎ 321/725–9790 ⊕ www.bahamasweb.com. **Bahamas Vacation Homes.** ☎ 242/333–4080 ⊕ www.bahamasvacationhomes.com. **Hope Town Hideaways.** ☎ 242/366–0434, 561/656–9703 ⊕ www.hopetown.com. **Villas & Apartments Abroad.** ☎ 212/213–6435 ⊕ www.vaanyc.com. **Villas of Distinction.** ☎ 800/289–0900 ⊕ www.villasofdistinction.com. **Villas International.** ⊠ 17 Fox La., San Anselmo ☎ 800/221–2260 ⊕ www.villasintl.com. **Wimco.** ⊠ Box 1461, Newport ☎ 888/997–3970 ⊕ www.wimco.com.

■ COMMUNICATIONS

INTERNET

Wi-Fi is becoming more available throughout the islands, but there are still pockets where service is impossible or difficult to get. If Internet is important, ask your hotel representative about service before traveling.

If you're carrying a laptop into the Bahamas, you should fill out a Declaration of Value form upon arrival, noting make, model, and serial number. The Bahamian electrical current is compatible with U.S. computers.

PHONES

Bahamas Telecommunications Company (BTC) and newcomer Aliv are the two phone companies in the Bahamas. Most visitors use their cell phones and Internet when they need to keep in touch; your best bet is to get a prepaid SIM card from either provider and top up as you need.

If you have a calling card from home, be sure to check with the provider about surcharges, and to see if your card will work in the islands (on the smaller cays it almost certainly won't). Ask your hotel which charges will apply when you make card calls from your room as these can be steep. There's usually a charge for making toll-free calls to the United States. To place a call from a public phone using your own calling card, dial 0 for the operator, who will then place the call using your card number.

When you're calling the Bahamas, the country code is 242. You can dial any Bahamas number from the United States as you would make an interstate call.

CALLING WITHIN THE BAHAMAS

Within the Bahamas, to make a local call from your hotel room, dial 9, then the number. Some 800 and 888 numbers—particularly airline and credit card numbers—can be called from the Bahamas. Others can be reached by substituting an 880 prefix and paying for the call.

Dial 916 for directory information and 0 for operator assistance.

CALLING OUTSIDE THE BAHAMAS

On in-room phones at larger resorts you'll find instructions for making international calls as well as costs, which differ from resort to resort. At smaller inns, like those in the Out Islands, you may not be able to get an international operator, but the hotel front desk can usually do this for you.

The country code is 1 for the United States.

Access Codes AT&T USADirect. ☎ 800/872–2881. **MCI Call USA.** ☎ 800/888–8000. **Sprint.** ☎ 866/313–6672.

Phone Company Aliv. ☎ 242/300–2548 ⊕ www.bealiv.com. **BTC.** ☎ 242/302–7700 ⊕ www.btcbahamas.com.

MOBILE PHONES

Some U.S. cell phones work in the Bahamas; check with your provider before your trip. The BTC has roaming agreements with many U.S. companies, including AT&T, T-Mobile, and Sprint. Roaming rates vary depending on the carrier but are typically very expensive.

In order to bypass hefty roaming fees, purchase a SIM card for about $15 at any BTC or Aliv location; this will allow you to use your own cell phone while in the Bahamas. Most gas stations, grocery stores, and convenience stores have top-up machines for both carriers. You can buy GMS cellular phones from companies such as Cellular Abroad, which charges $1.14 to $1.32 a minute on calls to the United States plus the cost of the phone, which stars at $79.95. They also offer rental plans starting at $70 per week plus a $29 recharge voucher. Service is improving but is still spotty, and on the Out Islands, cell phones may not work at all.

▮ CUSTOMS AND DUTIES

Customs allows you to bring in one liter of wine or liquor and one carton of cigarettes in addition to personal effects, purchases up to $100, and any amount of cash.

You would be well advised to leave pets at home, unless you're considering a prolonged stay in the islands. An import permit is required from the Ministry of Agriculture and Fisheries for all animals brought into the Bahamas. The animal must be more than six months old. You'll also need a veterinary health certificate issued by a licensed vet. The permit is good for one year from the date of issue, costs $10, and the process must be completed immediately before departure.

U.S. residents who have been out of the country for at least 48 hours may bring home $800 worth of foreign goods duty-free, as long as they have not used the $800 allowance or any part of it in the past 30 days.

Contacts Ministry of Agriculture and Marine Resources. ☎ *242/397-7400.* **U.S. Customs and Border Protection.** ⊕ *www. cbp.gov.* **U.S. Embassy.** ☎ *242/322-1181* ⊕ *www.nassau.usembassy.gov.*

▮ ELECTRICITY

Electricity is 120 volts/60 cycles AC, which is compatible with all U.S. appliances.

▮ EMERGENCIES

The emergency telephone number in the Bahamas is 919 or 911. Pharmacies usually close at 6 pm although some in New Providence are always open. Emergency medicine after hours is available only at hospitals, or, on remote Out Islands, at clinics.

Emergency Contacts Bahamas Air Sea Rescue Association. ☎ *242/325-8864* ⊕ *www.basra.org.* **United States Embassy.** ☎ *242/322-1181* ⊕ *www.nassau.usembassy. gov.*

▮ HEALTH

FOOD AND WATER

The major health risk in the Bahamas is traveler's diarrhea. This is most often caused by ingesting fruits, shellfish, and drinks to which your body is unaccustomed. Go easy at first on new foods such as mangoes, conch, and rum punch. There are rare cases of contaminated fruit, vegetables, or drinking water.

If you're susceptible to digestive problems, avoid ice, uncooked food, and unpasteurized milk and milk products, and stick to bottled water, or water that has been boiled for several minutes, even when brushing your teeth.

Drink plenty of purified water or tea; chamomile is a good folk remedy. In severe cases, rehydrate yourself with a salt-sugar solution (½ teaspoon salt and 4 tablespoons sugar per quart of water).

DIVING

Do not fly within 24 hours of scuba diving. Always know where your nearest decompression chamber is before you embark on a dive expedition, and how you would get there in an emergency. The only chambers in the Bahamas are in Nassau and San Salvador, and emergency cases are often sent to Miami.

Decompression Chamber Bahamas Hyperbaric Centre. ☎ *242/362–5765.* **Bahamas Medical Center.** ☎ *242/302–4610* ⊕ *www. bahamasmedicalcenter.com.*

INSECTS

No-see-ums (sand fleas) and mosquitoes can be bothersome. Some travelers have allergies to sand-flea bites. To prevent the bites, use a recommended bug repellent. To ease the itching, rub alcohol on the bites. Some Out Island hotels provide sprays or repellents but it's a good idea to bring your own.

SUNBURN

Basking in the sun is one of the great pleasures of a Bahamian vacation, but take precautions against sunburn and sunstroke.

MEDICAL INSURANCE AND ASSISTANCE

The most serious accidents and illnesses may require an airlift to the United States—most likely to a hospital in Florida. The costs of a medical evacuation can quickly run into the thousands of dollars, and your personal health insurance may not cover such costs. If you plan to pursue inherently risky activities, such as scuba diving, or if you have an existing medical condition, check your policy to see what's covered.

Consider buying trip insurance with medical-only coverage. Neither Medicare nor some private insurers cover medical expenses anywhere outside the United States. Medical-only policies typically reimburse you for medical care (excluding that related to preexisting conditions) and hospitalization abroad, and provide for evacuation. You still have to pay the bills and await reimbursement from the insurer, though.

Another option is to sign up with a medical-evacuation assistance company. A membership in one of these companies gets you doctor referrals, emergency evacuation or repatriation, 24-hour hotlines for medical consultation, and other assistance. International SOS Assistance Emergency and AirMed International provide evacuation services and medical referrals. MedjetAssist offers medical evacuation.

Medical Assistance Companies AirMed International. ⊕ *www.airmed.com.* **International SOS Assistance Emergency.** ⊕ *www. internationalsos.com.* **MedjetAssist.** ⊕ *www. medjetassist.com.*

Medical-Only Insurers International Medical Group. ☎ *800/628–4664* ⊕ *www. imglobal.com.* **International SOS.** ⊕ *www. internationalsos.com.* **Wallach & Company.** ☎ *800/237–6615* ⊕ *www.wallach.com.*

▌ HOURS OF OPERATION

Hours for attractions vary. Most open between 9 and 10 am and close around 5 pm.

Though most drugstores typically abide by normal store hours, some stay open 24 hours.

Most stores, with the exception of straw markets and malls, close on Sunday, although a number of Bay Street stores will open if cruise ships are in port

▌ MAIL

It's not unheard of for letters to take two to four weeks to reach their destinations. No postal (zip) codes are used in the Bahamas—all mail is collected from local area post-office boxes.

First-class mail from the Bahamas to the United States is 65¢ per half ounce; you'll pay 50¢ to mail a postcard. Postcard stamps good for foreign destinations are usually sold at shops selling postcards, so you don't have to make a special trip.

From the United States a postcard or a letter sent to the Bahamas costs 98¢.

Express Services Copimaxx. ☎ 242/328–2679. **FedEx.** ☎ 242/352–3402 Freeport, 242/322–5656 Nassau, 242/367–2817 Abaco, 242/368–2540 Andros, 242/332–2720 Eleuthera, 242/337–6786 Long Island, 649/946–2542 Grand Turk, 649/946–4682 Providenciales, 800/247–4747 U.S. international customer service. **Mail Boxes Etc.** ☎ 242/394–1508.

MONEY

Generally, prices in the Bahamas are slightly higher than in the United States. Businesses accept U.S. and Bahamian dollars as they are the same value, but they may not be able to give you change in U.S. currency. On the Out Islands, meals and simple goods can be expensive; prices are high due to the remoteness of the islands and the costs of importing.

ATMS AND BANKS

There are ATMs at banks, malls, resorts, and shops throughout the major islands. For excursions to remote locations, bring plenty of cash; there are few or no ATMs on some small cays, and on weekends or holidays, those that exist may run out of cash.

Banks are generally open Monday–Thursday from 9 or 9:30 am to 3 or 4 pm, and Friday from 9 am to 5 pm. On the Out Islands, banks may keep shorter hours—on the smallest cays, some are only open a day or two each week.

■**TIP**➜ PINs with more than four digits are not recognized at ATMs in the Bahamas. If your PIN has five or more digits, remember to change it before you leave.

CREDIT CARDS

Some smaller hotels in the islands do not take plastic.

CURRENCY AND EXCHANGE

The U.S. dollar is on par with the Bahamian dollar and is accepted all over the Bahamas. Bahamian money runs in bills of $1, $5, $10, $20, $50, and $100.

Because U.S. currency is accepted everywhere, there really is no need to change to Bahamian. You won't incur any transaction fees for currency exchange. Carry small bills when bargaining at straw markets.

PACKING

Between mid-December and April, prepare for the occasional cool evening. Some of the more sophisticated hotels require upscale attire, like jackets and dresses. The Bahamas' casinos do not have dress codes.

PASSPORTS AND VISAS

U.S. citizens need a valid passport when entering and returning from the Bahamas, but do not need a visa.

U.S. Passport Information U.S. Department of State. ☎ 877/487–2778 ⊕ travel.state.gov/passport.

SAFETY

There has been a significant spike in violent crime in Nassau, mostly in off-the-beaten-path locations. Exercise caution in these areas: be aware of your wallet or handbag at all times, and keep your jewelry in the hotel safe. Be especially wary in remote areas; always lock your rental vehicle, and don't keep any valuables in the car, even in the locked trunk.

Women traveling alone should be advised regarding walking unescorted at night in Nassau or in remote areas. Unwanted attention may be deterred via conservative dress.

General Information and Warnings U.S. Department of State. ⊕ www.travel.state.gov/travel.

TAXES

There's no sales tax in the Bahamas, but a 7.5% VAT is added to most goods and services; the $15 departure tax is usually included in the price of commercial airline tickets.

Tax on your hotel room is 6% to 12% in addition to VAT, depending on the island visited; at some resorts, a small service charge of up to 5% may be added to cover housekeeping and bellman service.

■ TIME

The Bahamas lie within the eastern standard time (EST) zone. In summer the islands switch to eastern daylight time (EDT).

■ TIPPING

In the Bahamas, service staff and hotel workers expect to be tipped. The usual tip for service from a taxi driver or waiter is 15% and $1 to $2 a bag for porters. Most travelers leave $1 to $3 per day for their hotel maid, usually every morning since the maid may have a day off. Many hotels and restaurants automatically add a 15% gratuity to your bill; if not, a 15% to 20% tip at a restaurant is appropriate (more for a high-end establishment). Bartenders generally get $1 to $2 per drink.

■ TRIP INSURANCE

Comprehensive policies typically cover trip cancellation and interruption, letting you cancel or cut your trip short because of illness, or, in some cases, acts of terrorism in your destination. Such policies might also cover evacuation and medical care. (For trips abroad you should have at least medical-only coverage. *See Medical Insurance and Assistance under Health*.) Some also cover you for trip delays because of bad weather or mechanical problems, as well as for lost or delayed luggage.

Another type of coverage to consider is financial default—that is, when your trip is disrupted because a tour operator, airline, or cruise line goes out of business. Generally you must buy this when you book your trip or shortly thereafter, and it's available to you only if your operator isn't on a list of excluded companies.

Insurance Comparison Information Insure My Trip. ☎ 800/487–4722 ⊕ www.insuremytrip.com. **Square Mouth.** ☎ 800/240–0369 ⊕ www.squaremouth.com.

Comprehensive Insurers AIG Travel Guard. ☎ 800/826–4919 ⊕ www.travelguard.com. **Allianz Global Assistance.** ☎ 866/884–3556 ⊕ www.allianztravelinsurance.com. **CSA Travel Protection.** ☎ 877/243–4135 ⊕ www.csatravelprotection.com. **HTH Worldwide.** ☎ 888/243–2358 ⊕ www.hthworldwide.com. **Travel Insured International.** ☎ 800/243–3174 ⊕ www.travelinsured.com. **Travelex Insurance.** ☎ 800/228–9792 ⊕ www.travelexinsurance.com.

■ VISITOR INFORMATION

Contacts Bahamas Ministry of Tourism. ☎ 800/224–2627 ⊕ www.bahamas.com. **Bahama Out Islands Promotion Board.** ☎ 954/475–8315 ⊕ www.myoutislands.com. **Caribbean Tourism Organization.** ⊕ www.onecaribbean.org. **Grand Bahama Island Tourism Board.** ☎ 800/545–1300 ⊕ www.grandbahamavacations.com. **Harbour Island Tourism.** ⊕ www.harbourislandguide.com. **Nassau/Paradise Island Promotion Board.** ⊕ www.nassauparadiseisland.com.

USEFUL WEB SITES

BahamasIslands.com. ⊕ www.the-bahamas-islands.com. **Bahamasnet.com.** ⊕ www.bahamasnet.com. **Bahamas Visitors Guide.** ⊕ www.bahamasvisitorsguide.com. **Nassau Guardian.** ⊕ www.thenassauguardian.com.

INDEX

PHOTO CREDITS

Front cover: Klein-Hubert / Media Drum World/Aurora Photos [Description: Pig standing with starfish, The Exumas, Bahamas]. 1, The Bahamas Ministry of Tourism. 2, Ray Wadia/The Bahamas Ministry of Tourism. 4, 5 (top and bottom), Bahamas Ministry of Tourism. 6 (top left), Beltsazar | Dreamstime.com. 6 (top right), Ron Nickel/age fotostock. 6 (bottom right), BlueOrange Studio/Shutterstock. 6 (bottom left), Bahamas Ministry of Tourism. 7 (top), Fowl Cay Resort. 7 (bottom), Worachat Sodsri / Shutterstock. 8 (top left), Stephen Frink Collection / Alamy. 8 (top right), Fowl Cay Resort. 8 (bottom left and right), Bahamas Ministry of Tourism. 9, Jocrebbin | Dreamstime.com. 10 (top left), Danita Delimont / Alamy. 10 (top right and bottom), Bahamas Ministry of Tourism. 11 (top), Danielbothaphoto | Dreamstime.com. 11 (bottom), BlueOrange Studio/Shutterstock. 13, The Bahamas Ministry of Tourism. **Chapter 1: Experience the Bahamas:** 16-17, Reinhard Dirscherl/age fotostock. 24 (left), The Bahamas Ministry of Tourism. 24(right), Mark gerardot/Tiamo. 25 (left), t.blue/Flickr. 25 (top right), Jonathunder/wikipedia.org. 25 (bottom right), Greg Johnston/Cape Santa Maria Beach Resort. 26 (left), Graycliff Hotel. 26 (top right), Steve Snodgrass/Flickr. 26 (bottom right), Henrik Bruun. 27 (left), Craig Dennis. 27 (right), Ramona Settle. 33, Dirscherl Reinhard/age fotostock. 34 and 35 (all), The Bahamas Ministry of Tourism. 36, frantisekhojdysz/Shutterstock. 38, Ray Wadia/The Bahamas Ministry of Tourism. 39 (both), 40, and 41 (top left and bottom left), The Bahamas Ministry of Tourism. 41 (right), Ray Wadia/The Bahamas Ministry of Tourism. 42, The Bahamas Ministry of Tourism. **Chapter 2: New Providence and Paradise Islands:** 43, Macduff Everton/Atlantis. 46, Daniel Korzeniewski/iStockphoto. 50, The Bahamas Ministry of Tourism. 56, Laurin Johnson/iStockphoto. 60, Ramunas | Dreamstime.com. 68, Graycliff Hotel. 73, Bruce Wolf. 77, Ramona Settle. 81, Walter Bibikow/age fotostock. 82 (left), biskuit/Flickr. 82 (right), Jef Nickerson/Flickr. 83 (top), Bahamas Ministry of Tourism. 83 (bottom), Peter Adams/age fotostock. 84, Shane Pinder/Alamy. 85(top), Erkki & Hanna / Shutterstock. 85 (bottom), Shane Pinder/Alamy. 88-89, Remedios Valls Lopez/age fotostock. 92, Lars Topelmann/The Bahamas Ministry of Tourism. **Chapter 3: Grand Bahama Island:** 97, Denis Jr. Tangney/iStockphoto. 100, Degas Jean-Pierre / age fotostock. 101 (top), Thomas Lorenz/Shutterstock. 101 (bottom) and 102, The Bahamas Ministry of Tourism. 108, Charles Stirling (Travel) / Alamy. 119, Our Lucaya Beach and Golf Resort. 120, The Bahamas Ministry of Tourism. 124, Davis James/age fotostock. 127, Dirscherl Reinhard/age fotostock. 131, The Bahamas Ministry of Tourism. **Chapter 4: The Abacos:** 135, SuperStock/age fotostock. 138, FLPA/age fotostock. 139 (top), flickerized/Flickr. 139 (bottom), Kate Philips/iStockphoto. 140, Patchai Panjatanasak/Shutterstock. 149, Sunpix Marine/Alamy. 154, DEA/A VERGANI/age fotostock. 165, Imagestate/age fotostock. 170, Ramona Settle. **Chapter 5: Andros, Bimini, and the Berry Islands:** 179, Greg Johnston/age fotostock. 182, Lars Topelmann/The Bahamas Ministry of Tourism. 190, Juliet Coombe/age fotostock. 205, Tiamo Resort. 209, BARBAGALLO Franco / age fotostock. 212, Mark Conlin/Alamy. 217, Larry Larsen / Alamy. 225, Amy Strycula / Alamy. **Chapter 6: Eleuthera and Harbour Island:** 227, The Bahamas Ministry of Tourism. 230, Erikruthoff81 | Dreamstime.com. 240, Greg Johnston/age fotostock. 248-49, The Bahamas Ministry of Tourism. 250, Bahamas Ministry of Tourism. 253, Alvaro Leiva/age fotostock. 256-57, Ian Cumming/age fotostock. **Chapter 7: The Exumas:** 259, ARCO/F Schneider / age fotostock. 262 and 263 (bottom), The Bahamas Ministry of Tourism. 263 (top), Ray Wadia/The Bahamas Ministry of Tourism. 264, The Bahamas Ministry of Tourism. 271, Cheryl Blackerby. 273, Ramona Settle. 275, Cheryl Blackerby. 278, Staniel Cay Yacht Club. 280, Bahamas Ministry of Tourism. 282, Staniel Cay Yacht Club. **Chapter 8: The Southern Out Islands:** 285, Greg Johnston/age fotostock. 288, Cheryl Blackerby. 289 (top), Patrick Swint/Flickr. 289 (bottom), stephan kerkhofs/Shutterstock. 290, Jeff Greenberg / Alamy. 291 (top), Cheryl Blackerby. 291 (bottom), mweichse/Shutterstock. 292, Greg Johnston/Cape Santa Maria Beach Resort. 300, Michael DeFreitas / age fotostock. 305, Greg Johnston/age fotostock. 308, The Bahamas Ministry of Tourism. 315, Greg Johnston/age fotostock. 321, Greg Johnston/Cape Santa Maria Beach Resort. 325 BARBAGALLO Franco / age fotostock. 330, Bahamas Ministry of Tourism. 333, Greg Johnston/Cape Santa Maria Beach Resort. **Back cover, from left to right:** travelpixpro/iStockphoto; frantisekhojdysz/Shutterstock; Daveallenphoto | Dreamstime.com. **Spine:** Kovnir Andrii/Shutterstock.

ABOUT OUR WRITERS

Born in Nassau and schooled in England, Bob Bower lived for seven years in Sydney, Australia where he co-partnered Blaze Communications, a successful PR firm. Returning to The Bahamas, Bob worked for 20 years at his family's Nassau-based business, Star Publishers Ltd., where he wrote and edited publications for the Bahamas Tourist News and two promotion board newspapers. For two years he was executive director of the Association of Bahamas Marinas, producing its Bahamas Cruising Map, and is now country manager for Waterway Guide Media. Bob loves travel, particularly the Bahama Out Islands. His further journeys have taken him to the Caribbean, Spain, Malta, France, Belgium, Ireland, the United Kingdom, the United States, and Canada. Since 1987 Bob has resided in Nassau with his wife and three children and loves his faith, reading, travel, and photography.

Sheri-kae McLeod is a freelance Caribbean travel writer, entertainment/lifestyle writer, and journalist. As a soon-to-be Communications graduate of The University of the West Indies, she has experience working for entertainment and lifestyle publications in Jamaica and in the United States, as well as travel writing experience for *The Culture Trip*, based in London. She has also worked as a Caribbean reporter for Magnetic Media, a three-time Telly Award–winning media production company based in Turks and Caicos.

Born in England and raised in the Bahamas, Jessica Robertson has traveled the world for work and play but calls Nassau home. She has visited just about all of the populated islands in the Bahamas, as well as some occupied only by hermit crabs and seagulls, and is happiest when she's paddling on, diving under, or lounging beside the ocean.

Ashleigh Sean Rolle was born in New Providence and grew up in Freeport Grand Bahama, The Bahamas. She's a columnist with the popular Bahamian site *10th Year Seniors* and a contributing blogger with *The Huffington Post*. She has a deep love for her people and her culture and lives to showcase them to the world. With travel being one of her greatest passions, she makes it a point to visit at least five new places every year. The Exuma Islands are her favorite in the archipelago of the Bahamas.

Dana MacKimmie spent nearly two decades braving Canadian winters as a line producer in the television industry before packing it all up and heading down to paradise—the Bahamas. She continues to freelance with the warm ocean breeze at her back.